Contents

When speaking of the country we, in this guide, use the word Netherlands as the word Holland applies to two of the country's 12 provinces.

*The **MICHELIN** publications you will need with this guide are*

Map **408**

at a scale of 1:400 000

Map **212**

at a scale of 1:200 000

"BENELUX"

Annual Red Guide
for hotels and restaurants

PRINCIPAL SIGHTS

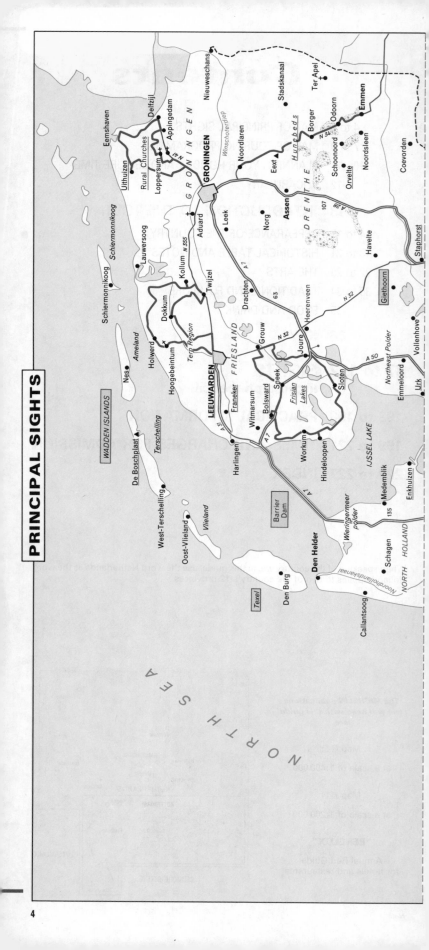

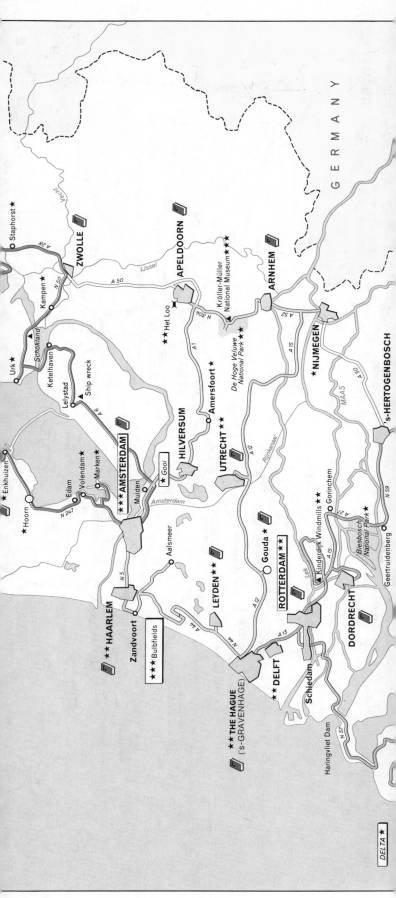

Staphorst ★

ZWOLLE

APELDOORN

ARNHEM

Kröller-Müller
National Museum ★★

De Hoge Veluwe
National Park ★★

Het Loo ★★

Kampen ★

Urk ★

Schokland ★

Ketelhaven

Lelystad

Ship wreck ▲

Enkhuizen ★

Hoorn ★

Edam ★

Volendam ★★

Marken ★

★★★ AMSTERDAM

Muiden

Gooi ★

Amsterdam

HILVERSUM ★

Amersfoort ★

UTRECHT ★★

Aalsmeer

★★ HAARLEM

Zandvoort

★★★ Bulbfields

LEYDEN ★★

Gouda ★

ROTTERDAM ★★

Kinderdijk Windmills ★★

Gorinchem

Biesbosch
National Park ★

Geertruidenberg

's-HERTOGENBOSCH

NIJMEGEN

★★ THE HAGUE
(' s-GRAVENHAGE)

★★ DELFT

Schiedam

DORDRECHT

Haringvliet Dam

DELTA ★

GERMANY

8

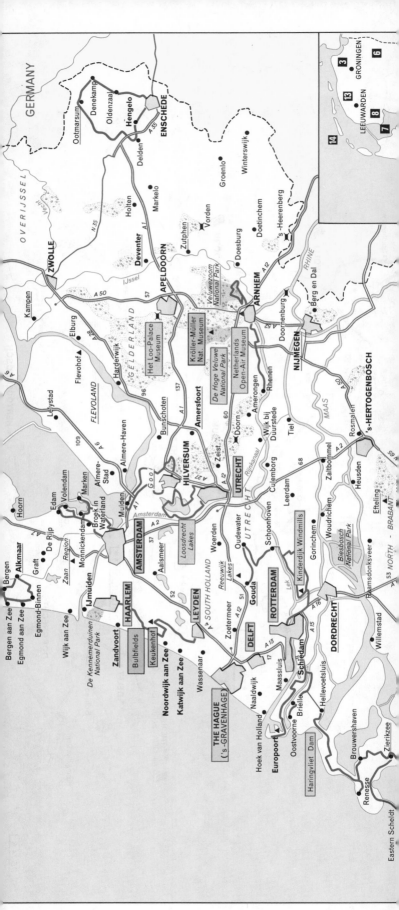

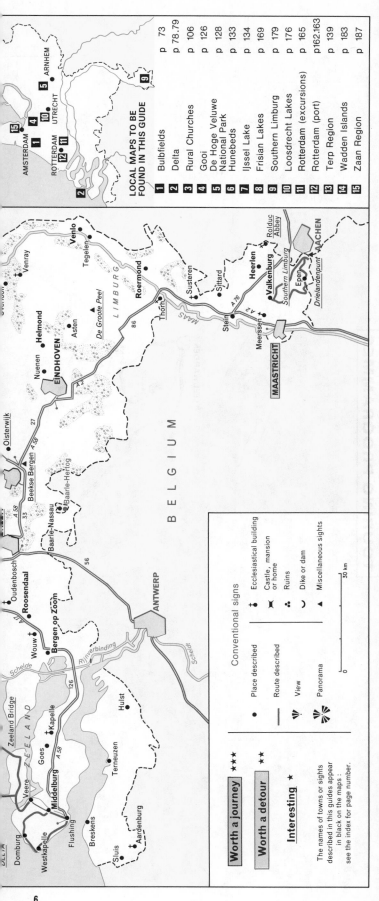

Worth a journey ★★★

Worth a detour ★★

Interesting ★

The names of towns or sights
described in this guides appear
in black on the maps :
see the index for page number.

Conventional signs

•	Place described	✝	Ecclesiastical building
	Route described	✖	Castle, mansion or home
▼	View	∴	Ruins
✹	Panorama	☽	Dike or dam
		▲	Miscellaneous sights

0 _____ 30 km

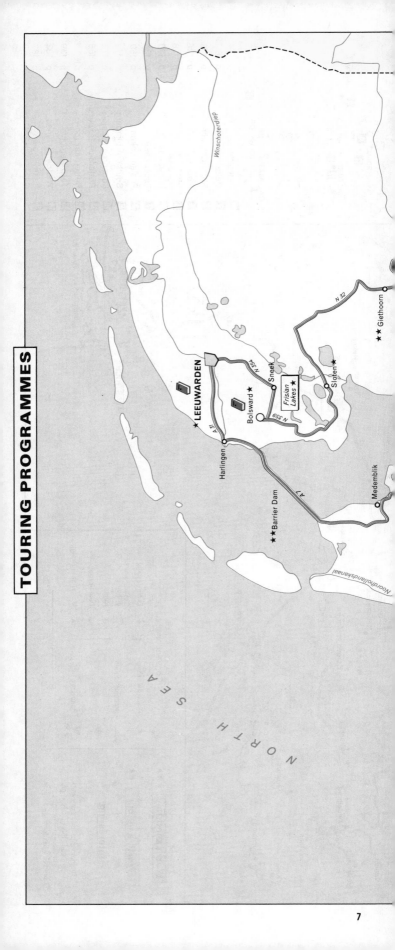

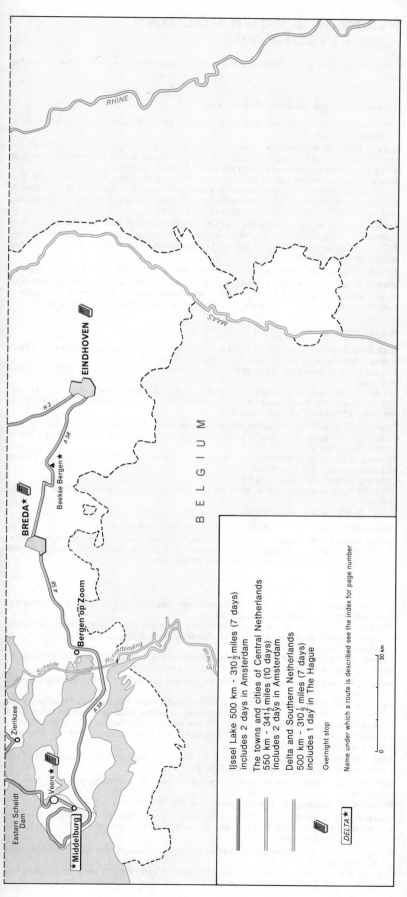

RHINE

MAAS

MAAS

BELGIUM

EINDHOVEN

N 2

A 58

Beekse Bergen ★

▲

BREDA ★

A 58

Bergen op Zoom ○

Scheldt

Riverbinding

A 58

Schelde

Zierikzee ○

Veere ★

Eastern Scheldt Dam

★ Middelburg

IJssel Lake 500 km - 310½ miles (7 days)
includes 2 days in Amsterdam
The towns and cities of Central Netherlands
550 km - 341½ miles (10 days)
includes 2 days in Amsterdam
Delta and Southern Netherlands
500 km - 310½ miles (7 days)
includes 1 day in The Hague

○ Overnight stop

Name under which a route is described see the index for page number

| | 0 | | | 30 km |

DELTA ★

PLANNING YOUR HOLIDAY
AND LEISURE TIME

For addresses and other details see the chapter Practical Information at the end of the guide.

When to visit the Netherlands?

The museums can be visited at any time of the year. However, each season has its particular characteristics.

Spring. – The bulbfields between Haarlem and Leyden and in the vicinity of Alkmaar, in particular, come out in magnificent colours *(from mid-April to end May)* while the foliage of the trees adds a green note along the canals crossing the towns.
Spring is the incubation period for birds and there are, consequently, many about. The region of the Betuwe, when the orchards are in blossom *(from mid-April to end May)* is also very beautiful, as well as the rapeseed fields in the provinces of Friesland, Groningen, Overijssel and Flevoland *(from mid-May to early June)*.

Summer. – Holidaymakers invade the vast beaches of the North Sea, Wadden Islands and holiday resort regions like the Drenthe and Southern Limburg, where it is, therefore, very difficult to find accommodation. Lakes and canals swarm with yachts. Flowering heather colours dunes and heaths.

Autumn. – The forests, like those of the Veluwe, are covered with splendid red foliage.

Winter. – Although, nowadays, it snows quite often; it is rare to have it sufficiently cold to be able to skate on frozen canals, lakes and ponds. But when it happens, everyone is on the ice and above all the children, who are given a day off to skate.

Accommodation

Hotels and restaurants. – To choose a hotel or restaurant, consult the current **Michelin Red Guide Benelux.** Breakfast is usually included in the price of the room.
It is essential to reserve a room, particularly over weekends and in very touristic towns and cities.
In a number of towns and cities it is possible to stay with a family, by first getting in touch with the tourist information centre (VVV); address and telephone number of local VVV in the current Michelin Red Guide Benelux.

Camping. – The country has about 900 organised sites, with facilities, divided into five categories. A leaflet including a map showing the position of the selected sites is distributed by the VVV.
There is a lot of caravanning. The Dutch have more than 580 000 caravans, that is 40 caravans per 1 000 inhabitants.
Camping outside official sites is forbidden.
On entering a camping site a form of identity (passport, drivers licence) must be shown.

Rental. – It is best to apply to the local tourist information centre (VVV).

Youth Hostels. – There are about fifty, accepting families and groups, as well.

Boarding houses for the young. – Large cities like Alkmaar, Amsterdam, Arnhem, Breda, Groningen, Nijmegen, Roosendaal, Rotterdam and Zwolle, offer cheap board to the young, but not very comfortable. Some are called "sleep-in".

Boating and fishing

The Dutch have more than 300 000 pleasure boats, that is about 1 boat per 47 inhabitants. There are about 950 pleasure boat harbours.
Water covers nearly $\frac{1}{6}$th of the country *(p 14)* and the lakes, ponds, canals, rivers and wide estuaries provide multiple possibilities. Friesland with its numerous lakes *(p 167)* is particularly favoured.
Another of the charms of sailing in the Netherlands is that it is sometimes possible to reach, by boat, even the centre of towns, which are crossed by canals.

Access. – Nearly all stretches of water can be reached by boat. However, there are certain restrictions.
A yacht with a mast which does not pull down can only take waterways which have lever bridges (some of them only open at certain hours). Some boats which have too great a draught cannot go to certain lake areas. To use a speed boat (speed over 20kph-12mph) an authorisation must be obtained. Finally, speed is limited on most stretches of water; motor boating can be forbidden.

Hiring. – Motor or sail boats can be hired. To hire for a long period of time, consult the leaflet on water sports or apply to the ANWB.

Sailing schools. – There are numerous sailing schools in the country (about forty in Friesland).

Wind surfing is becoming increasingly popular in the Netherlands.

Water skiing. – It is linked to pleasure boating, but is subject to stricter regulations: it is only authorised in certain areas. Furthermore, it is sometimes necessary to obtain authorisation from local authorities.

Angling. – To fish in the Netherlands, two documents are necesary: the *sportvisakte* and the *vergunning* (permit).
The first is on sale in post offices, while the second can be obtained from the Angling Associations *(Hengelsportverenigingen)*.

Walks

Walking, well organised in the Netherlands, is the object of many annual meetings as for example the Four Day Walks which take place in Apeldoorn and Nijmegen or the Tour of the Eleven Towns of Friesland, leaving from Leeuwarden.

Most of the woods belonging to the State are administered by the **Staatsbosbeheer** whose symbol *(opposite)* is easily recognisable. Laid out for tourists, they are usually equipped with cycling paths, picnic areas and footpaths. **Walking tours** are suggested: a sign at the start indicates the colour marking each route and the time needed.

Other Sports

Golf courses, gliding and racecourses are shown on Michelin map **212**. In addition on the insets found on Michelin map **408** covering the areas of Amsterdam and Rotterdam, various sporting and tourist areas are shown: golf courses, stadiums, swimming pools, bathing places, pleasure boat harbours, cycling paths, nature reserves and footpaths.

Traditional sports. – Some sports, particularly old or original ones, come from regional traditions.

Much enjoyed above all in **Limburg** is **shooting with a bow and arrow** or with an arquebus, an activity which dates from the troubled times when the bourgeois people were armed in the towns. An annual gathering is the occasion to see the procession of marksmen *(schutters)* wearing their traditional glittering uniforms.

In **Friesland,** apart from the **kaatsen,** a ball game with six players divided into two sides, and the **skûtsjesilen** *(qv),* sort of regatta the tradition of **pole vaulting** or *polsstokspringen* (*ljeppen* in Frisian) has been kept up, formerly played mainly by bird's egg hunters who crossed the canals by jumping over with the help of a long pole.

In Zeeland, at Middelburg, the **ringrijderljen** *(qv)* has been revived, a sort of tournament where the riders galloping on horseback have to aim their lances into a ring.

With milder winters the traditional custom of skating out of doors, as can be seen in the paintings of Hendrick Avercamp among other great 17C masters, was not only a diversion but a means of getting about and even a form of transportation; sleighs were used as well. They also played **kolfspel** on the ice. This game, played with a club *(kolf)* and a ball, has been a subject of controversy between the Dutch and Scots for centuries. An Act of Scottish Parliament mentions golfing in 1457, whereas the 17C Dutch landscapists painted winter scenes with men playing *kolfspel* (Avercamp, Van der Neer). It was during James I's (James VI of Scotland) reign that an embargo on golf balls from Holland was decreed.

Entertainment

The Netherlands has authorised gambling in **casinos** (Breda, Leeuwarden, Rotterdam, Scheveningen, Valkenburg, Zandvoort), which are open all year round. A leaflet can be obtained from tourist information centres stating precise information on the way they are run.

In **cinemas,** foreign films are shown in the original version with sub-titles in Dutch.

Amsterdam, notably, has well-known dance and opera companies, and a remarkable orchestra *(p 41).*

In the summer the Holland Festival offers a number of artistic events *(see the chapter Practical Information at the end of the guide).*

Make up your own itineraries

The map on pages 4-6 gives a general view of tourist regions, the main towns, individual sights and recommended routes in the guide.

The sights are described under their own name in alphabetical order (pp 37-192) or are incorporated in the excursions radiating from a nearby town or tourist centre.

*In addition the **Michelin Maps** **408** and **212** show scenic routes, places of interest, viewpoints, rivers, forests...*

VOCABULARY

Terms found when travelling and in towns are indicated in brown. For terms used in hotels and restaurants, see the more complete vocabulary in the current Michelin Red Guide Benelux.

abdij	abbey	**museum**	museum
alstublieft	please	**natuurreservaat**	nature reserve
begraafplaats	cemetery	**noord**	north
berg	mountain, hill	**Onze Lieve Vrouwe**	Our Lady
bezienswaardigheid	sight	**oost**	east
bezoek	visit	**open**	open
boerderij	farm	**opengesteld**	open, accessible
boot	boat	**orgel**	organ
brug	bridge	**oud**	old
dam	dam	**oudheidkamer**	antique museum
dank U	thank you	**paleis**	palace
dierenpark	zoo	**plas**	lake
dijk	dike	**plein**	square
doorgaand verkeer	crossroad	**poort**	gateway (to town)
duin	dune	**raadhuis**	town hall
eiland	island	**rechts**	right
fiets	bicycle	**rederij**	shipping company
fietsers oversteken	bicycle crossroad	**Rijks-**	of the State
fietspad	cycling path	**rondvaart**	boat trip
gasthuis	hospice, old hospital	**scheepvaart**	navigation
gemeentehuis	town hall	**parkeerschijf**	parking disk
gracht	canal (in town)	**verplicht**	obligatory
groot, grote	great	**schilderij**	painting, picture
grot	grotto, cave	**schouwburg**	theatre
gulden	florin	**singel**	ring canal
haven	harbour, port	**slot**	castle, fortress
heilige	saint	**sluis**	lock
heuvel	hill	**stad**	town
hoeveel?	how much?	**stadhuis**	town hall
hof	court, palace	**state**	castle
hofje	almshouse		(in Friesland)
huis	house, mansion	**stedelijk**	municipal
ingang; toegang	entrance	**straat**	street
jachthaven	pleasure boat harbour	**tegel**	earthenware tile
kaai, kade	quay	**tentoonstelling**	exhibition
kaas	cheese	**tuin**	garden
kasteel	castle	**uitgang**	exit
kerk	church	**veer**	ferryboat
kerkhof	churchyard	**verboden**	forbidden
kerkschat	treasury	**vest**	rampart
klooster	convent	**vogel**	bird
koninklijk	royal	**vuurtoren**	lighthouse
let op!	attention, beware!	**waag**	weigh house
links	left	**wal**	rampart
markt	market,	**wandeling**	walking tour
	main square	**weg**	path, road
meer	lake	**west**	west
mevrouw, mijnheer	Mrs., Mr.	**zee**	sea
molen	mill	**zuid**	south

TOWNS

's-Gravenhage; Den Haag	The Hague
Leiden	Leyden
Vlissingen	Flushing

PROVINCES

Noord Brabant	North Brabant
Noord Holland	North Holland
Zuid Holland	South Holland

Introduction
to the tour

Emboldened by centuries of living with the sea, the Dutch have befriended it.
As a sea-faring nation, they sailed far and wide founding trading posts in the Americas and East Indies.
They tamed it with the use of windmills, dikes and canals creating polders and vast water-sports centres.
Never far from it are the trim half-timbered and thatch-covered farms, moated and beautifully tended historic houses and mansions, picturesque flowered villages and ancient towns and cities, those celebrated centres of learning.
Criss-crossing the towns are those peaceful tree-lined canals which mirror the traditional water-gate, soaring bell tower with its pealing bells sounding far and wide and curving gables ennobling the patricians' houses.
With water another prominent feature of Dutch life is flowers: vast fields of flowers are transformed into a kaleidoscope of colours in spring, many attractive gardens and parks surround both the private houses and towns and the cheerful flower boxes and window displays enhance even the plainest façade.
This small, densely populated country is flat, yet never dull, as the constantly changing play of light between sea and sky inspires not only the great 17C masters but the 20C tourist as well.

Kinderdijk Windmills

Times and charges for admission to sights described in the guide are listed at the end of the guide.

The sights are listed alphabetically in this section either under the place – town, village or area – in which they are situated or under their proper name.

Every sight for which there are times and charges is indicated by the symbol ⊙ in the margin in the main part of the guide.

APPEARANCE OF THE COUNTRY

The territory of the Netherlands, which has immense stretches of water such as IJssel Lake and the Wadden Sea extends over 41 863sq km - 16 163sq miles, of which 33 937sq km - 12 895sq miles are drained. The longest distance from one end of the country to the other is 310km - 193 miles, i.e. from Rottum Island in the north of the Groningen province, to the south of Limburg.

The country is inhabited by 14 741 000 Dutch (census 1/1/89). The population of 434 inhabitants per sq km or 1 125 per sq mile makes it one of the most densely populated countries in the world (United Kingdom 233 inhabitants per sq km or 605 per sq mile). The population distribution is unequal: the most populated provinces are North and South Holland. These two provinces and the province of Utrecht form the **Randstad Holland,** a large conurbation comprising the country's four main cities: Amsterdam, Rotterdam, The Hague and Utrecht.

In 1988 out of 100 Dutch 24 % worked in industry, 62 % in the tertiary and government sectors, 5 % in agriculture, 3 % in fishing and petroleum related activities and 6 % were unemployed.

Agriculture in the Netherlands is intensive; its productivity is amongst the largest in the world. With stock raising, an activity favoured by the fertile land and elaborate irrigation system, agriculture, however, only counts for a small part of the national revenue. Industry, especially with the chemical industries, metallurgy and food processing, is mainly established in Randstad Holland, the Twente, North Brabant and Limburg. It often needs imported matter; on the other hand the export of byproducts is one of the country's main sources of revenue. Trade, particularly directed towards the transit between Europe and overseas, represents 50 % of the national revenue.

Holland and the Netherlands. – Over the years the name **Holland** has come to designate all the Netherlands. In fact, this old province – separated since 1840 into North Holland and South Holland supplanted the other regions of the United Provinces in the 17C due to its economic prosperity and its predominant political role. Napoleon I ratified the primacy of Holland by creating the short-lived kingdom of Holland in 1810.

In fact as early as the late Middle Ages, the plains stretching from Friesland to Flanders were called **Lage Landen** or **Nederlanden** (Low Countries). In 1581 the Verenigde Provinciën der Nederlanden (United Provinces of the Netherlands) came into being. In 1815 this was still the name used when William I took over the kingdom which included part of Belgium. The name has remained unchanged – Netherlands – despite the secession of Belgium in 1830, and Queen Beatrix has the title of "Koningin der Nederlanden" (Queen of the Netherlands).

Since January 1, 1986 the country has a new province: Flevoland *(qv)* consisting of the two polders of this name (North Flevoland and South Flevoland Polders and the Northeast Polder – *qv),* as well as that to the northeast and the old island of Urk. The Netherlands, together with the Netherlands Antilles *(qv)* form the kingdom of the Netherlands.

A "LOW COUNTRY"

The name Netherlands is very apt (*land* = country, *neder* = low). Nearly $\frac{1}{3}$ of its total area is below sea level, reclaimed by a persistent fight against water *(p 16);* without the protection of dikes and dunes at the time of high tides or river floods, more than $\frac{1}{2}$ the country would be under water. The lowest point in the country reaches 6.50m - 21.33ft at Alexanderpolder, near Rotterdam. However, a great difference can be noted between the west and the east. Half the west of the country is a plain which is less than 5m - $16\frac{1}{2}$ft above sea level. This is the most populated part of the country.

On the other hand, in the east, the Veluwe hills are 100m - 328ft high (106m - 348ft at Zijpenberg to the northeast of Arnhem), and **Drielandenpunt** is the highest point in the country, 321m - 1 053ft at the junction of the German and Belgian frontiers.

The Netherlands is an area deprived of the earth's crust which has been filled in by alluvial deposits from the Rhine and the Maas by moraines from the large Scandinavian glaciers and sand brought by the wind during the Quaternary Era.

The sea level in the Netherlands is called N.A.P (Normaal Amsterdams Peil).

The country of water. – The land above sea level represents only $\frac{5}{6}$th of the country.

In fact part of the country is covered by large rivers, whose estuaries form an immense delta *(p 78).* In addition, IJssel Lake, a large fresh water lake which replaced the Zuiderzee still covers 120 000ha - 296 400 acres, and ponds, small lakes, canals and streams abound in the country, above all in Friesland (its flag carries water lily leaves).

The percentage of land above sea level varies according to the region. There is much more from west to east since it is linked to the altitude. In fact, on the relatively high parts to the east of the country, water does not stay; it has on the other hand a tendency to accumulate in the plains and above all in the polders *(qv).*

LANDSCAPE

Apart from a few hilly regions, the soil, in general, forms an immense plain consisting of little varied material so that the natural landscapes are not of great diversity.

In addition the polder lands *(p 16)* marked by the determined intervention of man, can also appear somewhat monotonous. However, they contribute towards giving the country its originality, and by their light, colour and peaceful atmosphere form a land of poetic dimensions.

In the province of Groningen

Vast sandy areas. – Sand covers 43 % of the land. It extends mainly to the south and east of the country, notably in three regions, the **Kempenland,** area of North Brabant which is a continuation of the Belgian Kempenland, the **Veluwe** and the north of Overijssel and Drenthe. The moors of heather, broom, gorse, as well as the forests (around Breda, the Veluwe pine forests) cover the uncultivated expanses.

The hills of the Utrechtse Heuvelrug *(qv)* or the Veluwe, consisting of stones or erratic boulders, are the **moraines** of Scandinavian glaciers which covered the north of the country in the Quaternary Era. They have turned the flow of large rivers (Maas, Rhine) towards the west.

Here and there are a few **swamps** (De Peel, Biesbosch) or lakes, a large number appear in southern Friesland *(p 167)*. They have not been drained and transformed into polders, like those in Holland, because of their not very fertile sandy bottom.

Dunes. – Along the coasts the sand has formed offshore bars. The coastal **dunes** are of capital importance: they protect the plains against high tides. For this reason, they are supervised attentively by the State. Marram grass has been planted to consolidate them. In certain sectors, to avoid damaging the protective vegetation and prevent erosion, the public is not allowed to approach them.

When the chain of dunes is not sufficient, it is reinforced by dikes. Moreover, the dunes play the role of a water tower by absorbing the rainwater which feeds the underground water level.

Below the dunes and dikes, there are the vast beaches of seaside resorts.

The Wadden Islands, behind which is the Wadden Sea *(qv),* in fact, make a particularly important offshore bar.

Alluvium deposits. – Marine clay covers 28 % of the ground in the Delta, in the sea bays which still remain, or in those which have been reclaimed from the sea such as the Lauwers Sea and the Middelzee (which used to water Leeuwarden) partly transformed into polders.

Fluvial clay (10 % of the ground) spreads over the river region in the centre of the country, as well as in the Maas Valley, to the south of Venlo.

Peat bogs. – In the Netherlands, there exist two sorts of peat bogs. In lagoons, peat bogs have formed on top of sea clay. The peat used as fuel has been exploited, whereupon lakes formed which were subsequently dried out.

In the "upper country" peat formed in marshy areas. It was also exploited and the soil was then used for agriculture: they are called peat bog colonies *(veenkoloniën).* They are very common in the province of Groningen and in the Drenthe *(qv).*

Calcareous plateau. – Southern Limburg is an exception in the country not only geologically but physically, as well.

Its soil, limestone, covered with loess, is the same as that of Hesbaye in Belgium while in the extreme south there are a few rocks, last outcrop of the ancient Belgian Ardennes Massif.

The Limburg coalfields (closed down) are a continuation of those of Belgian Kempenland.

15

THE CLIMATE

The cloudy sky pierced by a few timid sun rays and the misty horizons whose beauty 17C painters were able to depict so well, are one of the features of the landscape.

The climate, oceanic, is humid and cool. An average of 750mm - 30in of rain falls each year, spread over more than 200 days. The temperature is fairly cool in summer without being very harsh in winter. Winters are warmer than in the past and the skating scenes seen in Avercamp's paintings attest to a quite different climate. The wind, which comes from the west, is often strong, and to protect themselves from it the farmhouses are surrounded by screens of poplar trees.

THE FIGHT AGAINST THE SEA *(see map p 17)*

The history of the country tells of the continuous fight by man against the elements, against river floods, against the sea and storms.

About 5BC the first dunes were formed, south of Haarlem. The line of dunes going from the Scheldt to the Eems appeared about 1000AD. Broken up at various points, this sand bar became the Wadden Islands *(qv)*, while the sea invaded the low peat bogs which became the **Wadden Sea.**

First stages: terps and dikes. – First inhabitants of the coastal areas as from 500BC, the **Frisians** were the forerunners in the fight against the sea. To protect themselves from high waters they built artifical mounds called **terps** *(qv)*.

They also built the first dikes as from 1200AD. Inside the dikes, between Leeuwarden and Sneek, they dried out a few parcels of land, already making a type of polder.

In the 13C there were 35 great floods, creating the Dollard and the **Lauwers Sea** in the north, and in the centre in 1287, the **Zuiderzee,** now called IJssel Lake *(qv)*.

Thanks to windmills: the first polders. – Starting in the 14C the swamps were drained and the lakes dried out by using **windmills** *(qv)*.

In the 15C in Zeeland, where the rivers had carved out islands and peninsulas, the shores crumbling at low tide and the lack of means of protection ended up in catastrophe: **St Elizabeth Flood** *(qv)*. This brought about the increase of windmills in the threatened plains. Thus, in North Holland small **polders** appeared, in Schagen in 1456 and in Alkmaar in 1564. **Andries Vierlingh** (1507-79) showed great skill in the building of dikes in coastal regions.

Creation of a polder. – A polder is land reclaimed from the sea, a lake or marshy soil. It is enclosed with dikes and its water level is artificially regulated by pumping. Since the beginning the creation of polders has gone through the same stages, despite the evolution of techniques.

In the peat bogs, along the rivers and along the coast, there are simple polders enclosed by a single dike. Their surplus water is directly returned into the sea or the river. When the polder extends above sea level it is sufficient at low tide to open the locks so that the water is evacuated into the diversion canals then into the sea. If not, pumping is necessary.

To dry out a lake a more complex type of polder is made. Around the lake a dike is built. This is surrounded by a canal which lines the ring dikes of the neighbouring polders. The polder is crossed with small canals linked to each other by collector canals. As soon as the desired water level is exceeded, the pump (formerly the windmill) forces the water back into the collector canals towards the peripheral canal and a whole network of lakes or canals serving as a temporary reservoir. The water is then discharged into rivers and in the sea either naturally, or by pumping. In the past when the lake to be dried out was deep, it was necessary to install several windmills in a row to force the water outside the polder.

17C: a series of polders. – In the 17C a name was associated with the drainage of inland water, that of **Jan Adriaensz. Leeghwater** *(qv)* (his name means low water). Under his supervision and with the help of 40 windmills reclamation work on **Beemster Lake** to the north of Amsterdam was satisfactorily carried out (1612). This process, crowned with success, encouraged the Dutch to continue the work. They created the polders of **Purmer** in 1622 and **Wormer** in 1626.

In 1631, Alkmaar undertook the drainage of **Schermer Lake** from Leeghwater's plans with the help of 50 windmills. It was completed in 1635. Leeghwater's projects also included the drainage of Haarlem Lake.

In 1667 Hendrik Stevin *(qv)* proposed drainage of the Zuiderzee in order "to evacuate the violence and poison of the North Sea". The project was completed only in the 20C.

In the 18C autonomous communities with hydraulic interests or **"waterschappen"** were responsible for the maintenance and construction of dikes, canals and locks. They still exist, though supplemented since 1798, by the **Waterstaat,** Ministry of Water and Highways.

A little before 1800 steam powered pumps began being used. They have the advantage of being able to force back water over the high dikes, therefore, replacing several rows of windmills and not being dependent on the wind.

Major work in the 19 and 20C. – The most spectacular period of land reclamation began in 1848 with the drainage of **Haarlem Lake** *(qv)*, completed in 1852 due to three enormous pumping stations, such as Cruquius's which has now been converted into a museum *(p 111)*.

Then, shortly after the great floods of 1916, it was the turn of the Zuiderzee itself, transformed into a lake, the **IJssel Lake** *(qv)* by the construction of the large **Barrier Dam** (Afsluitdijk) completed in 1932.

Several polders have progressively been created around the lake. The latest polder planned is the Markerwaard.

In addition other polders reclaimed in the 19 and 20C should be mentioned: the Prins Alexander Polder (1872) near Rotterdam, and the Lauwers Sea Polder *(qv)*.

THE FIGHT AGAINST THE SEA

- Polders : 14-18 C
- Polders : 19 C to the present
- Dike or dam : coastal or fluvial

The most recent disaster occurred on the night of 31 January-1 February 1953, brought about by a very strong wind blowing towards the land at very high tide; there were 1 865 deaths and 260 000ha - 642 200 acres devastated. Consequently engineers, encouraged by the successful closing of the Zuiderzee, looked for a means of protecting the islands of South Holland and Zeeland: the **Delta Plan** *(qv)*.

The water level in the canals which crisscross the polders is constantly checked and regulated *(p 16)*. This is so for most of the waterways in the country which have been converted into true canals by dikes and locks.

From the 13C to the present, about 7 050sq km - 2 745sq miles have been reclaimed from the sea of which 4 000sq km - 2 400sq miles due to coastal dikes, 1 650sq km - 644sq miles by creating the IJssel Lake and 1 400sq km - 546sq miles by other means. These figures do not include the territory, which was submerged during military operations and which subsequently also had to be reclaimed.

PROTECTION OF NATURE

In this very densely populated country with great industrial activity, there are certain groups which play a very active role in safeguarding nature. There is the Association for the Preservation of Nature, Vereniging tot Behoud van Natuurmonumenten, a large private organisation which undertakes acquiring land and looking after it. It has 150 parks covering 46 000ha - 113 620 acres of varied landscape (woods or moors, dunes or swamps). They are signposted **Natuurmonumenten** and entry, usually authorised, is subject to very strict rules.

As to woods belonging to the State, they are administered by the Staatsbosbeheer *(qv)*, a sort of Forestry Commission, and are often laid out for leisure activities.

Birds

The Netherlands, due to their innumerable ponds and swamps, and their long seashores bordered with dunes, is a land chosen by numerous species of migrating or sedentary birds. The **lapwing,** a small round bird about 30cm - 12in long and covered with rather lustrous bronze plumage, inhabits the grassland particularly in Friesland. It is almost considered the national bird. Its eggs are much appreciated *(p 35)*.

On the seashores there are many **terns, sea-gulls** and other **gulls,** particularly the black-headed gull *(illustration p 89)* which often nests on dry land; there are also colonies of **oystercatchers,** a small black and white wader. Another wader, the **grey heron** can be seen along canals. The **spoonbill** *(illustration p 185)* is rarer as is the **white stork** which is bred to prevent its extinction.

All sorts of **ducks** abound in canals, ponds and swamps: the wild duck or mallard and the sheldrake with multicoloured plumage are perhaps the most commonly seen in the country.

To protect certain species of birds, a multitude of **nature reserves** have been made, near the coast as well as inland. These natural areas make it easy for birds to nest and look for food, at the same time providing ornithological research. Most of the reserves are open to the public. Their access, however, is strictly controlled and some are partially forbidden during brooding time.

HISTORICAL TABLE AND NOTES

Events in italics indicate milestones for local history

Prehistory

BC	
30 000	First traces of human occupation in the east of the country.
4500	An agricultural people come to Limburg, whose pottery belongs to Spiral-Meander Ware culture.
3000-2000	In the Drenthe, the hunebed *(qv)* civilisation.
2200	North of the big rivers a nomadic people settle who make Stroke-Ornamented Ware.
2000	Bell-Beaker civilisation, notably in the Drenthe. The alluvial areas of the delta start being inhabited.
1900	Bronze Age. The dead are buried in burial mounds.
800	In the east the people cremate their dead and bury them in urnfields.
750-400	First Iron Age: Hallstatt Period.
500	First **terps** built in Friesland and in the Groningen region *(p 139)*.
450	South of the big rivers, Second Iron Age: La Tene Period.
300	Arrival of Germanic and Celtic tribes south of the Rhine.

Romans, Vikings

57-1	South of the Rhine **Caesar** defeated the Celtic tribes (Menapii, Eburones) which were part of Belgica.
12	The **Batavians** are found along the big rivers.

AD	
69-70	Batavian revolt *(p 151)* against the Romans.
3C	The **Franks,** a group of Germanic tribes, appear along the Rhine. With the **Saxons** and the **Frisians** they are the main tribes occupying the country.
End 3C	The areas south of the Rhine are part of the Roman province of Germania Secunda (capital Cologne).
4C	Fight between the Romans and the Salian Franks.
382	St Servatius transfers his bishopric from Tongeren to Maastricht, marking the beginning of Christianity in the country.
Early 6C	Under Clovis (465-511) the Merovingian kingdom extends from the north of Gaul to the Rhine.
561	Division of the Merovingian kingdom into Neustria (west of the river Scheldt) and Austrasia (east of the river Scheldt; present Netherlands).
End 7C	**Willibrord** tries to evangelise Friesland *(p 171)*.
800	**Charlemagne** emperor. His immense empire, centred at Aachen covers the whole country.
834	First raids of the **Vikings** at Dorestad *(qv)*.
843	**Treaty of Verdun.** Division of the Carolingian empire into three kingdoms: one Germanic, one French and a middle kingdom stretching from the North Sea to the Mediterranean and including the present Netherlands. Later amputated from the south, this middle kingdom became **Lotharingia.**
879-882	Great Norsemen invasion: the Vikings with Utrecht as their base make raids into the surrounding regions.
925	Lotharingia is united again to Germany by Henry I, the Fowler.
959	Lotharingia is separated into Upper Lotharingia (Lorraine) and Lower Lotharingia covering nearly all the present country.

Formation of Counties (comitatus) and Dukedoms

10C	Under Bishop Balderic (918-976) the **Utrecht** bishopric expanded.
Early 11C	Formation of the **Brabant** Dukedom by Lambert, Count of Louvain.
1066	*William the Conqueror lands in England.*
11C	Birth of the **Gelderland** county.
End 11C	Extension of the **Holland** county, at the expense of the county of Flanders (in Zeeland) and the Utrecht bishopric (to the east).
Early 13C	The Gelderland county expands to include the Zutphen and the Veluwe counties.
1215	*Magna Carta.*
Late 13C	**Floris V,** Count of Holland, conquers West Friesland.
1323	Holland takes Zeeland from Flanders.
1337-1453	*Hundred Years War.*
1350	Beginning of the civil war between the **Hooks** (*Hoeken*-backed by Margaret of Bavaria) and the **Cods** (*Kabbeljauwen*-backed by her son William V).

Burgundian Ascendancy

Late 14C	The Duchy of Burgundy stretches towards the north: **Philip the Bold,** acquires Limburg and rights over Brabant.
1428	Philip the Good gets hold of the counties of Holland and Zeeland from **Jacoba** *(qv)*.
1473	**Charles the Bold** obtains Gelderland. All the territory except Friesland is now in the hands of the Burgundians.

The Hapsburgs

1477	Death of Charles the Bold. His daughter, Mary of Burgundy marries Maximilian of Hapsburg.
1492	*Christopher Columbus discovers America.*
1494	Philip the Fair, their son, reigns over the Low Countries.
1515	Charles I of Spain, son of Philip the Fair, inherits the Low Countries. In 1519 he becomes Emperor of Germany under the name of **Charles V.** He enlarges the Low Countries by adding **Friesland** in 1523; in 1527 he receives the Utrecht bishopric; in 1528 he takes Overijssel and, in 1536 he seizes Groningen and Drenthe.
1543	The Duke of **Gelderland** abandons his Dukedom to Charles V who thus rules over nearly the whole of Europe.
1548	Charles V groups the 17 provinces of the Low Countries and the Franche-Comté into the independent "Burgundian Kreis".

Spanish Netherlands

1555	Charles V abdicates his claims to the Low Countries to his son Philip II, soon to be King of Spain.
1566	The **Breda Compromise** *(qv)*; the Beggars protest against the Inquisition. **Iconoclastic Fury** *(qv)*.
1568	**William the Silent** *(qv)* raises an army: it is the beginning of the Eighty Years' War.
1572	**Capture of Brielle** by the Sea Beggars *(qv)*.
1579	**Union of Utrecht** *(qv)*: alliance of the Protestant provinces.

The United Provinces

1581	Creation of the **United Provinces,** a federation of seven provinces, independent of Spanish rule.
1584	Assassination of William the Silent in Delft.
1585	Maurice of Nassau (became Prince of Orange after the death of his elder half-brother Philip William in 1618) succeeds his father as Stadtholder of Holland and Zeeland.
1596	Arrival of Cornelis de Houtman in Java *(qv)*.
1598	*Promulgation of the* Edict of Nantes.
1602	Founding of the **Dutch East India Company** *(qv)*.
1609	**Twelve years Truce** with Spain. Henry Hudson sails up the river, which bears his name, in his ship the *Half Moon*.
1614	The name New Netherlands is first used for the colony founded in the New World.
1618	**Synod of Dort** *(qv)*. Reprobation of the Remonstrants.
1619	Founding of Batavia (p 130) in the Dutch East Indies.
1620	*Pilgrim Fathers land at Plymouth, Ma.*
1621	Founding of the **Dutch West India Company.**
1624-54	Occupation of northeast Brazil.
1625	The Dutch settlement in Manhattan is called Nieuw Amsterdam.
1626	Peter Minuit, of the Dutch West India Company, buys Manhattan from the Indians for the equivalent of $24.
1634	Occupation of Curaçao in the Antilles by the Dutch West India Company.
1648	*Treaty of Westphalia* puts an end to the Thirty Years War, also called the Eighty Years' War. In the **Treaty of Munster,** Philip IV of Spain recognises the independence of the United Provinces.
1651	The English promulgate the *Navigation Act,* ill-fated for Dutch trade.
1652	Jan van Riebeeck *(qv)* founds the Cape colony.
1652-4	**First Dutch War** led by Admiral Tromp *(qv)*.
1653-72	Stadtholderless Period: **Johan de Witt** *(qv)* Grand Pensionary runs the State.
1658-1795	Occupation of Ceylon (now called Sri Lanka).
1664	English take Nieuw Amsterdam and rename it New York (after James II).
1665-7	**Second Dutch War** where Admiral de Ruyter *(qv)* distinguishes himself. In the *Treaty of Breda,* Dutch Guiana (present Surinam) ceded to the Dutch in exchange for Nieuw Amsterdam.
1667-8	War of Devolution led by Louis XIV; *Treaty of Aachen.*
1672	**William III,** Stadtholder of Holland and Zeeland.
1672-8	War of Louis XIV against the United Provinces. **Peace of Nijmegen** *(qv)*.
1685	*Revocation of the* Edict of Nantes.
1689	William III becomes King of England.
1701-13	Spanish War of Succession: alliance of several countries, including the United Provinces, against Louis XIV. **Peace of Utrecht** *(qv)*.
1702	The Stadtholder William III dies without an heir. The title of Prince of Orange passes to the Frisian Stadtholder John William Friso.
1714-27	*George I's reign.*
1747	**William IV,** son of the latter, is the first hereditary Stadtholder of the United Provinces.
1751-95	**William V** son of the former Stadtholder.
1776	*American Declaration of Independence.*

French domination

1789	*George Washington chosen as first President of the United States.*
1795	Conquest of the country by a French revolutionary army led by Pichegru. The French make the United Provinces into the **Batavian Republic.**
1806	The King **Louis Bonaparte** is at the head of the **Kingdom of Holland** with Amsterdam as the capital.
1810	Louis Bonaparte abdicates. The country is attached to the **French Empire** by Napoleon.

Union with Belgium

Dec. 1813	William of Orange, son of William V, last Stadtholder of the United Provinces, becomes sovereign of the Kingdom of the Netherlands.
1815	Battle of Waterloo; Napoleon's fall. At the Congress of Vienna William of Orange is recognised as King of the Netherlands (including Belgium), under the name **William I.** In addition he becomes Grand Duke of Luxemburg.
1820-37	*George IV's reign.*
1824	*Lafayette visits America.*
1828	The west side of New Guinea is occupied.
1830	Revolution in Belgium. Belgium becomes independent.

An independent kingdom

1831	Division of Limburg and Brabant with Belgium. William I only ratifies the treaty in 1839.
1837-1901	*Victoria's reign.*
1890-1948	Reign of **Queen Wilhelmina.**
May 1940	The country is invaded by the German army. The Queen leaves for London.
5 May 1945	Surrender of the German army (p 62). Return of the Queen.
1948	Queen Wilhelmina abdicates in favour of her daughter **Juliana** (b in 1909).
Dec. 1949	Independence of the Dutch East Indies which become the Republic of **Indonesia.**

1954	Autonomy of Dutch Guiana or Surinam and the archipelago of the Dutch Antilles.
1957	The Netherlands joins the EEC.
1960	The **Benelux** economic union comes into effect.
Nov. 1975	Independence of Dutch Guiana, becoming the Republic of **Surinam**.
30 April 1980	Queen Juliana abdicates in favour of her daughter **Beatrix**.

THE HOUSES OF ORANGE AND STUART

This chart is selective; it shows the association between the two houses.
For monarchs after William V see Historical Table and Notes.

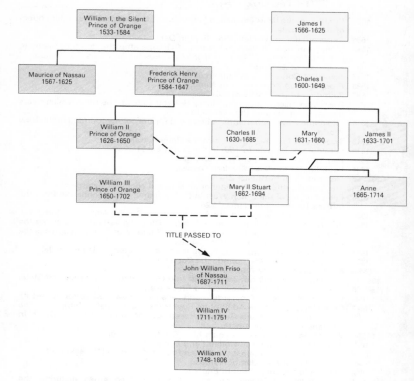

THE BRITISH AND DUTCH TIES

Two small sea-faring nations with a strong Protestant voice, in an otherwise predominantly Catholic world, were the Netherlands and Britain. They were linked politically, religiously, commercially, intellectually and artistically long before William III's reign and yet it was during his reign that their friendship reached its peak.

William III, Prince of Orange, nephew and son-in-law to King James II (1685-8) of England was Stadtholder of the United Provinces. He had married Mary, James's daughter in 1677. In England King James set about establishing Catholicism creating unrest and dissent throughout the nation. The British wrote to William in June 1688 asking him to restore peace and unity to the country. William landed in October 1688, James abdicated; the throne being vacant, Mary, the nearest Protestant claimant, with her husband William, were jointly crowned in April 1689; with their reign (1689-1702) a vogue for all things Dutch developed.

Political decisions were closely linked to commercial interests (Dutch Wars) and the Dutch, English and Scots had been exchanging naval techniques and trading together for years (Dutch trading English wool, weavers invited to England to teach their craft, with Scotland exchange of luxury goods existed, shipbuilding...).

Once commercial relationships had been established between the two countries, Dutch goods and influence began appearing in Britain (bricks and gables, sash windows, Dutch-style gardens, marinescapes and portraits, interior decorative detail...). Dutch influence reached its peak during William and Mary's reign with the transformation of Hampton Court and Kensington Palace: the influence of their Dutch residence, Het Loo, is apparent. They employed Grinling Gibbons (carvings), Daniel Marot (architect and interior decorator) and Sir Godfrey Kneller (portraitist) all in someway related to the Netherlands. Attention to interior decoration (carvings, tulip-vases, laquerware cabinets, upholstered cabriole-legged chairs...), Mary's obvious love of porcelain and William's for gardens were duplicated in many stately homes (Belton, Ashdown, Easton Neston, Breamore...) of that time.

The Dutch tradition of religious tolerance and freedom of expression attracted thinkers (Erasmus, Spinoza, Grotius, Voetius...), printers (English books printed and translated into Dutch) and scholars (Jonson, Boswell...) and enabled the English Bill of Rights to exist. Political (mid-17C Royalists, 1st Earl of Shaftesbury, Bishop Burnet...) and religious (Presbyterians, Separatists, Congregationalists...) refugees were welcomed.

With the reign of William and Mary, a wave of tolerance spread through Britain rendering exile to the Netherlands unnecessary.

OVERSEAS EXPANSION

In the middle of the 16C Amsterdam traders went to Antwerp to obtain goods brought back from the Indies by Portuguese ships. The mouth of the Scheldt being cut off by the Sea Beggars the traders started sailing to Lisbon in 1580, the same year that Philip II of Spain invaded Portugal. In 1585 he put an embargo on Dutch trade in Spain and Portugal. The Dutch merchants, forced to take care of shipments themselves, clashed with the Spanish, Portuguese and above all the English, fearsome competitors in overseas markets.

On the spice route. – When looking for access to India from the north of Europe, **William Barents** *(qv)* discovered Spitsbergen in 1596. The same year **Cornelis de Houtman** *(qv)* landed in **Java**.

To coordinate the ever increasing trading companies, in 1602 Johan van Oldenbarnevelt founded the **Dutch East India Company** *(qv)*. This institution which obtained a monopoly over shipping and trade to the east of the Cape of Good Hope kept going until 1798.

In 1619 the foundation of **Batavia** by **Jan Pieterszoon Coen** *(qv)* marks the beginning of the colonisation of Java. **Malacca** was taken from the Portuguese in 1641. The following year Tasman discovered **Tasmania** and **New Zealand,** then Australia (1644) but did not reside there.

In 1652 **Jan Anthonisz. van Riebeeck** *(qv)* founded the **Cape Colony.** Originally a stopping point on the way to India, it grew into a rambling but vigorous community which subsequently became an independent settlement, expanding and spreading inland. Finally **Ceylon** was occupied from 1658.

The Americas. – At the same time Dutch trade turned towards the New World.

In 1609 the **Hudson** *(qv)* expedition took place. In 1613 the **Guiana** coast was occupied by traders. **Willem Schouten** *(qv)* discovered Cape Horn in 1616.

The **Dutch West India Company,** created in 1621, covered both Africa and the Americas.

In **Brazil, John Maurice of Nassau** (1604-79) was appointed governor general (1636-44). Patron of arts and science, he surrounded himself with a team of scientists, painters and draftsmen who assembled abundant documentation on the country.

The settlement called **Nieuw Amsterdam** (New Amsterdam) was founded in 1625 on the eastern coast of North America. **Peter Stuyvesant** *(qv)* soon became its Governor. In the Antilles, the Dutch India Company founded the colony of **Curaçao** in 1634.

Many of these conquests were only temporary. However, the Dutch suceeded in making lasting settlements in Java, Guiana and in the Antilles; the **Netherlands Antilles** (capital: Willemstad), still belongs to the Kingdom of the Netherlands.

RELIGIONS

The Protestant proverb which says: "One Dutchman, a theologian; two Dutchmen, a Church; three Dutchmen, a schism" has been borne out over the years. Dutch interest in doctrines and theology, linked to a certain taste for tolerance, explains the proliferation in the country of different beliefs and the most diverse movements.

A mystic trend. – In the 14C the mystical writings of the Flemish **Jan van Ruysbroeck** are the origin of a spiritual movement, the **devotio moderna,** which developed within the Order of the **Brethren of the Common Life** *(qv)* due to the theologian **Gerhard Groote.**

The Reformation. – The Lutheran doctrine, born in 1517 and condemned by the Diet of Worms in 1521, spread quickly over the Low Countries.

In 1530 the **Anabaptist** movement appeared. A few fanatics joined up with **John of Leiden** *(qv)* and formed a community of a slightly revolutionary type in Munster, in Germany. In Friesland, **Menno Simonsz.** *(qv)*, a Catholic priest, founded in 1536, the Anabaptist sect, the **"doopsgezinden"** (Mennonites), which gathered together the faithful remaining in the country. The Anabaptists were persecuted for nearly a century.

However, it was **Calvinism** which obtained the upper hand in the Low Countries. This doctrine spread over the country from 1550 through France.

In the 16 and 17C Protestant refugees coming from Belgium and France established the **Walloon Churches** *(qv)* using the French language.

Quite early, the religious convictions of the Calvinists became the symbol of the struggle against the Spanish Catholics. Soon after the *Breda Compromise (qv),* the Iconoclastic Fury broke out in 1566.

Clandestine Catholicism. – After the fight for independence, Calvinist fanaticism grew stronger. Holland and Zeeland considering the Calvinist religion as official, forbade other religions in 1579 *(p 171)* and Catholics, in particular, were obliged to practise their cult in **clandestine churches** up to 1798, however, they were not persecuted.

From the 17C to today. – The Synod of Dort from 1618-9 gave a new cohesion to the Dutch Reformed Church (successor to the Dutch Reformed Church; changed to the Reformed Church of the Netherlands in 1816 by King William I). And yet its unity was established to the detriment of the Arminians or **Remonstrants** *(qv)*. They were the object of persecution for several years, as can be seen by the arrest of Oldenbarnevelt *(qv)*.

Towards the end of the 17C the **Labadist** *(p 97)* movement was born.

Persecuted in France, the Jansenists took refuge in Utrecht where they contributed to the establishment of an independent Catholic church, the **Old Catholics Church** *(qv)*.

In the beginning of the 18C the **Moravian Brothers** *(qv)* sect was created.

Presently the **Protestants** of the Netherlands belong either to the Reformed Church of the Netherlands (Nederlands Hervormde Kerk) which dates from the 1619 Synod of Dort and has nearly 2.5 million members, or to the group of Reformed Churches in the Netherlands (Gereformeerde Kerken in Nederland) founded in 1892 and which counts about 820 000 members.

The **Catholics,** numerous in the south of the country, represented 38% of the population in 1985.

THE ARTS

In the domain of the arts, the Netherlands has made a first-rate contribution to Western civilisation.

Sculpture, most likely due to lack of material more or less up to the 20C, and music occupy a relatively modest place in the Dutch artistic heritage. But architecture, at certain epochs very remarkable, and above all paintings, make the Netherlands a place of pilgrimage and inspiration.

Romanesque Art

It can be seen in several regions far apart from each other.

Rhenish-Mosan Art. – This developed in the Maas Valley and in particular at Maastricht, (which belonged to the Diocese of Liège). The style is very similar to the Rhine Valley style, hence its name.

Architecture. – Maastricht was an important town in the Roman era and then a place of pilgrimage – the relics of St Servatius, who died in 384, are venerated there. It has magnificent buildings such as St Servatius's Basilica and the Basilica of Our Lady.

In its early days Mosan art borrowed a lot from **Carolingian architecture.** Apart from St Nicholas's Chapel at Nijmegen, whose shape imitated the octagonal basilica of Charlemagne in the cathedral at Aachen, Carolingian churches usually have two chancels, an imposing westwork, and a chapel called the emperor's room, Keizerszaal, situated upstairs on the west side. Inside the wooden ceiling is flat, the pillars square.

Towards 1000AD the construction of **St Servatius's** was started, with a westwork with two large towers decorated with Lombard arcading. The **Basilica of Our Lady,** of the same period, also has a massive westwork, flanked by round turrets. St Amelberga's at **Susteren** *(qv)* built in the second half of the 11C is still very plain.

In the 12C Mosan architecture mellowed and decoration increased. Sculpture started appearing on the capitals, low reliefs and portals. It was the period when St Servatius's was altered, as well as the basilica of Our Lady (both in Maastricht), where the chancel, seen from the nave, is one of the most beautiful Romanesque achievements of the country. **Rolduc Abbey** in Kerkrade, shows by its original trefoiled plan, Rhenish influence.

The Church of Our Lady at **Roermond,** although restored, has kept Rhenish-Mosan characteristics. The crypts of these edifices are often very beautiful.

Gold and silversmith's work. – As in the rest of the Diocese of Liège, in Belgium, Mosan art has produced masterpieces of gold and silversmith's work. Thus, St Servatius's Basilica in Maastricht has preserved the gilded copper **shrine** of the saint, with richly decorated enamel work, cabochons, and: Christ and St Servatius (on each end), and the Apostles (on the sides).

(After photo Stichting Schatkamer St.-Servaas)

Shrine of St Servatius
in St Servatius's Basilica, Maastricht

It should also be mentioned that there is a lovely 11C Mosan Christ in bronze which belongs to the Het Catharijneconvent Museum in Utrecht.

Other regions. – It was normal that **Utrecht,** an important bishopric in the Middle Ages, was embellished with religious buildings in the Romanesque period. However, apart from St Peter's, a good example of the local style (1148), there are only a few remains of the lovely Romanesque series conceived by Bishop Bernulphus.

Among the edifices built in the Diocese of Utrecht, the Great Church at **Deventer** has preserved the remains of a double transept and a westwork (c1040) which links it to Mosan churches.

At **Oldenzaal,** the great St Plecheln's Basilica is later (early 12C) and has a nave with vaulting supported by strong pillars.

Utrecht keeps **gold and silverware** objects in its museums which are witness to the prosperity of its bishops from the Romanesque period: monstrances, pyxs, shrines, processional crosses and gospel books with engraved binding.

Beginning in the mid-12C the Romanesque style appeared in a particular regional manner in **Friesland** and in the **province of Groningen** in the village churches where the outside walls were enlivened by **brick decoration** *(pp 106 and 139)* and inside there are often fresco remains.

Gothic Art

Gothic art appeared only in the 14C and mainly in the 15C under Burgundian rule. Many religious buildings, as well as a few town halls date from this period.

Churches. – North Brabant, a province where the majority of the inhabitants are Catholic, has most of the large churches and **cathedrals** in the country. These buildings were built in the **Brabant Gothic style** similar to a number of edifices in Belgium and similar to Flamboyant Gothic: exterior – many openwork gables and crocket spires, tall windows, flying buttresses, tall belfry porch on the west side; interior – a slender central nave with pointed vaulting resting on round columns with crocket capitals and a triforium.

The Great Church in **Breda** is a typical example of Brabant Gothic as is St John's Cathedral in **'s-Hertogenbosch,** started in the 14C and one of the most beautiful and greatest achievements in the country. Contrary to other edifices, the vaults of the latter do not rest on columns but on a cluster of small columns without capitals.

The Brabant Gothic style influenced the construction of many other churches in the country. In Holland, the stone vault was rare and the church was covered with a wooden ceiling, flat or barrel vaulted. The only exception is the Great Church in Dordrecht. A number of lovely Gothic buildings worth noting include: in Leyden St Peter's and St Pancras's, in Alkmaar the Great Church or St Lawrence's, in Amsterdam the New Church, in Gouda St John's and in Haarlem the Great Church. The cathedral in Utrecht, unfortunately, did not survive the great storm of 1672. There still exists, however, a harmonious bell tower, the **Dom Tower,** similar in outline to many bell towers which can be seen in the country, as at Amersfoort.

In the diocese, the Church of St Nicholas in Kampen is also interesting.

Town Halls. – Two town halls in the Flamboyant Gothic style are particularly remarkable. That of **Gouda** is delightful with its façade where a multitude of pinnacles and slender spires rear up. That of **Middelburg,** more sumptuous, built by Belgian architects shows the influence of the Brussels town hall.

Sculpture. – Not as abundant as in Belgium, church furnishings have, however, some interesting 15 and early 16C wood carvings.

The groups by **Adriaen van Wesel** (late 15C) shown in the Rijksmuseum in Amsterdam *(qv)* are carved with a remarkable sense of composition and a great strength of expression.

The **Brabant altarpieces** are triptyches in the Flamboyant style, with a central panel in wood, carved on several levels, showing very animated scenes with

Gouda's Town Hall

comical details and flanked by two painted panels (altarpieces of St John's Cathedral in 's-Hertogenbosch and the Church of Our Lady in Roermond).

The **stalls,** often carved with satirical themes are a pleasure to see in several churches in the country, as in St Martin's in Bolsward or the Great Church in Breda.

The Renaissance

The Renaissance reached the Netherlands late.

Architecture. – This influence only appears in the mid-16C. Brought by Italian artists such as **Thomas Vincidor of Bologna** who designed Breda Castle (as from 1536); it was then taken up by local architects.

In fact, Renaissance elements were used without important architectural change and the traditional plan was often retained. It was especially through the details that a new contribution was made: shell-shaped window tympana, dormer windows overburdened with pinnacles and blind arcading, octagonal turrets...

Hans Vredeman de Vries (1527-c1603), a great adept of Renaissance decoration applied to architecture, did not remain long in his country.

Lieven de Key *(qv)* worked a great deal in Haarlem, his native town. The old meat market (1603) is his most complete work.

Hendrick de Keyser (1565-1621) is at the same time sculptor and architect. He built notably in Amsterdam several churches (Zuider Church, Wester Church), large town houses (Bartolotti House) and, in Hoorn, the weigh house. His style already forecasts the baroque; more monumental and heavier, the buildings became severe and imposing.

The Renaissance manifested itself particularly in **Friesland** where the taste for geometric decoration, for cheerful and picturesque details, already appearing in Romanesque churches, can once again be found in many buildings.

The town halls (Franeker, Bolsward), the Law Courts (Leeuwarden's Chancellery), fortified gateways (Sneek's water-gate: *illustration p 167),* all have the imprint of the new style. The east and south of the country remain a little apart from these influences, though the weigh house in Nijmegen is a good example of the Renaissance.

Sculpture. – **Mausoleums** in the Italian Renaissance style multiply.

Thomas Vincidor of Bologna made the tomb of Count Englebert II of Nassau in Breda; the four Romanesque figures at the corners and the contrasts of colour in material convey a new contribution.

Hendrick de Keyser continued this style in the early 17C with the tomb of William the Silent in Delft. He is also responsible for the sober statue of Erasmus in Rotterdam.

In **Friesland** the Renaissance style is expressed in woodwork. The **pulpits,** finely decorated, have symbolic panels (carved and added on St Martin's in Bolsward, Great Church in Dokkum).

The remarkable 17C stalls of Dordrecht's Great Church are also inspired by the Renaissance.

Finally, the magnificent stained glass of St John's in Gouda is one of the finest examples of Renaissance art.

The Golden Age: 17C

Beginning in the middle of the century the grace and lightness of the Renaissance style is over. The style called baroque, which reigns in architecture of exceptional sobriety in comparison with other countries, is sometimes called classic.

Architecture and Sculpture. – One of the most famous architects of the Golden Age is **Jacob van Campen** (1595-1657), designer of **Amsterdam's town hall** (1648) which subsequently became the royal palace. Quadrilateral in shape, with its slightly severe lines, it is barely restrained by the slight projection of the fore-part, its sculptured pediments and bell tower. It is a majestic work which greatly influenced architecture in the whole country. **Pieter Post** (1608-69) who built the royal palace (Huis ten Bosch) and the Mauritshuis in The Hague after the plans of Van Campen, and the town hall in Maastricht, follows this trend. **Jacob Roman,** also in the same style, built Het Loo Palace (1685) in Apeldoorn *(qv)* in collaboration with Daniel Marot *(see below).*
This art which reveals undoubted prosperity can be found in the **town houses** which are built along Amsterdam's main canals *(illustration p 48).* One of the most representative models of this solemn style is the Trippen Huis *(p 50)* built by **Juste Vingboons** (c1620-98) who worked a great deal with his brother Philip.
Many of the Protestant **churches** of this period are built on a central plan, and are sometimes topped by a dome (New Lutheran Church of Amsterdam, 1671).
The Antwerp sculptor **Artus I Quellin the Elder** (1609-68) decorated in a particularly baroque style, the pediments and the interior of Amsterdam's town hall *(p 48).*

Gold and silversmiths' work, pottery. – Beginning in the 16C, but mainly in the 17C, the guilds and the bourgeois had magnificent silver objects made for their banquets and reunions, finely engraved and chased, most of which are in museum collections: hanaps (a metal standing drinking vessel), goblets, large dishes, ewers, **nautilus shell cup** (a cup made with a nautilus shell mounted on a silver stem), chains of office *(illustration p 152).* The most famous gold and silversmiths were the **Van Vianen** brothers.
Protestant churches also have their silver goblets which are filled with wine when celebrating the Last Supper.
Frisian silverware is particularly remarkable. Beautiful **brandy bowls,** oval in shape with two handles and highly decorated, held brandy; to drink one dipped a silver chased spoon. The 17C is also an important period for pottery *(p 75)* and above all earthenware tiles *(illustration p 129).*

18-19C

Daniel Marot (c1663-1752) from France, builder in The Hague of patrician residences (Lange Voorhout 34, 1736) continued the Golden Age trend. However, he allowed the rococo style to make a timid appearance in the sculptures of façades (porch pediments, statues) and in the grilles and imposts which, above the gateways, usually formed an elegant decoration.
In the 19C architecture declined. **P.J.H. Cuypers** (1827-1921) introduced a certain form of neo-Gothic in a number of monuments (Rijksmuseum, central railway station in Amsterdam) and effected daring restoration work on medieval buildings.

20C

This century has seen the renewal of architecture in the Netherlands, as well as a passion for sculpture.

Architecture. – At the end of the 19C **Berlage** (1856-1934), in building Amsterdam's Stock Exchange, became the precursor of an architectural movement where importance is given to material and the use of space for a determined function. **De Bazel** (1869-1923) used the same formula (Algemene Bank Nederland in Vijzelstraat in Amsterdam).
The **Amsterdam School** (c1912-23) *(qv)* reacting against Berlage, turned towards a less austere architecture and **Michel de Klerk, Peter Kramer** and **J.M. van der Mey** were the enlightened craftsmen in the renovation of the town.
At the same time, the **De Stijl movement** *(qv)* was founded by **Mondrian, Theo van Doesburg** (1883-1931) and **J.J.P. Oud** (1890-1963). Architects like **G. Rietveld** drew their theories from it; their concrete buildings consist of cubic spaces which are superimposed or juxtaposed forming a whole (Rietveld Schröder House in Utrecht, 1924); he was also interested in furnishings and designed armchairs with very original shapes.
A little on the fringe of these movements, **Dudok** (b1884), influenced by the American Frank Lloyd Wright, is above all known for designing the town hall in Hilversum *(p 126);* he is also responsible for the theatre in Utrecht.
After 1950, during the reconstruction of **Rotterdam**, the town planners showed a desire to adapt to human desires: the Lijnbaan (1952-4) by **J.B. Bakema** (1914-81) was the first pedestrian precinct in Europe.
The present trend is to integrate architecture with nature by giving a very important role to openings as well as gardens and lakes.

Sculpture. – In most of the towns in the Netherlands the pedestrian precincts and parks are embellished with structures in bronze, ceramic, concrete or plastic, and the modern façades with geometric lines are enhanced with mosaics, coloured elements or bronze indentations.
Often figurative, the sculptures depict people *(illustration p 65)* or animals *(illustration p 159).*
Mari Andriessen (1897-1979) one of the most remarkable present-day sculptors, is responsible for the statue of a Docker near the Portuguese Synagogue in Amsterdam, the Volkspark monument in Enschede, as well as the statue of Queen Wilhelmina in Wilhelmina Park in Utrecht.

PAINTING

In the beginning, very similar to Flemish painting, then for a while influenced by Italy, Dutch painting had its Golden Age in the 17C with the country's freedom: from then on it blossomed along with the bourgeois society it painted.

Primitives. – Amongst the greatest, a fantastic painter appeared in the 15C in 's-Hertogenbosch, **Hieronymus Bosch** *(qv)*. His work, original for his country and epoch, remains mysterious and is subject to many interpretations. Still medieval in the portrayal of a world haunted by sin, Bosch by his realism is, however, a forerunner of 17C painting, and by his imagination, Surrealism.

The other painters are closer to the Flemish Primitives, such as **Geertgen tot Sint Jans** *(qv)* the delicate and serene painter of *The Adoration of the Magi* (in the Rijksmuseum) which has a beautiful and skilfully painted landscape in the background; **Cornelis Engebrechtsz.** *(qv)*, a painter of turbulent scenes with numerous people, and a remarkable colourist, whose work can be seen in the De Lakenhal Municipal Museum in Leyden, and finally **Jan Mostaert** *(qv)*.

Renaissance. – **Jan van Scorel** *(qv)* a pupil of **Jacob Cornelisz. van Oostsanen** (c1470-1533) on his return from Rome in 1524 introduced the Renaissance in the northern Netherlands. He is the first of the Romanist painters (northern artists who went to Italy and were greatly influenced by Italian Renaissance art). He painted portraits of great sensitivity (*Portrait of a Young Scholar*, in the Boymans-van Beuningen Museum in Rotterdam), as well as religious paintings, rather Manneristic in style. **Maarten van Heemskerck** *(qv)* his pupil was also a painter of refined portraits and religious scenes.

Lucas van Leyden *(qv)*, pupil of Cornelis Engebrechtsz., was also influenced by the Renaissance. He painted notably large harmonious compositions such as the *Last Judgment* in the De Lakenhal Municipal Museum in Leyden, and the *Adoration of the Golden Calf* (c1525) in the Rijksmuseum in Amsterdam.

Pieter Aertsen (c1509-75) was not at all affected by the Romanist influence. This great Amsterdam artist, who lived for a time in Antwerp, painted rustic or interior scenes with a certain subtlety and embellished the scenery with still lifes.

Antoon Mor acquired fame under the Spanish name of **Antonio Moro** *(qv)* by becoming Charles V's official painter and then Philip II's. He went to England as Sir Anthony More to paint the portrait of Queen Mary (exhibited in the Prado, Madrid) for her bridegroom Philip II. He died in Antwerp in 1575.

The Golden Age. – Dominated by great figures such as Rembrandt, Frans Hals, Vermeer and Jacob van Ruisdael, the 17C also includes a plethora of painters with very diverse talents. Whereas the Flemish still painted many religious scenes (due to the Spanish-Catholic influence), a large part of Dutch art was destined to decorate rich bourgeois interiors, consequently the subjects were more profane and of great variety. They are, at the same time, a remarkable record of the daily life of the period.

Guild portraits. – Civic guards, syndics, surgeons, almshouse regents, wished to immortalise their features, therefore, guild portraits were tremendously in vogue.

Bartholomeus van der Helst *(qv)*, apart from portraits of the bourgeois or members of the House of Orange, painted numerous group portraits, severe and classic. Less conformist, **Frans Hals** *(qv)* had the ease of genius. Most of his large guild paintings are in the Frans Hals Museum, in Haarlem, where he lived. He also painted striking portraits full of life (*Jolly Toper*, Rijksmuseum in Amsterdam).

Rembrandt and his pupils. – **Rembrandt** *(qv)* also painted guild portraits such as the famous *The Anatomy Lesson of Doctor Tulp* which is in the Mauritshuis in The Hague, but the best known example is the *Night Watch,* in the Rijksmuseum in Amsterdam. This museum, furthermore, has an excellent collection of this master's work, notably Biblical scenes, portraits and self-portraits, where the light shines on solemn people looming up from a mysterious darkness.

Rembrandt had a number of pupils: **Gerrit Dou** *(qv)* who did chiaroscuro genre paintings; **Ferdinand Bol** *(qv)*, one of the closest to the master in style; **Nicolaes Maes** *(qv)* who used warm colours to paint calm interior scenes; **Samuel van Hoogstraten** *(qv)*; **Aert van Gelder** *(qv)*; **Carel Fabritius** (1622-54) who died young, was the most gifted of all; **Philips Koninck** *(qv)*, mainly a landscape painter.

Landscape and seascape painters. – Although Rembrandt drew and etched admirable landscapes, he painted few. Numerous artists, on the other hand, specialised in this genre. In the early 17C **Hercules Seghers** (1589/90-1638) and **Salomon van Ruysdael** *(qv)* are painters of nature, as well as **Van Goyen** *(qv)*. Wide horizons, peaceful rivers, clouds filtering through the sun's brightness, silhouettes of trees, churches, windmills, fill their luminous and serene compositions. The greatest landscape painter of the time, **Jacob van Ruisdael** *(qv)*, nephew of Salomon, depicts slightly romantic sites.

Meindert Hobbema *(qv)* is the painter of large trees with vivid green foliage where the light plays. **Cornelis van Poelenburgh** *(qv)* had a preference for Italian-like landscapes with the setting sun.

(After photo Kröller-Müller Stichting)

The Old Oak Tree by Van Goyen,
Kröller-Müller National Museum

Sometimes landscapes are only a pretext to bring in people as with **Aelbert Cuyp** *(qv)*, shepherds and their flocks with **Nicolaes Berchem** *(qv)*, or cows and horses as with **Paulus Potter** *(qv)*, horses (and their riders) with **Philips Wouwerman** *(qv)*.

Hendrick Avercamp *(qv)* is slightly different: with an art which is similar to that of miniatures and with subtle colours he brings back to life the picturesque world of ice skaters. **Aert van der Neer** (1603/4-77) also paints winter scenes and rivers in moonlight.

Willem van de Velde the Elder and above all his son **Willem van de Velde the Younger** *(qv)* who ended their lives in the English court, were remarkable marine painters, as was **Ludolf Bakhuizen** (1631-1708), **Jan van de Cappelle** (1626-79) and the Ghent painter **Jan Porcellis** (1584-1632).

Pieter Saenredam (1597-1665) and **Emanuel de Witte** (*c*1617-92) whose work was highly appreciated during their lifetime, depict church interiors with much studied composition. **Job** (1630-93) and his younger brother **Gerrit** (1638-98) **Berckheyde** are known as painters of architecture.

Genre scenes. – Apart from certain of Rembrandt's pupils a number of painters specialised in interior scenes. **Gerard Terborch** *(qv)*, **Frans van Mieris the Elder** *(qv)*, **Gabriel Metsu** *(qv)* recreate intimate atmospheres with delicate brushwork. **Pieter de Hooch** *(qv)*, a remarkable colourist and virtuoso of perspective effects depicts the daily occupations of rich bourgeois.

Vermeer *(qv)*, a painter long neglected, is today considered as one of the greatest. He painted mainly interior scenes, realistic but tinged with a surprising poetry, simple in appearance but revealing a subtle research for colours, composition and light effects.

Country scenes, more popular and animated, are the speciality of **Adriaen van Ostade** *(qv)*, painter of rustic life influenced by the Flemish painter Adriaen Brouwer, and his pupil **Jan Steen** *(qv)* whose cheerfulness and humour show a certain moralising intention.

In Utrecht where the Italian influence was widespread in the 16C, **Abraham Bloemaert** continued this trend. One of his pupils, **Hendrick Terbrugghen** introduced Caravaggism into the country, as did **Gerrit van Honthorst**: the contrast between light and shadow, half-length portraits of common folk, and musical scenes characterise their work. A pupil of Frans Hals, **Judith Leyster** *(qv)*, wife of the painter Jan Molenaer, is also influenced by the Caravaggists.

Still lifes. – The tradition of still life painting of Flemish origin (Fyt, Snyders) is resumed in Haarlem by **Pieter Claesz.** and **Willem Claesz. Heda** *(qv)*. Their favourite subject was a table covered with the remains of a meal, and glasses and dishes brought into light. Less exaggerated than those of the Flemish paintings, more monochrome, their compositions follow a skilful geometry.

The works of **Willem Kalff** (1619-93), **Abraham van Beyeren** (1620/1-90) and **Jan Davidsz. de Heem** *(qv)* are more colourful and baroque.

Drawings and engravings. – Much appreciated by collectors, numerous drawings and engravings, notably etchings, were done by 17C painters. Rembrandt, himself, excelled in this genre.

From the 18 to 20C. – In the 18C a decline set in. **Cornelis Troost** (1697-1750), however, stands out, a painter from Amsterdam who inspired by the theatre, evokes Watteau and Hogarth. **Jacob de Wit** (1695-1754) is known for his *grisailles* (in Dutch: *witjes*) which decorate a number of bourgeois homes. **Wouter Joannes van Troostwijk** who died young (1782-1810) is the painter of Amsterdam.

In the 19C, with **The Hague School** *(qv)* directed by **Jozef Israëls** (1824-1911) there is a rebirth of Dutch art. Nature, the beaches, dunes and fishermen's life constitute countless subjects for paintings by artists of this school.

Living mainly in France, **J.B. Jongkind** (1819-1891) a partisan of Impressionism gives importance to light and a certain atmosphere in his paintings, as does **George Hendrick Breitner** (1857-1923), known also as a painter of horsemen and of old Amsterdam.

Isaac Israëls (1865-1934), son of Jozef, painted beach scenes and numerous portraits.

At the end of the 19C **Vincent van Gogh** *(qv)* first painted in a sombre manner, but under the influence of Impressionism, which he discovered in Paris, his canvas became lighter and more colourful.

Starting in 1886 he worked mainly in France – in Paris and in Provence near Arles – but his masterpieces can be seen in the Kröller-Müller Museum or the Van Gogh Museum in Amsterdam.

Jan Theodoor Toorop, called **Jan Toorop** (1858-1928) born in Java, was first an Impressionist, before turning to Symbolism, a movement in which he held an important place in Europe as did **Johan Thorn Prikker** (1868-1932). Later Toorop went through a pointillist and divisionist period and also took an interest in the Art Nouveau movement, doing number of posters in this style.

Mondrian *(qv)* was one of the greatest innovators of his period. Instigator of the De Stijl movement and the newspaper which was the movement's mouthpiece with **Theo van Doesburg** and **J.J.P. Oud** he contributed to the birth of Constructivist art.

Jan Sluyters (1881-1957), **Charley Toorop** (1891-1955), daughter of Jan, **Hendrik Chabot** (1894-1949) are Expressionist artists.

Kees van Dongen *(qv)* became well-known in Paris.

The **Magic Realism** or Neo-Realism theorists, **Raoul Hynckes** (b 1893), **Pyke Koch** (b 1901), **Carel Willink** (1900-83) by their near-photographic art tinged with Surrealism or the fantastic, influenced many young artists.

The poetic street scenes, somewhat medieval, by **Anton Pieck** (b 1895) illustrate many children's books.

The **COBRA** (a contraction of Copenhagen, Brussels and Amsterdam) movement (1948-51) founded by an international group, notably a Dane, Asger Jorn, a Belgian, Corneille and two Dutch, **Karel Appel** (b 1921) and **Constant** (b 1920) also known for his plan of a futurist town (New Babylon), reacted against the conformism of the De Stijl movement via a free and spontaneous creation.

MUSIC

Music has always held a very important place in the life of the Dutch, whether it is played at home, in churches or even in the street.

Musicians. – The most famous musician is **J.P. Sweelinck** (1562-1621), organist of the Old Church in Amsterdam, composer, precursor of J.S. Bach. During the same period **Constantijn Huygens** (1596-1687), statesman and poet, took an active interest in musical composition.

In the 19C, **Johannes Verhulst** (1816-91) was a composer and conductor, and **Richard Hol** (1825-1904), conductor, pianist and composer of cantatas and symphonies.

A student of Hol's, **Johan Wagenaar** (1862-1941), organist and unusual composer taught **Willem Pijper** (1894-1947) composer, who was also known for his essays on music.

Presently, the Dutch with the Concertgebouw Orchestra in Amsterdam and the Residentie Orchestra in The Hague, have two of the greatest orchestras in the world.

The first conductor of the Concertgebouw Orchestra was **Willem Mengelberg** (1871-1951) who took an active interest in many composers of his time, such as Mahler.

The Holland Festival *(see the chapter Practical Information at the end of the guide)* gives rise to important musical events.

Organs. – Created in Byzantium, imported into Western Europe in the 9C, the organ took a large place in Catholic liturgy as from the 12C. The instrument was made by monks. Soon spreading into private houses, the organ was spared the Iconoclastic Fury.

However, organ music was at first despised by the Calvanist religion. It was only in the middle of the 17C that it spread into Protestant churches.

Numerous instruments were made at this period and the following century. In the 18C the sons of the famous German organ builder **Arp Schnitger**, living in Groningen, perfected the instrument in the Netherlands and built the great organ in **Zwolle's** Great Church. The great organ of St Bavo's in **Haarlem** (18C) built by **Christiaan Müller** is one of the best known in the country.

Most of the organ cases dating from the baroque era are sumptuous achievements: crowning the pipes are statues and carvings.

A few organ concerts are indicated under the locality's heading.

Barrel organ. – In the Netherlands the streets often resound with a cheerful and familiar music, that of barrel organs as well as carillons. Whereas the barrel organ has practically disappeared in other European countries, a number of Dutch towns still have kept theirs – with its picturesque name, painted and carved face – which can be heard Saturdays in the shopping streets as well as on feast days.

The barrel organ, which appeared in the 18C, invented by an Italian, is a **cylinder-type organ.** A pinned barrel, turned by a handle, raises levers which admits wind to a set of organ pipes. Mounted on wheels, this organ became widespread in 19C Europe. In 1892 Gavioli built the first **book organ** *(pierement)* which took the place of the cylinder-type organ. The handle works a perforated music book which releases a mechanism. Use of a music roll made it possible to have an unlimited repertoire, and when linked to the use of a pneumatic system which improved it, thus its distribution increased.

Barrel organ

A builder of barrel organs, **Carl Frei** set up in Breda in 1920, but most of the instruments were imported from abroad, from Belgium (Mortier) and France (Gasparini and the Limonaire Brothers).

At the end of the 19C, the dance-hall organ became popular, a magnificent, very large sculptured instrument. In the beginning of the 20C fair organs produced loud music intended to be heard above the hubbub. Finally, after 1945 an electronic dance-hall organ appeared, a real animated orchestra with all sorts of instruments.

In Utrecht, the National Museum "from the musical clock to the barrel organ" contains an interesting series of barrel organs.

Carillons. – There are countless churches and town halls in the Netherlands which have a carillon (bronze bells in fixed suspension).

The carillon, which has probably existed since the 15C in Belgium is activated, like the organ, by a cylinder driven originally by the movement of a clock.

In the 17C **François and Pierre Hemony** from Lorraine, the famous bell founders, played a primordial role in their development in the Netherlands. There still exist, amongst many others of theirs, the carillons of the Tower of Our Lady in Amersfoort, the Martini Tower in Groningen and the Dom Tower in Utrecht.

A little on the decline in the 18 and 19C, there is a renewed interest in carillon music today. In 1941 a bell founder in Heiligerlee (province of Groningen) invented an **electromagnetic system,** replacing the cylinder. This is used in several towns.

Since 1953 there is the Netherlands School for Carillonneurs at Amersfoort.

Finally, Asten has an interesting National Carillon Museum *(p 89).*

In the text of localities and at the end of the guide we indicate some of the carillon concerts.

FURNITURE

With each epoch there is a style which spreads over the whole country and yet, certain local products are interesting by their uniqueness.

The Late Gothic period produced carved oak chests, credence tables, a sort of small side-table with shelves, and dressers decorated with pointed arches and fan-tailed motifs.

Beginning in 1550 the Italian Renaissance inspired a few credence tables with carved panels depicting medallions and grotesques. Heavy tables in the Flemish style *(bolpoottafels)* with turned feet widening into vase-like shapes appear. These tables first had rectangular struts but later were characterised by their H-shaped cross-bars, then beginning in 1650 the cross-bars were shaped like two forks.

Elegant stools with highly decorated backs and divergent legs belong to the Renaissance period. The Dutch chandelier of voluted copper *(kaarsenkroon)* is part of the 17C interior; it is also frequently found in churches, as seen in several of the church interiors painted by Saenredam and De Witte.

(After photo Rijksmuseum, Amsterdam)

Renaissance wardrobe

Wardrobes in the Golden Age. – The most beautiful Dutch productions at the end of the 16C and the Golden Age are linen wardrobes.

The **Dutch Renaissance wardrobe** *(Hollandse kast)* is perhaps the wardrobe seen the most often. It has very varied decoration: lion muzzles, caryatids, friezes of foliated scrolls and grotesques, and flat panels later replaced by geometric embossed designs. It has a wide plinth, four doors (those below usually divided into two panels) and a heavy cornice decorated with a frieze of plants. Its uprights consist of fluted pilasters, and subsequently columns: it is then called a columned wardrobe *(kolommenkast)*.

By the second half of the 17C magnificent and imposing wardrobes in various kinds of wood were made called **kussenkast wardrobes** because of the bulging shape (*kussen* means cushion) of their panels, usually veneered with ebony. The wardrobe rests on enormous ball feet. Five Delft vases often potbellied were frequently placed on the cornice.

The **Zeeland wardrobe** *(Zeeuwse kast)* wider than it was high, with four of five doors, is low and has few raised designs, but its Renaissance decoration, which is like that of the Dutch wardrobe, is very finely worked.

Frisian wardrobes have two doors. The panels are enhanced by engraved decorations between the uprights, formed by engaged columns similar to the columned wardrobes. The cornice is very thick and decorated with a finely engraved frieze.

In the **Gelderland,** wardrobes have two large doors with relief designs on the panels and fluted uprights, precious wood inlays, and a projecting cornice, simply decorated with gadrooning (convex curves).

The **Utrecht wardrobe,** which, in fact, is made in the province of Holland, is like that of the Gelderland: the panels are topped by an arch outlined with ebony inlay.

(After photo Gemeente-Archief, Middelburg)

Zeeland wardrobe

In town as well as in the country, at that time, people usually slept in box beds, the wooden panels matching the style of the room.

(After photo Rijksmuseum, Amsterdam)

Kussenkast wardrobe

(After photo Fries Museum, Leeuwarden)

Frisian wardrobe

Marquetry and inlaid work. – Beginning in the 17C and particularly in the 18C, there is an increased taste for marquetry and above all inlay of ebony, tortoise-shell, metal and ivory, which can be seen, as in Flanders, in writing-desks and cabinets, with numerous drawers intended to hold precious objects.

The *sterrekabinet* is inlaid with ivory motifs or with marquetry depicting stars *(sterren)* enclosed in circles or ovals.

18 and 19C wardrobes. – The Louis XV style, imported by the French Huguenots after the Revocation of the *Edict of Nantes* (1685), was very much in vogue in the 18C, but interpreted with a certain liberty. The **18C wardrobe** with two doors has a base with drawers, which in the middle of the century, had a characteristic bulge *(buikkabinet)*. It is topped with an undulating cornice.

Inlaid work and marquetry were also appreciated.

Finally, the English influence was quite important due to intensive commercial relations with England *(p 20)*.

At the end of the 18C furniture was influenced by the Louis XVI style, more austere, which was very faithfully reproduced.

In the 19C, influence of the Empire style was

(After photo Rijksmuseum, Amsterdam)

18C wardrobe

felt (under Napoleonic domination), due to the presence in the country of Louis Bonaparte and Queen Hortense, very attached to Parisian fashions.

Painted furniture. – Several localities in the north of the country specialised in the production of painted furniture in the 18C. It was mainly in the old ports of the Zuiderzee where, during the months of forced inactivity, that the fishermen worked and painted wood according to the methods seen during their journeys in the Baltic or in the East.

This furniture has particularly indented outlines; the wood is covered with very crowded paintings in a more or less popular and naive style. In the Zuiderzee ports (Hindeloopen, Enkhuizen), in the Zaan area, in the Wadden Islands, painting covers, wardrobes, fold-away tables, box beds, chairs, etc.

Longcase and pendulum clocks. – After the discovery in 1656 by Christiaan Huygens of the pendulum principle (pendulum serves to control the time in clocks) a **longcase clock** (also known as a grandfather clock) can be found in all wealthy looking interiors. Its tall clockcase has a fair amount of decoration and is topped by a rectangular head with an arched cornice. The clockface is often painted with an astral representation below with people or boats on the sea moving about. Amsterdam was a great longcase clock-making centre in the 18C. However, clocks in the Louis XV style or cartels (hanging wall-clocks) were also appreciated.

(After photo Zuiderzeemuseum)

Assendelft wardrobe, Zuiderzee Museum

In the provinces of Friesland, Groningen and Drenthe, the **clocks** called *stoeltjesklokken* are adorned with fanciful open-worked decoration, similar to that of the painted furniture *(see above)* and have a special mechanism installed on a small console. The clocks in the Zaan region are of a more precious type.

Several museums have lovely clock collections: in particular the Gold, Silver and Clock Museum in Schoonhoven and the Clock Museum in the Zaan Quarter.

A number of Dutch museums have a decorative arts section where rooms, *stijlkamers*, have assembled furniture belonging to a particular style, period or region. Furthermore the **doll houses,** which can be seen in certain museums, are detailed reproductions, making it possible to visualise the bourgeois interior in Holland during the Golden Age.

DUTCH FURNISHINGS

Dutch furnishings can be admired throughout the country. Listed below is a selection of museums:

Assen	– **Drenthe Museum: Ontvangershuis**	**Middelburg**	– **Zeeland Museum**
		Rotterdam	– **Schielandshuis Historical Museum**
Enkhuizen	– **Zuiderzee Museum**		
Hindeloopen	– **Museum**	**Utrecht**	– **Central Museum**
Leeuwarden	– **Frisian Museum**	**Zwolle**	– **Overijssel Museum**

TRADITIONS AND FOLKLORE

COSTUMES

In the past the variety of costumes in the Netherlands was remarkable.

Apart from Marken and Volendam where, in season, all the population wears the traditional costume for the tourists' pleasure, costumes, today, are only worn in very few areas regularly and mainly by women.

However, by their variety, originality and the way they are assembled, which is slightly ritual in colour and motif, the costumes and headdresses still worn in the Netherlands are of exceptional interest.

Fabrics. – Women's jackets and shawls, and also men's shirts worn under their black jackets are made out of traditional, brightly coloured textiles striped with checks, or flowers. In the latter case it is most often of **chintz**.

Starting in the 17C the Dutch East India Company imported enormous quantities of chintz from the East. This fabric, whose Dutch name *sits* comes from the Indian word *chint*, which means multi-coloured, is cotton decorated with a coloured pattern done by hand, using a special technique. Greatly appreciated not only for its suppleness and lightness but for its colours and designs, this material was soon the rage in the Netherlands. Interiors are decorated with it (bedspreads, curtains, wall hangings) and it is used to make all kinds of clothes. The women of Hindeloopen even make their traditional coat called *wentke* and other women happily replace their plain jacket by one in *sits* with shimmering colours.

At the end of the 17C chintz was made in the Twente *(qv)* and printed mechanically.

The female costume. – In spite of its variety, it retains certain unchanging features. It consists of a skirt, an apron and a jacket done up in front, often with short sleeves. Over the jacket some women wear a stiff bodice as in Bunschoten-Spakenburg, or a shawl as in Staphorst. The costume worn on Sundays is always more elegant than that on other days. Whit Sunday is particularly honoured: that day the women usually dress up in their most beautiful attire.

Volendam woman in costume

Headdresses. – Although a young girl in wooden shoes wearing a cap with wings, typical in Volendam *(see illustration above)*, often symbolises Dutch folklore for foreigners, there exists a wide variety of headdresses through out the country.

The most spectacular are those worn on the island of South Beveland, particularly in Goes *(qv)* on weekly market days.

Many headdresses have the distinctive feature of including golden ornaments: they conceal a head band ending in rings (Scheveningen), by animal heads (Urk) or by amusing types of spiral-shaped antennae raised up in front (Walcheren, Axel, Arnemuiden). Pins with a golden head or ending in a pearl are sometimes put into the headdress above the ears.

The magnificent lace work of these headdresses is admirable.

The male costume. – It only exists now in a few ports, such as Urk, Volendam and in South Beveland. Today it is nearly always black, whereas in the past brighter colours were worn. It consists of a jacket, often double breasted and wide or baggy trousers (Zuiderzee). The shirt, rarely visible, is made of brightly coloured cotton with a striped or checked pattern. Its straight collar closes with two gold buttons. They are the costume's only ornaments, except in Zeeland (South Beveland) where two lovely silver chased buckles hold up the trousers.

The man wears a small cotton scarf round his neck. On his head he wears black headgear: a round hat in Zeeland, a sort of military cap in Urk, or a plain cap. He often wears wooden shoes.

Belt buckle from Zeeland

Where can one see the costumes? – The main centres where costumes are worn by the population (men, women and children) daily are **Volendam** and **Marken,** but the custom is less respected in winter than in summer. In **Staphorst** and in the neighbouring village of **Rouveen,** women and young girls wear a very unique costume as do a few inhabitants of **Bunschoten** and **Spakenburg.**

In the Zeeland islands of **Walcheren** and **South Beveland,** a number of women still remain faithful to their costume and headdress to such a point that in 1975 they revolted against the wearing of a crash helmet when riding a motorcycle.

Other places which should be mentioned are **Scheveningen, Urk** and a few places in the Overijssel (Rijssen, Bathmen, Dalfsen, Den Ham, Raalte).

In a few cities women wear the traditional clothes mainly for the Sunday church service or the weekly market. Sometimes during the festivals and folklore markets, there is the possibility of seeing the Dutch decked out in their regional costumes *(see the chapter Practical Information at the end of the guide).*

The costumes are described in the guide under the locality's heading. Several museums make it possible to admire the detail.

FARMHOUSES

The lovely farmhouses which are scattered over the countryside are part of the country's familiar landscape. It is in the polder areas that they are largest in size.

Frisian farmhouses. – Surprising by the large size of their roofs, they can be seen all over Friesland or in the territories which formerly belonged to it (north of the province of North Holland) and in the province of Groningen.

Pyramid-shaped farmhouses. – There are a lot in the north of the province of North Holland (beyond the North Sea canal) where they are called *stolp;* they can also be seen in the south of Friesland, where they are called *stelp.* Their enormous four-sided

Pyramid-shaped Frisian farmhouse

pyramid-shaped roofs, bring to mind that of a haystack. Grouped under the same roof are the stables, a barn and living quarters. On one of the sides of the roof, thatch takes the place of tiles forming a decorative pattern resembling a mirror, called *spiegel.* Sometimes in wealthy farmhouses the façade is embellished with a richly decorated brick pediment.

Head-neck-trunk farmhouses. – They are called *kop-hals-rompboerderij,* a farmhouse with head-neck-trunk. They can be seen in the north of Friesland and a few in the province of Groningen.

Made up of three parts (thus head-neck-trunk), they consist of the living quarters (head), linked by a narrow part (neck), to a large building (trunk). The latter includes the cowshed, stable and barn.

The living quarters are covered with tiles whereas the barn is roofed traditionally with reeds. They are often built on a *terp* (p 135).

Frisian head-neck-trunk farmhouse

At the top of the roof over the trunk part – shed, barn... – is a **uilebord,** a wooden triangular panel pierced with holes which owls *(uil)* pass through, when living in the hay. It is often decorated with carved wooden motifs depicting two swans.

Kop-romp farmhouses. – In Friesland, as in the province of Groningen, there is also a type of farmhouse, which is a combination of the others (*kop* = head; *romp* = trunk): a tiled roof

covers the living quarters as in the head-neck-trunk farmhouse, but as in the pyramid-shaped farmhouse, a few rooms remain in the barn, under the large reed roof. The house is also sometimes joined to the barn by a series of projections characteristic of the Oldambt farmhouse.

Oldambt farmhouses. – From the Oldambt area, to the east of the province of Groningen, they can be seen all over the province. They are linked to the barn by a progressive widening at right angles to the house. Sometimes too, this model is combined with the head-neck-trunk type.

Kop-romp farmhouse

The house, high and wide, often has a main entrance surrounded by stucco mouldings, which gives it a rather solemn appearance. There is also a side entrance. A floor with low windows serves as a granary. The living quarters, covered in tiles can be distinguished from the barn, which is usually roofed with reeds.

Due to the richness of the harvest in the province, the Groningen farmhouse often has two or even three barns side by side, with no divisions inside.

Hall-farmhouses. – They are the most widespread type found in the Netherlands and particularly in the provinces of Drenthe, Overijssel, Gelderland and Utrecht; they can also be seen in South Holland and in the Gooi (North Holland).

Inside the timberwork is supported by two rows of beams which delimit, as in hall-churches, a wide central nave and two narrower side aisles.

Twente farmhouses. – In the Twente (Overijssel) and east of Gelderland towards Winterswijk, the walls, formerly of cob are now of brick, sometimes keeping the check-pattern half-timbering. The roof is wide, with two sides, and a wooden gable.

Los hoes farmhouses. – They can still be found in the Twente, but rarely. Originally all the hall-farmhouses were like this one.

Los hoes means open house: inside, to begin with, there were no partitions. The farmers and cattle shared the same space, the hay being heaped up on to planks halfway up. There was an open fire on the ground.

The parents' house, called *eendskamer*, sometimes consisted of a small independent building joined to the façade.

A *los hoes* farmhouse has been reconstructed in the Twente National Museum in Enschede.

Drenthe farmhouses. – It has an elongated shape. Today it is still very often covered with thatch. The same roof, with four sides, covers two distinct parts: the living quarters with high windows, and the barn-stable where the carts entered at the back through a carriage entrance whose opening was cut into the thatched roof.

Drenthe farmhouse

Beginning in the 18C in certain farmhouses in the southwest of the Drenthe and to the north of Overijssel, the carriage entrance at the back had been replaced by side doors in order to increase the space in the barn. It is like this in Wanneperveen *(qv)* where however, because the houses were set too close together, the doors were placed at the corners.

T-shaped farmhouses. – In Gelderland and notably in the region of Achterhoek, in the region of IJssel (province of Overijssel), in the provinces of Utrecht and South Holland, and in Gooi (North Holland), the house is set crosswise to the barn, hence its name *T-huis,* that is to say: t-shaped house. Prosperity brought about this type of farm-

T-shaped farmhouse

house which lies on fertile river banks. The farmer wished to enlarge his living quarters by two living rooms, *pronkkamer* and *royale opkamer,* overlooking the road; he put these two rooms under a roof which formed a transept. The carriage entrance to the farmhouse was at the back.

In the Veluwe (Gelderland) farmhouses are complemented by a separate hay shed and sheep pen. In Gooi, the hay was formerly heaped up at the back of the house, the doors being on the side; subsequently, in the 19C, it was also stored in an annexe.

In the provinces of Utrecht and South Holland (near Woerden), cheese-making farms had a dairy and cheese dairy in the basement of the dwelling.

Hall-type farmhouses can also be seen in Staphorst *(qv)*, Giethoorn *(qv)* Lopikerwaard (province of Utrecht); and in the province of South Holland, the farmhouses of Krimpenerwaard and Alblasserwaard *(qv)* possess the distinctive feature of having the living quarters on raised ground, due to the risk of floods.

Transversal farmhouses. – These farmhouses, where the longest side was the façade, consist of juxtaposed rooms, the living quarters set at right angles to the work area. They can be seen in Limburg and in the east part of North Brabant.

(After photo Off. Nat. Néerl. du Tourisme, Paris)

Southern Limburg farmhouse

Limburg farmhouses. – Today, the farmhouses stand out by their closed-in layout, unique in Holland. The buildings often form a square round a courtyard which only opens to the outside by a large carriage gateway. Near this stands the dwelling house. This layout came about progressively: originally there was only a barn at right angles to the house.

In Southern Limburg some of the buildings often have half-timbered walls emerging from white roughcast.

Brabant farmhouses. – They present a very long façade facing the road, with a line of doors, hence their name of long façade farmhouses.

Their long roof is covered in part by tiles and in part by thatch.

Rather small, these farmhouses were often of small capacity. It was then elarged by a barn in Flemish style, with wooden partitions and a thatched roof, set in the place of the door.

Brabant farmhouse

Zeeland farmhouses. – They consist of isolated buildings where the wooden barn is the most typical construction, with its tarred partitions and its doors and windows emphasised by a frame of white paint.

WINDMILLS

Perched high on the old ramparts of the town or on the dikes of polders or rivers, or else erected at the entrance to villages or along waterways, the numerous windmills (about 950) which still exist in the Netherlands contribute towards giving the landscape's characteristic aspect.

The best known and greatest concentration of windmills are those of Kinderdijk *(qv)*.

Windmill language. – The sails turn counter clockwise. When stopped, their position means something. The windmill speaks and sends its message afar:

– two vertical sails (+): rest for a short time during a working period.

– two diagonal sails (×): rest for a longer period, if it is a polder windmill.

– upper sail just to the right of vertical (⊁): celebration.

– upper sail just to the left of vertical (⊀): mourning.

On the occasion of a marriage, the windmill sails are abundantly decorated with garlands and symbolic motifs.

During the last war the windmills sent signals to the Allied pilots and maintained the population's morale.

Windmill decorations. – Many wooden windmills are painted green, with white frames. Where the sail crosses, there is usually a starred motif painted, yellow and red, or else blue and white. Below, on a carved panel, there is often the windmill's name and the date of its construction.

Post mill, Asten

Main types of windmills. – There are two kinds of windmills, the polder windmills and industrial windmills.

The **polder mill** serves, or served to pump water *(p 16)*. There are none to be found in the east of the country where the height above sea level ensures the drainage of water.

Industrial mills – about 500 – mill wheat, extract oil, hull rice and pepper, saw wood, etc. Several are still in use.

Precursor – the post mill. – To begin with the only mills known in the Netherlands were the watermill and the cattle power mill. Similar to those in Persia or Arabia, where they are used to mill grain, the first windmills appeared in the middle of the 13C (their existence is vouched for in 1274). Contrary to oriental mills, built of stone, these are of wood. Called *standerdmolen* or *standaardmolen,* they are post mills where the body turns with the sails round a heavy wooden pillar post made out of a tree trunk. Inside, the millstone moves when the sails move. Outside, on the side opposite the sails, a tail pole joined to the post and operated by a wheel made it possible to turn the windmill round on itself. The ladder fixed to the main body of the windmill is also drawn by the movement. Few windmills of this type remain in the country.

First polder mills. – The first windmill used for drainage, in about 1350, was the post windmill *(see above)*. Converted for this use, the central pillar post was replaced by a hollow post where the axis of the sails pivoted, it became the **hollow post mill** or **wip mill**, the first known dating from 1513. The upper part was reduced, but the base was larger, making it possible to install a scoop wheel to circulate the water,

(After photo Jos. P. Faure, Amsterdam)

Wip mill, Hellouw, Gelderland

however, quite often this remained outside and the base was used as living accommodations, particularly in South Holland.

The **sleeve windmill** *(kokermolen)* is easier to position, the pillar post was replaced by a heavy hollow post about which the top can turn with the sails.

A miniature variant of the wip mill is the **spinnekop** or spinbol which looks like a spider *(spin)*. There are many in Friesland. In North Holland, the small meadow mill, **weidemolentje** is even smaller.

In Friesland and Overijssel, the **tjasker**, very rare, has a primitive system where the sails are fixed directly to the device drawing up water.

Mills with rotating caps. – The **bovenkruier** (literally cap winder) in South Holland is a large windmill topped by a small cap which pivots alone. If the winding geer, which makes the cap and sails move, is outside, the windmill belongs to the **buitenkruier** type (the outside winder type). It is the most usual type, but in North Holland, there is also the **binnenkruier** (the inside winder type) which differs with the winding geer placed inside, giving it a more massive silhouette.

The mills with rotating caps are always built of wood, often **thatch** covered and octagonal; in this case the base is of brick. Sometimes the framework is also covered with **brick** and has a truncated shape *(illustration p 165)*.

Octagonal-shaped
polder mill, Amstelveen

Industrial mills. – In the 16C the windmill was adapted for industrial purposes.

In 1582 the first oil windmill worked in Alkmaar. In 1592 Cornelis Corneliszoon of Uitgeest (North Holland) built the first **saw mill**. Improved, it became the first **paltrok saw mill** which has a mobile base *(p 187)*.

Then **husking mills** were made to husk grain (barley, then rice after journeys to the Orient): the first was built in 1639 in Koog aan de Zaan.

Paper mills (invented *c*1600), developed in 1673, when French manufacturers withdrew to the Zaan region. Up to the 19C the greatest concentration could be found in the **Zaan region** *(qv)*, specialising in making paper and sawing wood for boat building. Most of the different types of windmills developed there, such as snuff mills (for tobacco snuff), hemp mills for ropes, tan mills for leather, spice mills mainly for mustard, fulling mills for textiles.

Many of them, which included a workshop, were very tall with a handrail.

(After photo Off. Nat. Néerl. du Tourisme, Paris)

Industrial mill, Zaan Quarter

Tall windmills. – Industrial windmills, often built in towns, had to be tall to catch the wind and were, therefore, several storeys high. The sails were operated from a circular stage with a handrail called *stelling* or *balie*, placed halfway up. It is the *stellingmolen*, tower mill with a stage often called a **stage mill.**

When it was built on a rampart *(wal)*, it was called *walmolen* or **wall mill.** The miller's living quarters and the granary are usually located under the handrail.

Other tall windmills stand in an artificial mound and are surrounded by an embankment (*bergmolen* or *beltmolen*) which facilitates the operation and avoids the need of constructing a handrail.

The stage mill is usually of brick and truncated, but in the province of Groningen it is built on an octagonal brick base, and in the Zaan on a workshop made of wood.

A few proverbs relating to windmills:

Hij heeft een klap van de molen gehad: *he was struck by a mill (he is a bit mad).*

Hij loopt met molentjes: *he functions with small mills (he is a little simple-minded).*

Dat is koren op zijn molen: *it is grain for his mill: (it brings water to his mill).*

Stage mill, Kromme Zandweg in Rotterdam

DUTCH LITERATURE

Dutch is the official language for about 20 million people, in the Netherlands, in their overseas possessions (Antilles), in Surinam and a part of Belgium. Together with Frisian and German it stems from the western Germanic linguistic branch. Starting in the 13C, in Flanders and the Brabant, this language was used by writers of talent.

In the 16C **Erasmus** *(qv)*, then in the Golden Age (17C) the theologian **Jansenius** (1585-1638), the jurist **Grotius** *(qv)* and finally **Spinoza** *(qv)* all wrote in Latin. But Dutch literature stands out with the poet **P.C. Hooft** *(qv)* and the poet and tragedian **Joost van den Vondel** (1587-1679). On the decline in the 18C it revived in the following century. Eduard Douwes Dekker, known under the pseudonym of **Multatuli** (1820-87) is the well-known novelist of *Max Havelaar* (1860) in which he expressed his opposition to colonialism in the Dutch Indies. After him, to mention a few of the better known names: the author **Louis Couperus** (1863-1923) who wrote *Old People and the Things That Pass* in 1906, the historian **Johan Huizinga** (1872-1945) known for his work *The Waning of the Middle Ages,* the novelists **Simon Vestdijk** *(qv)*, **Gerard Reve** (born in 1923) who wrote *Nights* in 1947 and **Simon Carmiggelt** (1913-87).

In Friesland, Frisian has remained alive. Frisian literature also has its followers. Use of the Frisian language in literature goes back to the time of **Gysbert Japicx** *(qv)*, 17C poet.

In **Limburg,** near Maastricht, the population speaks a particular dialect.

LORE

St Nicholas Day. – Before Christmas, which remains essentially religious, St Nicolas Day (6 December) plays a particularly important role, above all for children to whom the saint is supposed to bring presents. Coming from Spain by boat, **Saint Nicholas** (Sinterklaas) landed in Amsterdam where he made his official entry *(see the chapter Practical Information at the end of the guide)*. Riding a white horse and dressed as a bishop, he is always attended by one or two black devils or **Zwarte Piet** (Black Peter) who, armed with canes, must punish all naughty children. In the houses, the scattering of small cakes called **pepernoten,** indicate the passing through of Zwarte Piet.

The day before St Nicholas Day, 5 December, families meet in the evening and place shoes by the fireplace, which during the night are filled with presents. Adults have the custom of giving small poems full of humour as well as anonymous presents.

It is also the occasion to eat a number of specialities like the **borstplaat,** sweets that melt in the mouth, **speculaas** (speculos), brown sugar girdle cakes, **taai-taai,** aniseed biscuits in the shape of different figures, **vrijer,** equally with aniseed, and also initials in almond paste *(boterletters)* or chocolate *(chocoladeletters)*.

34

FOOD AND DRINK

An enticing breakfast. – Breakfast (*ontbijt,* pronounced ontbeyt) in the Netherlands is similar to an English or American breakfast: in most hotels, coffee, tea or chocolate is served with a boiled egg, thin slices of cheese, ham, sometimes salami, paté, and always *boterhammen* (literally slices of bread) of different kinds (rye bread, sandwich loaf, raisin bread, gingerbread) with butter and jam.

A quick lunch. – For lunch the Dutch often content themselves with a cold meal (without a cooked dish) or a very light meal and a cup of coffee. It is the time for a sandwich which is made of a soft roll or **broodje.** They also like the **uitsmijter** which consists of slices of buttered sandwich loaf, covered with ham or roast beef and two fried eggs, served with a sweet gherkin. As to **koffietafel,** mentioned on many menus, it is a kind of breakfast eaten for lunch, with coffee (*koffie,* hence its name) or tea.

A copious dinner. – The main meal is in the evening (between 6 and 7pm) and fairly plentiful. Soup is liked and notably, in winter, the traditional green pea soup, **erwtensoep** which must be sufficiently thick so that a spoon can stand up in it...
Oysters and mussels from Zeeland (Yerseke) are served in some restaurants.
Smoked eel (*gerookte paling*) and **red herring** (*bokking*) or a herring (*haring*) marinated in vinegar are eaten as starters. In the streets of Zuiderzee's old ports, they are sold on bread rolls. "Green" herring, **maatje** (or *groene haring,* or *nieuwe haring*) is eaten in May-June, raw and flavoured with chopped onions. It is also sold (in Amsterdam) by peddlers: it is then eaten by holding it by the tail and throwing ones head back. The first cask of herrings is offered each year to the Queen, who conforms to the tradition.
From 15 March to 10 April (a week later in Friesland) **lapwing's eggs** (*kievietseieren*) (p 17) served in jelly on a bed of watercress with pink radishes make a choice starter.
Limburg asparagus (Venlo), in season (*May-June*), are also much liked as starters. Limburg mushrooms are eaten fried, or with snails.
The main course – meat, poultry or fish – is served with vegetables, generally covered with plenty of sauce, and with a salad. The **vegetables** are varied: potatoes, cauliflower, green beans (*snijbonen*) cut into long strips, carrots or peas. Greenhouse cultivation makes it possible to have fresh vegetables all year long. Salads (lettuce, tomatoes, cucumbers, etc) are usually served with mayonnaise. As in Great Britain some meat dishes are served with apple or rhubarb compote.
Fish is a rare dish, and varies little: the menu usually offers fried **sole** (*tong*), sometimes plaice (*schol*) or turbot (*tarbot*).
A few family dishes are rarely found on restaurant menus: the **boerenkool,** mashed potatoes and green cabbage, often served with sausages (*worst*); **hutspot,** a sort of beef stew with mincemeat (or rib of beef), potatoes, carrots, turnips and onions, the origin of which dates back to 1573 (p 140).
Ham (*ham* in Dutch) and **sausages** (*worsten*) from the Veluwe are well-known.

Indonesian cooking. – In most towns, it is possible to satisfy an urge for exoticism by eating in an Indonesian restaurant, often called *chinees-indisch restaurant.*
The best known dish is the **rijsttafel.** It is a complete meal, the basis of which is a plate of rice accompanied by a minimum of about ten dishes: meat, fish, vegetables, fruit (bananas, pineapples) seasoned with spiced and aromatic sauces, sometimes sugary, and sprinkled with powdered coconut.
The **nasi goreng** has a fried rice base accompanied by numerous ingredients.

Cheese. – Rarely served at the end of the meal, cheese on the contrary is the main ingredient of breakfasts and cold meals. Creamy when they are fresh (*jonge*), they subsequently become dry and pungent when they are ripe (*oude*): **Gouda cheese** (*qv*) is cylindrical and flat, **Edam cheese** (*qv*) is ball-shaped with a yellow skin which is given a red covering when exported. They are the two cheeses found in the Alkmaar market (*qv*). The **Leyden cheese** (*Leidse kaas*) has caraway seeds which makes it a tasty cheese with drinks. That of **Friesland** (*Friese kaas*) is flavoured with cloves.

Desserts. – The Dutch are very fond of ice-cream and pastries, abundantly covered with whipped cream (*slagroom*).
The **vlaaien** are delicious tarts with Limburg fruit (Weert, Venlo).
All over the country small doughnuts called **poffertjes** and shortbread called **spritsen** are made.
In Friesland, the **suikerbrood** is a tasty bread roll with sugar.
Finally, amongst the numerous sweets, there are the **kletskoppen** a round crunchy cake with almonds (Gouda, Leyden); the **Haagse hopjes** coffee caramels, a speciality of The Hague and the **Zeeuwse babbelaars,** hard caramels of salted butter, made in Zeeland.

Drinks. – **Coffee** (*koffie*) is the preferred drink, with milk (*melk*). Black coffee made in a percolator is called "espresso". Beer is also enjoyed.
The usual aperitif is sherry, but there are local specialities such as **advocaat,** a thick type of egg-nog, or **gin** (*jenever*), a small glass (*borrel*) of it is usually drunk before meals.
Liqueurs such as kummel with a caraway seed base, anisette, apricot brandy, and above all **curaço** made with alcohol and bitter orange peel, are also appreciated.

Key

★★★ **Worth a journey**
★★ **Worth a detour**
★ **Interesting**

Sightseeing route with departure point indicated
on the road   in town

⛌ ∴ Castle, mansion – Ruins	⛪ 🏛 Ecclesiastical building / Building with main entrance
⛪ ✝ Chapel – Wayside cross or calvary	●━● Ramparts – Tower
☀ � Panorama – View	⦂ Gateway
🏮 ✹ Lighthouse – Windmill	⊚ Fountain
⌣ ✿ Dam – Factory or power station	▪ Statue – Small building
☆ ∪ Fort – Quarry	Gardens, parks, wood
▲ Miscellaneous sights	**B** Letters giving the location of a place on the town plan

Other symbols

❶ ❸ Motorway (unclassified)	▮▮ Public building
Dual carriageway	⊞ Hospital
Major through road	⬡ Covered market
Tree-lined street	⌇⌇⌇⌇ Cemetery
Stepped street	⛇ ⛳ Racecourse – Golf course
Pedestrian street	⛲ Outdoor or indoor swimming pool
Unsuitable for traffic or under construction	⛸ ⏛ Skating rink – Viewing table
Footpath	⬢ 15 Lever bridge – River ferry (load limit in tons)
⌐ 12 ⌐ Distances on roads (in kilometres)	Stadium – Water tower
△ 300 Altitude (in metres)	Tramway
Detailed plan – Simplified plan	▮▮▮ Railway station
Reference grid letters for town plans	✈ ⊚ Airport – Metro station
A B	Ferry services: Passengers and cars / Passengers only
③ Reference number common to town plans and MICHELIN maps	⊠ 平 Main post office with poste restante / Telegraph, telephone
	🛈 Tourist information centre (VVV)
	℗ Car park

MICHELIN maps and town plans are north orientated.
Main shopping streets are printed in a different colour in the list of streets.

Abbreviations

G Gendarmerie (Marechaussee)	P Provincial local authorities (Provinciehuis)	E International E-road (Europaweg)
H Town Hall (Stadhuis, Raadhuis)	POL. Police station (Politie)	A Motorway (Autosnelweg)
J Law Courts (Gerechtshof)	T Theatre (Schouwburg)	N Other roads
M Museum	U University (Universiteit)	ℙ Provincial capital (Hoofdplaats provincie)

⊙ **Times and charges for admission are listed at the end of the guide.**

Each year the Michelin Red Guide Benelux
presents a multitude of up-to-date facts in a compact form.
Whether on a business trip, a weekend away from it all
or on a holiday take the guide with you.

SIGHTS

listed alphabetically

★ **AALSMEER** North Holland   Pop 21 456

Michelin map **408** fold 10

Aalsmeer, a centre for growing flowers in greenhouses, is on the edge of Haarlemmer Lake *(qv)* a drained lake criss-crossed with canals and the larger Westeinder Plassen Lake. The town is mainly known for its flower auction where most Dutch florists buy their flowers and, thanks to the proximity of Schiphol airport *(qv)*, foreign buyers, as well. About 80% of sales are exported.

More than 2.8 milliard cut flowers were sold in Aalsmeer in 1986, amongst which 243 million carnations and 944 million roses, added to which were 204 million potted plants.

The procession of floral floats which takes place from Aalsmeer to Amsterdam is renowned *(see the chapter Practical Information at the end of the guide)*.

SIGHTS

★★ **Flower Auction** (Bloemenveiling). – It takes place in a large building decorated with
Ⓥ a tulip, the headquarters of the Aalsmeer Flower Auction, the **V.B.A.** (Verenigde Bloemenveilingen Aalsmeer), whose estate extends over 100ha-247 acres.

Inside **footbridges** make it possible to watch the activity in the market and the auctioneering.

Part of the hall is reserved for the arrival of cut flowers and potted plants which takes place the day before or early in the morning; another part is used for distribution. Packing and loading on to trucks takes place further away.

In the centre of the hall there are two amphitheatres, one for cut flowers, the other for potted plants. There retail buyers are installed in tiers facing dials which are linked to a computer. A cart carrying flowers in bunches is taken to the foot of each dial. On the dial a number indicates the price in units *(above)*, the number of the cart *(at the bottom)* and the quantity of flower bunches it contains *(on the left)*. The first buyer, who, by pushing a button in front of him, stops the hand moving on the dial from 100 to 0 stops the auction, and thus fixes the price. His number then appears on the dial *(above the number of the cart)* as well as the number of the bunches bought *(on the right)*.

Westeinder Plassen. – This vast lake is one of the most frequented water sports centres near Amsterdam. The road which goes round it by Kudelstaart has lovely views.

---

*With this guide use the **Michelin Maps** shown on p 3.*

★ **ALKMAAR** North Holland   Pop 87 034

Michelin map **408** fold 10

A historic town, Alkmaar owes its present reputation to its picturesque weekly cheese market.

Inside its surrounding moat, used partly by the canal, Noordhollandskanaal, the old town has more or less preserved its 17C plan and a number of old façades. The old fortifications have been transformed into a garden. Alkmaar is now the centre for the agricultural regions of North Holland peninsula.

HISTORICAL NOTES

Alkmaar was founded in the 10C in the middle of marshes and lakes. Its name means "all lake" or "auk lake" from the name of a bird, a kind of penguin which lived in the marshes.

A heroic siege. – During the Eighty Years' War, which began in 1568, Alkmaar was besieged in August 1573 by 16 000 Spaniards commanded by Dom Frederico of Toledo, son of the Duke of Alba. Heavy autumn rain, flooding the surrounding countryside, obliged the assailants to withdraw on 8 October, after seven weeks of siege. Alkmaar was, thus, the first town to resist the Spanish: "It was in Alkmaar that victory started" has been said for centuries.

Ⓥ **Boat trips.** – A tour of Alkmaar's canals as well as excursions to Amsterdam and in the Zaan Region *(qv)* are offered.

ALKMAAR★

★★ CHEESE MARKET (KAASMARKT) (B) *time: ½ hour*

⊙This traditional market, known since the early 17C, is held on Waagplein.
Early in the morning loads of cheese from Edam *(qv)* or Gouda *(qv)* are carefully piled
up. At 10am the buyers start tasting
and comparing the different cheeses
and bargain, then they make a deal
with a vigorous gesture of the hand,
to seal their agreement with the
seller.

Then immediately the famous **cheese
porters** *(kaasdragers)* take over, wearing the traditional white clothes and
straw hats; together they form an
ancient guild. It is divided into four
companies each identified by a different colour (green, blue, red, yellow)
and consisting of six porters and a
weigher or stacker *(tasman)*.
Once a batch of cheese is sold, it is
placed on a stretcher with the
company's colour.

Cheese porters

The porters then run with the load (weighing up to 160kg-353lbs) to the Weigh House
where the *tasman* officiates. Finally the cheese is taken to the trucks.

ALKMAAR

ADDITIONAL SIGHTS

Weigh House (Waag) (B M¹). – It is the former Chapel of the Holy Ghost, built at the
end of the 14C and transformed in 1582 into a Weigh House: on the east side, the
chancel has been replaced by a Renaissance building with a finely worked gable,
which since the 19C, is decorated with a painting, on Auvergne lava, depicting trade
and industry.
The tower, which was built at the end of the 16C, modelled on that of the Old
Church in Amsterdam *(p 54)*, has a **carillon** and automata of knights jousting every
hour.
⊙The Weigh House contains a **Museum of Dutch Cheese** (Hollands Kaasmuseum). The tour
starts on the 2nd floor, which is devoted to the history and making of cheese and
butter. Note the lovely decorated wooden cheese moulds.
Documentation on the 1st floor shows present cheese making procedures, on
the farm, in the dairy, as well as the importance of dairy products in the Dutch
economy. On the ground floor there are pamphlets etc (in several languages) and
cheese tasting.

Cannonball House (Huis met de Kogel) (B D). – Overlooking the canal the house has a
corbelled wooden façade and on its gable there is a Spanish cannonball which
remains from the battle in 1573 *(p 37)*.
From the neighbouring bridge there is a fine **view** of the Weigh House.

Mient (B 19). – On this square and along the canal, one can see numerous old façades.
To the south there is the fish market (Vismarkt).

Langestraat (AB). – This pedestrian precinct is the town's main shopping street.

⊙**Town Hall (Stadhuis) (A H).** – Its charming Gothic façade with a flight of steps, flanked
by an elegant octagonal tower streaked with limestone, is built onto a 17C façade.
Inside it has a porcelain exhibit.

Ⓥ **Great Church** or **St Lawrence's** (Grote- of St.-Laurenskerk) (A E). – A Protestant church, it is a beautiful edifice with three naves, transept, and ambulatory dating from the end of the 15C and beginning of the 16C. It was built by members of the Keldermans family, famous architects from Mechlin in Belgium. The imposing interior is roofed with wooden vaults from which hang beautiful 17C chandeliers. A plain triforium runs above the large arcades. Under the chancel vault there is a painting, the *Last Judgment*, by Cornelis Buys (15-16C), known as the Master of Alkmaar.

The case of the **great organ★** made in 1645 by Jacob van Campen *(qv)* is decorated with panels depicting the Triumph of David. On the ambulatory's left the **small organ★** dates from 1511: it is one of the country's oldest instruments.

The consistory, the room where the ministers met to discuss the service, has kept its original style.

On the south side of the transept there is a brass memorial plaque of Pieter Palinck and his wife. Numerous stone slabs can be seen on the church floor. There is also the tomb built in memory of Count Floris V, assassinated in 1296.

Ⓥ **Municipal Museum** (Stedelijk Museum) (A M²). – It is installed in the historic 16C building of the Archers Guild, the Nieuwe Doelen. It has interesting collections with respect to the town's past: excavated objects, sleighs, dolls and games, and gold and silversmiths' work. Among the paintings displayed there is a portrait of William the Silent, dated 1583, a picture of the siege of Alkmaar by the Spanish, a view of Alkmaar in the 16C and a view of Egmond Castle *(see below)*. The museum has exhibitions on contemporary art and on the town's history. In the interior courtyard there are sculptures and ancient façade stones *(p 48)*.

EXCURSIONS

The dunes. – *Round tour of 35km - 21½ miles – about 1½ hours. Leave by ⑤ on the town plan.*

Bergen. – Pop 14 099. Called also Bergen-Binnen (*binnen:* interior) as opposed to the neighbouring seaside resort, Bergen is an agreeable holiday resort where the wealthy-looking villas stand in rows along tree-lined avenues. It has a popular university installed in the former manor-house of the lords of Bergen.

Towards 1915 the **Bergen School** was formed; its members (Leo Gestel, the Wiegman brothers) were influenced by the French painters, Cézanne and Le Fauconnier. Bergen still has numerous artists living here. Their work is exhibited in the Noordhollands Kunstcentrum *(on Plein)* or in the summer in open-air markets.

The battle of Bergen took place in September 1799 with the Anglo-Russians (British soldiers under the command of Abercromby) against the troops of the Batavian Republic commanded by Brune. Subsequently, the Alkmaar convention was signed by which the invaders left the country.

Ⓥ At the crossroads with the road to Egmond, is the entrance to the **Noordhollands Duin Nature Reserve,** a private nature reserve of 4 760ha-11 757 acres covering the dunes up to the sea. Numerous birds live here.

Bergen aan Zee. – The seaside resort is located on a coast lined with high dunes dotted with villas. From the boulevard there is an extended view over the desolate landscape

Ⓥ of dunes, with trees lining the horizon. The **aquarium** (Zee-Aquarium) has a lovely collection of exotic fish, and a small pool where seals swim.

Egmond aan de Hoef. – The village is set in the bulbfield region which extends south of Alkmaar. To the east, on the Alkmaar road, beyond the church, the ruins of the moated **Egmond Castle** (Slot van Egmond) can be seen. Among its proprietary lords was the famous count executed in 1568 in Brussels *(p 74)*.

Egmond aan Zee. – This small seaside resort is in the middle of the dunes. At the foot of the lighthouse a statue of a lion symbolises the heroism of **Lieutenant Van Speijk,** who on 5 February 1831 near Antwerp, blew up his gunboat with all its occupants rather than surrender to the Belgians.

Return to Egmond aan de Hoef.

Egmond-Binnen. – In 1639 Descartes stayed here. The famous **abbey** of Egmond, destroyed by the Beggars *(qv)* in 1572, was rebuilt in 1935.

Return to Alkmaar by ④ on the town plan.

Graft - De Rijp. – Pop 5 345. *17km - 10½ miles to the southeast by ② on the town plan.*

These two localities merged in 1970. **Graft** has kept its beautiful town hall (raadhuis) built in 1613, with crow-stepped gables. **De Rijp,** an important centre for herring fishing and whale hunting in the 16 and 17C also has a town hall (1630) and houses

Ⓥ built in the regional style with wooden gables and a **church** (Hervormde Kerk) decorated with 17C stained glass windows. It is the birthplace of **Jan Adriaensz. Leeghwater** (1575-1650) *(qv)*.

Make up your own itineraries

– *The map on pages 7 to 9 gives a general view of tourist regions, main towns, individual sights and recommended routes in the guide.*

– *The above are described under their own name in alphabetical order (pp 37-192) or are incorporated in the excursions radiating from a nearby town or tourist centre.*

– *In addition the Michelin Maps nos 408 and 212 show scenic routes, places of interest, viewpoints, rivers, forests...*

Michelin map **408** fold 11
Plan of built-up area in the current Michelin Red Guide Benelux

Set in Gelderland Valley, at the confluence of two waterways which form the navigable Eem River, Amersfoort is a quiet town of melancholy charm surrounded by woods and moors. To the south, the hills of **Utrechtse Heuvelrug** are the ancient moraines of a Scandinavian glacier.
Well preserved within its double ring of canals, Amersfoort has kept its medieval character.

Historical notes. – The town developed round the castle, founded in the 12C, which no longer exists. Its city rights were granted in 1259. Its first town wall dates from the 13C; it is surrounded by canals.
In the 15 and the 16C Amersfoort became very prosperous due to the cloth and wool trade and, also, to the production of its numerous breweries. A second town wall was built c1400 reinforced by a ring of canals, now partially replaced by the Stadsring, a wide circular boulevard. Besides Koppel Gate (p 41), interesting remains can be seen at the far end of Kamp (**BZ**), the town's main street.
The town's industries: metallurgical (mechanical engineering), chemical food processing, graphics, construction and a few service sectors, are the main activities in Amersfoort which has widely developed beyond its original centre.
The town is the headquarters of the Netherlands School for Carillonneurs.

Two Celebrities. – Amersfoort is the birthplace of **Johan van Oldenbarnevelt** (1547-1619). **Grand Pensionary** (top civil servant) of Holland, the most important province in the United Provinces; he was at the origin of the country's power, by his will to ensure its development in all spheres (12-year truce in 1609, founding of the Dutch East India Company in 1602, etc). Unfortunately, he clashed with Maurice of Nassau, son of William the Silent and stadtholder as from 1584, who had him imprisoned in 1618; he was executed in The Hague in May 1619.
The painter Pieter Mondriaan, called **Piet Mondrian,** was born in Amersfoort in 1872. After attempting all kinds of painting and a stay in Paris (1911-4) where he experimented with cubism, Mondrian founded the abstract art movement called **De Stijl** (meaning style) with **Theo van Doesburg** and **J.J.P. Oud**. He passionately expounded his theories in the art periodical De Stijl, first published by Van Doesburg.
Abandoning all subjectivity, his painting, thereafter, only had vertical and horizontal lines and primary colours – red, blue, yellow – to which he added neutral – black, white and grey. Mondrian unremittingly pursued his research in this method, called Neo-Plasticism. In 1940 he moved to New York where he died in 1944. He is considered one of the founders of geometric abstraction. His influence can also be seen in architecture. Buildings designed by **G. Rietveld** (1888-1964), like the **Zonnehof** (**AZ**) of 1959, or the Schröder House in Utrecht (p 176) are directly inspired by his theories.

★ THE OLD CITY time: 4 hours

The tour is clearly defined running along the first town wall's layout, where in the 15C the famous **Muurhuizen**★ (**BZ**) were built. These town wall houses on the ramparts or leaning against them are one of the town's typical scenes.

The Boulder (De Amersfoortse Kei) (**AZ A**). – On a lawn of Stadsring there is an enormous glacial boulder of about 9 metric tons. Found in a nearby wood where it had been left by a Scandinavian glacier, it was transported in 1661 to Varkensmarkt, in the town centre. It has since been moved again.

Varkensmarkt (**AZ 34**). – It is the former pig market. At the beginning of Langestraat there is a lovely view on the left over the shaded canal and the Tower of Our Lady.

Krankeledenstraat (**AZ 22**). – In this street old façades can be seen, one of which is part of the **Kapelhuis** (**AZ B**), a house in the Late Gothic style.

★**Tower of Our Lady (Onze Lieve Vrouwe Toren)** (**AZ C**). – It stands in a large and calm
⊙ square, Lieve Vrouwekerkhof. In brick, ending in an octagonal stone floor with an onion-shaped dome, this beautiful 15C Gothic tower 100m - 328ft high is the old tower of a church which was destroyed in 1787 by the explosion of a gun powder mill.
It has a carillon made by François Hemony (qv).
At the corner of the square and Lieve Vrouwestraat there stands a beautiful old façade (**AZ Y**).

Take the small footbridge crossing Lange Gracht, the town's central canal.

Hof (**BZ**). – This large square still lined with a few old façades (no 24) (**BZ D**) is congested on Friday mornings and Saturdays by an important market.

⊙ **St George's (St.-Joriskerk)** (**BZ E**). – Built in 1243 in the Romanesque style, this church caught fire in 1370, was subsequently rebuilt and then enlarged in 1534.
The interior of this hall church with its three naves has preserved from its primitive Romanesque edifice: a few superimposed arcades, the porch tower against which lean the Gothic naves and on a west wall traces of frescoes (St George). The chancel is separated from the nave by a lovely finely sculpted Gothic (late 15C) **rood screen** (in sandstone). By the chancel, the capitals and consoles depict people and animals (monks, angels, lions, stags). Affixed to the wall not far from the rood screen is the funerary monument to Jacob van Campen (1595-1657), famous for having built the old town hall in Amsterdam (now the Royal Palace – p 48). The 14C baptismal font near the pulpit should be seen, and a small Jack (Klockman) of 1724 on a 15C clock. An annexe contains a 17C surgeons' room (chirurgijnskamer).

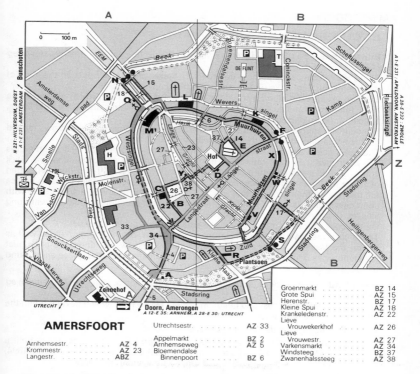

Groenmarkt (BZ 14). – Several lovely old houses have been restored, in particular in the angle formed by Groenmarkt and the neighbouring Appelmarkt. An **antiques market** is held on this square.

By Langestraat, go to the Kamperbinnen Gate.

Kamperbinnen Gate (Kamperbinnenpoort) (BZ F). – Called the Kampen interior gateway, this ancient town gateway of brick, flanked by octagonal turrets, was built in the 13C a little outside the first town wall on the road to Kampen.
On the 1st floor of the west turret there is a **pewter foundry.**
To the west, the road runs alongside the first Muurhuizen (**BZ K**), restored, which are of smaller size here.

By Bloemendalse Binnenpoort go to the Havik.

Havik (AZ). – This is Amersfoort's old port situated near the ford where the town was founded. The quays are lined with lovely restored houses. Every Friday morning there is a flower market.

Return to Bloemendalse Binnenpoort.

There are some interesting and particularly impressive **Muurhuizen★ (AZ L)** to be seen between nos 217 and 243.

★ Koppel Gate (Koppelpoort) (AZ N). – This beautiful double gate built *c*1400 includes a fortified bridge over the Eem forming a water-gate, a fulling mill for working cloth in the centre, and the gateway itself, flanked by turrets. The Guild of Boatmen used to meet here. Today there is a **puppet theatre** *(poppentheater)* inside.
On the quay of the nearby lock or **Kleine Spui**, at no 8 (**AZ Q**), note two façade stones, one of which depicts a boat.

Flehite Museum (AZ M¹). – This museum houses collections mainly concerned with the town's past and the Flehite canton: archaeology, history, local arts and crafts and souvenirs of Johan van Oldenbarnevelt *(qv)*.

By Westsingel, the last part of which is a pedestrian precinct, return to and cross Varkensmarkt; then on the right reach the old ramparts.

Pass in front of the **Mariënhof (BZ R)**, a former Ursuline convent. This lovely 16C building (restored) is used by the National Archaeological Excavation Service.

Plantsoen (BZ). – The garden, laid out on the old ramparts, has erratic blocks and monoliths offered by various countries, set out on its lawns.

Monnikendam (BZ S). – This graceful water-gate (1430) spaning the large ring canal overlooks the verdant gardens of the patricians' houses.

By Herenstraat, reach Zuidsingel and follow it to the left.

The lovely shaded Zuidsingel **canal** waters the gardens of the Muurhuizen; crossing it one comes again to some Muurhuizen. The **Korte Gracht** bridge (**BZ**) is particularly picturesque, overlooked by the **Tinnenburg (BZ V)**, an impressive wall house.

't Latijntje (BZ W). – On the right, also called Dieventoren or Plompetoren, this 13C tower is a relic of the first town wall. It houses the exercise keyboard of the Netherlands School for Carillonneurs.
A remarkable group of **Muurhuizen★ (BZ X)** are lined up from the tower to Langestraat.

EXCURSIONS

★ **Bunschoten.** – Pop 18 079. *12km - 7½ miles to the north. Leave by Amsterdamseweg* (**AZ**).

Bunschoten forms a single built-up area with **Spakenburg**, a small port on the edge of the freshwater Eem Lake (Eemmeer: eel fishing).

The two villages run along a street for more than 2km - 1 mile, which divides in the north to form the quays of a canal. The canal then widens into a dock where old boats, typical of the Zuiderzee, sometimes moor.

Opposite the church in Bunschoten, there is a charming house with side crow-stepped gables and a door decorated with a shell.

The two villages are famous for their traditions. Some women, as well as little girls still wear a very unusual **costume★**. The skirt is long, black and covered with a black apron. The distinctive feature of the costume is the bodice stiff and flowered, often of chintz *(qv):* a tartan band marks the centre. Widows wear a violet or black bodice for the rest of their lives, if they do not marry again. It covers a black shirt with short check sleeves. In the winter some women wear a cotton overblouse with long sleeves.

On the back of the head they all wear a small white crocheted bonnet.

These costumes can be seen on Saturday afternoons, during the market, as well as during the last two Wednesdays of July and the first two Wednesdays of August (Spakenburgse Dagen), when handicrafts are on sale on the market place and around the port.

Heathland. – *41km - 25½ miles to the south – about 3½ hours. Leave by Arnhemseweg* (**AZ**).

The road crosses the forest and heathland called **Leusder Heide,** which developed on the edges of terminal moraines.

At the Utrecht-Woudenberg crossroads turn right.

Austerlitz Pyramid (Piramide van Austerlitz). – Napoleon's soldiers, unoccupied, built a sand pyramid here in 1804. Hidden under vegetation, it was discovered in 1894, restored, equipped with a staircase and topped by a small memorial.

Doorn. – *Description p 84.*

Wijk bij Duurstede. – Pop 14 434. This town, near the Lek, is former **Dorestad,** a great trading community which was abandoned after its destruction by the Vikings in 863. The city was reborn in the 15C through the Bishop of Utrecht's influence, who chose it as his place of residence.

Markt, the great square, is overlooked by the church with its incompleted square tower and the town hall (1662).

⊙ In an adjoining street *(Volderstraat 15-17)* a small **museum** (Kantonnaal en Stedelijk Museum) has been opened, which retraces the history of the town and recalls, notably, the excavations undertaken on the site of ancient Dorestad.

Near the Lek, a **stage mill** (Molen Rijn en Lek), where the base forms an arch, has a striking resemblance to the one which Jacob van Ruysdael painted in one of his works exhibited in the Rijksmuseum in Amsterdam.

On the outskirts of town, the ruined and moated **castle** (Kasteel Duurstede), still has the remains of a square keep and a 15C round tower.

Amerongen. – Pop 6 652. A peaceful place in the Lower Rhine (Neder Rijn) region, where tobacco was formerly cultivated; typical wood tobacco drying sheds can be seen. Its Gothic **church** is overlooked by a tall 16C tower of sandstone with limestone courses. On the square, with lovely rustic houses, an oak tree was planted in 1898 in honour of Queen Wilhelmina's coming of age.

⊙ Not far away, in Drostestraat, there is a famous **castle** (Kasteel Amerongen).

Louis XIV at war with the United Provinces had it burnt down because its owner had abandoned it in 1672. Only the foundations were spared by the fire. A new, sober and elegantly proportioned edifice was built between 1673-8 in the classical style. This quadrilaterally-shaped building is surrounded by double moats. From 1918-20 Kaiser Wilhelm II of Germany lived here before he went to live in Doorn *(qv).*

North of **Leersum,** on the Maarsbergen road, the Het Leersumse Veld Nature Reserve is ⊙ situated on the heathlands of an old glacial moraine. Here, near the lakes **Leersumse Plassen,** seagulls come to breed.

In order to give our readers the most up to date information the times and charges for admission to sights described in the guide are listed at the end of the guide.

The sights are listed alphabetically in this section either under the place – town, village or area – in which they are situated or under their proper name.

Every sight for which there are times and charges is indicated by the symbol ⊙ in the margin in the main part of the guide.

Michelin map ⁴⁰⁸ folds 10, 27 and 28 (inset) – Local map p 134
Plan of built-up area in the current Michelin Red Guide Benelux

Capital of the Netherlands, Amsterdam is not the seat of the government. The sovereigns are enthroned here but do not live here.

The town is built on the banks of the IJ and the Amstel on about a hundred islets of moving sand linked up by a thousand bridges.

Its network of canals like a spider's web, its tall and narrow brick houses with stepped or voluted façades, its port, its intense commercial and cultural activity, its museums, give Amsterdam a pronounced and very fascinating charm.

Practical information. – For the young there are several brochures on sale with all sorts of useful information.

Transportation. – Due to the narrow quays and parking problems, traffic is difficult in Amsterdam and congestion is frequent.

Public transportation by bus, tramways and undergrounds can be useful to the tourist. In the tourist information centre or VVV *(Stationsplein 10)* a small practical leaflet is distributed concerning public transportation.

⊘ **Taxi-boats,** maximum 7 passengers, are a pleasant and quick way to get around the city.

⊘ The **hiring of bicycles** allows you to choose your own itinerary without having to cope with parking.

Entertainment. – In cinemas, films are shown in the original version, with sub-titles in Dutch.

The ballet companies (Het Nationaal Ballet), the Netherlands National Opera (Nederlandse Opera) and the Concertgebouw Orkest give excellent performances for those who do not know the language. Apart from the Concertgebouw *(p 53),* Amsterdam has a modern auditorium, the Muziektheater with 1 600 seats.

The VVV edits a small weekly brochure *(Amsterdam This Week),* in English only, where the city's entertainment, and where it takes place, is indicated.

Meals. – All Dutch and international specialities are served in Amsterdam. The town also has a large number of Indonesian restaurants *(p 35).*

Markets. – Apart from the various markets mentioned in the text, there is a stamp market which takes place twice a week *(Wednesday and Saturday afternoons)* to the south of Nieuwezijds Voorburgwal.

Festivals. – Among the most important are the Holland Festival, the floral float procession, and the official entry of Saint Nicholas, a national event *(see principal festivals pp 197-198).*

HISTORICAL NOTES

Legend has it that Amsterdam was founded by two Frisian fishermen who had landed on the shores of the Amstel in their small boat. They had a dog with them. The boat and the animal are depicted on the town seals (15C).

In fact the city's existence was only known from 1275: Count Floris V of Holland granted trading privileges to this fishing village situated on a jetty or dike *(dam),* at the mouth of the Amstel. Amsterdam developed in stages round the original village centre, now Dam *(p 48).* Towards 1300 it was awarded its city charter, then in 1317 it was annexed by William III, to the county of Holland.

In 1345, following a miracle (an Eucharistic host was found intact in a brazier), Amsterdam became a place of pilgrimage.

In 1428 the town, with the county of Holland, passed into the hands of the Duke of Burgundy, Philip the Good.

The imperial crown shown on its coat of arms was granted in 1489 by Emperor Maximilian, widower of Mary of Burgundy, the daughter of Charles the Bold, for the support given by the city to the Burgundian-Austrian monarchs.

The beginning of prosperity. – The end of the 16C marked the beginning of a brilliant period for Amsterdam. After the town had been pillaged by the Spanish in 1576, the rich merchants from Antwerp took refuge in Amsterdam; they brought their diamond industry with them.

Once freed from Spanish dominance by the *Union of Utrecht* (1579) the town became very prosperous; the new immigrants actively contributed.

Then at the end of the 17C, the Marranos arrived from Spain and Portugal, they were Jews, who had been converted by force to Catholicism but continued to practice their own religion in secret. To encourage the trading activities of the latter, the authorities granted them extensive privileges.

The Golden Age (17C). – This century marked the height of Amsterdam's glory.

Following in the wake of the Portuguese, the Dutch undertook their overseas expansion. In a few years their boats plied all over the Far East. In 1602 they founded the East India Company (Verenigde Oostindische Compagnie, or V.O.C), then in 1621 the West India Company. It is the Englishman Henry Hudson *(qv),* who was sailing for the Dutch India Company, who is credited with discovering Manhattan in 1609.

The Bank of Amsterdam, created in 1609, became one of the first European credit establishments. The Stock Exchange was built 1608-11 by Hendrick de Keyser.

In 1610 it was decided to build the three main canals, Herengracht *(illustration p 48),* Keizersgracht and Prinsengracht. They were soon lined with the mansions of the rich bourgeois traders.

The town was surrounded with a high wall on which windmills were placed.

Rembrandt, born in Leyden *(qv)* went to live in Amsterdam in 1630 (d 1669). He was buried in Wester Church (**JX**).

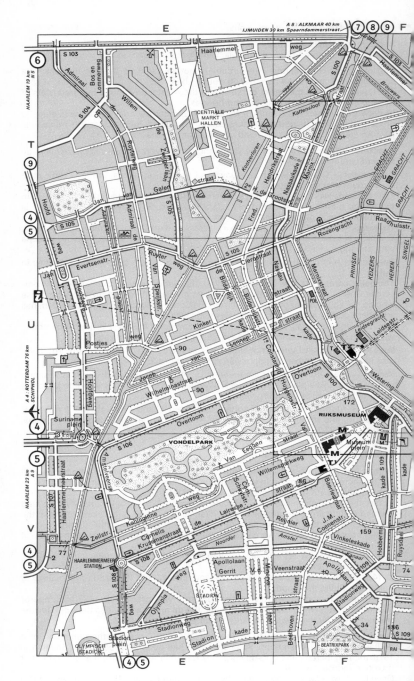

In 1648, with the *Treaty of Munster,* ending the Eighty Years' War with Spain; the independence of the United Provinces was officially recognised.

The development of navigation led to the making of maps and globes; it became Amsterdam's specialty.

The Revocation of the *Edict of Nantes* in France in 1685 brought about the immigration of a large number of Huguenots who joined in the town's commercial activity. At the end of the 17C, however, Dutch maritime power was on the decline and so was textile manufacturing.

French occupation. – The accumulated wealth was such that Amsterdam for a long time resisted the effects of the economic decline which occurred in the 18C.

Although in 1672 Amsterdam had been able to repel the attack of Louis XIV's troops by opening the locks which protected it, it could do nothing in 1795 against Pichegru's army. In 1806 Napoleon made his brother Louis Bonaparte, King of Holland. He settled in Amsterdam, which became the capital of the kingdom.

Reunited to France in 1810, decreed by Napoleon as the third town of the French Empire and seat of the local government of the Zuiderzee *département,* Amsterdam was then hit by the Continental System which ruined its trade.

In November 1813, the population revolted and recognised the Prince of Orange, William I, as sovereign on 2 December.

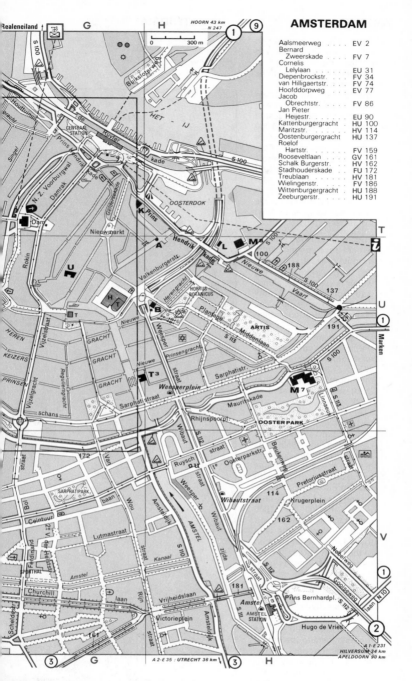

Economic reawakening. – It is only in the second half of the 19C that the town emerged from a long period of economic lethargy.

The bastioned ramparts which, by Singelgracht, demarcated the inner town, were razed in the 19C.

In 1876 a new canal was opened linking it to the North Sea (Noordzeekanaal) which facilitated the shipping trade.

The Central Station (LX) in the neo-Renaissance style was built in 1889 on 8 657 wooden piles laid on the IJ islands.

Thanks to foreign and government aid the diamond industry rapidly redeveloped. Here, in the City of Diamonds, such diamonds as the Cullinan and Koh-i-Nohr were cut. A number of **diamond cutting workshops** are open to tourists.

Amsterdam in the 20C. – In 1903 the new Stock Exchange by **Berlage** was completed, inaugurating a modern era in architecture.

A little before World War I, the town started expanding and new quarters were built. Several architects grouped together into the **Amsterdam School** which spread an original style of building (Navigation House) and developed mainly after World War I, with **Michel de Klerk.** Until his death in 1923 he built, together with **Peter Kramer** and **J.M. van der Mey,** a great number of houses, particularly to the south of Sarphatipark (**GV**) and to the west of Spaarndammerstraat (**FT**). They show a desire to break the monotony of façades by asymmetry and differences in levels and reduce the severity of straight lines with sections of curving walls.

The last war hit the town badly. Under the German occupation which lasted five years nearly 80 000 Jews were deported (only 5 000 survived). In February 1941 the heroic dockers' strike, protesting against the massive deportations, had no effect. A statue commemorating this event was sculpted by Mari Andriessen *(p 54)*.

Post-war period. – Amsterdam rose magnificently from its ordeals.

The large industrial city, which is part of the Randstad Holland *(qv)* is now devoted to metallurgical, graphic, and food industries.

On Europaplein the RAI (**FV**) is a large congress and exhibition centre. The World Trade Centre, near the South Station (Station Zuid) was inaugurated in 1985.

The canal from Amsterdam to the Rhine (Amsterdam-Rijnkanaal), completed in 1952, has contributed to the development of the port which has increased its trade with Eastern Europe.

A road tunnel for cars built under the IJ in 1968 has made communication easier between the old town and the area situated to the north of the port. An underground was opened in 1976. Schiphol airport, which can be reached by rail has furthered Amsterdam's activity.

The town has grown with such modern suburbs as Buitenveldert to the south, and Bijlmermeer to the southeast. However, housing problems remain which explains why house-boats have multiplied; there are about 2 400 alongside 36km - 22 miles of quays.

As tolerant as it was in the 17C and readily avantgarde, Amsterdam with two universities totalling 39 000 students and also numerous higher educational institutions, is very open to new ideas and allows freedom of expression to the young who represent 30% of the population. There is a continual feeling of optimism in the air drawing the young from all over the world.

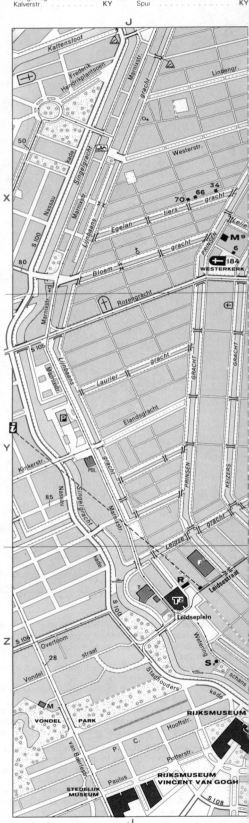

★★★ OLD AMSTERDAM *time: allow 1 day*

★★★ The canals (Grachten). – Most of the town houses which stand behind the trees, lining the canals in the centre of the town, were built in the 17 and 18C by wealthy merchants. Somewhat similar in appearance with their narrow façades and front steps, and yet they differ by the colour of their brick – pink, blue, violet or grey – and by the gable decoration.

Beams with pulleys project over the pediments: the too steep and too narrow staircases make it impossible to bring in furniture, so it is not unusual to see a piano, a wardrobe or a sideboard being hoisted upwards.

Gables and façade stones. – *See illustration below.* Gables have the most varied shapes. The oldest ones, concealing a two-pitched roof, are plain (a legacy from wooden houses), with pinnacles or crow-steps (Leeuwenburg House, *p 54*).

Then the gable gets taller. It is sometimes in the shape of a bell *(klokgevel)* **(A)**, or else that of a neck *(halsgevel)* **(B)**: it is then topped by a triangular or curved pediment and often framed with fine sculptures.

The wealthiest houses stand out by the width of their façade. The roof is then hidden by a large pilaster gable ending in a triangular pediment **(C)** or if the roofing is parallel to the street, by an emblazoned balustrade crowned with statues.

Finally a large type of house developed with pilasters and topped with a triangular carved pediment **(D)** where the façade, sometimes in stone, is often decorated with garlands.

On some façades there is a small sculptured stone: it is the emblem of the owner or the symbol of his trade, for example a bunch of grapes indicated the location of a wine merchant. The **façade stones** *(illustration p 54)* in Amsterdam outdo each other in extravagance. Many have disappeared but some have been recuperated and regrouped on the walls throughout the city.

To the north, near the port, there is a long line of **warehouses,** with the characteristic wooden shutters.

Herengracht

★ Boat trip (Rondvaart). – The boat trip gives an excellent view of the most important canals as well as part of the port (the evening trip is recommended). The route varies according to the opening of the locks. They make it possible to regulate the water level in the canals and ensure their cleanliness (canals are pumped clean every couple of days) due to the circulation of water pumped from IJssel Lake.

Leave from Dam.

Dam (KY). – The Dam, Amsterdam's main square, is at the junction of the two large central thoroughfares: Damrak and Rokin *(p 50)*, on the site of the dike (dam) on the Amstel. Overlooking this very animated square, there is the Royal Palace and the New Church.

The **National Liberation Monument (KY A)** (1956) by the sculptor Raedeker, symbolising suffering humanity bent under the scourge of war, is the rendez-vous of strollers.

The café at no 11 **(KY)** is the oldest house, **De Wildeman** (the wild man) in the square; it has a charming red brick façade, dating from 1632.

★ Royal Palace (Koninklijk Paleis) (KY). – The old town hall (burned down in 1652), known thanks to the painting by Saenredam in the Rijksmuseum, had become too small and was in disrepair, therefore, Jacob van Campen was called in to design a new town hall, whose construction began in 1648. It became the Royal Palace in 1808 under the reign of Louis Bonaparte.

It is a heavy classical construction, quadrilateral in shape, and built on 13 659 wooden piles. The east and west façades are topped by tympana carved by Artus I Quellin the Elder from Antwerp, who also did the building's interior decoration.

On the ground floor is the Hall of Justice (Vierschaar) where the death sentence was pronounced. The judges sat on a marble bench, above which were marble reliefs depicting Misericordia, Wisdom and Justice, and they sat facing statues of Prudence and Justice. This lay-out shows, symbolically, the cross-examiner and the judges. The people could follow the case through grilles. In the citizens' gallery (1st floor), the flooring illustrates the two hemispheres east and west and the north firmament. There is also the famous sculpture by Artus I Quellin the Elder of Atlas holding up the celestial globe. It was in the Aldermans' Gallery that Queen Juliana abdicated in 1980. Above the chimney admire the painting by Ferdinand Bol (qv), one of Rembrandt's pupils, of Moses coming down from Mount Sinai.

★ **New Church** (Nieuwe Kerk) (KX). – A Protestant church, the New Church or St Catherine's is to the Dutch what Westminster Abbey is to the English. It is here, in fact, that sovereigns are enthroned: Queen Wilhelmina was crowned here on 6 September 1898, her daughter Queen Juliana 50 years later, day for day, her granddaughter Queen Beatrix on 30 April 1980.

This lovely Late Gothic church was several times pillaged and gutted by fire. After a fire in 1645, its tower, designed by Jacob van Campen, remained unfinished.

It has a wooden vault, a **pulpit**★ in mahogany carved by Vinckenbrink in the 17C and a copper chancel screen, which is one of the masterpieces of Johannes Lutma, Amsterdam's famous gold and silversmith. The main organ case (c1650) was built from Van Campen's drawings; the whole has been greatly restored.

Dutch Admirals have their mausoleums here, in particular that of De Ruyter by Rombout Verhulst of Mechlin (Belgium). The poet Joost van den Vondel, as well as the famous bell-founders François and Pierre Hemony are also buried in this church.

Kalverstraat (KY). – A very busy and picturesque pedestrian precinct this is the most important shopping street in Amsterdam.

★★ **Museum of Amsterdam History** (Amsterdams Historisch Museum) (KY). – In this modern museum, in a former orphanage (Burgerweeshuis), Amsterdam's history unfolds.

The entry into the enclosure is by a small porch topped with the town's coat of arms. On the left is the orphanage boys' playground: they used to put their personal belongings in the cubby-holes: opposite, a building in classical style holds temporary exhibitions.

Then on the left, in the glass **gallery** there are portraits of civic guards who united to defend the town in 1580.

On the right is the porch leading to **St.-Luciensteeg** (St Lucy's alleyway) (KY 166), which takes its name from the convent which preceded the orphanage. On the wall near the porch a large number of picturesque **façade stones** from the city's old houses are gathered here.

Entrance to the museum is in the second courtyard, which was reserved for the girl orphans.

One follows in order the museum's 17 rooms spread over various levels (the room number is in parenthesis).

In the 1st room, an amusing illuminated map shows the extraordinary growth of the city and at the same time a mobile column shows the population growth.

The city built on sand, constructed a town hall (2) and devoted itself to trade (3). In 1345 a miracle made it a pilgrimage town (4). Then Amsterdam was subjected to Spanish domination (4). It is also its period of expansion in the world (5). At its peak it built a new town hall, the present Royal Palace (6). Then came other buildings and several churches (10). The wealthy town did not forget its poverty-strikten: charitable institutions abound; their Regents commissioned their portraits (11). In the 18C Amsterdam could no longer face up to foreign competition (12); during this same period the production of Amsterdam porcelain is renowned (14). In 1795 the French arrived (16). In the 20C Amsterdam remains very dynamic (17).

On leaving, visit, on the left, the **Regent's Room** (Regentenkamer) where the directors of the orphanage sat and which has kept its original appearance.

By a passage in the courtyard, reach the Beguinage.

★★ **Beguinage** (Begijnhof) (KY). – It appears as a haven of peace in the heart of the town. Founded in the 14C, it is one of the rare enclosures of this type which remain in the Netherlands, together with the one in Breda (p 70). Beguines are women belonging to a lay sisterhood; although they take no vows, they do devote themselves to religious life and wear a uniform.

Its tall 17 and 18C façades, preceded by a small flowered garden, is arranged round a meadow where the ancient church of the Beguines stands. It belongs to the Presbyterian Reformed Church, which has been using the English language since 1607.

Lovely sculptured façade stones can be seen at nos 11, 19, 23 and 24. No 26, a tall and elegant house was for the Mother Superior of the Beguinage. At no 31 there is a hidden Catholic chapel, built by the Beguines in 1665. Not far is the town's oldest house (15C) with its wooden façade; note in the left courtyard the façade stones.

★ **Madame Tussaud's** (KY M[1]). – Created in 1970 this extraordinary waxwork museum is a subsidiary of the one in London (see Michelin Green Guide to London).

Madame Tussaud is in the entrance, after a portrait she did of herself in 1842 at the age of 81. In the hall Queen Wilhelmina presides. In the Hall of Mirrors there is a crowd of well-known people from all over the world, past and present, who make startling appearances. Two sections have contemporary Dutch personalities. There is also an amusing carousel.

Three scenes illustrate the life and work of Rembrandt. Further on there is Vincent van Gogh and the Russian writer Solzhenitsyn with a recording of his voice.

Muntplein (KY 127). – This square, called Mint Square, is an animated crossroads dominated by the **Mint Tower** (Munttoren).
The tower, the remains of a 17C gateway, is crowned with a spire, which was added by Hendrick de Keyser and has a **carillon**. In 1672 during the war against France money was minted here.

★ **Flower Market (Bloemenmarkt)** (KY). – There are many flower sellers in Amsterdam and the sight of the shop windows and carts is a pleasure to the eye, but without doubt the most picturesque sight is that of the open-air stalls, supplied by barges which ride along the Singel.
Some of the stalls are installed on the barge itself, transforming the barge into a floating greenhouse.

Singel (KY). – On this canal, at no 423, there is the **university library** (KY C) and a 17C Lutheran church, Oude Lutherse Kerk (KY D).

Herengracht (Lords' Canal) (KYZ). – *Illustration p 48*. It is one of the main 17C canals where wealthy merchants came to live. Their houses rival in richness and decoration, and most of all in the height of their gables.

Starting at no 364: Cromhout Houses★ (Cromhouthuizen) (KY E): built by Philip Vingboons in 1662 they form a harmonious whole. The classical style façades are enhanced by a more baroque decoration (note the *œil-de-bœuf* windows). One of them houses the Bible Museum *(p 56)*.

Nos 386 to 394 (KY): a lovely series of façades. At no 394, below a graceful gable, a charming façade stone depicts the four Aymon sons, legendary heroes of the Ardennes, mounted on their horse Bayard.

Further on the right Leidsestraat begins (p 53).

At the 2nd bend formed by the canal, vast solemn residences form the **Golden Curve** (Bocht) (KZ F). It was the opulent quarter where at the beginning of the 17C the elite society lived; they are now occupied by banks and consulates. It was during this period that façades widened, the pediments leveled out and adopted the classical style while still keeping their decorative exuberance: the balustrades which crowned them, topped by flame ornaments or statues, surrounded the armorial bearings or allegorical scenes.

No 475 (KY K) *(opposite shore):* residence with a stone façade, built by Daniel Marot and Jacob Husley and decorated by Jan van Logteren; note the sumptuous roof ridge. At the corner of Vijzelstraat, the Algemene Bank Nederland building, is the work of the architect De Bazel, Berlage's *(qv)* contemporary.

No 502: Burgomaster's House (Huis met de kolommen) (KZ L): built in 1672 for a rich merchant of the Dutch India Company and altered in the 18C (the balcony supported by columns dates from this period) this house is, since 1927, the mayor's *(burgemeester)* official residence and where distinguished guests are received.

Reguliersgracht (LZ). – From the bridge which crosses this canal, there is a lovely **view**★ to the right over it and the some seven bridges spanning it.
Going a little further up to Keizersgracht, there is another agreeable **viewpoint**★: note the picturesque group of old houses (LZ N). The Keizersgracht or Emperor's Canal takes its name from Emperor Maximilian's crown which tops Wester Church spire.

Return to Herengracht.
From the bridge which crosses it, there is a lovely **view**★ to the left and right.

Thorbeckeplein (LZ 177). – With its string of nightclubs, this square is very busy in the evening.

Rembrandtsplein (LY). – It is one of the Amsterdamers favourite squares for their evening stroll.
Round the square, with its statue of the painter by Royer (1852), there are several large brasseries.

Rokin (KY). – This dock is situated at the far end of the Amstel, the continuation having been filled in. At the far end of the dock stands the equestrian statue of Queen Wilhelmina (KY R) by Theresia van der Pant.
By Langebrugsteeg one plunges into Amsterdam's oldest quarter around which the town developed.
Crossing Oudezijds Voorburgwal, one sees the old houses and warehouses which line this canal.

University (LY U). – The **Agnieten Gate** (LY Q) is the former entrance to the **Illustrious Atheneum,** a college which, founded in 1632, became a university in 1877. The chapel and the nearby buildings still belong to the university.
Walk alongside the university and its inner courtyard by the vaulted passageway, where second-hand booksellers are installed. One comes out on to **Kloveniersburgwal.** At no 29 (LY), the **Trippen House** (huis) is a large classical edifice built 1660-4 by Juste Vingboons for cannon manufacturers: the chimneys are in the shape of mortars.

Weigh House (Waag) or **St Anthony's Gateway** (St.-Anthoniespoort) (LY P). – This imposing fortified gateway (1488) flanked by towers and turrets, served as a weigh house in 1617 and was restored in the 19C.
To the west of Nieuwmarkt near Oudezijds Voorburgwal *(p 53)* is the red light district.

Return to Dam by Oude Hoogstraat and Damstraat.

PRINCIPAL MUSEUMS *time: allow 1 day minimum*

★★ **Rijksmuseum** (JZ). – This national museum was founded by Louis Bonaparte in 1808
⊙ but the present building was constructed between 1876-85 by P.J.H. Cuypers in the
neo-classical style. It includes an exceptional collection of 15 to 17C paintings with, as
well, sculpture and decorative arts, history, prints and Asian art collections.

15 to 17C Paintings (Schilderkunst 15de - 17de eeuw). – *1st floor, east wing; room
numbers appear in brackets.* In the collection of **Primitives** there are works by: **Geertgen
tot Sint Jans** (room 201), the *Holy Family* of delicate drawing and exquisite colours, *The
Adoration of the Magi* in a lovely landscape; Jan Mostaert, whose *Adoration of the
Magi* (202) is set in an Italian Renaissance scene; the Master of Alkmaar, *(qv),* famous
for his *Seven Works of Charity* (202); Jacob Cornelisz. van Oostsanen shows elegant
draughtsmanship with his *Adoration of the Magi* (203); Cornelis Engebrechtsz. (204)
is a rather touching painter.

In the **Renaissance, Lucas van Leyden** in his *Adoration of the Golden Calf* (204) shows great
art of composition and an expressive and lively technique; **Jan van Scorel** depicts a *Mary
Magdalene* (205) of very Italian elegance.

The art of Pieter Aertsen is more realistic while a certain reserve emanates from
Antonio Moro's portraits. There are works by Cornelis Cornelisz. van Haarlem, a
Mannerist painter like Abraham Bloemaert, a still-life of flowers by Velvet Bruegel; as
well as some lovely landscapes by the Antwerp painter, Momper (all in room 206).

In the **Golden Age**, painting styles varied. **Frans Hals** painted excellent portraits like *The
Couple* (209) or *Jolly Toper* (210) which reminds one of Impressionism. Several rooms
(211, 215, 221a, 224, 229, 230) are devoted to **Rembrandt**. *The Stone Bridge* (1638) is one
of the rare landscape paintings by the master. The portrait of his mother reading the
Bible (1631) in a meditative atmosphere can be compared with that of his pupil Gerrit
Dou, who treats the same subject with more severity (all three paintings in room 211).
By Hals's pupil, Judith Leyster there is a genre scene, *The Serenade* (213). Saenredam
liked portraying monuments like Amsterdam's *Old Town Hall.* There were numerous
landscape painters as well: Van Goyen *(Landscape with Two Oaks)* and Salomon van
Ruysdael (*River Landscape with Cattle Ferry;* all in room 214).

Portraits were popular at the time as is exemplified in Rembrandt's *Maria Trip* (c1640),
a luxuriously dressed young woman, as well as a work by one of his contemporaries
Ferdinand Bol, the fine *Portrait of Elisabeth Bas* (both in room 215).

Other painters turned to depicting animals as did Paulus Potter or happy domestic life
as did Jan Steen in the *Feast of St Nicholas* (both in room 216).

More landscapes are rendered in the works of **Jacob van Ruisdael** with *The Windmill at
Wijk bij Duurstede* (217) and the *View of Haarlem* (218) and Hobbema (*Watermill* -217).
While Adriaen van Ostade turned more towards villagers, catching them in scenes of
their daily life *Peasants in an Interior: The Skaters* (218).

Philips Wouwerman (220) and Adam Pynacker (221) are good landscape painters.
There are also admirable seascapes and naval battles by Willem van de Velde the
Younger (220). Another of Rembrandt's portraits is his *Portrait of Titus* (c1660) with his
son posing in a monk's habit; next to it is the lovely *Girl at a Window: The Daydreamer*
by one of Rembrandt's contemporaries Nicolaas Maes (both room 221a).

By **Vermeer**, the extraordinary colourist, the four paintings exhibited (room 222) are
masterpieces: *The Little Street,* painted from the windows of his house (c1658), *The
Kitchen Maid,* pouring milk with a measured gesture (c1658). *The Young Woman
Reading a Letter* (c1662) with luminous blue tones, and finally *The Letter* (c1666).
Another intimist painter worth noting is Pieter de Hooch with his sober, geometric
settings *(The Pantry).* The more objective architectural painter Emmanuel de Witte is
represented by his religious building interiors *(Oude Kerk, Synagogue)* (also in room
222). Then in room 222a there are portraits by Terborch and a self portrait with a pipe
by Gerrit Dou and a sentimental scene by Metsu *(The Sick Child).*

One room (room 223 for information on the work) is devoted to the Company of
Captain Frans Banning Cocq called **The Night Watch** (Nachtwacht) (224). Commissioned
by the arquebusiers, this enormous painting was completed in 1642 and throned in
the guild headquarters, the Doelen, in Kloveniersburgwal *(p 50)* until it was transferred
to Amsterdam's town hall in 1715. At that time, it was made smaller by cutting off
60cm - 23½in on the left, 10cm - 4in on the right, 20cm - 8in from top and bottom.
Owned by the Amsterdam Municipality, the painting was lent to the museum as soon
as it was founded, but hidden during World War II in caves near Maastricht *(qv).* It
owes its name (night) to the layers of varnish which darkened it until 1947, but it in fact
depicts the civic guards coming out in full daylight.

The guards, shown in great agitation, in a very disorderly group, are taken by surprise:
the captain is giving the departure signal and the guards, some of whom have their
faces half hidden, make a very original group portrait.

A few details add to the spontaneity of the whole: the little girl who is crossing the
group a bird attached to her belt, the barking dog, the dwarf running, the man with a
helmet covered with leaves. Spots of bright colour enhance the rather grey tones of
the guards' uniforms: bright yellow dress of the small child and the lieutenant's
costume, red outfit of the guard who is reloading his gun, red scarf of the captain.

One room (225) is reserved for the **foreign paintings' collection.**
From the Italian School, amongst numerous Primitives, there is a *Virgin and Child* by
Fra Angelico as well as a *Mary Magdalene* by Crivelli (225). Portraits by the Florentine
painter Piero di Cosimo are interesting, as are the views of Venice by Guardi. From
Spain there is a lovely *Virgin and Child* by Murillo and the portrait of *Ramon Satue* by
Goya, the only painting by this artist in the Netherlands. The Flemish are present with
two works by **Rubens.** The great gallery (229-236) contains paintings by the Dutch
masters from the second half of the 17C; note Rembrandt's late works (229, 230).

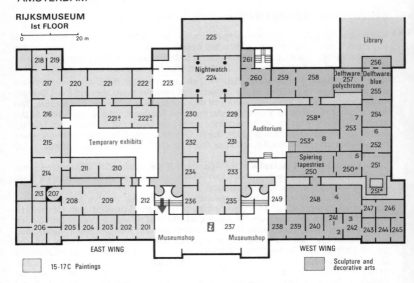

RIJKSMUSEUM
1st FLOOR

Rembrandt's portrait of himself as St Paul (1661) appears as a disenchanted old man. Whereas the portrait of a couple called *The Jewish Bride* (1668-9) gleams with light and is bathed in tenderness (both in room 229).

The Sampling Officials of the Drapers Guild of 1662, grouped behind a table enhanced by a red carpet, have serious faces, but are very alive.

The Anatomy Lesson of Doctor Joan Deyman which should not be confused with *The Anatomy Lesson of Dr Tulp* (Mauritshuis, The Hague) is composed round the figure of a foreshortened corpse (both in room 230).

Once again Maes, Rembrandt's contemporary, is represented with his *Old Woman in Prayer* (231). Greatly influenced by the master was his pupil, Aert de Gelder *(Portrait of Ernst van Beveren* - 232).

Aelbert Cuyp tended more to paint landscapes filled with both people and animals (234).

Sculpture and Decorative Arts (Beeldhouwkunst en Kunstnijverheid). – *1st floor, ground floor and basement, west wing.* This extensive section takes up numerous rooms, which are richly furnished and decorated with *objets d'art* (sculpture, paintings, gold and silversmith's work, glassware and tapestries) dating from the 15C to the 1900s. As regards local production, amongst the sculptures there are: **The Meeting of Saints Joachim and Anne**, a moving, late 15C work in wood, anonymous (1); the groups by **Adriaen van Wesel** of the same period, full of life and elegance, such as the *Death of the Virgin* (2) and the *Music Making Angels* (3): there is also a rood screen executed *c*1500 (4).

Also notable, from the 17C, are tapestries by the Flemish, Spiering, from his Delft workshops (250), a terracotta bust by **Hendrick de Keyser** (5) a Renaissance oak cabinet, a type widespread in the country (6) *(illustration p 28),* a lovely bouquet painted by Velvet Bruegel (7), engraved glassware (253), a Ceylanese colonial bed (8), gold and silversmith work by the Van Vianen brothers and Johannes Lutma (254), Delftware both blue (255) and polychrome (257) and a *kussenkast* cupboard (9) *(illustration p 28).* On the ground floor and in the basement, there is 18 to 20C furniture and lovely collections of pottery, glassware, lace, doll's houses, etc.

Dutch History (Nederlandse Geschiedenis). – *Ground floor, east wing.* The history of the country, from the Middle Ages, is pleasantly illustrated, notably by *objets d'art.*

The large room is devoted to the Golden Age, its wars, sea battles and daily life. There is a portrait by Van Dyck of the young Prince William II and his wife Henrietta Mary Stuart; he was 15 and she was 9 when they were married in 1641, The Stadtholders, in particular, are evoked in a series of portraits, as well as the Batavian Republic, the domination of Napoleon, the Battle of Waterloo and the monarchy.

Print Room (Rijksprentenkabinet). – *Ground floor, west wing.* The museum possesses a large number of drawings and engravings, from the 15C to the present, which are exhibited in rotation. **Temporary exhibitions** of drawings and prints of foreign origin also take place.

18 and 19C Paintings (Schilderkunst 18de en 19de eeuw). – *Ground floor, southwest wing.* This section has paintings and a few ceramic collections.

Cornelis Troost *(An Amsterdam Town Garden)* is the best of the 18C Dutch painters (room 136).

At the beginning of the 19C, Wouter Johannes van Troostwijk (143) painted Amsterdam with much poetry while artists of **The Hague School** (Jacob Maris, Anton Mauve, Jozef Israëls) observed the country and the sea in their landscape paintings. One room (138) is devoted to Islamic art.

Asian Art (Aziatische Kunst). – *Basement, southwest wing. Direct access by 19 Hobbemastraat or else by the 18 and 19C Paintings section.* This section houses some works of art from the Far East (China, Japan, Korea), India, Ceylon, Southeast Asia and Indonesia. Chinese and Japanese art are beautifully exhibited.

Rooms 20 to 22 give a good overall view of Chinese porcelain. In room 15 a polychrome wooden sculpture, of the Sung dynasty (960-1279), depicting the Chinese bodhisattva (future Buddha), Kuan-Yin, bears witness to the height reached by Chinese sculpture of this period. Amongst the Japanese collections, note the ceramic objects used for the tea ceremony (rooms 14 and 23) and the lacquer-work (room 13). Two fragments from a series of stone low reliefs from eastern Java show a curious landscape. The 12C bronze sculpture showing Śiva in a cosmic dance (room 17) comes from Southern India.

From Java there is a small carved Buddha (room 18), which either comes from Southern India or Ceylon, and dates from the 8C.

★★★**Vincent van Gogh National Museum** (Rijksmuseum Vincent van Gogh) (JZ). – The ⊘ museum contains the archives and collections of the Vincent van Gogh Foundation, which includes nearly 200 paintings and 500 drawings by Vincent van Gogh (1853-90), 50 works by his contemporaries, which belonged to his brother Theo, as well as 600 letters.

The painting collection enables the visitor to follow the artist's development: somber canvases at the beginning evolving into the violent tonalities of his last years.

Born in Zundert, south of Breda, Van Gogh sketched right from childhood, but he only became conscious of his vocation at age 27; he then drew with passion before taking up oil painting the following year in The Hague.

He started with dark landscapes of the Drenthe with its thatched cottages. Then came the Nuenen period, the village where Vincent lived in his parents' presbytery *(p 154)*. A series of portraits of peasants, striking by the intensity of their expression, served as studies for *The Potato Eaters* (1885).

After staying in Antwerp he went to Paris in February 1886. His palette became more luminous (1887-8) under the Impressionist influence with the *View over Paris* from Vincent's atelier *Rue Lepic,* the *Grande Jatte Bridge,* the *Seine at Asnières,* and numerous self-portraits including the *Self-Portrait in Front of an Easel.*

He also worked on painting landscapes in the style of Japanese engravings.

Orchards in Provence, the *Zouave,* the *Drawbridge,* and *Sunflowers* emphasise his determination to depict the violence of colour contrasts under the Arles sky (February 1888-May 1889).

Frenzied wheat fields, tormented olive trees, cypress trees twisted by the *mistral,* and more subdued tonalities reveal the troubles which caused his hospitalisation in Arles and then to the asylum in St-Rémy-de-Provence (May 1889-May 1890), from where he painted from memory his room in Arles. Finally, after a calm spell in Auvers-sur-Oise, near Paris, he painted in 1890 the dramatic composition, *Wheat Fields with Crows.* The same year, in which, on 27 July, he wounded himself in a despairing gesture, which two days later ended his brilliant but short-lived career.

In the museum there are also lithographs, watercolours, drawings (changing exhibitions) showing sketches of his major works, and among Theo's collection the works of Adolphe Monticelli (1824-86), Hendrik Koning, etc.

ADDITIONAL SIGHTS

Vondel Park Quarter

★★**Municipal Museum** (Stedelijk Museum) (JZ). – Built in 1895 and enlarged in 1954, this ⊘ modern art museum is continually being renewed with works of art covering the period from 1850 to the present.

There are also paintings by Cézanne, Monet, Picasso, Léger, Malevitch, Chagall as well as Mondrian and Van Doesburg, who represent the De Stijl *(qv)* movement. The most recent trends in European and American art are well represented.

In summer all the rooms exhibit the leading collections (latest acquisitions).

On Van Baerlestraat there is the **Concertgebouw** (FV T^1), built in 1888.

Leidseplein (JZ). – It is a lively square with a shaded terrace, very busy in the summer and lined on the north side by a row of old gabled houses (JZ R). All around there are theatres, including the well-known municipal theatre, **Stadsschouwburg** (JZ T^2), restaurants and discos: this quarter specialises in pop music. To the east on Weteringschans (no 6), the Paradiso (JZ S), a secularised church, has been converted, by the municipality, into a youth centre and is a well-known meeting place for music lovers.

Leidsestraat (JKZ). – In this long and pleasant pedestrian street linking Leidseplein to the centre, a barrel organ *(qv)* plays popular tunes daily.

⊘ **Vondel Park** (Vondelpark) (EUV). – Vondel Park, named after the great 17C Dutch poet, Joost van den Vondel (1587-1679), stretches from the large Singelgracht to Amstelveenseweg. There is an open-air theatre in summer.

Oudezijds Voorburgwal Quarter

This is the famous red light district. Lovely old houses line its narrow canals.

★ **Amstelkring Museum "Our Lord in the Attic"** (Museum Amstelkring Ons' Lieve Heer op ⊘ Solder) (LX M^5). – Since the *Union of Utrecht (qv)* the Catholics, driven out of their churches by the Reformation, celebrated mass in private houses. This secret chapel fitted out in the attics of three houses was used for Catholic worship from 1663 until the construction of the new St Nicholas Church in 1887, whereupon it was converted into a museum for the Amstelkring Foundation. Certain ceremonies take place here; concerts are sometimes held here.

The staircase leading to the 2nd floor passes in front of the hall (sael) which is in the pure 17C Dutch style and the abbot's room with a box bed. The **church,** where the two superimposed galleries correspond to the 3rd and 4th floors, has interesting 18C furnishings. In one room, on the confessional floor, there is an interesting exhibition of liturgical objects in silver, some of them from this secret chapel.

Opposite the museum, at no 19, the house's gable is framed with enormous dolphins.

⊙ **Old Church (Oude Kerk)** (LX). – This church, dedicated to St Nicholas, was built in the 14C. It is the oldest in the city. In the 16C the bell tower was topped by an elegant spire whose carillon was in part cast by François Hemony.

Very damaged inside by the Iconoclasts (qv), it still has in its 16C Lady Chapel three elegantly designed 16C stained glass windows. In 1642 the remains of Saskia, Rembrandt's wife, were brought here (stone slab no 29). Numerous famous people are buried here (the painter Pieter Aertsen, the writer Roemer Visscher, etc).

Leeuwenburg House (Huis) (LX V). – 14 Oudezijds Voorburgwal. This picturesque 17C rust coloured brick façade with a crow-stepped gable and lattice windows with red shutters, is decorated with a carved stone depicting a fortified castle sheltering a lion. On a nearby wall some very lovely **façade stones** have been embedded (LX W).

Façade stone

On the bridge over the lock where two canals meet, there is a picturesque **view★**: on one side, the Oudezijds Kolk where old houses lie shrouded and overlooked by the dome of the Catholic church of St Nicholas (1887), on the other side the Oudezijds Voorburgwal, which frames a lovely series of old façades, further on is the Old Church tower.

Weeping Tower (Schreierstoren) (LX X). – Folklore relates that near the old rampart tower, sailors' wives came to say goodbye to their husbands.

A low relief evokes the Englishman, **Henry Hudson,** who in 1609 for the Dutch East India Company, sailed up the river which now bears his name, Hudson River in New York (see the Michelin Green Guide to New York City).

Rembrandt's Quarter

★ **Rembrandt's House (Museum Het Rembrandthuis)** (LY M⁶). – It is situated in Jodenbree-
⊙ straat, the old Jewish quarter's main street.

When it was built in 1606 this house had one floor less. In 1639 Rembrandt bought it for 13 000 florins payable over 6 years; he lived here until he was evicted by his creditors in 1659.

The house has a collection of the master's graphic works. Exhibited beside two lovely ancient pieces of furniture are about 250 etchings, giving an insight into his work. Drawings can be seen in small temporary exhibitions.

There are also a few canvases by one of his professors, Pieter Lastman, as well as works by his pupils.

Waterlooplein (LY). – The Catholic **Moses and Aaron Church** (Mozes- en Aäronkerk) (LY Y), overlooking this large square, is used in the summer as a centre for entertainment and
⊙ metaphysical reflection. A **flea market** is held here, as well as an **antique market.**

South of Jodenbreestraat, on the former Vlooyenburg Island, two recently constructed buildings are worth noting: **Muziektheater** (LY T), which opened its doors in 1986, and the new **town hall** both designed by the Austrian architect Wilhelm Holzbauer.

The Muziektheater, the entrance of which is decorated by a pink granite sculpture by André Volten (born in 1925), is the seat of the National Opera and the National Ballet Company. From the foyer there is a good view of the Amstel and its bridges.

★ **Museum of Jewish History (Joods Historisch Museum)** (LY M¹⁵). – South of Jonas Daniel
⊙ Meijerplein stand four restored Ashkenazic synagogues. The first one, Great Syna-
gogue, was built in 1671 by D. Stalpaert; as it became too small the Obbene (1686), Dritt (1700) and New Synagogue (1752) were successively added.

The New Synagogue is easily identified by its Ionic columned entrance and dome. The exhibition inside covers different aspects of the Jewish identity: religion, Zionism, persecution and survival, culture, environment and history. In the **Great Synagogue,** where a fine white marble ark of the Covenant (1671) is worth admiring, Judaic themes – the Jewish year and its religious celebrations and the steps into adulthood are complemented by cultural and ceremonial objects (silverware, lamps, clothing and ornaments accompanying the Torah, drapes...). Note, as well, the two recepticles for ritual bathing (mikwe).

⊙ **Portuguese Synagogue** (HU B). – This massive building, lit by tall windows, was built in 1675 (since restored) by Elias Bouman for the worshipping of the three Portuguese Jewish congregations which had just united.

The interior remains as shown in the painting by Emmanuel de Witte (can be viewed in the Rijksmuseum) with wide wood barrel vaults supported by very high columns, galleries for the women, the ark of the Covenant, and large copper chandeliers as the only decoration.

Near the Portuguese Synagogue, the **statue of a Docker** by Mari Andriessen commemorates the strike launched by the dockers against the German occupying forces on 25 February 1941.

Bridge to the south of Oude Schans (LY Z). – From this bridge there is a fine **view** over the Oude Schans basin and **Montelbaan Tower** (Montelbaanstoren) (HU A). This tower, as well as St Anthony's Gate *(p 48)* was part of the town's curtain wall in the 16C.

Zuider Church (Zuiderkerk) (LY). – The first church (no longer used) built in Amsterdam after the Reformation was built between 1603 and 1611 from a plan by Hendrick de Keyser; it is flanked by a **tower** (1614).

Further along, at 69 St.-Antoniesbreestraat, there is the **De Pinto House** (huis) (LY) which was built c1600 and once belonged to a rich Portuguese Jew. It is now a public library.

Groenburgwal (LY). – In a picturesque site, a wooden **lever bridge** crosses this shaded canal which in earlier days went through what used to be the dyers' district. There is a lovely **view** of the Zuider Church tower from here.

Near the bridge, at 7b Staalstraat, is the former seat of the Drapers' Guild, immortalised by Rembrandt.

Damrak, Rokin, Amstel

Stock Exchange (Beurs) (LX). – Built by Berlage between 1897 and 1903, this is the principal work of this Amsterdam architect enamoured by functionalism and pioneer of modern architecture in the Netherlands. This brick building has a sober exterior. Inside, the open steel framework supports a glass roof.

Since 1987, this former Commodity Exchange (stock market is located in a neighbouring building) serves as a cultural centre (exhibitions, concerts).

★ **Allard Pierson Museum** (KY M²). – It is the archaeological museum of Amsterdam University and contains a remarkable collection of antiquities from Egypt, the Near East, Cyprus, Greece, Etruria and the Roman world.

1st floor. – Egypt (coffins with mummies), Near East (Iranian pottery), Crete and Mycenae as well as Cyprus are represented. Room 7 is reserved for the Coptic art collection: textiles.

2nd floor. – It is devoted to Greece, Etruria and the Roman world: a stone head, Greek Archaic art, statues of the Classical period (Aphrodite, c400BC), funeral stele from Attica (c400BC), pottery, a Roman sarcophagus (c300AD). Room 20 has jewellery from Iran, Greece and Egypt.

Blauw Bridge (Blauwbrug) (LY). – It is a copy of the Alexandre III Bridge in Paris *(see Michelin Green Guide to Paris)*.

★ **Magere Bridge (Magere Brug)** (LZ). – This fragile 18C wooden bridge (*magere* means thin) crossing the wide Amstel canal evokes the bridges dear to Van Gogh.

The large building to the east is a **theatre** (Theater Carré, GHU T³) dating from 1887 (circus, opera, operetta, variety shows). Standing beside the bridge one can see several bell towers, including that of Zuider Church.

At the corner of Prinsengracht and Amstel quay, a former wine shop has a bunch of grapes over the door.

Wester Church Quarter

Anne Frank's House (Anne Frank Huis) (JX M⁹). – This narrow building erected in 1635 stretches back and has a house behind, which was enlarged in 1740. It is here that Anne Frank's father, a German Jew who emigrated in 1933, hid his family and friends in July 1942. Betrayed and deported in August 1944 with the other refugees, he alone returned from Auschwitz. The moving diary *(Diary of Anne Frank)* kept by his 13 year old daughter was found in the house, and reveals a rare sensitivity. The Anne Frank Foundation spreads her message of peace throughout the world.

A secret passage hidden by a revolving bookcase leads to the barren rooms where all lived. On the 2nd floor of the neighbouring house, documentation and photographs retrace the history of persecutions all over the world.

Wester Church (Westerkerk) (JX). – This church was built in 1631 by Pieter de Keyser, after the plans of his father Hendrick. The **bell tower** dating from 1638, topped by the Imperial Crown commemorating Maximilian of Austria is 85m - 279ft high and has a remarkable carillon by the Hemony brothers.

Rembrandt was buried here in 1669, next to his son Titus who died the year before, On the neighbouring square, **Westermarkt** (JX), **Descartes** lived at no 6 in 1634.

Theatre Museum (KX M¹⁰). – Belonging to the Netherlands Theatre Institute, the museum is installed in a house, which was built in 1618 and converted in 1638 by Philip Vingboons. It has a fine stone façade decorated with the coat of arms of its earlier owner, Michel de Pauw.

The interior, fitted up c1730 in Louis XIV style, preserves a valuable decoration of stuccos, mural frescoes and ceilings painted notably by Jacob de Wit.

A section presents one of the greatest theatres in Amsterdam, "Amsterdamse Schouwburg" with the celebrated miniature stage created by Hieronymus van Slingelandt.

The museum's library is in part of the neighbouring house (no 170) or **Bartolotti House** (KX C), built by Hendrick de Keyser c1617. Its fairly wide brick façade, topped by a very decorative gable, is enlivened by a multitude of decorations carved in white stone.

House of Heads (Huis met de Hoofden) (KX D). – It is a lovely brick house dating from 1624 (restored) and where the façade, a little like that of the Bartolotti House *(see above)* is decorated with six sculptured heads representing the gods of Roman mythology.

The Central Canals

⊘ **Willet-Holthuysen Museum** (LZ M¹¹). – This patrician house built *c*1687 has kept a series of elegantly furnished rooms, evoking the life of rich merchants of that time. There are also collections of pottery, glassware and gold and silversmiths' work.

⊘ **Van Loon Museum** (KZ M¹²). – Built in 1671-2 (altered in the 18C) on the edge of Keizersgracht by Adriaan Dorstman, this fine mansion belonged to the painter Ferdinand Bol (1616-80). The refined interior contains numerous portraits.
At the bottom of the garden, there is a Renaissance style coach house.

⊘ **Fodor Museum** (KZ M¹³). – This old bourgeois house (19C) on Keizersgracht presents **exhibitions** by contemporary Amsterdam artists.

⊘ **Bible Museum** (Bijbels Museum) (KY M¹⁴). – Installed in the **Cromhout Houses** *(p 50)*, this museum gives information on Judaic religious life, history of the Bible in the Netherlands, and life in Palestine in Biblical times.

New Lutheran Church (Nieuwe of Ronde Lutherse Kerk) (KX E). – Built in 1668-71, this church with its high dome stands on the edge of the Singel. Disused, it has been
⊘ converted into a **concert hall** and conference centre.

Nearby, no 7, is the narrowest house in Amsterdam.

The Jordaan

Efforts are being made to enhance this popular area which dates from the 17C. At that time it was inhabited by French immigrants, whence its name which is a deformation of the French word *jardin* (garden). Most of its canals bear the names of flowers.

Brouwersgracht (Brewers' Canal) (KX). – This canal, perpendicular to the three main canals, is lined with picturesque quays and old houses and warehouses.
The **De Kroon warehouse** (no 118) has been nicely restored. On its façade, it has a carved stone depicting a crown *(kroon)*.
Near the bridge at the confluence of Prinsengracht there are many old façades (KX F), two with crow-stepped gables are notable.

Noorder Church (Noorderkerk) (KX). – Built in 1623 by Hendrick de Keyser, this church is in the shape of a Greek cross.
On Noorderplein there is a **bird market** (Saturday mornings).
In the neighbouring Westerstraat a large rag market is held (Monday mornings). In the
⊘ summer a **fruit and vegetable market** (not treated) also takes place.

Egelantiersgracht (JX). – At no 34, the **Claes Claesz. Hofje** is an old 17C almshouse (JX) *(enter by Eerste Egelantiersdwarsstraat)* surrounding a picturesque little courtyard. At nos 66-70, near a bridge, there are three trim houses (restored), lit on the ground floor by numerous windows, and with a gable in the shape of a neck *(p 48)*.

Quarters to the East

★ **Artis** (HU). – This is Amsterdam's **Zoological Garden,** its name, Artis, is an abbreviation
⊘ of the name of the company which founded it in 1838, Natura Artis Magistra (Nature, Mistress of Art). In a large well cared for park more than 7 000 animals can be seen as well as an **aquarium** where 700 aquatic species and invertebrates live.
The building for nocturnal animals *(nachtdieren)* has lighting conditions where day and night have been reversed, which allows you to observe these animals in activity. Note also the buildings for small mammals (lemurs, otters, etc) reptiles and bears and hippopotamuses. An incubator shows the different stages of chicks' hatching.

★ **Tropical Museum** (Tropenmuseum) (HU M⁷). – Life in the tropical and subtropical
⊘ regions of Africa, Asia, Middle East, Oceania and Latin America is shown with the help of *objets d'art* and a wide variety of everyday objects, reconstructed dwellings and, often, very primitive shops. Photographs and slide shows complete the exhibit. Temporary exhibits and gamelan (Indonesian orchestra) concerts are held.

The Quays of the Port

★ **Netherlands Maritime History Museum** (Nederlands Scheepvaart Museum) (HU M⁸). –
⊘ This large maritime warehouse installed in the old arsenal was built in 1656 on 18 000 piles in the waters of the Oosterdok.
It has interesting collections concerning Netherlands' shipping: maps and globes, ship models, nautical instruments, paintings and prints.
A seaport with ships of Dutch design is underway.
Opposite the museum, the **Pollux boat** (HU L) is moored; it is an elegant three-masted training ship intended for the apprenticeship of pupils of the merchant navy.

Prins Hendrikkade (HTU). – On the quay running alongside the Oosterdok at the corner of Binnenkant, there are the immense buildings of **Navigation House** (Scheep-vaarthuis) (GHT K). Built in 1913 by the principal architects of the Amsterdam School – Van der Mey, Michel de Klerk and P.L. Kramer – it is representative of their style.
From the bridge to the east, there is a fine **view** of Montelbaan Tower *(p 55)*.

Realen Island (Realeneiland) (GT). – This is one of the islands in the west quarter of the port, lined with warehouses.
On **Zandhoek**, a row of 17C houses have been restored, whose façades, decorated with sculptured stones, overlook the Westerdok.

EXCURSIONS

South of Amsterdam. – *24km - 15 miles to the south – about 1 hour. Follow Amsteldijk* (HV) *and the west bank of the Amstel.*

Rieker Mill (Rieker Molen). – *Illustration p 33.* Formerly located in the Rieker Polder, this lovely thatched polder mill *(qv)* with a rotating cap has been transferred to the banks of the Amstel.
The bronze statue depicting Rembrandt drawing, reminds one that the artist often walked along the Amstel seeking inspiration.

Ouderkerk aan de Amstel. – This picturesque village is very often visited on Sundays by Amsterdamers.
To the north is a **stage mill.**

Amsterdamse Bos. – This is Amsterdam's woods, an immense park strewn with lakes (boating, fishing with permit).

Amstelveen. – Pop 68 581. A modern residential city which contains several **botanical gardens** (heemparken) devoted to the country's flora.
The most well known is **Dr. J.P. Thijsse Park** *(between Amsterdamseweg and Amsterdamse Bos).*
One can also visit a **cheese dairy:** Kaasboerderij Clara Maria *(Bovenkerkerweg 106).*

Schiphol. – Built 4.5m - 14ft below sea level in an old cove of dried-up Haarlem Lake *(qv),* Amsterdam's airport, Schiphol, is one the continent's great stop-overs.
Not far from the runways is the **Aviodome,** a strange parachute in mat aluminium, honeycombed with stars, which houses the National Aviation Museum's collection. Various airplane models, some of them old, showing technical evolution can be seen as well as space-craft and an exhibition on civil aviation.
A movie theatre is installed in the basement.

Round tour of 65km - 40 miles. – *About 4 hours. Leave Amsterdam by Mauritskade* (HU). *After the second bridge (Schellingwouderbrug) near the locks (Oranjesluizen), turn towards Schellingwoude then pass under the road and go towards Durgerdam.*

Durgerdam village

Just before reaching **Durgerdam** there is a lovely **view★** of the village.
The houses painted in different colours sometimes with a wooden gable, and an amusing square building with a pyramid-shaped roof topped with a pinnacle, are on the shore of a small cove.
After Durgerdam, the dike road, very narrow and winding, which goes along the former Zuiderzee coast, offers lovely views. Opposite lies, perhaps, what may become Markerwaard polder *(see map p 17).*

★ **Marken.** – *Description p 148.*

Monnickendam. – Pop 9 909. This small pleasure boat harbour was renowned in the past for its eels. Like several ports on IJssel Lake, smoked herrings are eaten here. The town is overlooked by the 16C brick **Speel Tower** (Speeltoren). Opposite, the **town hall** (Stadhuis) is an 18C patrician house with a decorated pediment; note the entrance ramps shaped like a serpent. In the same street (Noordeinde) and in Kerkstraat, several houses have picturesque gables and façade stones. Not far, in Middendam, stands the **weigh house** (Waag), a small building *c*1600, which is decorated with pilasters and a heavily carved gable.
To the south, the Gothic **Great Church or St Nicholas** (Grote- of St.-Nicolaaskerk), a three-naved hall-type church, contains a lovely 16C chancel screen of carved wood.

★ **Volendam.** – *Description p 182.*

Edam. – *Description p 87.*

Broek in Waterland. – Pop 2 725. Near a lake, the Havenrak, this flowery village with freshly painted houses has always been known for its cleanliness: in the past was it not necessary to take off one's wooden shoes before entering? It is said that Napoleon took off his boots when he came here for a friendly meeting with the mayor on 15 October 1811.
Several 17 and 18C wooden houses can be seen in the village. Some of the 17C ones are U-shaped. Some have two doors, the one on the façade being used only for marriages and funerals.
On the edge of the lake is the pavilion where Napoleon was received (Napoleonhuisje). Dating from 1656 it is a small white pagoda-shaped wood construction.
Near the canal, the **church** (kerk) set on fire by the Spaniards in 1573 was rebuilt between 1585 and 1639. In the north aisle, there is an interesting stained glass window *(c*1640) in harmonious and original colours, which recalls the tragic event and the church's reconstruction.
A model **cheese dairy,** De Domme Dirk *(Roomeinde 17)* allows one to taste and buy Edam cheese.

Return to Amsterdam by ① *on the town plan.*

Michelin map ▨▨▨ fold 12
Town plan in the current Michelin Red Guide Benelux

A real garden-city, Apeldoorn is situated in the heart of the Veluwe *(qv)* which seems to continue right into the city; it is cut by wide avenues lined with great trees and endowed with numerous parks.
Apeldoorn has a few industries; in addition, due to the very pure spring water it has become a laundering centre.

⊙ A **steam train** (De Veluwsche Stoomtrein) runs between Apeldoorn and Dieren *(23km - 14 miles).*

★★ **HET LOO PALACE MUSEUM** (RIJKSMUSEUM PALEIS)

Access by ⑧ on the road to Amersfoort.

Surrounded by a **park** of 650ha - 1 626 acres, Het Loo Royal Palace and its gardens were opened to the public in 1984 following extensive restoration work.

HISTORICAL NOTES

When **William III** (1650-1702), Prince of Orange and Stadtholder of the United Provinces bought the 14-15C Het Oude Loo Castle in 1684, this ardent huntsman began fulfilling his dream. In 1685 the first stone of Het Loo Palace was laid, about 300yds from the site of the old castle, by William's wife Princess **Mary Stuart**, daughter to James II.
The palace was intended for the princely couple with their court and guests, as well as their large hunt. The presence of spring water made it possible to provide water for horses and dogs and decorate the gardens with fountains. Situated in the heart of the Veluwe and abounding in game, it had a privileged location.
The Royal Academy of Architecture in Paris supplied the plans of the palace while **Jacob Roman** (1640-1760) pupil of Pieter Post *(qv)* can be considered as the main architect. The interior decoration and the creation of the gardens were given to **Daniel Marot** (1661-1752) a Parisian Huguenot, who probably arrived in Holland shortly after the Revocation of the *Edict of Nantes* (1685).
In 1689 William III was proclaimed King of England after having chased his father-in-law and uncle, James II, out of the country. The Het Loo Palace was to become a royal palace, and had to be enlarged: the colonnades which linked the main part of the building to the wings were replaced by four pavilions and further embellished the gardens.

Notable Events

1684	**William III,** Prince of Orange and Stadtholder of the United Provinces, buys Het Oude Loo.
1685	Building of Het Loo Palace starts. Revocation of the *Edict of Nantes.*
1688-97	War of the League of Augsburg.
1689	William and Princess Mary Stuart crowned King and Queen of England.
1692	Extension of the palace.
1694	Princess Mary Stuart dies in England.
1702	The Stadtholder-King William III dies without a successor.
1747-51	**William IV,** son of John William Friso, hereditary Stadtholder of the United Provinces.
1751-95	**William V,** son of the precedent stadtholder.
1795	Conquest of the country by the French army; William V flees to England. Het Loo siezed by the French, does not escape from the destructive rage of the soldiers.
1795-1806	The Batavian Republic.
1806-10	Louis Bonaparte, King of Holland, puts rough-cast on the palace façade and makes an English garden.
1810	The Kingdom of Holland attached to the French Empire.
Oct. 1811	Emperor Napoleon stays briefly in Het Loo Palace.
1815	Het Loo, now State property, is offered to **King William I** as a summer residence.
1840	In Het Loo Palace, William I abdicates in favour of his son **William II.**
1849-90	Reign of William III.
1890-8	Regency of **Queen Emma.**
1898	**Wilhelmina,** only daughter of William III and Emma, accedes to the throne.
1901	Marriage of Queen Wilhelmina to Duke Henry of Mecklenburg-Schwerin.
1904-14	The State decides on extensive work of rearranging and enlarging of the palace.
1948	Abdication of Queen Wilhelmina, who retires to Het Loo Palace.
1962	Death of Princess Wilhelmina.
1967-75	Princess Margriet, daughter of Queen Juliana, and her family were the last members of the royal family to live in Het Loo.
1969	Queen Juliana gives up the use of the palace by the royal family and the creation of a museum is decided.
1977-84	Restoration of the palace and gardens.
June 1984	Opening of the **National Museum.**

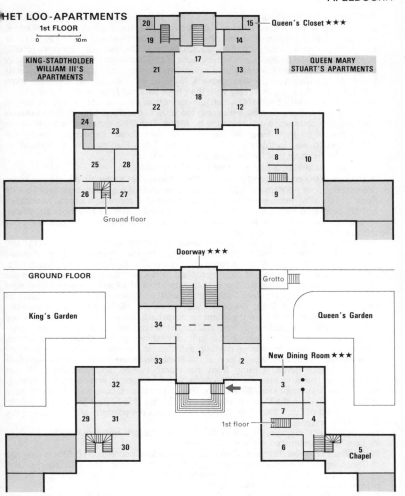

HET LOO - APARTMENTS

1st FLOOR

0   10m

KING-STADTHOLDER
WILLIAM III'S
APARTMENTS

QUEEN MARY
STUART'S APARTMENTS

Queen's Closet ★ ★ ★

Ground floor

Doorway ★ ★ ★

GROUND FLOOR

King's Garden

Queen's Garden

Grotto

New Dining Room ★ ★ ★

1st floor

Chapel

⊘ TOUR *time: about 3 hours*

It is advisable to choose a sunny day to visit the palace in order to better appreciate certain badly lit rooms.

After having walked alongside the **royal stables** (fine series of cars and sleighs, late 19 – early 20C) one reaches a large path, where the beech trees form a magnificent vault; then one reaches the vast brick building flanked with long wings which surrounds the main courtyard.

A grille, painted blue and gold, closes the main courtyard, where a fountain decorated with dolphins was used to water horses.

The finely proportioned building, built on an north-south axis, is impressive by its somewhat severe sobriety, characteristic of the Dutch baroque style. The only decorative elements are the tympana in sandstone of hunting scenes, and the window sills. The east pavilions were intended for Queen Mary Stuart while those situated to the west included those of the King Stadtholder William III. The sash windows of the main part of the building and the pavilions were a novelty often believed to be a Dutch invention and characteristic of English Georgian style.

East Wing. – It contains a collection of historical documents, ceramics, paintings and prints as well as *objets d'art* regarding the most illustrious members of the House of Orange. Many of the documents were written in French, the language used by the Dutch court until the regency of Queen Emma (1890).

West Wing. – On the ground floor there is a **video film show** on the palace's history and restoration.

On the 1st floor the **Museum of the Chancery of the Netherlands Orders of Knighthood** (Museum van de Kanselarij der Nederlandse Orden) exhibits insignia, uniforms, Dutch and foreign Orders.

Apartments. – *Access by a staircase on the side of the steps leading to the main building.*

From the vaulted cellars a staircase leads up to the **great hall (1)** where two 17C garden vases, after drawings by Daniel Marot, are exhibited.

The **old dining room (2)** is decorated with 17C Antwerp tapestries. Note the cabinet (Antwerp, 1630), with biblical scenes painted by Frans Francken the Younger.

The remarkable **new dining room**★★★ (3) (c1692) is a very good example of Marot's contribution to the palace's interior decoration. The white columns and pilasters, decorated with gold bands and the coffered ceiling gives this room, hardly bigger than the old dining room, a majestic character. On the walls, the Brussels' tapestries (c1690) depict the armorial bearings and monograms of William III and his Queen, as well as a mirror (1689), in finely carved gilded wood, which comes from Honselaarsdijk Castle (south of The Hague, since disappeared). Here, as in other rooms, there are some admirable Dutch chairs (late 17C) with their high backs of finely worked wood.

At the end of the **white corridor** (4) which has portraits of members of the Nassau family, who lived in Friesland (p 136), a staircase leads up to the **chapel** (5) where **organ concerts** are held. The coffered stucco ceiling is by Marot. The Bible exhibited is a gift by the Dutch people to their king, William III, who had shown generosity during the 1861 floods. It was in this chapel where many Dutch filed past to bid farewell to Princess Wilhelmina (her funeral took place in Delft - qv).

Go back down the stairs and take the left corridor.

At the end of the corridor and on the left **Prince William IV's Chamber** (6), a luminous room due to the yellow silk damask, has, apart from portraits of the stadtholder and his wife Anne of Hanover, Princess of England, daughter of George II, a crystal chandelier (c1747) decorated with the coat of arms of the United Provinces and those of William and Anne. The walls of the **Frisian Cabinet** (7), opposite, are covered with gilded leather (18C); portraits of the Frisian Nassaus.

On the 1st floor one passes through the **library** (9), laid out after Marot's drawings and decorated with a stucco ceiling inlaid with mirrors, to reach the **gallery** (10). In its lovely decor of panelling and green damask, this gallery, with magnificent chandeliers, contains a lovely collection of paintings. Next to the window giving on to the main courtyard, there are portraits of René de Chalon (qv) and his wife Anne of Lotharingia (1542); William the Silent (two first portraits on the left) inherited the Principality of Orange from René de Chalon. Adriaen van de Venne (1589-1662) has depicted the sons and nephews of William the Silent on horseback. On either side of the chimney there are William III and Mary II, King and Queen of England, Ireland and Scotland, by G. Kneller. The portrait above the chimney showing the king-stadtholder on horseback, is a study for a large painting exhibited in Hampton Court in London.

After having crossed the **drawing room** of the **Stadtholder William V** (11) where a porcelain chandelier from Berlin is hung from the stucco ceiling, and portraits (1795) of William V and his wife, Princess Wilhelmina by John Hoppner, one enters the drawing room of the first Dutch king, **William I** (12). The Empire chairs, covered in blue and gold cloth, were made in the Dutch workshop of A. Eeltjes (1751-1836) for Het Loo Palace at the request of Louis Napoleon. On the walls there are portraits of the king and his daughter Marianne.

One then visits the apartments of Queen Mary Stuart and the King-Stadtholder William III, reconstructed in their 17C layout.

In **Mary Stuart's Bedroom** (13) the sumptuous canopied four-poster bed (c1685) is covered in Genoa velvet; it comes from Kensington Palace in London. The decoration on the ceiling, where the four elements and the four cardinal virtues are depicted, is by the painter Gerard de Lairesse (1641-1721).

Mary Stuart's Dressing Room (14), where the walls are covered with 17C Dutch tapestries, adjoins the **Queen's Closet**★★★ (15), which is decorated mainly in red and green. This lovely little room, where Mary had a splendid view over the gardens, has a lacquer cabinet (1690) made in England as well as Delft and Chinese porcelain.

The **grand staircase** (17), designed by Marot, has been reconstructed by W. Fabri at the request of Queen Wilhelmina.

The landscapes on the walls of the **great hall** (18) were painted by J. Glauber (1646-1726); this room with lovely grisailles on a golden background is where King William I abdicated in 1840.

A passage with gilded leather hangings (19) leads to the **King-Stadtholder William III's Closet** (20). There is a fine Dutch writing-desk (late 17C).

In **William III's Bedroom** (21) the colours are again blue and gold, the colours of the House of Orange-Nassau. The table, the two guéridons and the mirror in silver and gilded silver (c1700) are the work of an Augsburg gold and silversmith, J. Bartermann.

The next room (22) was laid out according to the taste of **King William II**, with neo-Gothic rosewood furniture (c1845). On the right of the king's portrait, there is a portrait of his wife, Princess Anna Pavlovna by J.B. van der Hulst.

When reconstituting **Sophia's Drawing Room** (23), Princess of Würtemberg and first wife of William III (1817-90), the watercolours painted at the queen's request, which depict this room, were an excellent reference. The 19C German artist Franz Xaver Winterhalter painted the portrait of Queen Sophia in a black dress.

The small room (24) which gives on to the king's garden (p 61) was the **King-Stadtholder William III's Closet**. At the request of the sovereign, Melchior d'Hondecoeter (1639-c95) painter of still lifes and animals, decorated the mantelpiece.

The furnishings in **King William III's Bedroom** (1817-90) (25) in walnut and ebony, inlaid with ivory, brass, mother-of-pearl and semiprecious stones was made by the Swiss cabinetmaker E. Baud.

The following three small rooms contain, respectively, objects relating to **Prince Henry** (1820-79) (26), brother of William III, a **collection of watercolours** (27) (note the painting on the left showing the palace's back façade with the English garden), and toys and furniture which had belonged to **Queen Wilhelmina as a child** (28).

On the ground floor **Queen Sophia's Closet** (29) has been fitted out in Moorish style. There is also the **exhibition room of hunting trophies** (30) of Prince Henry, husband of Queen Wilhelmina. On the left of the windows there is the prince in hunting costume (1917) by J. Kleintjes.

Queen Emma's Drawing Room (31), second wife of William III, and that of **Prince Henry (32)** are furnished according to the tastes of the time. The palace visit ends with **Queen Wilhelmina's Drawing Room and Office (33 and 34)** arranged as they were when she was alive. The statuette on the chimney in the second room is of Gaspard de Coligny (father to William the Silent's fourth wife, Louise) who led the Huguenots in the 16C.

> *Go down to the vaulted cellars, then pass between the two staircases and turn right, then left to reach the gardens (tuinen).*

On your way, do not miss seeing the small **kitchen** covered in Delft tiles. Queen Mary Stuart used this room, when she prepared jam with fruit from her garden. The small **grotto**, restored, has shells, fine stones and marble decoration.

Gardens. – *Go up to the terrace.* The superb **doorway★★★** in gilded wrought iron was used in the past to enter the terrace. With only the techniques of the time, it took two years for a Dutch craftsman to recreate this masterpiece designed by D. Marot. Under the crown can be seen the initials of William and Mary (W and M), and in the lower part, orange trees and acanthus leaves.

The terrace, flanked by two statues in sandstone, symbolising the rivers which edge the Veluwe, has a fine view over the gardens (6.5ha - 16 acres).

Documents of the time as well as ruins discovered under the layers of sand in the 19C English garden have made it possible to reconstitute the 17C gardens. In addition the choice of plants decorating the flower beds has been limited to species known at the time.

There are four gardens:

The **lower garden,** bordered with slopes, consists of four *parterres de broderie* (embroidery-like pattern) and four English-style parterres decorated with statues representing Flora and Bacchus *(east side)*, Apollo and Juno receiving a golden apple from the son of Ceres *(west side).*

Amongst the fountains note the one in the centre – whose Venus is a copy of a work by Gaspar Marsy (1625-81) which is in Versailles, and the terrestrial and celestial globes; the first reflects the world as it was known in Europe at the end of the 17C, whereas the positioning of the second corresponds to that of the sky above Het Loo at the birth of Princess Mary Stuart. The waterfall in the middle of the east slope is decorated with a very graceful statue of Narcissus gazing at himself in the water, the copy of a work by the Belgian sculptor Gabriel de Grupello (1644-1730).

Beyond the path lined with a double row of oak trees which led to Het Oude Loo Castle (a few turrets can be seen) extends the **upper garden.** This is delimited by colonnades – go up the staircase to see the view – and amongst the large trees in the English-style garden, there is a tulip tree, recognisable by its leaves ending not in a point but in a V-shaped notch. The king's fountain symbolises the power of the sovereign William III who wished it to be higher than those of his rival Louis XIV.

Distinguished people have witnessed to the qualities of the water: contrary to the water of Versailles, that of Het Loo was limpid and odourless.

The **King's Garden** *(to the west of the palace)* where blue and orange are the dominant colours, has a lawn, once a bowling-green.

For the **Queen's Garden** *(to the east of the palace)* of more intimate character with its arbour of greenery, flowers in pastel shades have been chosen, as well as fruit trees (orange, apricot, cherry-plum, morello cherry trees).

ADDITIONAL SIGHT

⊙**Marialust Historical Museum (Historisch Museum Marialust).** – *Verzetsstrijderspark 10.* Installed in the Marialust mansion, overlooking a park, it is devoted to the region's past, from prehistory to *c*1930.

ARNHEM Gelderland P   Pop 127 671

Michelin map **408** fold 12
Plan of built-up area in the current Michelin Red Guide Benelux

Arnhem is the capital of Gelderland province, a former duchy. Situated on the Neder Rijn or Lower Rhine, one of the branches of the Rhine which separated from the IJssel, Arnhem is an important road junction near one of the country's major trunk roads.

⊙**Boat trips.** – On the Gelderland's rivers.

HISTORICAL NOTES

A coveted duchy. – Residence of the Counts of Geldern, who fortified it in the beginning of the 13C and granted it city rights, Arnhem, in the Middle Ages, was a prosperous town dealing in the trade of goods along the Rhine and the IJssel; it was part of the Hanseatic League *(qv).* Gelderland became a duchy in 1339.

Arnhem was taken by Charles the Bold in 1473, then by the Emperor Maximilian (Charles the Bold's son-in-law) in 1505. Invaded by Emperor Charles V, the duchy was defended by Charles of Egmond, who was killed in battle in 1538. His successor ceded his rights to the duchy to Charles V in the *Treaty of Venlo* (1543). In 1585 under the reign of Philip II (Charles V's son), the town was taken from the Spanish. It passed into the hands of the French during, the 1672-4 War *(p 19),* then 1795-1813 the Austrians possessed it.

Arnhem is the birthplace of Professor Lorentz (1853-1928), who, with his former pupil Zeeman, received the Nobel Prize for Physics in 1902.

The garden-town. – Due to its numerous parks and above all its advantageous position on the last hills of the **Veluwe** region *(qv)*. Before the last war, it was one of the favourite retirement places for colonials returning from the Dutch Indies (Indonesia): their lovely residences are dispersed throughout the woods.

The Battle of Arnhem (17-27 September 1944). – The name Arnhem is linked to one of the most tragic episodes in the liberation of the Netherlands *(1)*.

On 17 September 1944 more than 10 000 men of the 1st British Airborne Division were parachuted into **Oosterbeek**, west of Arnhem. They were to march to Arnhem to create a bridgehead on the Neder Rijn and hold it until the 20 000 Americans (18th, 101st and 82nd US Airborne Divisions) and the 3 000 Poles parachuted to the south, could ensure the movement of troops over two important canals to the north of Eindhoven, then the Maas at Grave and the Waal at Nijmegen. General Montgomery, who directed this operation, called **Market Garden,** counted on a surprise attack to disorganise the enemy. In this way he hoped to reach IJssel Lake, cut the country in two and isolate the German troops located to the west (preventing them from fleeing back to Germany), then reach the Ruhr. It was a failure.

On the 18th a thick fog enveloped Arnhem making help impossible. Only a few batallions of parachutists from Oosterbeek had reached the town. After 9 days of very hard fighting the **Red Devils,** who had not managed to get hold of the bridge, left 2 000 dead and more than 5 000 wounded or missing in the destroyed town. On the other hand 500 soldiers were hidden by the inhabitants and 2 300 were evacuated towards the south during the night of 25-26 September.

In the meantime the progress of troop armoured divisions effecting a junction had been held up by several German attacks. The crossing of the Maas at **Grave** (on 19 September) and the Waal at **Nijmegen** (the 20th) made it possible for the Allies to come within sight of Arnhem, but it was too late. The bridge over the Neder Rijn was, according to General Browning "a bridge too far".

If the operation had been successful, the terrible famine which occurred during the winter of 1944-5 in the country's western provinces could have been avoided. Arnhem was liberated by the Allies on 8 April 1945, shortly before the German capitulation.

Arnhem today. – The town is an active city which lives by its textile manufacturing (synthetic fibres) and its metallurgical industries. The tertiary sector occupies a major position with, notably, technological research institutions and research consultancies. It also plays an important administrative role in the east of the Netherlands.

A speciality of the town are *Arnhemse meisjes,* small puff-pastry biscuits.

★★ NETHERLANDS OPEN-AIR MUSEUM
(NEDERLANDS OPENLUCHTMUSEUM) *time: 4 hours*

⊙This folklore museum situated in a beautiful undulating, wooded park of 44ha - 109 acres (**BX**) evokes the architecture and rural activites of the Netherlands's provinces, due to the restoration of about a hundred farmhouses, mills, workshops and barns.

Inside each building, the typical furnishings, exhibitions (pottery, carts) and demonstrations (bread-making, paper-making, various handicrafts) make the visit particularly interesting.

At the entrance to the park, in front of the restaurant, there is a fine view over a large clearing where several **mills** stand including grain and polder mills *(p 33)*.

Some buildings are grouped together, such as the handsome half-timbered ones from the province of Limburg (nos 100-104), or the farmhouses from the Gelderland province (nos 1-19) but the most attractive corner is that of the **Zaan Region** *(qv)* with its wooden houses painted green and lovely decorated gables. Nearby, the stretch of water is reminiscent of the Zaan. It is crossed by a wooden lever bridge; two mills, one for grain, the other for sawing wood, are reflected in the water. Do not miss the pavilion where there is an **exhibition of regional costumes** (no 125). Costumes and objects are exhibited in rotation. Tableaux with models wearing traditional costumes (sometimes still worn) illustrate scenes of daily life in typical interiors.

---

(1) For more details, read A Bridge Too Far, by Cornelius Ryan.

ADDITIONAL SIGHTS

Markt (AZ). – This long square is bordered by the **Law Courts (AZ J)** and, at the end, by the Gelderland government seat, **Het Huis der Provincie (AZ P)**. Destroyed during the war, this building was reconstructed in 1954 by the architect J.J.M. Vegter. In rather severe style, it encloses an interior courtyard.

Adjoining this building is the **Sabels Gateway (AZ C)**, a 14C fortified gateway (altered in 1645), which is all that remains of the town's ramparts.

⊙ **Great Church** or **St Eusebius** (Grote- of Eusebiuskerk) **(AZ A).** – Near Markt, this church was erected in the 15C on the site of an old Romanesque church.

Destroyed during the Battle of Arnhem, it, as well as its tower (93m - 305ft), were rebuilt in the Gothic style; the summit was reconstructed in a more modern style.

The church has an organ (1793) which came from an Amsterdam church.

The mausoleum of Charles of Egmond *(qv)*, Duke of Gelderland, was built in 1538.

The tower has a modern carillon with 54 bells. It also has a carillon of seven bells, four of which were cast by the Hemony brothers.

Devil's House (Duivelshuis) **(AZ B).** – This fine Renaissance edifice, built in 1645 and much restored in 1829 was spared during the war.

It takes its name from the strange statues and grotesque heads which decorate its walls. It was the last dwelling place of the blood thirsty general **Maarten van Rossum,** chief of the armies of the Duke of Gelderland, Charles of Egmond, and adversary of Emperor Charles V. According to legend, Van Rossum, had these demons carved to offend the magistrates of Arnhem, who refused to allow him to pave the steps of his perron with gold.

Formerly the town hall, this house is still occupied by certain municipal services.

Behind is the new **town hall (AZ H)** built in 1964 from the architect J.J. Konijnenburg's plans.

★**Municipal Museum**
⊙ **(Gemeentemuseum) (AY M).** – Situated on a hill overlooking the Rhine, in an old 19C mansion, topped by a rotunda, and with a modern new wing added, this museum contains interesting collections on the art and history of Gelderland. Modern and contemporary art exhibitions are organised regularly.

The rooms with 15-18C decorative arts are particularly rich: wardrobes and clocks, gold and silversmiths' work either liturgical or of guild corporations, 18 and 19C Arnhem ceramics and Chinese porcelain. There is also a doll's house in the shape of a wardrobe, a fine carved wood group (c1500) depicting St John the Baptist among the Pharisees, a still life by Jan Davidsz. de Heem and a *View of Arnhem* by Van Goyen.

Prints as well as paintings by more contemporary artists are displayed with notably Carel Willink (1900-83) and Dick Ket (1902-40) who painted in the Magic Realist style.

The basement is devoted to items of regional archaeological excavations: prehistory, Roman times (glass, coins), Middle Ages (earthenware).

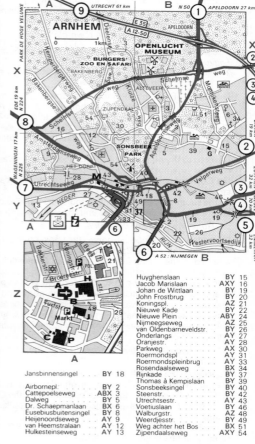

On the 1st floor there are 19 and 20C *objets d'art:* glass, gold and silversmiths' work, Delft ceramics, Chinese porcelain.

A large bay window on the 1st floor gives a magnificent view over the river.

There are contemporary sculptures in the garden.

★ **Sonsbeek Park (ABY).** – This park of 75ha - 185 acres together with the Zijpendaal Park which prolongs it, is one of the most beautiful parks in the Netherlands. It is an undulating countryside covered with woods and vast meadows and lined with a string of lakes.

Two castles stand here, and near a large farm, a 16C watermill (De Witte Molen).

⊙ **Burgers' Zoo and Safari Park** (Burgers' Zoo en Safari) (AX). – It is a wood of 25ha - 62 acres divided into four parks. In the **Savannah**, a vast clearing, giraffes, zebras, ostriches, rhinoceroses, antelopes and crowned cranes stroll. The wild beast enclosure has a number of lions and their females. In **Burgers' Bush** a vast hall has been arranged into a tropical forest and three different itineraries allow the visitor to observe tropical fauna (caimans, snakes, birds, insects, etc) and flora.

EXCURSIONS

★ **Veluwezoom National Park** (Nationaal Park Veluwezoom). – *Round tour of 20km - 12 miles. Leave Arnhem by Rosendaalseweg* (BX 34).
The Veluwezoom National Park is a vast area (4 600ha - 11 362 acres) of forests (pines, silver birches) and deeply undulating heathland situated to the north of Arnhem on the edge *(zoom)* of the Veluwe *(qv)*. Numerous car parks, foot and cycling paths, make for a pleasant outing.

⊙ The **De Heurne reception centre** (Bezoekerscentrum), has been fitted out in an old farmhouse on Schietbergseweg, the road from Rheden to Posbank.

⊙ **Rosendael Castle** (Kasteel Rosendael). – This small 16C castle is flanked by a tower from the Middle Ages, which is reflected in a lake in the heart of the large **park**.
The road rises in the forest. It crosses **Beekhuizen**. Then the road divides into two, separated by a row of magnificent beech trees, and continues to the national park. Nearly 100m - 328ft in height, around **Posbank**, several belvederes have vast **panoramas ★** on the right over rolling hills covered in heather with winding paths to stroll on.

One then goes down towards De Steeg and IJssel Plain.

⊙ **De Steeg.** – To the east of the village, amongst the woods, the 17C **Middachten Castle** (Kasteel Middachten) raises its severe walls in the middle of wide moats. There is a fine view on the west side, from the restored garden. The interior courtyard *(access forbidden)* is surrounded by the outbuildings.
Returning to Arnhem by the main road one can see on the left, on entering Velp, **Biljoen Castle** (Kasteel Biljoen) also surrounded by water.

Enter Arnhem by ② on the town plan.

The southern edge of the Veluwe. – *25km - 15½ miles to the west – about 2½ hours. Leave by ⑦ on the town plan.*
The route follows the north bank of the Neder Rijn where the last hills of the Veluwe are sprinkled with numerous villages.

Oosterbeek. – To the north of this small town, on the road to Warnsborn, a little beyond the railroad, the **war cemetery** (Airborne kerkhof) of Allied troops who fell during the battle of Arnhem have more than 1 700 stelae (1 667 British and 79 Polish).
⊙ The **Hartenstein villa** *(Utrechtseweg 232)* was General Urquhart's (Commander of 1st British Airborne Division) headquarters in September 1944. It houses the **Airborne Museum**, previously at Doorwerth.
Devoted to the Market-Garden operation and the Battle of Arnhem *(qv)*, this museum contains memorabilia of the parachuting of the airborne troops, notably in the Oosterbeek area. In a cellar, General Urquhart's headquarters have been reconstructed.
To the south, on the banks of the Rhine, the terraces of **Westerbouwing** (restaurant inside) offer a fine **view** over the river and the Betuwe with its orchards.

Go to the banks of the Rhine.

Doorwerth. – Near a wood, Doorwerthse Bos, on the river's edge, Doorwerth was badly hit in 1944 during the Battle of Arnhem.
⊙ Situated in the meadows near the river, **Doorwerth Castle** (Kasteel Doorwerth) built in 1260, was enlarged c1600 and consists of a high square building and outbuildings, the whole surrounded by moats. The fortified walls open by a fine door with armorial bearings. Several furnished rooms in the north and east wings are open to visitors. The south wing houses the **Netherlands Hunting Museum** (Nederlands Jachtmuseum), which contains information on hunting and the way of life of animals which interest hunters. Fine collections of weapons, stuffed animals, pictures and photographs are attractively displayed.

Go towards Renkum and pass under the motorway to take the road to Wageningen.

Wageningen. – Pop 32 418. This industrial town is known for its **Higher School of Agriculture** (Landbouwhogeschool); in the surrounding country there are orchards and nurseries. In the De Wereld building *(Gen. Foulkesweg 1)*, the Germans signed their capitulation on 5 May 1945 in the presence of General Foulkes, commander of the Canadian troops.
In the Belmonte Arboretum *(Gen. Foulkesweg 94)*, the Higher School of Agriculture cares for a fine collection of shrubs.
5km - 3 miles from Wageningen, opposite a Netherlands military cemetery, situated on the Grebbeberg, a path leads to the **Koningstafel** or king's tableland; view over the Rhine and the Betuwe. It was one of King Frederick V of Bohemia's favourite walks; he took refuge in the Netherlands after having been beaten by the Austrians in 1620.

⊙ **Rhenen.** – Pop 16 541. This locality contains the **Ouwehands Dierenpark Zoological Garden**, which houses nearly 800 animals spread over a park of 15ha - 37 acres. An enormous aviary of exotic birds, an exhibition of parrots and dolphins, and an aquarium add to the interest of the visit, made easy by the presence of a monorail. It is also a recreation centre with a swimming pool, a lake and attractions for children.
⊙ **Cunera Church's** (Cunerakerk) lovely tower, bombed in 1945, has been restored.

Michelin map ⁗⁗⁗ fold 6 – Town plan in the current Michelin Red Guide Benelux

Assen owes its existence to a nunnery, founded in the 13C, of which one can see the chapel, the old town hall, on the main square or Brink. Today, this modern and spacious town is laid out beside **Asserbos,** a pleasant wood to the south. It is an area rich in megalithic monuments *(p 132).*

Until 1602 members of the States, or Provincial Assembly of Drenthe met out of doors, in the Germanic style, at the Balloërkuil *(see below)* where they dispensed justice. Due to its central location Assen was chosen as capital of the Drenthe in 1809, under the reign of Louis Bonaparte.

To the south of town, a motorcycle **racing circuit** (Tourist Trophy Circuit or T.T.C) is used for the Dutch Grand Prix *(p 198).*

Drenthe. – For a long time this province was ill-favoured. The Scandinavian glaciers, which lingered in the north of the Netherlands, left a sandy and not very fertile soil. In places it is covered with **heath** vegetation with a few clumps of oak or pine. In the more humid areas, **peat** covered the surfaces left by the glaciers. Drenthe was the largest peat-producing region. Its extraction has left traces on the land, which remains criss-crossed by a multitude of canals which were dug out in order to transport the peat. Today much clearing and the use of fertilisers has modified the landscape. The sheep moors are rarer, making place for pastures or plantations of conifers. The peat bogs, with the help of fertilisers, sand and the upper layer of peat can make a good arable soil (potatoes, cereals, market garden produce); colonials have settled here. Farmhouses in Drenthe, very picturesque with their vast thatched roofs, are for the most part hall farmhouses *(pp 31-32).*

Many villages have kept their original Saxon layout: in the centre is the **Brink,** the tree-lined main square, often with a church.

★ **Drenthe Museum (Drents Museum).** – Brink 1. The old Provincial House (1885) contains Ⓞ this regional museum. On the 1st floor, it has a particularly interesting **archaeological section★**. It displays excellent documentation on prehistoric times: geology, population, *hunebeds (qv)* and has assembled a large number of objects discovered in the province, either in the *hunebeds,* burial mounds, fields of funeral urns, or in the peat-bogs which lends to the preservation of these objects.

Apart from tools, instruments and pottery, there are also a great variety of other pieces: a small boat of 6300BC (discovered in Pesse, 23km - 14 miles south of Assen), mummies of the 3 and 5C, Celtic and Merovingian jewellery, Roman and Merovingian coins.

On the ground floor there is regional silversmiths' work, as well as drawings and prints (views of Drenthe villages).

In the adjoining abbey church, agricultural life over the ages in Drenthe province is evoked.

Belonging to the same museum, the **Ontvangershuis★** *(Brink 7)* former residence of the general tax collector, has been turned into a decorative arts museum. One goes through elegant rooms decorated with beautiful 17 and 18C furniture, a regional kitchen with box beds as well as a delivery room.

Behind the garden of the Ontvangershuis, there is a charming statuette of the young **Bartje,** famous local hero of the regional novelist Anne de Vries (1904-64). It was sculptured by Suze Berkhout (the original is in the town hall).

Bartje

EXCURSIONS

Rolde. – Pop 6 030. *6km - 3½ miles by ② on the town plan, local map p 133.* To the west of Rolde, in a wood, one can see the **Balloërkuil** *(see above),* a sort of vast terrace dug into the ground.

Beyond the church, turn left into a paved path indicating *hunebeds (qv).* In a wood there are two **hunebeds** (D 17/18); one of them is covered with seven slabs.

Midwolde. – *27km - 16½ miles to the northwest by ⑤ on the town plan; then turn right.*

Norg. – Pop 6 562. This charming village in Drenthe with numerous thatched roofed cottages is a holiday centre. It is built round a Brink, a large shady square on which stands a small Gothic church, preceded by a bell tower with a saddleback roof.

Leek. – Pop 17 708. To the north of town in a vast park surrounded by a moat stands **Nienoord Manor** (Huis "Nienoord"). Rebuilt in Ⓞ 1886, it houses the **National Carriage Museum** (Nationaal Rijtuigmuseum).

Inside exquisite small vehicles are exhibited: small carriages pulled by goats, royal children's carriages, and 17 and 18C sledges. In the outbuildings, in season, there are carriages with dummies wearing period costumes.

Further on in the park, near a pavilion built *c*1700, whose walls are covered with shells, a modern building contains a collection of stage coaches.

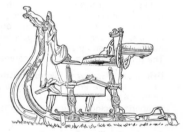

(After photo Nat. Rijtuigmuseum, Leek)

Sledge

⊙ **Midwolde.** – The small brick **church** with a saddleback roofed bell tower has the fine marble **funerary monument**★ made by Rombout Verhulst in 1669 at the request of Anna van Ewsum. The young woman is leaning with a gracious gesture over the mortal remains of her husband.

The cherubs in white marble, symbolise the family's children. In the place of the seventh cherub there is now a statue of Anna van Ewsum's second husband, which was made by Bartholomeus Eggers in 1714.

Note the carved pulpit (1711), the tall stalls (c1660-70) and the small organ (1630) with lead pipes.

GREEN TOURIST GUIDES

Picturesque scenery, buildings
Attractive routes
Touring programmes
Plans of towns and buildings.

BERGEN OP ZOOM North Brabant   Pop 46 353

Michelin map **408** fold 16 or **212** fold 14 - Local map p 79
Town plan in the current Michelin Red Guide Benelux

Centre of two important annual fairs in the Middle Ages, Bergen op Zoom, starting in 1287, was the main town of an independent lordship. The old port, today partially filled in, was linked to Eastern Scheldt *(p 78)*. In 1533 the lordship of Bergen op Zoom was changed into a marquisate.

The town has remained famous for its invincibility as it victoriously withstood two sieges against the Spanish, in 1588 by the Duke of Parma, Alessandro Farnese, then in 1622 when it was invested by troops commanded by Spinola.

Its fortifications were reinforced c1700 by **Menno van Coehoorn** (1641-1704), an engineer who made numerous strongholds in the country. However, Bergen could not hold out against the French army in 1747 during the Austrian War of Succession.

The ramparts were demolished in 1868 but the boulevards' location recalls the layout.

Bergen op Zoom, set in the middle of woods, is renowned for its carnival *(see the chapter Practical Information at the end of the guide)*. The sandy land around the town is used for growing asparagus.

SIGHTS

⊙ **Town Hall (Stadhuis).** – It is on Grote Markt and consists of three houses: the one in the middle and the one on the right have been decorated, since 1611, with a lovely stone façade preceded by a perron bearing the **town's arms;** two savages stand on either side of a shield, topped by the marquis's crown; the shield bears three of St Andrew's crosses and a mountain with three peaks *(berg:* mount).

Near Grote Markt, there is a massive stone **bell tower** (14C). Familiarly called De Peperbus, (the Pepperpot), due to the shape of its 18C lantern turret, it is the remains of **St Gertrude's,** which was destroyed in 1747 by the French *(see above);* after being rebuilt it burned down in 1972. The outside walls of the nave, the transept and chancel (15C), as well as a second transept (16C) were all spared by the catastrophes.

★ **Markiezenhof.** – *Steenbergsestraat 8.* – This is the former palace *(hof)* of the
⊙ marquisate of Bergen op Zoom. Dating from the 15 and 16C, the work of Anthonis Keldermans, architect from Mechlin (Belgium), it was inhabited by the marquises until 1795 and has been restored. Its façade, decorated with bands of stone, forming an elegant effect, has a stone base ornamented with large latticed windows and topped with brick crow-stepped gables and dormer windows.

The inside has been turned into a cultural centre, with, notably, the **Communal Museum.** The small courtyard with arcades is picturesque. The large palace hall or **Hofzaal** *(concerts)* is particularly remarkable with its carved stone chimney-piece (St Christopher) of 1522, its portraits of Bergen's marquises, a 16C Brussels tapestry *(Charlemagne in Rome)*, paintings and gold and silversmiths' work.

In the wing, renovated in the 18C, there are lovely rooms with **decorative arts** (Louis XIV, Louis XV and Louis XVI styles). The 2nd floor is devoted to fortifications, a scale model of the town in 1747, a copy of the one made for Louis XV. One room has ancient art objects. One can also see objects and banners for processions, as well as ceramics made in Bergen op Zoom.

The ground floor rooms are reserved for exhibitions.

Prisoners' Gateway (Gevangenpoort) or Our Lady's Gateway (Lieve Vrouwepoort). – *Access by Lieve Vrouwestraat leaving from Markiezenhof.*

Of the 14C, this is the only gateway, which remains from the medieval town's ring of ramparts. Facing the town its brick façade is flanked with bartizans; facing out it has two large stone towers.

Ravelin (Ravelijn) "Op den Zoom". – *To the northeast of town.*
Near the lovely **park** (A. van Duinkerken Park) surrounding a lake, there is a small fortified moated outwork, witness to the fortifications built by Coehoorn.

EXCURSION

Roosendaal. – *15km - 9 miles to the northeast by ② on the town plan - local map p 79.*

⊘ **Wouw.** – Pop 8 325. In the Gothic **church,** rebuilt after World War II, there are some lovely statues. The 17C baroque **statues** belonged to the stalls, which disappeared during the war. They are placed in the chancel (on consoles) and in the aisles where they surround the confessional boxes. The figures are shown in very lively attitudes.
The stained glass window on the west side of the tower, depicting the Resurrection, is a work by Joep Nicolas (1937).

Roosendaal. – Pop 57 930. It is an important railway junction and industrial city with a modern commercial quarter, De Rozelaar.
Nearby there are several nature reserves, notably the **Visdonk** and **De Rucphense bossen** (1 200ha - 2 964 acres).

⊘ The **Golden Rose Museum** (De Ghulden Roos) is a regional museum installed in an 18C presbytery *(Molenstraat 2)* called **Tongerlohuys.** It houses an interesting artistic collection, notably gold and silversmiths' work belonging to the guilds (corporations), pottery, Chinese porcelain, stoneware, as well as various objects such as Brabant bonnets, agricultural tools, children's toys, a velocipede of the Michaux type. The interior of an old sweet shop has been reconstructed.

★ BOLSWARD Friesland   Pop 9 851

Michelin map **408** fold 4 - Local map p 169

Bolsward or Boalsert in Frisian, is one of the oldest Friesland towns. Its existence was known in 700AD. Its origin is disputed: was it founded by Princess Bolswina? Or, does its name come from the Frisian word *bodel,* which means depth and would apply to the canals which surround it?
Situated in the past on the Middelzee, an inland sea linked to the Zuiderzee, Bolsward was rich and powerful. In the 11C it was granted the privilege of minting coins and became a Hanseatic town.
Today it is a peaceful town, which becomes animated each year (October) during the presentation of the Frisian literary prize, which alternatively bears the name of Dr. Joost Halbertsma (1789-1869), and that of **Gysbert Japicx** (1603-66) who, born in Bolsward, contributed to the development of Frisian literature.
Situated in the centre of a rich pastoral region, Bolsward is also the seat of the National Dairy School.

SIGHTS

★ **Town Hall (Stadhuis).** – An elegant early 17C construction, it has a lovely façade in the
⊘ Renaissance style with, in the centre, a projecting central block with a gable and a lovely 18C perron, decorated with two lions bearing the town's coat of arms. At the top there is a tall octagonal pinnacle with a **carillon.**
Inside, the **Council and Marriage Hall** opens by a magnificent carved door (1614) by Japicx Gysberts, the town hall's presumed architect; the lovely wooden chimneypiece is surrounded by stone telamones.
A room on the 1st floor, with enormous beams supporting the weight of the tower, holds the **Museum of Antiquities:** Frisian silverwork, traditional costumes, objects from archaeological excavations, etc.

⊘ **St Martin's (Martinikerk).** – This large Gothic church, today Protestant, was built in the middle of the 15C. It is preceded by a tower capped with a saddleback roof, like most Frisian bell towers.
Inside, the vaults of the three naves rest on thick cylindrical pillars.
In the chancel, the **stalls★** (late 15C) are remarkable for their sculptures full of truth and naivety. The scenes which are shown on the lateral partitions are admirable:
– bench against the south wall:
– Manna, a saint; on the other side: St Catherine and the philosophers, St Barbara;
– St Christopher; on the other side: St George and the dragon;
– Moses and the Jews, baptism of Christ, spies and the bunch of grapes.
– against the north wall, bench near the nave:
– Judgment of Salomon, St Martin, Abraham's sacrifice; above the lectern: an alchemist.
– St Peter and St Paul, heaven and hell; on the other side: God and angel musicians, the Last Judgment.
– against the north wall, bench near the apse:
– the Virgin crushing the dragon; on the other side: Judith beheading Holopfernes;
– dragon, Bolsward's coat of arms, Temptation of Christ.

Equally interesting are the figures on the high backs, the picturesque illustrations of parables shown on the misericords, the figures on the cheekpieces, and the grotesque figures of the lecterns.
The **pulpit★** (17C), crowned with a tiered canopy is decorated in the Frisian manner with elegant motifs added on. The central panel depicts a Bible and the signs of the zodiac; the other panels depict the seasons. Above there is a frieze of fruit and vegetables; below a series of shells.
The ground is strewn with tombstones. The organ was made in 1775 by Hinsz of Groningen. The church's remarkable acoustics has made it possible to record concerts.

EXCURSION

Witmarsum. – *10km - 6 miles to the northwest.* Near the main road there is the statue of **Menno Simonsz.** (1496-1561). Born in Witmarsum, he became vicar of Pingjum, then the parish priest of his native town and, finally, in 1536, broke away from the Catholics and turned towards the Anabaptist doctrine, founding the *doopsgezinden* brotherhood or **Mennonites.** In 1539, a work summarised his doctrine, more pacifistic than that of John of Leiden *(qv)*; belief in the Bible, rejection of the baptism of children, accent on personal piety, refusal to obey all the established Church's dogma. The Mennonite religion extended over Germany, Switzerland and North America (the largest groups are in the United States and Canada) where it still has its followers.

The Mennonites of Witmarsum meet in a small **church** (Menno-Simonskerkje) *(located on Menno-Simonsstraat),* rebuilt in 1961.

One can see the prayer room with the portrait of Menno Simonsz. and the sacristy. Further on, in the same street, set in a small wood, is a monument in memory of Menno Simonsz., on the site of his first church.

★ BREDA North Brabant   Pop 119 427

Michelin map **408** fold 17 or **212** fold 6
Plan of built-up area in the current Michelin Red Guide Benelux

At the confluence of the Mark and the Aa, Breda was formerly one of the country's main fortified towns and the centre of an important barony. Today it is a dynamic city and a great commercial and industrial centre. Benefiting from its position on one of the main access routes into the country, it is a welcoming stopping place with large pedestrian precincts.

With numerous parks, Breda also, has very attractive suburbs where large woods like the **Liesbos** to the west and the **Mastbos** *(qv)* to the south have been laid out for leisure activities. To the east, **Surae** is a recreational park with a swimming area.

In February *(see the chapter Practical Information at the end of the guide),* Breda holds its well-known **carnival★**. Around Easter there is the Antiques Fair, in May, the international classical jazz festival and an international horse show. In mid-August the Great Church houses the Breda floral exhibition. At the end of August there is the Taptoe, a military music festival in the castle *(see the chapter Practical Information at the end of the guide).*

HISTORICAL NOTES

The Nassau fief. – Breda obtained its city rights in *c*1252. It became part of the Breda barony, but in 1404, this came into the possession of the Nassau family, who made the town its seat. The 13C fortifications were rebuilt (*c*1535) by Count Henry III of Nassau, and the ring canals still show the location of the walls, which were destroyed a little after 1870.

The Compromise of Breda. – Decided in September at Spa in Belgium, the Compromise of the Nobility or of Breda was signed in Breda Castle in 1566. Its aim: to abolish the Inquisition.

Following this reunion about 300 nobles went in delegation to Brussels to see the governor Margaret of Parma to ask her for a convocation of the States General in order to change the edicts against heretics (i.e. Protestants). Whereupon, she burst into tears; her counsellor, the Count of Berlaymont responded in jest with the phrase: "What, Madam, afraid of these *gueux* (beggars)?" This statement did not displease the Calvinists, who from then on took the name **beggars** for their movement and the beggars bowl as the symbol of their fight against Spanish rule. The Calvinists then thought they could do anything: in the month of August the **Iconoclastic Fury** started: churches were pillaged and statues destroyed, the direct consequence of which was the arrival in 1567 of the terrible Duke of Alba.

An ardently disputed stronghold. – In 1581 Breda was pillaged by the Spanish, who occupied the castle belonging to William the Silent.

In 1590, Maurice of Nassau took the town by surprise, 70 of his men having been able to enter by hiding under a load of peat in a barge belonging to Adriaan van Bergen. In 1625, Breda, after a long siege surrendered to the Spanish commanded by the Marquis of Spinola. This episode was immortalised by Velázquez in *The Surrender of Breda-Las Lanzas* (1634-5). The town was recaptured in 1637 by the Prince-Stadtholder Frederick-Henry.

Upon the *Treaty of Breda* which, in 1667, put an end to the Second Dutch War the Dutch gave New Amsterdam, to the English which became New York. They, in exchange were given Guiana (now Surinam). The negotiations and the signature of the treaty took place in the castle.

During the French Revolutionary Wars, the town was taken by Dumouriez in 1793. He had to evacuate it after the defeat of Neerwinden (Belgium), which obliged him to withdraw from the Netherlands.

Besieged again in 1794 by Pichegru, Breda surrendered only when the whole country was occupied. It became part of the Deux-Nethes *département* (county town Antwerp) until 1813: that year, at the approach of the Russian vanguard the French garrison sallied out but the population of Breda stopped it from returning.

On 11 and 12 May 1940 Breda marked the furthest point of the Allied advance in the Netherlands: the Dyle Manœuvre, an operation where the Franco-British forces tried to make a breakthrough to the north to protect Amsterdam, failed.

A scholarly soldier. – During the siege of Breda by Spinola, a young mercenary belonging to Maurice of Nassau's army passed through the town's Grote Markt.
There he saw a group gathered around a poster written in Dutch. His neighbour, head of Dordrecht College, translated the text for him. Since it was a question of finding the solution to a geometry problem, he asked the soldier if he had the intention of bringing him the solution; the latter promised and kept his word. It was René Descartes *(qv)*.

Charles II's restoration. – With the death of Cromwell (d1658), the Protectorate (1653-9) weakened under his son's rule, and in May 1660 Charles II was called back. It was here, in Breda, that Charles II issued the Declaration of Breda which set the terms upon which he would accept the throne, re-establishing the English monarchy.

★ GREAT CHURCH OR CHURCH OF OUR LADY

(GROTE OF ONZE LIEVE VROUWE KERK) (C B) *time ¾ hour*

It is an imposing 15-16C edifice in the Gothic Brabant style. With three naves, it was enlarged in the 16C by a few chapels and an ambulatory. Its tall **bell tower★** of 97m - 318ft with a square base and octagonal top is surmounted by an onion-shaped dome.
The **carillon** has 49 bells.
The interior with typical Gothic Brabant style columns – their capitals decorated with crockets – and with a triforium, contains numerous tombs. The most striking one is the **tomb★** of Engelbert II of Nassau (1451-1504) and his wife in the Chapel of Our Lady, to the north of the ambulatory. This Renaissance alabaster monument was carved in the Michelangelo style, probably from a project by Thomas Vincidor of Bologna. The recumbent statues are placed under a slab held up by fine figures at each corner; they depict Julius Caesar (military courage), Regulus (magnaminity), Hannibal (persever- ance) and Philip of Macedonia (prudence). Above the slab the armour of Engelbert II is shown. In the vault under the tomb, René de Chalon *(qv)*, Henry III of Nassau and Anna van Buren, William of Orange's first wife, are buried. In the ambulatory is the 15C tomb of Engelbert I and John IV of Nassau. Note some of the Renaissance epitaphs as well as the memorial slabs covering the floor.
The 15C wooden chancel stalls are carved with satirical motifs illustrating vices, proverbs, etc. Other unusual reliefs were added after 1945.
In the north transept there is a triptych by Jan van Scorel where the central panel illustrates the Finding of the True Cross. At the end of the south aisle there is a bronze baptismal font (1540) made in Mechlin (Belgium) of Gothic construction with Renaissance motifs. The organ case is decorated with a 17C painting depicting David and Goliath and the Ark of the Covenant. The organ, a fine instrument, with its oldest parts dating from the 16C, can be heard during **concerts**.

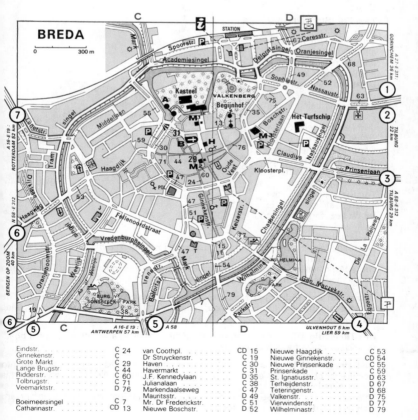

ADDITIONAL SIGHTS

Leave from the crossroads of Nieuwe Prinsenkade and Prinsenkade.

From here you have a lovely view of the Great Church's bell tower.

Het Spanjaardsgat (C A). – The remains of the fortifications, known as the Spanish Gap, consist of two large towers with small onion-shaped domes flanking a water-gate, which was used for the evacuation of water round the castle.

⊘ Hidden behind these walls is the **castle** (kasteel). It is an immense building with numerous windows, surrounded by a moat, and where the north façade (visible from the Academiesingel) is flanked by octagonal turrets. Since 1828 it is occupied by the Netherlands Military Academy.

An old fortified castle, it was altered, as from 1536, on the plans of Thomas Vincidor of Bologna, and was William the Silent's favourite retreat until his departure for the revolt which was declared in 1567. It was here that the *Compromise of Breda (qv)* was signed by the nobles.

The castle's present aspect dates between 1686 and 1695, under Stadtholder William III of Orange who continued Vincidor's original plan.

Havermarkt (C 31). – This charming little square at the foot of the Great Church, formerly 'hay market', is now invaded by the clients of its numerous cafés.

⊘ **Ethnographical Museum (Rijksmuseum voor Volkenkunde) Justinus van Nassau (C M¹)**. – Installed in the town governor's former residence, Justin Nassau, it is possible to travel around the world via about fifteen rooms where scenes of daily life are depicted and collections of weapons, jewellery and masks are exhibited.

All the continents are represented with emphasis on Asia (Indonesia, India and Tibet).

In front of the museum is an equestrian statue of the Stadtholder William III.

★**Valkenberg (D)**. – This old castle park, shaded by lovely trees is very pleasant.

Nearby is the **Beguinage** (Begijnhof) enclosure. Founded in 1267 the Beguinage *(p 49)* was transferred here in 1531 and groups 29 houses of sobre aspect, arranged round a courtyard with a medicinal plant garden and a chapel.

At the entrance to the Beguine convent is their old chapel, which has become a **Walloon Church** (Waalse Kerk). The Frisian, **Peter Stuyvesant** (1592-1672) was married here; it was he who became the last Dutch governor of Nieuw Amsterdam (New York) from 1647-64 *(see the Michelin Green Guide to New York City)*.

Grote Markt (C 29). – From the middle of this large square there is a fine **view** of the Great Church.

⊘ **Town Hall** (Stadhuis) (CD H). – Dating from the 17C, the town hall was altered in 1767. It contains a reproduction of the **Surrender of Breda - Las Lanzas**, the historical composition by Velázquez, the original being in the Prado Museum in Madrid *(see Michelin Green Guide to Spain)*.

Opposite, at the corner of Reigerstraat, there is a lovely house with a crow-stepped gable.

To the south of the square, at no 19, is **Het Wit Lam**, former meat hall and premises of

Grote Markt

the crossbowmen guild, where the Municipal and Episcopal Museum is installed *(see below)*. On the façade's (1772) pediment St George is slaying the dragon.

Grote Markt, where pedestrian precincts converge, has a food market on Tuesday and Friday mornings and a flea market on Wednesdays.

⊘ **Municipal and Episcopal Museum (Stedelijk en Bisschoppelijk Museum) (C M²)**. – The collections show the history of Breda: religious art, gold and silversmithing, guilds and daily life.

Het Turfschip (D). – This congress and exhibition hall is called after the "peat boat" *(turfschip)* which freed Breda in 1590.

⊘ **De Beyerd (D M³)**. – This building, a former almshouse, has been transformed into a centre for plastic arts (Centrum voor beeldende kunst). A collection of modern art is shown here in rotation.

The centre also organises temporary exhibitions: international contemporary art, architecture, photography and design.

EXCURSIONS

Ⓥ **Bouvigne Castle (Kasteel Bouvigne).** – *4km - 2½ miles. Leave by ⑤ on the town plan then Duivelsbruglaan and turn right.*
On the edge of the **Mastbos** *(qv),* a lovely wood of pines and beech crisscrossed with cycling or horse-riding paths, is Bouvigne Castle; the name derives from the word *boeverije* meaning low meadow. Built in 1612 it is flanked with a high octagonal turret with an onion-shaped dome and surrounded by a wide moat.

Baarle-Nassau. – Pop 5 823. *37km - 23 miles to the southeast by ④ on the town plan.*
This localilty shares its territory with a Belgian district (Baarle-Hertog) consisting of several enclaves in Dutch territory. In the 12C the village of Baerle was divided into two. The south part came back to the Duke of Brabant (Baarle-Duc or Baarle-Hertog). The north part, united to the Breda barony, was called Baarle-Nassau from the time when Breda, in the beginning of the 15C, became the Nassau family fief. The boundary of the districts is very complicated. Presently, each one has its own town hall, church, police, school and post office. Houses of different nationalities are mixed together: their nationality is identified by the numbered sign with the national flag.

Willemstad. – *50km - 31 miles to the west. Leave by ⑥ on the town plan and turn right at Etten-Leur.*
Ⓥ **Hoeven.** – Pop 7 894. The **Simon Stevin Observatory** (Volkssterrenwacht) is located here. It is named after the Flemish scientist, Simon Stevin (1548-1620). There is also a **planetarium.**

Oudenbosch. – Pop 12 378. The town is overlooked by the enormous St Agatha and St Barbara **Basilica** (basiliek van de H.H. Agatha en Barbara). It was built by P.J.H. Cuypers in 1867-80, a replica of St Peter's in Rome, but smaller in size. The dome, however, reaches 48m - 223ft (St Paul's in London apex of internal dome: 66m - 218ft). The façade (1892) is a copy of the façade of the Basilica of St John Lateran in Rome. The interior was decorated by an Antwerp sculptor.

Ⓥ A **Museum of Pontifical Zouaves** (Nederlands Zouavenmuseum) has been set up to honour the 3 000 Dutch, who, in the 19C, contributed to the defence of the Papal States in Italy.

By Standdaarbuiten, then by the A 59 and the A 29, reach Willemstad.
Willemstad. – *Local map p 79.* Pop 3 276. This fortified town in the shape of a seven-pointed star, dating from 1583, owes its name to its founder: William the Silent. Today it is a pleasure boat harbour much frequented by tourists, and commands the lock giving access to the Volkerak.
The octagonal-shaped **church** surrounded by a shaded cemetery and encircled by a small moat was completed in 1607; it was the first Protestant church in the Netherlands.
Near the port the **old town hall** (17C) (voormalig raadhuis) is topped by an octagonal tower. It contains a **Ceramics Museum** (Ceramisch Museum).
The **mill** (D'Orangemolen), a white wall mill, truncated in shape, dates from 1734.
Ⓥ Northwest of town, in a park, the town hall (gemeentehuis) is in the **Mauritshuis,** built in the 17C for Prince Maurice of Orange. It houses a small historical collection.

★ **Biesbosch National Park.** – *50km - 31 miles to the north by ① on the town plan.*

Raamsdonksveer. – Very near the motorway exit there is a modern building housing the
Ⓥ **National Automobile Museum** (Nationaal Automobielmuseum). The collection exhibits more than a hundred cars (from the end of the 19C to the present) motorcycles, bicycles, 18C coaches and sledges, as well as fire engines. Note the Spijker, a well-known Dutch car at the beginning of the century. There are also posters and reconstructions of old shops.

Geertruidenberg. – Pop 6 615. An old fortification on the Amer, this small town is organised round a triangular **square** overlooked by the massive tower of St Gertrude's. The **town hall** (stadhuis) has a lovely 18C façade overlooking the square. Nearby a baroque fountain splashes.

Drimmelen. – Well situated on the banks of the Amer, excellent for water sports since the Delta Plan *(qv),* Drimmelen has become a tourist centre. Its **pleasure boat harbour** can accommodate 1 400 boats; it is also frequented by anglers.

★ **Biesbosch National Park.** – The Biesbosch (or Biesbos) consists of four parts, three of which are criss-crossed by roads. The fourth (Zuidwaard) is entirely surrounded by water.
Ⓥ The **boat trip**★ gives a good overall view of the region.
This region of 40 000ha - 98 000 acres suffered in the St Elizabeth Flood in 1421. Due to important diking work undertaken during the last five and a half centuries, the submerged parts are no longer more than 6 000ha - 14 820 acres. Although very frequented by pleasure boats, the Biesbosch has an abundant aquatic wild-life. One sees not only coots, godwits and redshanks, but also plovers, herons and pheasants. On the islets, reeds, rushes and grassland are the main vegetation, but numerous other species grow there as well: willows, ash, loosestrife, willow for wickerwork, hogweed, arrowhead, valerian and cress.
The closing of the Haringvliet estuary *(p 79)* led to the disappearance of tides in this part, as well as the appearance of a transitory phase in the growth of willow. Several sports are available in the Biesbosch (rowing, sailing, canoeing).
There is a project underway to make the Biesbosch a national park. Several recreation areas have been made, as well as a bird sanctuary and three water reservoirs (spaarbekkens) which supply the Rotterdam and Dordrecht regions.

Michelin map **408** folds 16 and 23 (inset) or **212** fold 4 – Local map p 162

An old fortified town on Voorne Island, Brielle, generally known as Den Briel (pronounced bril), was an active port at the mouth of the Maas.

On 1 April 1572 the Sea Beggars (*Gueux de Mer* or *Watergeuzen*), mercenaries, backed by William the Silent left England and landed at Brielle. This was the signal for the uprising of Holland and Zeeland against the Spanish occupation. In July, 19 priests were executed in Brielle of which 16 had just been made prisoners by the Sea Beggars at Gorinchem. Known as the "martyrs of Gorkum", they have been canonised.

Each year, on 1 April, the seizure of the town by the Sea Beggars is commemorated by historical sketches.

Brielle is the birthplace of Admiral **Maarten Tromp** (1598-1653).

Today, Brielle is a tourist centre benefitting from the proximity of **Brielle Lake** (Brielse Meer) to which it is linked by a ferry for pedestrians and cyclists.

The city has kept from its past the remains of fortifications, laid out as an esplanade, and peaceful quays bordered with old houses, like **Maarland** to the north of the town. At the far eastern end of Maarland, beyond a bridge, there is a fine view over the docks and the tower of the Gothic church of St Catherine.

⊙ **Tromp Museum (Trompmuseum).** – Behind the 18C town hall, on the **Wellerondom,** a picturesque square with its old façades, fountain and canon, this small museum, installed in the weigh house, is devoted to the town's history and its famous son, Admiral Tromp. Admiral Tromp is famous for his victory against the Spanish during the Thirty Years War at the Battle of Downs in 1639, which ended Spanish supremacy at sea. He was knighted in 1642 by Charles I. He died in battle (near Scheveningen) in August 1653 and was buried in the Old Church in Delft *(p 76).*

⊙ **Great Church or St Catherine's (Grote- of St Catharijnekerk).** – Built in the 15C, it remains unfinished. In Brabant Gothic style, it is preceded by a massive stone belfry porch 57m - 187ft high. The carillon cast in 1660 by one of the Hemonys has been enlarged and now has 48 bells.

★★★ **BULBFIELDS** South Holland

Michelin map **408** fold 10

Between Leyden and Haarlem extends the famous area devoted to the cultivation of flowering bulbs (known as *bollenvelden*). In the spring it is transformed into a vast, multicoloured checkerboard.

An original speculation. – The tulip is said to have been brought from Turkey by Ogier Ghislain de Busbecq (1522-92) the Austrian ambassador, who gave bulbs to Charles de l'Ecluse (1526-1609), better known under the name of **Carolus Clusius,** a scientist, who at the time was in charge of the Emperor's garden of medicinal plants in Vienna.

Professor at the University of Leyden in 1593, Clusius started to cultivate tulips on the sandy and humid soil which stretched along the North Sea between Leyden and Haarlem. This cultivation was a great success.

Meanwhile other flowers such as hyacinths and gladioli had been introduced but it was the tulip which attained the highest bids. Between 1634 and 1636 speculation reached insane proportions. A rare tulip bulb was sold for 6 000 florins. Buyers even went to exchanging one bulb for a coach and two horses, for acres of land or for a house. The Dutch States put an end to this speculation in 1636 and the flower industry was regulated. At the end of the 17C the tulip craze was taken over by that of the hyacinth.

A few figures. – Today bulbs cover an area of 15 564ha - 38 458 acres in the country. The main production areas are in the south of Haarlem (2 900ha - 7 166 acres) and to the north of the line formed between Alkmaar and Hoorn.

The bulbs are exported in both hemispheres and the total of these exports represents about 950 million florins per annum. West Germany, the United States and France are the best clients (for quantities bought).

Bulb cultivation. – The most widespread species in the Netherlands are the tulip, gladiolus, narcissus, lily and iris but numerous other flowers are cultivated such as the hyacinth, crocus, anemone and freesia.

Towards mid-March the bulbfields take on their first colour with the blossoming of orange and violet **crocuses,** which are followed by white and yellow **narcissi** (end March). Mid-April the **hyacinths** flower as well as the early **tulips.** A few days later the most beautiful tulips open out. It is, therefore, at the end of April that the plain is usually at its most beautiful. Divided into multicoloured strips separated by small irrigation canals, it looks like an immense patchwork. It is the time of the floral floats on the road from Haarlem to Noordwijk *(see the chapter Practical Information at the end of the guide).* The fields are then covered by irises, then **gladioli** (August). Another floral float procession takes place in September *(see the chapter Practical Information at the end of the guide)* between Aalsmeer and Amsterdam.

Shortly after blossoming the stems are cut off by mechanical means, in order to strengthen the bulb. Once harvested, the large bulbs are sold. The bulblets are replanted in autumn.

⊙ Crossing the bulbfields by railway offers lovely views; flying over them in an **airplane** is highly recommended.

★★★ KEUKENHOF (NATIONALE BLOEMENTENTOONSTELLING) *time: 2½ hours*

⏱ In the heart of the bulb-fields, this park is in a way the sanctuary of flowering bulbs.

It is visited by more than 900 000 people each spring. It extends over 28ha - 69 acres in a lovely wooded setting. Formerly it was the hunting domain of Jacqueline of Hainaut *(p 95),* whose castle still stands to the west. Contrasting with the geometrically patterned bulbfields surrounding it, Keukenhof is more an English style parks: hilly with small sinuous canals running through, scattered with lakes where swans swim, and with the most beautiful varieties of flowers, above all tulips, hyacinths, and narcissi, which form small isolated clumps and create magnificent patches of colour on a green grass and leafy background. A few sculptures add to its embellishment.

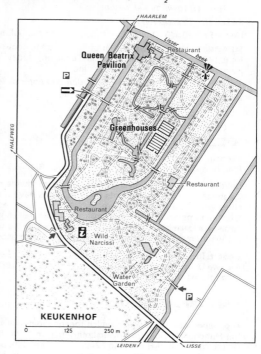

The most fragile species are shown in large greenhouses.

From the mill there is a splendid **view**★★ over the neighbouring bulbfields.

FROM HAARLEM TO LEYDEN *46km - 28½ miles – about ½ day*

★★ **Haarlem.** – *Time: 3 hours. Description p 108.*

> *Leave Haarlem by ③ on the town plan.*

A few fine properties border the road, then the first bulbfields appear. On the right there is a 17-18C mansion, Manpad House (Huis te Manpad).

> *Take the first road on the right towards Tulipshow and cross the level crossing, then turn right.*

★ **Tulipshow.** – *1.5km - ¾ mile*
⏱ *to the north of Vogelenzang.* This floral centre has, since 1789, a hothouse, a garden and large cultivated fields which one can visit.

One can also see a maker of wooden shoes at work.

Vogelenzang. – This village is set in a wooded region near the coastal dunes. Several fine private houses are located here.

To the south of De Zilk one can see the coastal dunes, their pale tints, contrasting with the brightly coloured carpet of flowers.

On leaving Noordwijkerhout, the road rises before the interchange. It then overlooks the bulbfields offering splendid **views**★.

> *Turn left towards Sassenheim then, after the railway line, left again.*

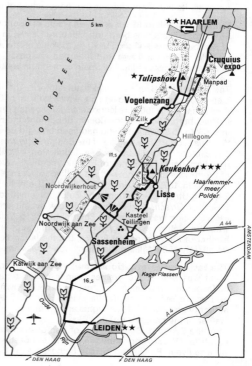

BULBFIELDS★★★

From the bridge over the railway line there are lovely **views**★ over the bulbfields.

Turn left towards Keukenhof.

★★★ **Keukenhof.** – *Description p 73.*

Lisse. – Pop 20 449. One of the main towns of the bulbfield region.

Sassenheim. – Pop 14 013. A great bulb cultivation centre.

Near here is **Teilingen Castle** (Kasteel Teilingen), today in ruins, where Jacqueline of Hainaut spent the last years of her life.

Take the motorway to reach Leyden and enter by ④ on the town plan.

★★ **Leyden.** – *Time: 5 hours. Description p 140.*

★★ DELFT South Holland Pop 87 736

Michelin map **408** south of folds 9 and 10
Plan of built-up area in the current Michelin Red Guide Benelux

Delft earthenware has given to the city its worldwide renown.
Its shaded canals, monuments and museums have made Delft one of the country's cities which has retained the most character. A refined city inspiring daydreaming... It is the homeland of the jurist Grotius *(qv)*, as well as Vermeer *(qv)* and the naturalist **Antonie van Leeuwenhoek** (1632-1723) who, thanks to the microscopes, which he himself perfected, made a multitude of discoveries in microscopic plant and animal life.

★ **Boat trip on the canals.** – *Landing stage: Wijnhaven 6* (CZ). The boat follows ⏱ Nieuwe Delft formed by Hippolytusbuurt and Voorstraat. It passes near the Old Church then returns by Oude Delft and Koornmarkt.

HISTORICAL NOTES

A prosperous city. – Delft, which means moat, was probably founded by Godefroy the Hunchback, Duke of Lower Lothringen in 1074. It obtained its city rights from Count William II of Holland in 1246; and reached its peak in the 13 and 14C by cloth work and its breweries. At the end of the 14C, in order to export its products, it established a waterway link with the mouth of the Maas, where it soon established a port, Delfshaven, which in 1886 became part of Rotterdam.
In 1428 Jacqueline of Hainaut *(qv)* signed the *Treaty of Delft* here; she gave all her possessions (Holland, Zeeland, Hainaut) to Philip the Good and kept the title of countess.
In the 15C fortifications gave the town the layout which it kept until the 19C.
Extensively damaged by the large fire of 1536, it has few edifices dating before the 16C. In 1654, the explosion of a powder magazine completed the destruction.
Today Delft is an intellectual centre, due to its schools of Natural Sciences, its hydraulic laboratory and its Technical University. A nuclear reactor to be used for research was installed in 1963. The modern university buildings are in the new quarters to the southwest of the town.
Amongst its industries there is the manufacture of leaven.

William the Silent (Willem de Zwijger). – Son of Count William of Nassau and Juliana of Stolberg, William was born, in Dillenburg Castle, in Germany, in 1533. On the death of his cousin **René de Chalon** (1544) he took his motto *Je maintiendrai* (I shall maintain), his title of **Prince of Orange** and inherited his possessions in France and in the Low Countries. In 1559, Philip II of Spain named him **Stadtholder** of the provinces of Holland, Zeeland and Utrecht.
The measures taken by Philip II to reinforce the repression against the Calvinists created an opposition movement, which William of Orange and the **Counts of Egmont and Hornes** headed. In 1566 the Iconoclastic Fury began *(qv)*. William feeling threatened fled to Dillenburg (1567) but the Counts of Egmont and Hornes were executed in Brussels in 1568. In 1570 William, who had been brought up as a Catholic, became a Calvinist. With his support the struggle of the Beggars *(qv)* was organised, both on land and sea. The capture of Brielle by the Sea Beggars on 1 April 1572 marked the beginning of a merciless fight. The States of Holland meeting in Dordrecht in July *(p 84)*, approved of the revolts and acknowledged William of Orange as Stadtholder.
Starting in 1572 the prince often lived in Delft. In 1579 several provinces (Holland, Zeeland, Utrecht, Gelderland and Zutphen) joined forces in the fight with the famous *Union of Utrecht (qv)* followed closely by the other provinces. A reward for his assassination was offered by Philip II in 1581; William of Orange defended himself with the well-known *Apologie*. He sought support and asked François of Anjou, brother of King Henry II of France, but the latter died (1584) shortly after.
On 10 July 1584 William the Silent was assassinated in the Prinsenhof in Delft.

The father of international law. – Born in Delft, Hugo de Groot or **Grotius** (1583-1645) was one of the greatest minds of his time. At the same time theologian philosopher and occasionally poet, he is best known for his legal writings and notably his *De Jure Belli ac Pacis (On the Law of War and Peace* – 1625) which was an accepted authority on matters of civil rights and earned its author the right to be considered as "father of the people's rights".
After the Synod of Dort, Grotius, of Remonstrant religion and follower of Oldenbarnevelt *(p 82)*, was imprisoned in Loevestein Castle *(qv)*. He managed to escape and went to live in Paris, then in 1634 he became the Swedish Ambassador to France.

Vermeer of Delft (1632-75). – Delft and its inhabitants were this painter's universe who, born in Delft and dying there practically unknown, is one of the great masters of the Netherlands.

Applying himself to painting scenes of daily life, he is one of those who, without breaking with tradition and without giving up realism practiced at the time, revolutionised pictorial art. With Vermeer the anecdote disappeared, the subject would be banal and everyday if it were not developed by an extraordinary science of composition, geometry, the use of unctuous matter, vivid tones (lemon yellow, sky blue) remarkably blended, and above all, by the marvellous light effects for which Vermeer is the great virtuoso.

This play on light is particularly fine in the famous *View of Delft* as seen from Hooikade (CZ) or in the portraits of women suffused with light and grace like the *Young Girl with a Turban* and *The Lacemaker*.

The Mauritshuis in The Hague and the Rijksmuseum in Amsterdam are the two museums in the Netherlands with the greatest number of works by Vermeer, whose work, in fact, was not very prolific.

His contemporary, **Pieter de Hooch** or **Hoogh** (1629-84) born in Rotterdam, spent a long time in Delft before going to Amsterdam. He depicts the life of the well-to-do bourgeois seen in interiors with doors and windows open, creating clever perspectives and light effects on the floor.

A serious pretender. – It being impossible to substantiate the death of the Dauphin, son of Louis XVI and Marie-Antoinette in the Temple prison in 1795 in Paris, numerous candidates to the throne of France under the reign of Louis XVIII, tried to pass as the young prince.

Amongst them, the clockmaker **Naundorff** gathered round him a circle of followers who, impressed by the precision of his declarations about the Court and the royal family, recognised him as the legitimate sovereign until his death in 1845. His descendant has kept, by privilege, the title of Duke of Normandy.

Delftware. – In the Netherlands, at the end of the 16C, the vogue for stoneware coming from the Rhine was taken over by that of majolica, from Italy. The main centres, Haarlem and Amsterdam, made useful objects then, together with Makkum *(qv)* and Harlingen, started to produce earthenware tiles for wall decoration. In the 17C contacts with the Orient (via the Dutch East India Company) brought new sources of inspiration, in both form and colours taken from Chinese porcelain.

In the second half of the 17C Delft acquired a reputation which soon spread over all of Europe.

Heir of the Italian majolica techniques, Delftware is tin-glazed earthenware and characterised by its remarkable lightness and its particularly shiny aspect, due to the application of a translucent coating.

Firstly, Delft is known for its monochrome painting of blues on a white background; this characteristic defines Delftware still to this day.

At the end of the 17C, the production became more varied, polychromy appeared, and there was not a design or shape, coming from China or Japan, which the Delft artists did not try out in order to satisfy the tastes of European clients fascinated by the Orient.

In the 18C the influence of Sèvres and Dresden porcelain expressed itself in objects with mannered outlines and decoration, while some of the pieces remained faithful to traditional Dutch scenes where one sees small boats sailing on the canals spanned by humpback bridges.

In the beginning of the 18C, Delftware reached its peak. But a decline set in rapidly, caused mainly by English competition; production continues in several factories.

★★HISTORICAL CENTRE AND THE CANALS

time: $\frac{1}{2}$ day – town plan p 77

Markt (CY 13). – This vast esplanade where the market takes place (Thursdays) stretches between the New Church and the town hall.

★ **New Church** (Nieuwe Kerk) (CY A). – This Gothic church (1381) has a brick tower ⊙ crowned with a lovely stone spire. The carillon has bells cast by one of the Hemonys. The church contains the crypt of the princes of the House of Orange. Only a few members of this family were not buried here: Stadtholder and King of England, William III lies in Westminster Abbey, John William Friso in Leeuwarden, Philip-William, eldest son of William the Silent, in St Sulpice in Diest (Belgium).

The interior with three naves is plain. The squat columns support pointed arches, more acute in the chancel. Under the vault of dark wood, the high windows of the nave overlook a floor of blind lancet windows while in the chancel runs a triforium.

The light of the nave contrasts with the rich stained glass windows of the transept and the wide ambulatory. Put in between 1927-36, they depict figurative motifs in warm colours. Only the stained glass window of Grotius, in the north transept, by the master **Joep Nicolas** (1897-1972) stands out by its muted grey and blue tones.

The **mausoleum of William the Silent★** stands in the chancel, above the royal crypt. This imposing Renaissance edifice in marble and black stone was made by Hendrick de Keyser from 1614-21. In the middle of a peristyle cantoned with great allegorical figures, the prince lies in full-dress uniform, under the eyes of a bronze Fame. At his feet lies his ever faithful dog. At the head of the marble recumbent statue, a bronze statue depicts William the Silent in armour.

In the centre of the chancel, the entrance to the House of Orange's crypt is indicated by a large emblazoned slab.

In the ambulatory, paved with tombstones, there is the mausoleum of King William I by William Geefs (1847) and in the north aisle that of Grotius (1781).
Behind the chancel, a chapel is consecrated to a retrospective of royal funerals up to 1962, date when Princess Wilhelmina was buried.

⊙ **Access to the tower.** – From the next to last platform there is a **panorama★** over the new town, beyond the ring canal, with the Technical University and the nuclear reactor, and on the horizon, Rotterdam and The Hague.

Town Hall (Stadhuis) (CY H). – Burnt down in 1618 it was rebuilt in 1620 by Hendrick de Keyser. Restored in 1965 it has recovered its 17C aspect with its mullioned windows set in lead and its low shutters.
The façade overlooking the square, decorated with shells, is dominated behind by the old 15C keep, all that remains of the original town hall.
Turn round, there is a fine view of the New Church's tower.

Weigh House (Waag) (CY T). – This building (1770) has been transformed into a theatre. From here one can see the **meat market** (vleeshal-CY B), whose façade has two ox heads (1660).

Koornmarkt (CZ 10). – *Cross the canal.* The landing stage for boat trips is located here *(p 74).*
At no 81 (CZ C) there is a lovely Renaissance house with medallions, called De Handboog (the bow). At no 67 (CZ M⁴), the 18C patrician house, where the painter **Paul Tetar van Elven** lived (1823-96), is now a museum *(p 78).*
⊙ At no 1 Korte Geer, prolongation of Koornmarkt, is the **Royal Netherlands Army Museum** (Koninklijk Nederlands Leger en Wapenmuseum) (CZ M⁶). It is housed in the **Arsenal** or Armamentarium, which includes two depots of 1602 and 1692 and a warehouse (c1650) of the Dutch East India Company *(qv).* The exhibition illustrates the Low Countries's battles from prehistory to the present through arms, armour, uniforms, models, etc...

★ **Oude Delft (CZ).** – The somber water of the canal shaded by lime trees, the humpbacked bridges and the elegant façades form a lovely decor.
At no 39 the lovely **house of the Dutch East India Company (CZ E)** has been restored. The façade carries the company's coat of arms and its initials: VOC.

> *Turn back and follow the quay.*

One soon sees the slightly leaning spire of the Old Church. In sombre brick, it is

Oude Delft

flanked by four pinnacles. On the opposite quay there is a charming Gothic chapel of the Sisters of the Holy Ghost (Kapel van het H. Geestzusterhuis - CY F). From Nieuwstraat Bridge there is a fine **view★** over the canal. At no 167 the **Delft Water Board** (Hoogheemraadschap van Delfland) (CY K), an old patrician house (c1520), displays a sumptuous Renaissance stone façade decorated with sculptured tympana. The portal is topped with polychrome armorial bearings. No 169 has a fine façade with the arms of the House of Savoy and contains the local archives.

★ **Prinsenhof (CY M¹).** – *No 183. Access by St. Agathaplein, a small square situated*
⊙ *beyond the porch.*
The sculptured stone above the porch is a reminder that in the 17C the Prinsenhof was converted into a cloth hall. It was originally a convent (St Agatha) before becoming, in 1572, the residence of William the Silent, who was assassinated here in 1584.
The palace (Prinsenhof: the Prince's Court) now houses a **museum.** It contains souvenirs of the Eighty Years' War and collections concerning the House of Orange-Nassau, notably numerous historical portraits. The buildings in the 15C Flamboyant Gothic style are arranged round two courtyards. One is flanked by the chapterhouse (room II), the other by the refectory (room IV), opposite the chapel (room XIV). The latter is now used as a Walloon church *(qv).* Held each year in the Prinsenhof is an Antique Fair *(see the chapter Practical Information at the end of the guide).*

⊙ **Old Church (Oude Kerk) (CY N).** – Dedicated to St Hippolytus, this 13C church, which is reflected in the waters of Oude Delft was enlarged four times. Since the 16C it has three chancels and the beginning of a transept. The tower, which leans, embedded in the main nave, is built on the foundations of a watch tower. It has the biggest bell in the Netherlands (9 metric tons).
Numerous memorial slabs (16-18C) are set in the pavement. The finely carved Renaissance pulpit is like the one in the Great Church *(p 115)* in The Hague.
The stained glass windows (1972) in the chancel, the transept and at the end of the side aisles, made by Joep Nicolas have lovely figurative compositions.

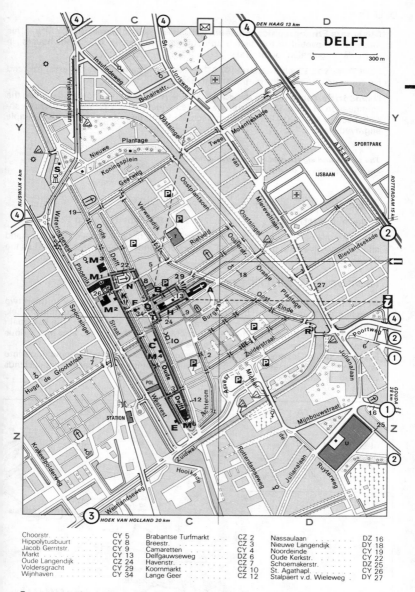

DELFT

0   300 m

DEN HAAG 13 km

SPORTPARK

IJSBAAN

Famous people are buried in this church. In the main chancel Admiral Piet Hein *(qv)* is shown lying in his armour: it is the work of Pieter de Keyser, son of Hendrick.
In the chapel near the north chancel, the mausoleum of Admiral Tromp *(qv)* by Rombout Verhulst is baroque. The low relief depicts the naval battle of Terheyde, where the admiral was killed in 1653.
To the north of the tower, near the stained glass window depicting William the Silent, (no 25) there is the monument to Van Leeuwenhoek *(qv)*.

Hippolytusbuurt (**CY 8**). – This shaded canal is one of the oldest in Delft. Along the quays florists display their wares (Thursdays). On the corner of Hippolytusbuurt and Camaretten is the fish market, next to which stands the former meat market *(p 76)*. Opposite this is a lovely 16C house (Kaaskop) (**CY Q**) with crow-stepped gables.

Voldersgracht (**CY 29**). – This is a picturesque canal, edged on the south by a few corbelled houses.
From the second bridge, there is a fine view of the New Church tower.

ADDITIONAL SIGHTS

★**East Gate** (**Oostpoort**) (**DZ R**). – Formerly called St Catherine's Gate, it is the only one remaining from the town walls. It is a lovely dark brick construction, flanked with two slender octagonal turrets dating from the 15 and 16C. There is a fine view from the picturesque white lever bridge which is in front of it. A canal passes under the annex.

⊙**Lambert van Meerten Museum** (**CY M³**). – This 19C mansion has a magnificent collection of **earthenware tiles★** from the 16 to 19C. Note on the staircase a naval battle against the English and a panel of tulips; upstairs, a series of birds, flowers and a long panel illustrating the various stages in boat building.

DELFT★★

⊘**Nusantara Ethnographical Museum** (Volkenkundig Museum "Nusantara") (CY M²). – This museum is devoted to the history and culture of Indonesia. One room houses, in particular, a gamelan (orchestra).

⊘**Paul Tetar van Elven Museum** (CZ M⁴). – Furniture, paintings by the artist *(qv)* and his contemporaries and ceramics are on display.

Naundorff's Tomb (Graf van Naundorff) (CY S). – At the end of Noordeinde canal, the continuation of Oude Delft, there is a shaded square where Naundorff *(qv)* the so-called son of Louis XVI lies. A railing decorated with fleur-de-lis surrounds a simple engraved slab.

*The towns and sights described in this guide
are shown in black on the maps.*

★ **DELTA** South Holland - Zeeland

Michelin map 408 folds 15 to 17 and 22 to 25 or 212 folds 2 to 5 and 12 to 14

At the mouths of the rivers Rhine, Maas and Scheldt, the provinces of South Holland and Zeeland give onto the North Sea a series of islands and estuaries: known as the Delta.

HISTORICAL AND GEOGRAPHICAL NOTES

At the mouth of three large rivers. – The **Rhine** crosses the country forming two branches, the Neder Rijn and the Waal. The **Neder Rijn** (Lower Rhine) becoming the Lek, then Nieuwe Maas, runs into the New Waterway (Nieuwe Waterweg). The **Waal,** main arm of the Rhine, flows into the Lek and the Maas. The **Maas,** which also has various names (Bergse Maas, Amer), flows into the Hollands Diep.
Eastern Scheldt (Oosterschelde) is an old estuary of the **Scheldt** which now flows into Western Scheldt (Westerschelde). The rivers make their way between several islands which sometimes become peninsulas.

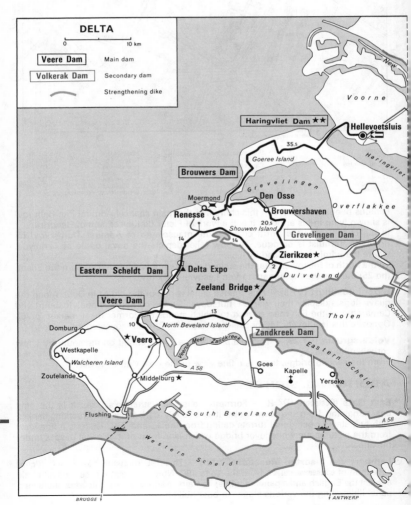

A threatened region. – The Delta's islands, won from the sea by alluvial deposits at the end of the Middle Ages, are very low in altitude. A great many of them are situated below sea level or less than 5m - 16½ft above. The coastal front is protected by high dunes but the shores of estuaries are only edged by dikes. Several times in history these have shown to be fragile when, at the moment of spring tides the water surges in with violence.

On 19 November 1421, date of the **St Elizabeth,** a terrible flood devastated all the Delta and reached Dordrecht *(qv)* and the Biesbosch *(qv)*.

During the night of 31 January-1 February 1953 there was another catastrophe. Under the effect of spring tides, combined with low atmospheric pressure, a tidal wave broke the dikes in several places, flooding the islands, bringing about 1 865 deaths and 500 000 disaster victims and devastating 260 000ha-642 200 acres of land. Its effects were felt in the interior of the country as far as Hollandse IJssel.

The Delta Plan (Het Delta Plan). – Three years after the tidal wave of 1953, two solutions were proposed in order to prevent the recurrence of similar catastrophes: heighten the old dikes or block the Delta's channels (project adopted by the Senate in 1958). Four **main dams** two of which had locks facing the North Sea and several **secondary dams** situated behind, closed off the estuaries. The presence of secondary dams, preventing the formation of too violent currents was necessary during the construction of the main dams. Afterwards their role became less important but they continue to serve as communication routes. No dam closes Western Scheldt which flows into the port of Antwerp, nor the New Waterway which flows into Rotterdam, the two ports having free access to the North Sea.

The dams shorten the coast by 700km - 435 miles, forming reservoirs of fresh water (dams: Haringvliet and to the east Philips and Oester), putting an end to the salinity of the land, avoiding floods, forming stretches of water for pleasure boats, furthering road networks and the region's rapid development.

The Delta Plan also included the raising of dikes along navigable waterways and the development of the Biesbosch.

To the east of the Delta, the canal from the Scheldt to the Rhine (Schelde-Rijnverbinding), completed in 1975, links Antwerp to the Volkerak, a distance of 37km-23 miles.

Dams and bridges. – Already, the Brielse Maas estuary, downstream from Rotterdam, had been transformed into a lake (Brielle Lake) *(p 72)* in 1950. But, because the New Waterway remained open for navigation, it was necessary to build a large **mobile storm surge barrier** (Stormvloedkering Hollandse IJssel) (1954-8) on the Hollandse IJssel near Krimpen aan de IJssel, which allowed river navigation when the sluice gate was raised. It was doubled by a lock of 120 × 24m - 394 × 79ft for ships of high tonnage and used to pass through when the main work was closed.

The Haringvliet estuary was closed by the enormous **Haringvliet Dam** *(p 80)*. Behind, on the Hollands Diep there was the **Volkerak Dam** (Volkerakdam). Built 1957-69 between Overflakkee and the province of North Brabant, it has three large sluices; it forms a Y with **Haringvliet Bridge** (Haringvlietbrug) which links it to Beijerland.

To the south, the Brouwershavense Gat Channel is closed by the **Brouwers Dam** (Brouwersdam) *(p 80)*, assisted by the **Grevelingen Dam** (Grevelingendam) made on the estuary of the same name. This latter dam, erected (1958-65) between Duiveland and Overflakkee, was completed by filling the last channel with stone blocks brought by cable-car. It forms a T with the **Philips Dam** (Philipsdam).

The **Eastern Scheldt Dam** *(p 80)* (Oosterscheldedam) between Schouwen and North Beveland closes off, since 1986, this estuary of the Delta, which is the widest (9km - 5½ miles) and the deepest (35m - 115ft). To the east of the estuary two dams, the Oester and the Philips *(see above)* spare the canal between the Scheldt and the Rhine from tidal flow. Eastern Scheldt is also crossed by **Zeeland Bridge** (Zeelandbrug) *(p 80)*. The salt water channel, Veersemeer, which runs along North Beveland to the south, is blocked by **Veere Dam** (Veersedam - *p 80*). This is doubled by a secondary dam, the **Zandkreek Dam** (Zandkreekdam). Built 1956-1960 on the salt water Zandkreek channel between North Beveland and South Beveland, it is 800m -2 625ft long and has a lock of 140 × 20m - 459 × 65½ft spanned by a bascule bridge making road connections possible. On the Western Scheldt estuary, which has not been closed, there are two regular boat services for crossings. The project to build a bridge is being studied.

Boat trips. – In the north part of the Delta, leaving from Rotterdam *(p 156)* and from Willemstad *(p 71)*; on the Eastern Scheldt, leaving from Zierikzee *(p 188)*.

FROM HELLEVOETSLUIS TO VEERE
99km - 61½ miles - allow 1 day - local map p 78

Hellevoetsluis. – Small port on the salt water channel of Haringvliet, it has pleasure boat harbours.

★★ **Haringvliet Dam** (Haringvlietdam). – Built between 1955 and 1971, it is a major work. To build it first an artificial island was made in the centre of the estuary. The final phase of construction was effected by use of a cable-car, a method already used for the Grevelingen Dam *(p 79);* the blocks of concrete were dropped in this way into the last channel to be filled in.

5km - 3 miles long, the Haringvliet Dam has 17 drainage locks of 56.50m - 185ft.

Their sluice gates work in 20 minutes due to a hydraulic press system with 68 presses situated in the 16 pillars and in the abutment-piers. Normally these sluice gates are closed and the water is driven back to the New Waterway. The drainage locks contribute to maintaining the equilibrium between fresh water and sea water. A shipping lock has been made near the small port to the south.

Brouwers Dam (Brouwersdam). – Built from 1963 to 1972 between the islands of Goeree and Schouwen, this large dam has no lock.

To complete the north segment, caissons with sluice gates were made, the same system which had been used, for the first time when building Veere Dam *(see below).* The south segment needed a cable-car, transporting 15 metric tons of concrete each time.

Between this dam and that of Grevelingen there is a salt water lake with no tidal flow.

Renesse. – This small locality situated on Schouwen Island has a lovely sandy beach.
⊙ 1km - ½ mile to the east is **Moermond Mansion** (slot Moermond), a fine brick construction of the 16 and 17C with a 14C porch.

Den Osse. – Dikes hide the installations of this new pleasure boat harbour.

Brouwershaven. – Pop 3 577. Formerly a prosperous port which imported beer from Delft (*brouwer:* brewer), today it is a small pleasure boat harbour. The city suffered from the 1953 floods.

It is the homeland of **Jacob Cats** (1577-1660). This statesman, nicknamed Father Cats, who was Grand Pensionary of Holland and West Friesland from 1636-51 is also known for his poetry.

⊙ Brouwershaven has a lovely 15C Gothic **church** (St.-Nicolaas) with a transept and ambulatory. Inside the pulpit and chancel screen are in the rococo style.

The **town hall** (stadhuis) of 1599 has a Renaissance façade in stone, highly decorated, and topped by a pinnacle.

★ **Zierikzee.** – *Description p 188.*

Eastern Scheldt Dam (Oosterscheldedam). – *For security reasons the dam road is closed during strong winds. If closed use Zeeland Bridge to cross Eastern Scheldt.*

Started in 1966, the dam was inaugurated in 1986. This impressive hydraulic undertaking 3km - 2 miles long was built across the estuary via 3 deep passes and two artificial islands (used as bases).

The project, which was to close the Eastern Scheldt completely off from the sea, was modified so that the estuary remained linked to the sea. The dam was made of 65 pillars (height: 40m - 131ft; weight 18 000 metric tons) between which 62 steel sluice gates (weight 300-500 metric tons) can slide. In case of a storm 1 hour is sufficient to lower the sluice gates, normally left open. The realisation of this new project, which only modifies by 15 % the tidal flow in Eastern Scheldt and makes it possible to continue oyster and mussle breeding, slowed down, however, the project's completion. On the other hand, the security measures and alarm systems have been improved in the whole Scheldt region.

⊙ On one of the Eastern Scheldt Dam's artificial islands, **Delta Expo** is held. This exhibition explains the evolution and extent of the work undertaken in the Netherlands in its fight against the sea.

Models, explanatory panels and slide presentations illustrate the different steps involved in the Delta Plan. The tour includes a visit to the pillars and the dam's
⊙ underground system and ends with a **boat tour.**

★ **Zeeland Bridge** (Zeelandbrug). – Completed in 1965, this toll bridge links Zierikzee to the former island of North Beveland. Since 1987, this roadway has been doubled by the Eastern Scheldt Dam. An impressive achievement, the bridge spreads its 50 arches across 5 022m - 16 476ft; the height above average water level 17m - 56ft.

A bascule bridge near Schouwen-Duiveland enables boats with high masts to pass through.

Veere Dam (Veersedam). – Built (1958-61) between the islands of Walcheren and North Beveland, neer Veere, it has an enclosing dike of 2 700m - 8 858ft which, in spite of the protection of a sandbank, is very exposed to storms, due to its northwest orientation. It was the first dam to be built with the help of caissons equipped with sluice gates; the caissons were placed at the bottom of the channel, all the sluice gates were then closed at the same time, which prevented the formation of a destructive current.

A small salt water lake, with no tidal flow, stretches between this dam and Zandkreek Dam.

★ **Veere.** – *Description p 179.*

DEN BOSCH See 's-Hertogenbosch

★ DEVENTER Overijssel

Michelin map **408** fold 12
Plan of built-up area in the current Michelin Red Guide Benelux

Right in the south of the Overijssel province and the Salland region, Deventer, formerly a Hanseatic town on the east bank of the IJssel, has kept its old character, witness to a rich past.

HISTORICAL NOTES

As early as the 9C it was a prosperous port. At the end of the 9C, the city became the residence of the Utrecht bishops, who fled from their town menaced by the Northmen. On Nieuwe Markt, the remains of an 11C episcopal palace have been found.

The town soon played an important religious role. The theologian **Gerhard Groote** (1340-84), born in Deventer, was the innovator of a spiritual movement, the *devotio moderna* (modern devotion). One of his pupils, Florentius Radewyns, following the wishes of his master, founded in Deventer c1384 the first monastery for the Order of the **Brethren of the Common Life,** a community devoted to the education and care of the poor, which had a large intellectual influence in Europe. Those who passed through his school were Thomas à Kempis *(qv)*, Pope Adrian VI *(qv)*, Erasmus in 1475-6 and Descartes in 1632-3.

In the 16C Hendrick Terbrugghen *(qv)* was born in Deventer. At the end of the 17C, Gerard Terborch, born in Zwolle *(p 191)*, came to work here, dying in 1681.

In the 16 and 17C printing was an important enterprise in the town: already in the 15C numerous incunabula were produced.

Today the metallurgical industry, as well as chemical, graphic and foodstuff industries are amongst the main activities of this town; a well-known gingerbread *(Deventer koek)* is made here.

In the heart of the city, in the pedestrian shopping precinct, a very large barrel organ, called the Turk, plays old tunes on Saturdays.

Deventer is an Old Catholic *(qv)* Episcopal See.

⊙ **Boat trips.** – Tours on the IJssel, offering fine views of the city, are organised.

TOWN CENTRE *time: 2 hours*

Brink (Z 15). – It is the main square of the town, so named, as in all localities of Saxon origin.

A market is held here (Friday mornings and Saturdays).

At nos 11 and 12, there is an early 17C façade decorated with shells.

The richly decorated **Penninck House** (Penninckhuis) (Z **D**) dates from 1590.

Weigh House (Waag) (Z **M¹**). – It is a large, slightly sloping edifice built in 1528 in the Late Gothic style and completed in 1643 by a tall perron supported by arcades. The roofing is flanked by four turrets and topped by a wooden pinnacle.

On the north façade an immense cauldron is suspended which, in the past, is believed to have boiled counterfeiters.

⊙ The building contains a **museum** (Museum De Waag). The museum's various collections concern the city's history: construction and expansion *(basement)*, social and economic features *(1st floor)*, art and culture *(2nd floor)*.

House of the Three Herrings (De Drie Haringen) (Z). – Dating from 1575, this merchant's house has a fine Renaissance façade with a façade stone depicting three herrings. It is used by the VVV *("i" on the town plan)*.

On the other side of the street no 69 (public library) has an elegant façade with pinnacles.

⊙ **Toy Museum** (Speelgoed– en Blik Museum) (Z **M²**). – This museum has collections of old toys and a museum of mechanical toys; a section contains old tinware.

Bergstraat (Z 8). – In this street of Bergkwartier or hill quarter, which has been restored, there are several fine old façades; lovely view over the two towers of St Nicholas.

St Nicholas (St.-Nicolaas) **or Bergkerk** (Z **B**). – It was started c1200AD in the Romanesque style and has kept from that time the two square towers of the façade, topped by spires. The rest was modified in the Gothic style in the 15C.

Grote Kerkhof (Z 27). – The Great Church and town hall are on this square.

⊙ **Town Hall** (Stadhuis) (Z **H**). – This complex (greatly restored) is in three parts: the actual town hall (Raadhuis), the Wanthuis (also giving on to Polstraat), and the Landshuis. The joint façade of the town hall and the Wanthuis dates from the 17C; its architect Jacob Roman also designed Het Loo Palace in Apeldoorn. The **Landshuis,** former headquarters of the Overijssel States has a lovely brick façade (1632) punctuated by pilasters and topped by a pinnacled gable.

In the hall of the town hall several 17 and 18C paintings of guilds are exhibited. A room on the 1st floor of the town hall has a lovely canvas by Terborch: The **Aldermen's Council** (in the koffiekamer) painted in 1657.

⊙ **Great Church or St Lebuin's** (Grote- of St.-Lebuïnuskerk) (Z **E**). – It bears the name of Lebuin, Saxon apostle, who built a church here in the 8C. The Romanesque church founded c1040 by Bernulphus, Bishop of Utrecht, was rebuilt as from 1235 and then again in the 15C in the Gothic style. It is a vast building flanked to the west by a tower topped with an octagonal lantern in wood designed by Hendrick de Keyser.

⊙ Its carillon, which was cast by one of the Hemonys, can be heard during **concerts.**

DEVENTER

Brink	Z 15	Bergstr.	Z 8	Noordenbergstr.	Z 58
Broederenstr.	Z 18	Binnensingel	Y 9	Ossenweerdstr.	Y 62
Engestr.	Z 23	Bokkingshang	Z 12	Pontsteeg	Z 65
Grote Poot	Z 30	Brinkpoortstr.	Y 17	Roggestr.	Z 67
Kleine Poot	Z 42	Graven	Z 25	Snipperlingsdijk	Z 69
Korte Bisschopstr.	Z 47	Grote Kerkhof	Z 27	Spijkerboorsteeg	Z 70
Lange Bisschopstr.	Z 48	Grote Overstr.	Z 28	Stationsstr.	Y 72
Nieuwstr.	YZ 56	Hofstr.	Z 33	Stromarkt	Z 73
		Hoge Hondstr.	Y 35	T.G. Gibsonstr.	Y 76
Bagijnenstr.	Y 4	Houtmarkt	Z 36	van Twickelostr.	Y 78
Bergkerkpl.	Z 5	Kapjeswelle	Y 40	Verlengde Kazernestr.	Z 79
		Kerksteeg	Z 41	Verzetslaan	Y 82
		Menstr.	Z 51	Zandpoort	Z 85
		Mr. H. F. de Boerlaan	Z 52	Zutphenselaan	Z 87

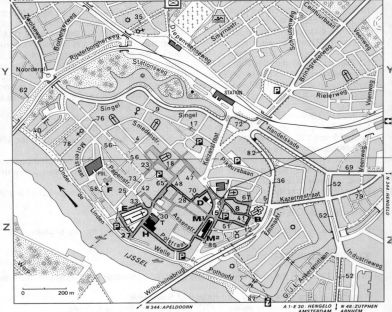

The hall-type *(qv)* interior has kept the remains of a double transept. The stellar vaulting has paintings round the keystones (16C). Other paintings can be seen, notably under the porch near the tower; the Bearing of the Cross dates from the 16C.

⊙ The 19C great organ has 3 000 pipes; **organ concerts** are held.

Under the chancel, the Romanesque crypt (1040) is remarkable with its six short pillars, cabled or decorated with geometric motifs.

⊙ **Access to the tower.** – From the top there is a lovely view of the city.

Return to Brink by the pedestrian precinct.

ADDITIONAL SIGHT

Buiskensklooster (Z F). – This early 15C building has recovered its brickwork walls. It is the former convent of St Agnes where the Sisters of the Common Life lived, following the rules set forth by Gerhard Groote *(qv)*. It contains the **town archives** (no 3)
⊙ and a **library** (Stads- of Athenaeumbibliotheek) where there are interesting exhibitions of books and manuscripts.

EXCURSION

Markelo. – *26km - 16 miles to the east by Snipperlingsdijk* (Z).

Holten. – Pop 8 634. This town, situated in the Salland region, attracts many tourists, drawn by the wooded and sandy heights of the **Holterberg** (alt 50m - 197ft), which marks the southern extremity of an old Scandinavian glacier.

⊙ On the Holterberg, there is a **museum★** (Bos Museum). About ten large **dioramas** bring to life various European animals, which can be found mainly in the region; some are shown in their winter coats. Note the diorama showing a group of Scandinavian elks being attacked by wolves.

In a nearby clearing is a beautifully landscaped **Canadian cemetery** (Canadese Militaire Begraafplaats) with 1 496 tombs of Canadians killed in World War II.

Markelo. – Pop 6 993. At the beginning of the century an important field of funeral urns was found north of Markelo.

Markelo has an **open-air theatre** (De Kosterskoele) where in summer *(see the chapter Practical Information at the end of the guide)* an 1830 country wedding *(boerenbruiloft)* is enacted.

If you are puzzled by an abbreviation or a symbol in the text or on the maps, look at the key on p 36.

DOESBURG Gelderland

Pop 10 559

Michelin map **408** south of fold 12

At the confluence of the IJssel and the Oude IJssel, Doesburg, an old stronghold of the Zutphen earldom, was a prosperous commercial town in the Middle Ages; and a member of the Hanseatic League in 1447. This lovely city of the Achterhoek *(qv)* has kept numerous vestiges of its past, notably the remains of ramparts dating from 1630 *(to the south)* and several Gothic and Renaissance façades.

⊙ **Boat trips.** – Excursions are organised on the IJssel.

SIGHTS

⊙ **Great Church or Martin Church (Grote- of Martinikerk).** – This Gothic church (15C) is lit by tall Flamboyant windows. Its high tower, destroyed in 1945, has been rebuilt and ⊙ has a **carillon.** Organ concerts are held inside in summer.

Weigh House (Waag). – Now a restaurant, this graceful building (*c*1500), under a gable decorated with pinnacles, has high picture windows with painted shutters, topped by tympana. Inside, in a typical setting, the weigh house scales can be seen.
There are other interesting houses in the same street, notably the **Baerkenhuizen** (nos 29-31), two Renaissance buildings of 1649 with voluted gables.

Town Hall (Stadhuis). – It stands opposite the weigh house. Dating from the 14C, it has an interesting façade on Roggestraat.
⊙ Next to it is a **museum** of local history and handicrafts ("De Roode Tooren" Museum voor Stad en Ambt Doesborgh). Reconstitution of a wooden shoe maker's workshop, a room where a cigar-maker chopped tobacco and an old grocer's shop *(1st floor)*. Note the scale model of a pontoon bridge: near Doesburg the banks of the IJssel were linked by this type of bridge until 1952.

⊙ **Mustard Factory (Doesburgsche Mosterdfabriek).** – *Boekholtstraat 22*. In this factory, founded in 1457, mustard is prepared according to old techniques using wooden mills.

EXCURSION

's-Heerenberg. – *22km - 14 miles to the southeast.*
Doetinchem. – Pop 40 682. On the banks of the Oude IJssel, this town, situated in the heart of the Achterhoek *(qv)* formerly belonged to the Zutphen earldom. It was badly damaged by a bombardment in 1945. Today, it is a modern industrial and commercial city with numerous pedestrian precincts. The traditional manufacturing of wooden shoes is still one of the specialties of the city and its vicinity.
Doetinchem has a large **wall mill** (1850) near the Oude IJssel (VVV inside).
6km - 3½ miles to the east of the town stands the large **Slangenburg Castle** (Kasteel Slangenburg), surrounded by moats and a beautiful **park;** it belongs to the Benedictine Order.
⊙ **'s-Heerenberg.** – The imposing **Bergh Castle** (Huis Bergh) dominates this locality.
Built in the 13C by the Van den Berghs, it was altered in the 17C. In 1946 its last owner bequeathed it and its contents to the State. The interior is embellished with antique furniture, paintings and carvings on wood and ivory. Nearby, the former Gothic castle chapel, has become the parish church.

DOKKUM Friesland

Michelin map **408** fold 5 – Local map p 139

Formerly a flourishing port, this small town in the north of Friesland, is hidden behind the remains of its shaded ramparts, from which emerge a few bell towers and tall mills. Built on a mound, it has several slightly sloping streets.
St Boniface, often called the Apostle of Germany, was executed here in 754 with his 52 companions. An Englishman, born in *c*675 of a Wessex, England family he came to convert the Frisians in 716 and then met St Willibrord *(qv)* in Utrecht. It was during his second mission to Friesland in 754 that he was killed. He is buried in Fulda, Germany, where he had founded a monastery.

SIGHTS

Zijl. – From this wide bridge, there is a fine **view** over Klein Diep (meaning small canal) bordered by a mill and the Groot Diep (meaning large canal). The 18C **town hall** (Stadhuis) is topped by a white pinnacle. Opposite, three lovely houses with crow-stepped gables dating from the early 17C have been restored.

Follow Diepswal to reach the museum; first road on the left, then the alleyway on the right.

⊙ **Admiralty House Museum (Museum Het Admiraliteitshuis).** – This regional museum is in the former Admiralty House (1618 - restored) and in the neighbouring 18C mansion; note the Admiralty House's small baroque portal.
The collections are very varied: Dokkum silverwork, a Frisian sledge of carved wood, a bone iceskate dating from the Middle Ages, Frisian folk art (19C toys), regional costumes; note the black Carolingian headdress found in a mound.

Weigh House (Waag). – This small building with two decorated pediments, one of which has the town's coat of arms (a crescent moon and three stars) stands on Grote Breedstraat.

⊙**Great Church or St Martin's** (Grote- of St.-Martinuskerk). – In commemoration of St Boniface's murder, a mound and a church were erected here. The present building, a Protestant church, is Gothic: the chancel dates from the 15C. Inside there is a very high gallery added above the aisle. A great number of tombstones are on the ground; note the Frisian pulpit with elegant carved panels (a lion, a pelican, a falcon).

St Boniface Chapel (Bonifatiuskapel). – *Leave town southwards towards Leeuwarden and after the bascule bridge take the second road on the left.*
On a square stands the statue (1962) of St Boniface; using his Bible, the bearded monk protects his head against the Frisian attack.
In the small park is a chapel (1934) where every year a great pilgrimage takes place *(see the chapter Practical Information at the end of the guide).*

DOORN Utrecht   Pop 10 323

Michelin map **408** south of fold 11

Situated on the edge of a wooded region, Doorn has a castle on the south side.

⊙**Castle** (Huis Doorn). – Surrounded by moats, set in the middle of a lovely park, this castle was the home of the ex-Kaiser of Germany **Wilhelm II**, from 1920 to his death in 1941.
Obliged to go into exile after his abdication in November 1918, he was first given refuge in Amerongen Castle *(p 42)*. Then, in May 1920, he and the Empress Augusta Victoria moved to Doorn Castle which he had acquired. His wife died the following year. In 1922 he married Hermine, Princess of Reuss.
The castle was built in the 14C by the Bishop of Utrecht to defend his territory (altered in 1780), remaining from the medieval castle is a turret on the southwest side.
Now a **museum**, the castle contains souvenirs of Wilhelm II, who had brought his **collections★** (paintings, tapestries) from the imperial palaces. These are shown in a setting which has remained unchanged since the Kaiser's death.
One room is devoted to Frederick the Great (Frederick II of Prussia, 1712-86), the most famous representative of the Hohenzollern family, who was a great art lover and collected paintings and pastels of the French School (Nicolas Lancret, Watteau's emulator) as well as snuff-boxes.
There is also a fine collection of silver, mainly consisting of presents received by the Hohenzollerns in the 19 and 20C as well as a fine collection of uniforms, helmets, boots and ceremonial sabres having belonged to Wilhelm II.
Kaiser Wilhelm's mausoleum stands in the park.

★ DORDRECHT South Holland   Pop 106 987

Michelin map **408** fold 17 or **212** folds 5 and 6
Plan of built-up-area in the current Michelin Red Guide Benelux

In the south of the province of South Holland, Dordrecht, which the Dutch familiarly call Dordt, is an important river centre between the Beneden Merwede, branch of the Rhine, the Noord, which links it to Rotterdam and the Nieuwe Maas, the Dordtse Kil, which links it to the Maas and the Oude Maas. It is also a great pleasure boat harbour where yachts are anchored at most of the town's docks, and more to the east, in the Wantij.
The old town has kept its colourful quays, its canals and its old façades, while the southern quarters rival with their bolder constructions.
It inspired many painters including Van Goyen (1596-1656); a number of 17 and 18C artists were born here *(p 85)*. **Ary Scheffer** (1795-1858), painter of biblical and religious scenes, was Louis-Philippe's court painter.

⊙**Boat trips.** – Dordrecht is the departure point for boat trips through the Biesboch *(qv)*.

HISTORICAL NOTES

According to the chronicles, the town was destroyed by the Vikings in 837.
In 1220 it acquired city rights from the Count of Holland, William I, and because of this, it is considered the oldest town in the earldom. It was fortified at the end of the 13C. The 14C was a period of great prosperity for Dordrecht due to the privilege of applying stop-over fees, which beginning in 1299, were levied on goods coming from the Rhine. The 15C, on the contrary, was disastrous; there was the unsuccessful siege in 1418 by Count John of Brabant as part of the fight between the Hooks and Cods *(p 96)*, the St Elizabeth *(qv)* tidal wave of 1421 which isolated the town making it an island, the big fire of 1457 and then its capture in 1480 by John of Egmont.
In the 16C the town recovered its splendour.

The cradle of independence. – In the Dordrecht Court of Justice (Het Hof), the first free assembly of the Holland and Zeeland States was held in July 1572, brought about by the capture of Brielle by the Sea Beggars in April of that same year *(p 72)*.
In Dordrecht the delegates of the twelve confederate states of Holland and the nobility decided to deliver the country from the Duke of Alba's armies, and proclaimed William the Silent as Stadtholder representing Philip II of Spain. In this way they laid the foundation for the future United Provinces *(qv)*.

Synod of Dort. – Dordrecht was also the meeting place in 1618-19 of the great synod of Protestant theologians who came to settle the controversy that had arisen between the moderate **Remonstrants** or Arminians, supporters of Arminius *(qv)* who upheld that the blessings of grace were open to all, and the **Gomarists,** supporters of Gomar or Gomarus, a strict Calvinist who defended the principle of predestination. The latter group won, with the help of Maurice of Orange, and carried out bloody persecutions on their opponents, such as Oldenbarnevelt *(qv)* and Grotius *(qv)*.

At this synod (attended by English representatives and a Scotsman sent by James I as well as Germans and Swiss), the union of all Protestant churches in the country took place, except for the Remonstrants, and a joint doctrine (canons of Dort) was established. The theologian **Episcopius,** who had pleaded the cause of the Remonstrants, then founded a Remonstrant Church in Antwerp (1619).

A 17C painters' breeding-ground. – A number of 17C painters were born in Dordrecht. Some of them were Rembrandt's students.

Ferdinand Bol (1616-80) went to live in Amsterdam where he worked in Rembrandt's studio. His works, notably the numerous portraits tinged with seriousness are very like those of his master, by the chiaroscuro, the abundance of impasting and the harmony between warm colours.

He also did the famous guild painting: *The Governors of the Leper Hospital* (1649), exhibited in the Museum of Amsterdam History *(p 49)*. One of his students, Sir Godfrey Kneller, became court painter to Charles II and subsequent Stuart kings and queens.

Nicolaes Maes (1634-93) was also influenced by Rembrandt, whose pupil he was from 1648-52, in Amsterdam. More realist than the latter, he chose simple people, modest subjects, scenes which he made somewhat touching and which he enriched by his science of chiaroscuro and reddish tones. The best known of his works is *Girl at a Window: the Daydreamer* in the Rijksmuseum in Amsterdam. At the end of his life, on the contrary, he painted fashionable portraits.

Samuel van Hoogstraten (1627-78) studied with Rembrandt, then after having travelled a great deal in Europe, returned to his birthplace. He mainly painted portraits and interior scenes which, by their effects of light and perspective can be compared to those of Pieter de Hooch *(qv)*. **Godfried Schalcken** (1643-1706) was his pupil.

Aert van Gelder (1645-1727) was first a pupil of Van Hoogstraten, then of the ageing Rembrandt, in Amsterdam. His biblical scenes owe a lot to the technique of the great master, notably the sumptuous clothes and the slightly theatrical composition.

Aelbert Cuyp (1620-91) influenced by Jan van Goyen *(qv)* painted landscapes of very studied composition with luminous backgrounds, immense skies and in the foreground horsemen or peaceful herds of cattle.

The De Witt brothers. – Dordrecht is the birthplace of the De Witt brothers, distinguished 17C statesmen.

Johan de Witt (1625-72) became the Grand Pensionary of Holland in 1653. An excellent administrator, he failed in international politics. He was unable to avoid the defeat of the Dutch fleet by England in 1654, the end of the First Dutch War. In addition, hostile to the predominance of the House of Orange, he had to confront popular opposition which supported the family.

After having won the Second Dutch War (1665-7) and withstood the War of Devolution led by Louis XIV (1667-8), Johan de Witt managed to get the **Perpetual Edict** of 1667 voted, which abolished the Stadtholdership and thus the Orangist power in the province of Holland.

However, the same year (1672) that Louis XIV and Charles II united against the United Provinces in the Third Dutch War, the people, feeling menaced, repealed the Perpetual Edict electing William of Orange, Stadtholder (under the name of William III) and army commander. Finally, **Cornelis,** brother of Johan de Witt and burgomaster of Dordrecht in 1666, was wrongly accused of conspiring against William III and was imprisoned in the Prison Gate in The Hague *(p 115)*. While visiting him, Johan de Witt was the victim of an uprising and murdered with his brother near the prison *(p 115)*.

From the 17C to the present. – In the early 17C Dordrecht was supplanted by Amsterdam, then, above all by Rotterdam. The town became French in 1795.

Presently it is an expanding city due to its advantageous position which attracts numerous firms.

Industry is very varied: chemical, metallurgical (shipbuilding, aeronautics, electronics) and the building industry. The tertiary sector is highly developed.

★THE OLD TOWN *time: ½ day*

★ Great Church or Church of Our Lady (Grote- of O.L. Vrouwekerk) (C B). – Legend has it that the church was started by a young girl, St Sura, who, wishing to build a chapel to the Virgin and possessing only three *daalders,* saw, each time she prayed that three new coins were miraculously added to her treasure.

In fact a chapel existed in the Middle Ages. It was enlarged in the 13C, then in the 14C, but a fire destroyed the building in 1457. The present church, which is Protestant, was built between 1460-1502 in Brabant Gothic style *(qv)*.

The massive **tower** has remained unfinished because it sags on the north side: it ends in a terrace with four clock faces outlining its square shape.

The carillon (1949) consists of 49 bells.

Interior. – It is very large (108m - 354ft long) and imposing with its 56 pillars topped in Brabant Gothic style with crocket capitals.

The oak choir **stalls★** are finely carved by the Fleming Jan Terwen between 1538 and 1542 in the Renaissance style, and are amongst the most beautiful in the country.

The low reliefs on top of the backs of the last row, north side, depict secular triumphs notably those of Emperor Charles V; south side, religious triumphs. There are also lovely cheekpieces and misericords carved with fantastic subjects.

The baroque chancel screen (1744) is elegant. In a chapel of the ambulatory on the east side, three stained glass windows depict episodes in the town's history: flood of 1421, fire of 1457 and capture of the town in 1480.

The pulpit (1756) with a marble base is in the rococo style. The **organ** was built in 1671 by Nicolaas van Hagen of Antwerp. 17 and 18C stone slabs pave the church floor.

Access to the tower. – 279 steps. On the way up there is a view of a 1626 clock. From the top terrace, there is a superb **view★★** over the old town where the houses huddle together along the canals and docks; note the length of the roofs: on the banks of the canals space was so costly that one preferred to build houses in depth. One can also see the rivers which circle round the town, spanned by large bridges, and modern Dordrecht.

To the right of the tower, the bridge (Leuvebrug) over the Voorstraathaven has four **low reliefs** sculptured in stone in 1937 by **Hildo Krop** (1884-1970); in naive style they depict a prisoner, a baker, a dairywoman and an apothecary-surgeon.

Blauw Gateway or Catharijne Gateway (Blauwpoort or Catharijnepoort) (C D). – Near this very simple gateway, dating from 1652, there are warehouses and a beautiful patrician house with a perron, the 18C **Beverschaep (C E)**: its door is topped by a naiad and a triton embracing; on the pediment a sheep *(schaap)* and a beaver *(bever)* frame the coat of arms.

Nieuwehaven (C). – Pleasure boats find shelter in this dock with shaded quays.

★Simon van Gijn Museum (Museum Mr. Simon van Gijn) (C M¹). – This lovely residence ⊘ (1729) was bequeathed to the town, with its contents, by the banker Simon van Gijn (1836-1922), a great art collector.

Inside one can admire an elegant decor, lovely fireplaces, rich furnishings, tapestries, paintings, silver, glass and porcelain show cases.

⊘ In the music room, on the ground floor, an **organ** (1785) has been restored.

On the 2nd floor, are scale models of ships (note the Bleiswijk, belonging to the Dutch India Company), costumes, earthenware, porcelain and toys, including dolls' shops and houses. The ground floor of the **toy house** is also interesting.

From the north bank of Nieuwehaven, there is a fine **view** over the dock overlooked by the Great Church with its clerestory, its transept and its massive tower. The view is also lovely over the Kuipershaven lined with warehouses.

Kuipershaven (CD). – Numerous barges are crammed into this old quay of coopers formerly devoted to the wine trade.

At nos 41-42, a barrel is shown on the grill forming a transom window above the door. In the transom window of no 48 a basket is depicted.

Groothoofds Gate (Groothoofdspoort) (D). – It was the main gate (1618) to the town. Topped by a dome it is covered on both sides with ornaments and low reliefs in sandstone. From the quay, situated on the north side, there is a fine **view★** over the wide confluence of the Merwede, the Noord and the Oude Maas Rivers. Boat traffic is particularly intensive as dusk falls.

On the other side of the gate near the lever bridge, the **Wijnhaven** (wine port) a dock for pleasure boats, and the chapel pinnacle make a colourful picture.

Wijnstraat (CD). – Another evocation of the wine *(wijn)* trade, this unevenly paved street is lined with picturesque houses, all lop-sided. Some are Renaissance, still with crow-stepped gables (nos 73-75; with the emblem of a cock: no 85), others in Louis XIV style (no 87).

Cross the canal.

Around this central canal are the city's oldest residences.

Voorstraat (CD). – Very commercial, this is the town's main street. There are some interesting façades: at no 178 the façade has a lovely rococo decor; at no 188 is **Munt Gate** (Muntpoort - **D K**) of 1555.

At the beginning of the pedestrian precinct, on the left, near the Augustijnen Church, (Augustijnenkerk), at no 214 a porch gives on to **Het Hof** (**D L**), the former Court of Justice where the States General met in 1572.

Opposite the Het Hof, at the corner of an alley leading to a bridge, there is a fine Renaissance façade with two-coloured tympana decorated with sculptured heads.

Scheffersplein (CD 42). – This is the market place; in the middle there is a 19C statue of the painter Ary Scheffer *(qv)*.

Visstraat (C 54). – This street which means Fish Street, leads to Dordrecht's very modern commercial quarter.

At no 7 there is a lovely small Renaissance house, **De Crimpert Salm** (**C N**) (1608). Very elaborate, it has a façade stone depicting a salmon *(zalm)* and is topped by a lion. As is usual in Dordrecht, the windows are framed with mouldings coming down to corbels.

Cross the bridge towards Groenmarkt.

Views over the canal, which is narrow here, and the old town hall, a white neo-classical building. On the bridge there is a monument (1922) to the De Witt brothers.

Groenmarkt (C 9). – Former vegetable market. On the right, at no 39, the **De Sleutel** house (**C Q**) has a façade decorated with a key *(sleutel)* and tympana with recessed orders. Dating from 1540, it is the oldest in the town.

At no 53, there is a fine façade with ogee-shaped tympana.

Grote Kerksbuurt (C 14). – The house at no 56 has a charming façade with crow-stepped gables.

ADDITIONAL SIGHTS

⊙**Museum of Dordrecht** (Dordrechts Museum) (D M²). – This museum contains an interesting collection of paintings.

Notably there are works of 17C painters born in the town, such as Aelbert Cuyp, Nicolaes Maes as well as Van Goyen and the works of The Hague School and the Amsterdam School. Among the works (paintings, drawings, sculptures) of the 18 and 19C there are a few canvases by Ary Scheffer *(qv)*. Several 20C art movements are also represented. The museum also holds temporary exhibitions.

Arend Maartenshof (D R). – This old almshouse (1625) has kept its original character with small low houses surrounding a courtyard.

EDAM North Holland   Pop 24 251 (with Volendam)

Michelin map **408** folds 10 and 11

An important cheese centre, Edam is a small, quiet and charming town, crossed by canals still lined with a few fine 17C houses. It is overlooked by **Speel Tower** (Speeltoren), a tall tower with a carillon, the remains of a church demolished in the 19C. In fact, it was formerly a busy port of the Zuiderzee, known for its shipyards.

Edam cheese. – Originally made in Edam, it is now made in several regions. Prepared with slightly skimmed milk, it is similar to Gouda *(qv)* with its smooth texture, but it differs by its easily indentifiable shape: a ball with a yellow crust, covered with a thin red coating if it is for export.

SIGHTS

Dam. – In the centre of town, and crossed by Voorhaven Canal, this, the main square, is overlooked by the 18C **town hall** (stadhuis), topped by a pinnacle.

⊙A lovely house (1540) contains the small local museum, **Museum of Edam** (Edams Museum).

Kaasmarkt. – On this square, the former cheese market, stands the **weigh house** (Kaaswaag) where cheese was weighed. Decorated with painted panels, the weigh

⊙house contains an **exhibit** concerning cheese making.

⊙**Great Church or St Nicholas's** (Grote- of St-Nicolaaskerk). – Dating from the 15C, the church has lovely early 17C stained glass windows and a fine organ.

Michelin map **408** fold 18 or **212** fold 18
Plan of built-up area and town plan in the current Michelin Red Guide Benelux

A very important industrial centre, and in constant development, Eindhoven had hardly 5 000 inhabitants in 1900. Since then it has grown, as well as its outlying area, into an industrial centre: there are now tobacco factories (cigars), paper making and textile industries, the largest factory for dairy products in the country, the large DAF Trucks automobile factories and electrical industries.

The "city of light". – It is mainly to the Philips Company that the town owes its spectacular expansion. Founded in 1891, this family firm's main activity was the manufacture of electric light bulbs; it then employed 26 workers. Today, in Eindhoven, it employs 40 000 people, 11% of the company's workforce throughout the world.
Its activities have considerably varied, apart from bulbs, it makes radios and televisions, video-tape recorders, tape recorders, record players, household appliances, audiovisual systems, electronic components, etc.
Eindhoven also has a well-known engineering school, the Technische Hogeschool.

A modern city. – Although industrial and laid out with a recent urban plan, Eindhoven is a pleasant city. Bustling commercial activity prevails, notably in the pedestrian precincts such as Demer.
The city is remarkably equipped with recreational activities, parks and green spaces, like the **De IJzeren Man**, to the east, and has a municipal theatre (built in 1964). The surrounding wooded areas of Kempenland *(qv)* offer numerous walks. 13km - 8 miles from the city, the **Eurostrand** recreation park provides the inhabitants of this large city with vast spaces for leisure.
The Eindhoven carnival is very animated *(see the chapter Practical Information at the end of the guide).*

★**EVOLUON** *time: 1½ hours*

Situated on the edge of town, Evoluon, created by the Philips Company, and designed by the architects Kalff and De Bever, is an immense building (1966) resting on 12 V-shaped concrete pillars and looking like a flying saucer.
It contains an important exhibition set on several superimposed rings, which is devoted to the evolution of science and technology. Various art objects embellish the decor.
On the vault, which is not held up by any pillar, there is a gigantic suspended reproduction of a polypropylene molecule.

(After photo Evoluon, Eindhoven)

Evoluon

The visitor watches with interest the different stages of the exhibition and manipulates the various scientific apparatuses, games and tests.

Take the elevator to reach the first balcony of ring 3 then continue the visit downwards.

Ring 3, the largest, with two balconies, is devoted to the problems of demographic expansion in the world and the influence of science and technology on life in society.
Ring 2, concerns technology and techniques, notably electricity and electronics.
Ring 1, the smallest, shows the role played by industry (manufacture of a television set).

★**VAN ABBE MUSEUM** (STEDELIJK VAN ABBEMUSEUM) *time: 1½ hours*

Separated from the town hall by the Dommel, which runs through its lovely gardens, this building was bequeathed to the town in 1936 by the industrialist H.J. van Abbe. Enlarged in 1978 the museum inside exhibits, in rotation, a rich collection of paintings and sculpture from 1900 to the present, concentrating especially on contemporary, as from 1945. The museum also has temporary exhibitions of contemporary art.
The permanent collection, which is never entirely shown, consists of the whole evolution of modern art through: the Cubism of Picasso, Braque, Juan Gris; Orphism or poetic interpretation of the real with Delaunay, Chagall, Fernand Léger; the De Stijl movement *(qv)* with Mondrian, Van Doesburg; Constructivism with a great number of works by El Lissitzky, Expressionism of Kokoschka, Kandinsky, Permeke; Surrealism with Miró, Ernst, Pieter Ouborg, Francis Bacon.
After the war the young Paris School was marked by abstract painters such as Bazaine, Sam Francis (born in California), Poliakoff. The COBRA movement *(qv)* is represented by Karel Appel, Asger Jorn, Corneille. Apart from subject-matter painters such as Dubuffet, Tàpies, there are also works by Vasarely, Lucio Fontana, Klein, the Zero group (Mack, Piene and Uecker), the Americans of Pop Art including Morris Louis, Robert Indiana, Frank Stella. Conceptual Art (Kosuth, Barry, Brouwn, Kawara), minimal art (Judd, Andre, Sol LeWitt) and contemporary German sculpture (Kiefer, Baselitz, Penck) are also represented.

ADDITIONAL SIGHTS

Town Hall (Stadhuis). – Not far from the old town hall, rebuilt in 1865 in the neo-Gothic style, this modern building, designed by the architect J. van de Laan, was built in 1965-9.

On the square stands a **monument** in memory of the Liberation carved by the Dutchman Paul Grégoire in 1954, it depicts three men leaping towards the sky in pursuit of a dove.

⊙ **Animali.** – *Roostenlaan 303.* This flower garden has, apart from flocks of swans and pink flamingos, a large collection of rare birds, as well as packs of monkeys.

⊙ **Kempenland Museum.** – *St.-Antoniusstraat 5-7.* Installed in the old church of St Anthony of Padua, this museum evokes the history and customs of the town and its surroundings, Kempenland *(qv).* The collections, exhibited in rotation, concern archaeology, beliefs, textile industry, handicrafts: note the clocks made in Eindhoven *c*1800.
Temporary exhibitions concerning history and art are organised.

EXCURSION

★ **De Groote Peel.** – *38km - 23½ miles. Leave by ② on the town plan.*

Helmond. – Pop 63 909. Helmond is mainly devoted to textile manufacture. The trade is very active here, particularly in the pedestrian precincts near Markt.

⊙ Set in the middle of a park, the medieval **castle**★ is an imposing quadrilateral surrounded by moats, cantoned with round towers and surrounding an interior courtyard. It contains the municipal museum.

Asten. – Pop 14 586. To the northwest, a modern building houses two museums.

⊙ The **National Carillon Museum**★ (Nationaal Beiaardmuseum) has information on bell making, a collection of small bells from all over the world, a series of weight-driven clocks and striking clocks, and a large drum carillon with visible mechanism.

⊙ The **Nature Museum** (Natuurstudiecentrum en Museum Jan Vriends) houses a series of stuffed animals, butterflies, insects, a reproduction of the land and fauna of De Peel and an aquarium with species found in the Peel lakes.
To the southeast of Asten stretches a large marshy zone called **De Peel** *(peel* means marsh). The lakes mark the site of former peat bogs.

★ **De Groote Peel.** – *Access to the south by Moostdijk, near*
⊙ *Meijelse Dijk.* It is a **national park** of about 1 300ha - 3 211 acres consisting of peat bogs, moors and large stretches of water. This environment which is humid and not very fertile attracts numerous birds.
Hundreds of **black-headed gulls** *(kokmeeuwen)* come to breed here (from mid-March to mid-July). This gull is about 40cm-16in long and is white but in summer, its head becomes completely black. It can be found on the coasts in winter, but it often comes to

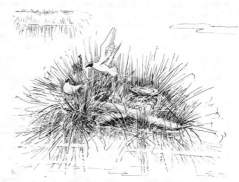

The black-headed gulls of De Groote Peel

nest inland, notably near the lakes. In early spring, black-headed gulls come in thousands to make very neat nests between the clumps of reeds which cover the submerged roots.
Males and females share the task of sitting on the eggs and jealously defending their nest. They make an unceasing noise with their strident and not very harmonious call.

⊙ A small **museum** (Bezoekerscentrum Mijl op Zeven) installed in a typical farmhouse in the Peel has documentation on the nature reserve's formation, which became a national park in 1985, and its flora and fauna.
Three signposted footpaths make it possible to discover this strange universe stirred by the shrill cries of the gulls.

Join us in our never ending task of keeping up to date.

Send us your comments and suggestions, please.

Michelin Tyre Public Limited Company
Tourism Department
Davy House – Lyon Road – HARROW – Middlesex HA1 2DQ.

Michelin map **408** north of fold 13 – Local map p 133

A prosperous market centre, Emmen is a pleasant town bordered to the north and the east by fine forests. The southern end of the Hondsrug *(qv)* has numerous *hunebeds (qv)*, prehistoric funerary monuments.

SIGHTS

★ **Hunebed of Emmer-dennen** (D 45). – *Access by Boslaan, direction Emmer Compascuum. It is situated near a large crossroads, and indicated.*

This remarkable *hunebed,* an alleyway covered with six enormous slabs encircled by uprights, was erected on a mound right in the forest. Its overall beauty attracts painters.

Hunebed of Emmerdennen

Hunebeds along the Odoorn road. – Several megaliths appear one after the other from the south to the north. *After the last farm bear left on a path signposted* "hunebed". Between the trees there is a **hunebed★** (D 43); the shape of the burial mound has been reconstructed and two covered alleyways are hidden. The whole is surrounded by uprights between which are piles of rocks which hold up the earth *(illustration p 132).*

A few hundred yards further to the north, on the left side of the road, there is a small *hunebed* (D 41) covered with capstones.

On leaving Emmen, on the right, a lane marked *hunebedden* goes through the forest to a large clearing of heather. Three *hunebeds* (D 38/40) stand in this lovely setting: one is half buried, the second, also buried, is in the shape of a square, the third is covered with fallen stones.

★ **Zoological Garden** (**Noorder Dierenpark**). – This zoo is interesting for the abundance and ⊘ variety of the species shown.

Several exhibit areas are particularly interesting. In an enormous aviary there are birds from South American tropical forests. A tropical garden houses more than a thousand butterflies. The seal pool and the "Africanium", which incorporates a series of greenhouses, a natural history museum, and an ethnographical museum, are other attractions.

Finally, on a vast strip of land (1.5ha - 4 acres) giraffes, zebras, antilopes, rhinoceroses, cranes, and impalas all live together.

EXCURSIONS

★ **Orvelte.** – *40km - 25 miles to the west – local map p 133.*

Noordsleen. – This charming village of the Drenthe, with a restored mill, has two **hunebeds**. *Access by the small road from Zweeloo and a lane on the right marked* hunebedden *(D 51).* On the left, is a small covered alleyway still topped by three capstones (four have disappeared). Further on the right, the **hunebed★** (D 50) shaded by a large oak which grows in its centre, is better preserved. Five slabs are still in place as well as the oval crown of upright stones. The entry pillars to the south, which have been leveled, are still visible.

Schoonoord. – *3.5km - 2¼ miles to the south of the locality,* in the woods near a riding centre, a *hunebed* (D 49) has been partially reconstructed. Between the uprights there are pebbles. Above, the heather-covered ground forms a mound and hides the large slabs which form the *hunebed's* roof. This *hunebed* is called **De Papeloze Kerk** (church without a priest); congregations met here at the beginning of the Reformation

★ **Orvelte.** – This museum-village situated in the heart of the Drenthe consists of a group of farmhouses, barns with thatched roofs, which, due to restoration, have kept their regional character. *Access forbidden to cars.*

With traditional agricultural activities (cow and sheep breeding, growing of maize), handicraft work has developed: blacksmiths, potters...

Coevorden. – Pop 14 208. *21km - 13 miles to the southwest.* An old fortified town, Coevorden has kept several interesting monuments.

The **castle** (kasteel) is a fine building flanked by a corner turret, with walls of rose-coloured roughcast and pierced in the left part of the façade (15C) by tall narrow windows. Part of it is occupied by the town hall; in the basement there is a restaurant.

Near Markt *(Friesestraat no 9),* there is a picturesque late Renaissance **house** with voluted gables and ornamentation: bright red shells, heads of women, cherubs, Moors, and inscriptions.

On Markt, facing the docks, are the three 17C roofs of the Arsenal (restored), which ⊘ contains the **"Drenthe's Veste" Museum.**

To the east, beyond Weyerswold (6km - 3½ miles) typical thatched cottages of the Drenthe stand beside innumerable small oil wells. In this respect the **Schoonebeek** region is in fact very rich.

Michelin map **408** fold 11

Enkhuizen was the residence of the Frisian chiefs until 1289, when West Friesland was united to the Holland earldom. It was a very flourishing port where herring fishing was most prosperous; the town has kept three herrings on its coat of arms.

Fortified in the middle of the 16C it was one of the first towns to revolt against the Spanish in 1572. Towards 1600 its walls were rebuilt. In the 17C it had a population of 50 000. The silting up of the port in the 18C, and the construction of the large IJssel Lake dike in 1932 put a stop to its shipping activity.

Since then it has turned towards its hinterland. The richness of the surrounding land has made it an important market town and bulb cultivation centre. Its ramparts have been made into an esplanade.

A dike road *(31km - 19 miles)* edging the future Markerwaard polder *(see map p 17)*, links it to Lelystad, Flevoland's main town.

Enkhuizen was the birthplace of **Paulus Potter** (1625-54), the famous animal painter, whose best known painting, *Young Bull,* hangs in the Mauritshuis in The Hague.

Ⓥ **Boat trips.** – Enkhuizen is the departure point for boat trips to Stavoren *(p 168)* and Urk *(p 154)* and Medemblik *(p 93)* in connection with the tourist railway *(p 93)*. *Departure: Spoorhaven.*

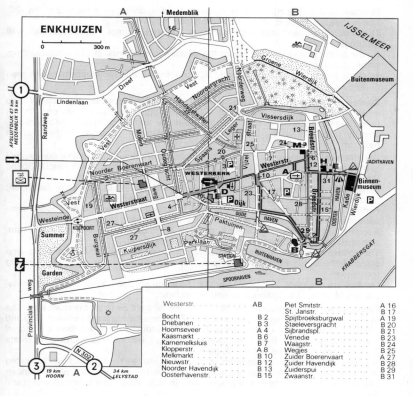

Westerstr.	AB	Piet Smitstr.	A	16
Bocht	B 2	St. Janstr.	B	17
Drebanen	B 3	Spijtbroeksburgwal	A	19
Hoornseveer	A 4	Staeleversgracht	B	20
Kaasmarkt	B 6	Sijbrandspl.	B	21
Karnemelksluis	B 7	Venedie	B	23
Klopperstr.	A 8	Waagstr.	B	24
Melkmarkt	B 10	Wegjes	B	25
Nieuwstr.	B 12	Zuider Boerenvaart	A	27
Noorder Havendijk	B 13	Zuider Havendijk	B	28
Oosterhavenstr.	B 15	Zuiderspui	B	29
		Zwaanstr.	B	31

★ OLD TOWN time: 5 hours

It has kept numerous 17C façades in the Renaissance style, their fine decoration bearing witness to its former prosperity.

Westerstraat (AB). – It is the town's main street. There are lovely façades, notably that of no 158 to the north, dating from 1617 with the town emblem on a gable: a young girl bearing a coat of arms depicting three herrings.

Ⓥ **West Church or St Gommarus's** (Westerkerk of St.-Gomaruskerk) (AB). – It is a 15 and 16C building. Its isolated wooden tower built in the 16C on a stone base was rebuilt in the 19C in the neo-classical style. The hall-type interior has three naves of equal height, covered with a wooden vault. There is also a fine wooden **rood-screen★** with six richly carved panels (16C), tympana, pulpit (both 16C), a replica of the one found in the Great Church in The Hague, and a 1547 organ case.

Opposite the church is the former **Mint** of West Friesland (West-Friese Munt) (**B E**) with a lovely, finely decorated 15C façade.

Further on at no 109 the façade of the **Orphanage** (Weeshuis) (**B D**) has been rebuilt after the original façade (1616).

Turn right to take Melkmarkt and Venedie.

Dijk (B). – This quay runs alongside the old port (Oude Haven). At no 32, a house (1625) displays the motto: "Contentement passe rychesse" (happiness is worth more than riches).

★ **Dromedaris** (B B). – This imposing and well-known building (now a restaurant) which
ⓣ was part of the town's enclosure was, like that of Hoorn *(qv)*, intended for keeping
watch over the entrance to the port. It consists of a semi-circular tower and an edifice
built on to it with a door. It has a carillon cast by Hemony, which is one of the best in
the country.

From the top there is a vast **panorama★** of Enkhuizen, its port, IJssel Lake and in the
distance Friesland.

From the quay to the south of the tower, there is a fine **view★** to the east over the docks
(Zuiderspui) and the backs of houses with picturesque wooden galleries overlooking
flowered gardens.

To the south is Buitenhaven, the pleasure boat harbour.

Zuiderspui (B 29). – This short street is lined with interesting façades: no 1 has
five polychrome coats of arms, from left to right can be seen those of Hoorn
(a horn), the House of Orange, West Friesland (two lions), Enkhuizen and
Medemblik.

Breedstraat (B). – Several houses have interesting façade stones notably: no 81,
called Den Kuiser Maegt (the young girl from Enkhuizen), depicting the town's coat
of arms, no 60 an old boat and no 59 a young girl also holding the town's coat of
arms.

Town Hall (Stadhuis) (B H). – It is an imposing building dating from the end of the 17C.
Above the door there is an excerpt from a poem by Vondel *(qv)*.

The interior is decorated with paintings, painted ceilings, tapestries and wall
paintings.

On the corner of Zwaanstraat stands the **old prison** (gevangenis) (B F) a small building,
whose picturesque façade dates from 1612.

From the bridge and over to the right, old boats, from Zuiderzee Museum, can be seen
docked along Oosterhaven quay.

★ **Zuiderzee Museum (Zuiderzeemuseum)** (B). – The museum is made-up of two
ⓣ museums: one is in the Pepperpot (Peperhuis) opposite IJssel Lake, on Wierdijk
(*wier:* seaweed); built in 1625, it is an old home and a warehouse, which subsequently belonged to the Dutch East India Company. The other is the open-air
museum.

★ **Indoor Museum** (Binnenmuseum). – On the corner, the house with a double crow-stepped
gable has kept its sculptured stone façade in the shape of a ship and the motto Spend
first to gain later *(De kost gaet voor de baet uyt)*.

In the **main hall** there are old boats, mostly **sailing ships** having sailed on the Zuiderzee;
note the flat-bottomed *tjotters* and the *ijsvlet* from Urk which slid on ice.

Further on, figureheads can be seen next to *hakkeborden,* a kind of wooden tympanum carved with religious themes, which decorated the ship's stern.

A large room contains magnificent **furniture** *(pp 28-29)* carved or painted as in Workum,
Jisp and Assendelft *(illustration p 29),* and sledges.

The following rooms house a handicraft section, models of fishing boats and
ships of the Dutch East India Company, as well as a section devoted to fishing
techniques.

Costumes are displayed in typical interiors: Terschelling, Zaan, West Friesland, Hindeloopen, Marken, Urk, Spakenburg and Volendam.

★★ **Outdoor Museum** (Buitenmuseum). – *Access to the car park via ② on the town plan.* The
open-air museum evokes daily life in the old Zuiderzee fishing ports between 1880 and
1932, completion date of the Barrier Dam (Afsluitdijk) *(qv)*. More than a hundred
houses and workshops from about twenty localities have been reconstructed to create
the picturesque quarters of this village-museum.

A meticulous and faithful rendition of the old Zuiderzee region has been recreated
in the house and shop interiors, garden layouts, the church from old Wieringen
Island and the reconstruction of Marken port in 1830, where the odour of tannin still
floats...

ⓣ **Weigh House Museum (Stedelijk Waagmuseum)** (B M³). – On Kaasmarkt, or cheese
market, this fine building (1559) with curved gables, painted shutters and polychrome
coats of arms, is the old weigh house where cheese and butter trading took place. It
is now the municipal museum.

There is a dentist's office of 1920 *(in the basement)* and an 18C delivery room. A spiral
staircase leads to the **surgeons room** installed in 1636; the members of this guild used
this fine room for their meetings.

Note the painted panelling, the rostrum and the small room where the students waited
before taking their exams.

The attic is used for temporary art exhibitions.

Return to Westerstraat.

In the eastern section of the street there are also lovely gables, shop signs and façade
stones (a cooking-pot, a bull's head, etc).

ⓣ **South Church (Zuider of St.-Pancraskerk** (B A). – It is flanked with a fine Gothic tower, the
wooden cap of which was added in the 16C. Its carillon was cast by the Hemony
brothers.

ADDITIONAL SIGHT

ⓣ **Summer Garden** (A). – Near the old ramparts, this lovely garden with attractive
parterres reminds one that the region is devoted to the cultivation of flowers.

EXCURSION

Medemblik. – Pop 6 890. *21km - 13 miles to the north* (A). Medemblik which was granted its city charter in 1289 became the capital of West Friesland; it was already part of the Hanseatic League. Today it is one of old Zuiderzee's *dode steden,* ghost towns. The dike which limits the Wieringermeer Polder *(p 134),* to the east, starts at Medemblik. To the north of the town the Lely pumping station is this polder's most important drying out station.

A **tourist railway** links the town to Hoorn *(p 92)* while boat service runs between Medemblik and Enkhuizen.

The town has kept some interesting old houses with lovely façade stones, particularly in **Nieuwstraat,** the main street (no 26: a 1613 façade which has a lintel bearing four coats of arms.

At the far end of this street, the **weigh house** (Waag) has a crow-stepped façade decorated with a carved façade stone depicting scales. The **Westerhaven,** a quay stretching along one of the port's two main docks, retains several fine houses (nos 9 to 14, with crow-stepped gables, no 16, no 20). In Torenstraat, which begins at Westerhaven, the old **orphanage** (Weeshuis) has a door topped with a naive low relief depicting four orphans (18C).

Finally **Oosterhaven**★ has some of the finest old façades. Note nos 22, 43 and 44 decorated with carved stones. At the far end of the quay there is a **view** over IJssel Lake.

⊘ **Radbod Castle** (Kasteel) stands on the opposite side of Oosterhaven. It was built in the 8C by Radbod, King of Frisia. About 1288 the Count of Holland, Floris V, fortified and altered it. Only one restored part exists today, surrounded by moats, the rest having been destroyed in the 17 and 18C.

The castle houses a small **museum:** coins, pitchers, etc from excavations.

ENSCHEDE Overijssel   Pop 144 227

Michelin map ▓▓▓ fold 13

Enschede, situated in Twente, a verdant area, is the largest town in Overijssel province. An important industrial centre, it specialises mainly in textiles.

Its rapid expansion due to the development of industry only started at the beginning of the century. Severely damaged by fire in 1862 and bombarded in 1944, it is, today, a modern city.

The vast campus of **Twente Technical University** (Technische Hogeschool Twente), established in 1964, lies northwest of town.

Twente and the textile industry. – Rich in running water which made it possible to wash the fibres and work the looms, Twente, formerly specialised in the processing of linen, which they cultivated, retted, spun and wove on the spot. **Almelo** *(qv)* was the centre of this activity. Twente linen was exported to Norway and to Russia where the Vriezenveen (7km - 4 miles to the north of Almelo) merchants had founded a colony near St Petersburg.

In the 18C, linen was replaced by cotton, less costly, at the same time they produced in large quantities a twill of linen and cotton called bombasine *(bombazijn).* In the early 19C weaving and spinning production were industrialised with the development of looms driven by steam-power.

The metallurgical industry also developed greatly at this time; in 1960, together with the textile industry, it represented 86% of industrial activity. Since then, the expansion in the production of artificial fibres, foreign competition and economic recession have considerably affected the textile industry.

Presently, alongside heavy metallurgy and that of processing, the building industry and the tertiary sector are developing.

★TWENTE MUSEUM (RIJKSMUSEUM TWENTHE) (Y M[1]) *time: 1 hour*

⊘ The building erected in 1930 from plans by Muller and Beudt has been largely converted. The museum has a fine series of paintings by a number of famous artists, from the Primitives to the present and ethnographical collections concerning the eastern part of the Netherlands and the frontier zone with Germany (prehistory, history, popular arts and traditions).

In the prehistoric section there are a number of objects discovered in the Twente, burial mounds and tombs as well as in the *hunebeds (qv)* which no longer exist.

A room of **sacred art** groups sculptures, paintings and *objets d'art.*

In the garden, a half-timbered farmhouse of the los hoes type *(p 32)* has been reconstructed, the interior being a vast space, without any partitions, shared by both men and beasts.

The rich **painting section,** both ancient and modern, includes portraits by Holbein the Younger, Cranach, a landscape by Momper, the *Wood Gatherers* by Bruegel the Younger, a *View of Nijmegen* by Van Goyen, etc.

Among the more recent works there is a canvas by Jongkind painted while he was staying in Rotterdam, a *View of the Cliffs Near Pourville* by Claude Monet, works by the members of COBRA *(qv)* and paintings and objects by contemporary Dutch artists.

The museum has a Lenten veil *(hongerdoek)* from Germany; it is a curtain which separates the chancel from the nave during Lent.

Manuscripts and incunabula can be seen next to champlevé ivory and enamel objects.

The museum houses a fine collection of Delftware tiles.

ENSCHEDE

ADDITIONAL SIGHTS

⊙ **Textile Industry Museum** (Textielindustriemuseum) (Z M²). – Located in an old textile mill – opened in 1900 and closed in the 1960s – the museum's collections illustrate the evolution of the textile industry encountered in the Twente *(qv)* over the past 150 years.

Workers' interiors, which have been recreated, show the results of this evolution on living conditions (cottage industry and rural life; then the move to the city to be closer to the factory with all it entails, increased comfort...). Also displayed are the tools used through the different periods: spinning wheels, winding machines and looms.

⊙ **Museum of Natural History** (Natuurmuseum) (YZ M³). – Well presented this museum contains remarkable collections.

On the ground floor are minerals, fossils, mostly discovered in the region, shells etc. The 1st floor is devoted to fauna: **dioramas** show the main species of mammals and birds found in the Netherlands, aquariums and small ponds for reptiles; one room evokes whale hunting.

In the basement there are precious stones as well as others which are radio-active and fluorescent.

Volkspark (YZ). – To the southeast of this park, one of the many green areas of Enschede, there is a monument (Z **D**) erected to the memory of victims of World War II: a group of bronze statues (a hostage, people in the Resistance, etc) by the sculptor **Mari Andriessen.**

Town Hall (Stadhuis) (YZ **H**). – Built by G. Friedhoff in 1933, it is inspired by Stockholm's town hall. This brick building, somewhat austere, is flanked by a high square bell tower with slightly bulging walls.

Reformed Church (Hervormde Kerk) (Y **A**). – This sandstone church stands on Markt, the town's main square. Begun *c*1200, it was enlarged in the 15C but has kept its great Romanesque **tower** (13C), with its paired openings. The spire was added in the beginning of the century.

EXCURSION

Round tour of 80km - 50 miles. – *Time: about 5 hours. Leave by ④ on the town plan.*

The route crosses the north part of **Twente.** Known for its industrial activities, Twente is also a verdant region where the land, cut by waterways, is divided into pastures and magnificent forests.

Scattered throughout the area are large farms with wooden gables and sometimes half-timbered walls.

Oldenzaal. – Pop 29 188. This small industrial town, near the German frontier, is an old, once fortified city, which has kept its concentric streets round a lovely Romanesque
ⓥ church, **St Plecheln's Basilica** (St.-Plechelmusbasiliek).

A sanctuary existed here in 770. Dedicated to the English and Irish saint, St Plecheln the present edifice, with three naves and transept, dates from the early 12C.

The square bell tower, its massive aspect characteristic of the region, was built in the 13C. Since 1950 the church has held the title of basilica.

The interior has a very robust appearance. The groined vaulting of the nave leans on thick square pillars. The chancel and the south aisle were rebuilt in the Gothic style in the 15C. The south arm of the transept has a triptych (Adoration of the Magi) attributed to the Fleming, Pieter Coecke van Aelst. The baroque pulpit has vigorously carved figures. The modern organ is used for concerts.

ⓥ Not far away is the **Het Palthe Huis Museum** (on Marktstraat).

This house with its charming baroque façade was bequeathed to the Oldenzaal antiquities collection by the Palthe family and displays traditional objects in 17C style rooms. There is also a reconstructed apothecary's shop, and in the attic a 17C chair where a murderer was held for 110 days.

Denekamp. – Pop 12 139. This small town, situated in one of the loveliest parts of Twente has kept its strange tradition of *midwinterhorens,* which translated means horns of mid-winter. They are horns of carved wood which are blown at the approach of Christmas *(see the chapter Practical Information at the end of the guide)* in Twente villages; their origin remains mysterious.

ⓥ Near town stands **Singraven Castle** (kasteel).

A lovely road runs alongside the Dinkel, a small shaded and calm waterway where
ⓥ there is the lovely 15C Singraven **water mill** (watermolen van Singraven); grain is still ground here and wood is sawn; the building on the left houses a restaurant. The 17C **mansion** flanked by a square tower is reflected in the Dinkel, one of whose branches waters the magnificent park. The furniture, tapestries (Beauvais, Aubusson), porcelain collections, paintings (Salomon van Ruysdael, Van de Capelle) all add to the refined atmosphere of the 18C interior.

★ **Ootmarsum.** – Pop 4 265. Built on a mound, round a Gothic church, this charming village with concentric streets has been restored; lovely, elaborately decorated Renaissance façades and wooden gables can be admired.

ⓥ On Kerkplein stands **St Simon and St Judas** (kerk van de HH. Simon en Judas). This church is in the Romanesque-Gothic transitional style, which is reminiscent of Westphalian churches by the use of stone and by its thick square tower to the west (partly demolished). The apse is Gothic as well as the fourth bay. Inside, the polychrome colours highlight the lines of the pointed arches, the small columns and ribs. At the end of the north side aisle, there is a lovely statue in wood of the Virgin (c1500); in the aisles the modern stained glass windows depict saints; in the chancel there is a silver lamp. The organ in Westphalian style, has been restored *(concerts)*. In the display cabinets are gold and silver liturgical plate and a lovely chasuble (1749) embroidered with the effigy of the church patrons. On the south side aisle a tomb is used as a columbarium.

Take the road to Almelo

Kuiperberg. – From the belvedere on top of the Kuiperberg (alt 65m - 213ft) there is a **view** over Ootmarsum and the wooded countryside. Next to it, near the tower ruins, there is an old Jewish cemetery.

Via Almelo and Borne, go to Delden.

Delden. – Delden is an important agricultural market centre. Former residence of the Counts of Wassenaar, **Twickel Castle** (kasteel) stands to the north of town. Founded in the 14C, it was altered in the 16C (main door) and the 17C. It is surrounded by moats
ⓥ and lovely **gardens**.

Great Church or **St Blaise** (Grote- of St.-Blasiuskerk), this Gothic style stone hall-church, has a heavy square tower in front.

ⓥ The old town hall *(Langestraat 21)* houses both the VVV and a **salt museum** (Het Zoutmuseum). Located not far from the country's main rock salt deposits, the museum explains salt's origin, extraction and use, as well as its importance to men, animals and plants.

Hengelo. – Pop 76 714. Town plan in the current Michelin Red Guide Benelux. This commercial and industrial town (metallurgy, electricity, electronics, chemicals) has modern buildings, in particular the **town hall** (stadhuis), the work of Berghoef (1963). Since 1972, to the east of town, a new experimental residential quarter is being built by the architect Piet Blom.

Return to Enschede by ③ on the town plan.

★ FLEVOLAND Flevoland

Michelin map **408** folds 11 and 12 – Local map p 134

Flevoland is in fact two polders which form the most recent achievements in the Zuiderzee reclamation project *(p 133);* that of East Flevoland and South Flevoland.

East Flevoland Polder (Oostelijk-Flevoland). – It is the third polder created on IJssel Lake, after Wieringermeer Polder *(qv)* and the Northeast Polder *(p 150).*

An area of 54 000ha - 133 380 acres, it was diked and drained between 1950-7. The main part of this polder is destined for agriculture (75% of the area) while 10% of the land has been turned into meadows and woods, 8% for dwellings and the rest alloted to canals, roads and dikes. Before being exploited, the land was first sown with reeds. Farmhouses hidden behind curtains of poplars and enormous barns are scattered over this flat country, criss-crossed by clusters of young trees. Tall trees indicate an already old dwelling-place. In the fields, drained by ditches, sheep, cows and ponies graze.

There are numerous lapwings, golden pheasants and water birds such as the coot, a small dark wader whose black head has a white spot.

Since 1960 towns and villages have sprung up: Lelystad, Dronten, Swifterbant, Biddinghuizen; piles placed on a sand bed ensure the stability of the construction. Large straight roads cut across the polder. Some have been built on the ring dikes. Lakes such as the **Veluwe**, separating the polder from the Zuiderzee's former coast, act as regulators and have become recreation lakes with beaches.

South Flevoland Polder (Zuidelijk-Flevoland). – It is separated from the East Flevoland Polder by a security dike, the Knardijk, parts of the road being forbidden to traffic. It is surrounded by a dike built between 1959-67. In 1968 this polder of 43 000ha - 106 210 acres had largely been drained. Half the area is devoted to agriculture, 25 % to dwelling areas, 18% for meadows and woods. The rest is taken up by canals, dikes and roads.

To the north, near Oostvaarders dike, there is a nature reserve **De Oostvaardersplassen**. Very marshy, it is a refuge for birds including some very rare species.

Since 1975, **Almere**, a town with a pleasure boat harbour, is being built to the south on Gooi Lake; it should accommodate 150 000 inhabitants. Its lay-out has been carefully studied.

Another residential area, Zeewolde, is being built level with Harderwijk; planned for 25 000 inhabitants it already has a large pleasure boat harbour.

SIGHTS

The tour – allow 1 day – is recommended in May-June, at the time when rape is in flower; the countryside is then tinted with spots of very vivid yellow.

⊙ **Ketelhaven.** – Near this pleasure boat harbour, a **Museum of Maritime Archaeology** (Museum voor Scheepsarcheologie) houses remains of ship wrecks found at the bottom of the Zuiderzee, together with their contents: cargoes of goods, pottery, weapons, coins, shoes, pipes.

The oldest wreck exhibited goes back to Roman times (2C).

In the middle of the museum there is the skeleton of a large 17C merchant ship.

Flevohof. – *Indicated from the Elburg and Harderwijk bridges.*

⊙ Covering 150ha - 370 acres, this **amusement park** embellished with flowers is devoted to agriculture.

A round tour (numbered) is conducted through the exhibition buildings where one can find out about intensive production methods used in agriculture and breeding and in the treatment of products (milk, eggs, meat, potatoes, sugar, cereals, beer); the tour ends with the latest techniques in greenhouse cultivation of flowers and vegetables. Nearby, one can visit a vast model farm devoted to breeding (cows, pigs), the cheese museum (tools for making butter and cheese), an agricultural company and a remarkable rose garden. Various exhibitions, gardens, tropical greenhouses, parks as well as a children's village complete the visit.

Lelystad. – Lelystad, capital of Flevoland, bears the name of the engineer Lely *(qv).* This new town built to accommodate between 80 000 and 100 000 inhabitants consists mainly of low buildings. The **Agora,** a community building built in 1976 by Frank van Klingeren, marks the centre of the town.

Linked to Enkhuizen by the dike *(31km - 19 miles)* which borders the future Markerwaard polder, Lelystad is also linked to Amsterdam by a canal, the Oostvaardersdiep, 300m - 984ft wide, access being controlled by two locks, the Houtribsluizen.

Ship wreck (Scheepswrak). – *To the south of Lelystad. Access by the Oostranddreef; at the rotunda turn left, then the first road on the right, right again at the next crossroads. Nearby a narrow lane leads to the wreck.*

In the middle of cultivated land the skeleton of a 23m - 75ft long ship has been left where it was found during drainage of the polder in 1967. Called De Zeehond (the seal), dating from 1878, it transported bricks, a pile of which can be seen nearby.

Some of the ship's contents are exhibited in Ketelhaven's Museum of Maritime Archaeology *(see above).*

Dronten. – In the heart of the polder this new town extends mainly round a church with an openworked tower, and a community centre, **De Meerpaal**.

This immense glass hall, built in 1967 by Frank van Klingeren (see Lelystad's agora), is a closed agora, a prolongation of the main square. Built for collective cultural and sporting activities, it also houses in winter, a weekly market.

★ FRANEKER Friesland

Michelin map **4.0.8** fold 4

This small Frisian town (Frjentsjer) had a famous university founded in 1585, where Descartes became a student in 1629. It was closed in 1811 under the reign of Louis Bonaparte.

SIGHTS

★ **Town Hall (Stadhuis).** – A splendid building in the Dutch Renaissance style, dating from ⊘ 1591, with a double gable, it is topped by an elegant octagonal tower.
The Council Chamber *(ground floor at the end of the corridor)* and the Registrar's Office (Trouwzaal; *1st floor*) are hung with 18C painted leather, in rich colours.

★ **Planetarium.** – At the time when a number of his contemporaries feared the ⊘ end of the world due to the exceptional position of the stars, the Frisian **Eise Eisinga** decided to show that the situation was not dangerous. This wool-comber, who had been interested in astronomy since childhood, built 1774-81, an ingenious system where the movement of stars was depicted on his living room ceiling. Eisinga represented with surprising precision the celestial vault as known by 18C astronomers.
This planetarium, whose movement can be seen in the attic, is the oldest one in working order in Europe.
At the end of Eisingastraat, a charming **House of Corn Porters** (Korendragershuisje) can be seen.

⊘ **'t Coopmanshûs Museum.** – *Voorstraat.* Installed in the **weigh house** (waag) and in the neighbouring houses, including the lovely **Coopmanshûs** (1746), this municipal museum evokes the memory of **Anna Maria van Schuurman** (1606-78). This illustrious entomologist and draughtsman belonged to the Labadist sect founded by the French emigre **Jean de Labadie** (1610-74), who proposed bringing Protestantism back to Primitive Christianity. The history of the town and its university is illustrated by engravings and a scale model.
The museum, also, has fine collections of Frisian gold and silversmith's work and ceramics. In the attic there is a collection of old vehicles (cycles, sledges) and regional costumes, which are also worth noting.
In the same street (at no 35), the **Martenahuis** was built in 1498.

Church (Martinikerk). – Gothic, the church has 15C paintings, and figures of saints on the pillars. The ground is strewn with finely sculptured tombstones in the Frisian style.

Orphanage (Weeshuis). – The former orphanage's door is topped with 17C inscriptions. Nearby, the **Camminga-Stins** is a lovely residence of the 15-16C, now used by a bank (on the 1st floor, exhibition room of coins and medals).

The layout diagram on page 3 shows
*the **Michelin Maps** covering the country.*
In the text, reference is made to the map
which is the most suitable from a point of view
of scale and practicality.

★★ GIETHOORN Overijssel

Michelin map **4.0.8** fold 12

In a marshy region stands the small town of Giethoorn. It owes its name to the great number of wild goat horns *(geitenhoorns)* found in the area by the peat-workers. It is located on the edge of canals, built for the transportation of peat, the massive extraction of which, over the past centuries, has created lakes.

⊘ **Tour.** – *The village is forbidden to cars: it can either be visited on foot (a path runs alongside the main canal or via different types of boats (dinghy, sail, motor, with or without helmsman).*

A lakeside village. – The pretty thatched cottages of Giethoorn are surrounded by canals spanned by humpback bridges or simple footbridges. Their façades, with a flowered lawn in front, gives on to the main canal. Although the bicycle is the inhabitants' favourite vehicle much transportation is via water often by boats with a double bow called *punters.* Breeding, reed cutting and the tourist trade are Giethoorn's main activities. Bridal processions also use the canals.

Kameeldak roofs. – The hall-type farmhouses *(p 31)* are remarkable for their thatched cambered roofs. The increase of harvests, due to the amount of land reclaimed from water, obliged the inhabitants of Giethoorn to enlarge their farmhouses. Due to the exiguity of the land, they were enlarged upwards and the working building was slightly raised above the dwelling house, creating a difference in level (called *kameeldak,* meaning camel-back).
As all transportation is on water, the farmhouse has no carriage entrance; the hay is stored in a barn situated above the boat shed.

The lakes. – The lakes which stretch to the east and to the south of the village, great bodies of water separated by small reed-covered islands, are populated with many birds.

EXCURSION

Blokzijl. – *26km - 16 miles.*

Wanneperveen. – In this small town which, like many peat-bog villages has a name which ends in *veen* (peat-bog), thatched cottages run for several miles alongside a road planted with pear trees.
Not far from the village's west entrance, one can see the **cemetery** with its isolated bell tower scantily built with a few beams, characteristic of Southern Friesland; note in main street, at no 94, a lovely house with a crow-stepped gable, the **old town hall** (vroegere stadhuis).

Vollenhove. – It was a port situated on the edge of the Zuiderzee, before the drainage of the Northeast Polder.
On **Kerkplein** stand a few fine monuments: **St Nicholas** (St.-Nicolaaskerk), a late Gothic church with two naves and its old isolated bell tower, the **Klokketoren** which was used as a prison; built on to the bell tower is the **old town hall**, a 17C brick and sandstone porticoed building converted into a restaurant; finally the lovely façade with crow-stepped gables of the **Latin School** (1627) (now used by the VVV and a bank) has an entrance with two carved stelae in front.
From the church's east end one can see the bastions of the old ramparts where pleasure boats are moored.
The new town hall is housed in **Oldruitenborgh** manor-house, set in a park near a church (Kleine Kerk).

Blokzijl. – It was formerly a prosperous port on the Zuiderzee, which was part of the Hanseatic League and used as a refuge for ships of the Dutch India Company in the event of storms. Witness to these riches is a row of lovely 17C houses (restored) along the now sleepy quays.
Kerkstraat, which leads to the 17C church, is also picturesque.

The practical information chapter,
at the end of the guide, regroups

– a list of the local or national organisations
supplying additional information

– a section on times and charges.

GOES Zeeland   Pop 31 497

Michelin map **408** fold 16 or **212** fold 13 – Local map p 78
Town plan in the current Michelin Red Guide Benelux

Former small port, which owed its prosperity to the salt trade and the madder industry, Goes, today, is the main centre of South Beveland. The town is surrounded by meadows and orchards.
A canal links it to Eastern Scheldt estuary.
Goes has preserved, through the location of its canals, the layout of its 15C ramparts.
⊙ A small **steam tramway** (stoomtram) runs between Goes and Oudelande.

Jacqueline of Hainaut or Jacoba. – Former residence of the Counts of Zeeland, who had a castle here, Goes has kept the memory of the turbulent Jacoba, daughter of William VI, Duke of Bavaria. On his death in 1417 she inherited the earldoms of Hainaut, Holland and Zeeland, and was envied by many. She had a bone to pick with the Cods *(qv).* In 1421 she left her second husband John IV, Duke of Brabant, who had dispossessed her of the Holland earldom giving it to John of Bavaria, Jacoba's uncle and supporter of the Cods. The following year she married Humphrey, Duke of Gloucester, fourth son of King Henry IV, brother to King Henry V of England.
Later, to escape from the intrigues of Philip the Good, who had invaded her territories, she took refuge in Goes. She was forced by Philip to sign an agreement in Delft in 1428, *Treaty of Delft,* in which she recognised him as heir and promised never to remarry. The promise was soon broken (1432) and Jacqueline lost her title of countess (1433); three years later she died in Teilingen Castle, near Sassenheim.

Market day. – The weekly market on Goes's Grote Markt (Tuesdays) gives the occasional opportunity of seeing the Zeeland costumes of Zuid-Beveland *(qv).* The headdresses, above all, are very beautiful, square for Catholics and in the shape of a vast aureola for Protestants.

SIGHTS

Grote Markt. – This, the town's main square, is overlooked by the 15C **town hall**, which was altered in the 18C and has a rococo façade.

⊙ **Great Church or St Mary Magdalene (Grote- of Maria Magdalenakerk).** – Part of it was built in the 15C, and rebuilt in 1621 after a fire. The main nave is very high. Similar to the two transept portals of the Hooglandse Church in Leyden, the **north portal** is finely decorated in the Flamboyant style, and has a wide window topped by an openworked gable.
⊙ Inside the church has a remarkable 17C **organ**, crowned with a canopy in the 18C.

Turfkade. – *To the north of Grote Markt.* This "peat" quay is lined with lovely crow-stepped gabled façades.

EXCURSION

Yerseke. – *15km - 9 miles east by ② on the town plan – local map p 78.*

⊙ **Kapelle.** – Pop 10 012. The **church** stands out by its imposing 14C bell tower, cantoned with pinnacles.
In the nave note the decorated balusters and heads of satyrs. The main chancel, decorated wiith Gothic blind arcading in red brick contains a 17C tomb.
Next to the village cemetery, to the west, there is a **French military cemetery** where French soldiers killed in the Netherlands in 1940 are buried.

Yerseke (or Ierseke). – This small port on the Eastern Scheldt specialises in oyster and mussel cultures and in the breeding of lobsters. The Eastern Scheldt Dam *(qv)* has floodgates which makes it possible for Yerseke to benefit from tides and continue its activities.

Except where otherwise stated,
all recommended itineraries in towns, are designed as walks.

GORINCHEM South Holland   Pop 28 016

Michelin map **408** folds 17 and 18 or **212** folds 6 and 7

On the borders of three provinces (South Holland, North Brabant and Gelderland) Gorinchem, often called **Gorkum** is an important waterway junction, at the confluence of two large rivers, the Waal (branch of the Rhine) and the Maas, as well as the Merwedekanaal and a small river, the Linge.
It has a large pleasure boat harbour to the west.

Hooks (Hoeken) and Cods (Kabeljauwen). – Gorkum dates from the 13C. Due to its strategic position it has suffered numerous sieges.
In 1417 it was the stake of a ferocious fight between the Hooks, supporters of **Jacoba** *(qv)* who had inherited the town, and **William of Arkel,** on the side of the Cods. The latter wished to reconquer the town, which had belonged to his father. He lost his life during a skirmish in the city.
Gorkum was one of the first strongholds wrested from the Spanish by the Beggars in 1572.
Amongst the prisoners taken by the Beggars, there were sixteen priests who were executed at Brielle *(qv)* the same year; they are the martyrs of Gorkum.
It was the birthplace of the 16C painter, Abraham Bloemaert *(qv)* who lived mainly in Utrecht.

⊙ **Boat trips.** – Gorinchem is the departure point for boat tours in the Biesbosch *(qv)*.

THE OLD QUARTER *time: ¾ hour-town plan p 100*

Surrounded by water, the old quarter has kept the shape of its bastions and ramparts which have been transformed into an esplanade. It is crossed by the Linge, which forms a picturesque harbour, the **Lingehaven.**

Grote Markt and Groenmarkt. – On the first of these squares stands the town hall;
⊙ on the other stands the **Great Church or St Martin's** (Grote- of St-Maartenskerk) (**A**). Dating
⊙ from the 15C, it is mainly remarkable for its tall early 16C Gothic **tower** (St.-Janstoren) which is slightly curved in shape; as a matter of fact while being built it was noticed that the edifice was collapsing so the upper walls were straightened, these are the only vertical ones.
On Grote Markt, at no 23, a small baroque **door** called Hugo de Grootpoortje (**B**) is the place where the illustrious Grotius took refuge after having escaped from Loevestein Castle *(qv)*.

⊙ **Bethlehem House (Dit is in Bethlehem) (M).** – Formerly a shop, it has a lovely façade with decorated window tympana, topped with a voluted gable dating from 1566. Bethlehem House now houses a small regional **museum** (Museum Oud-Gorcum), which exhibits collections regarding the history of Gorkum, scale models, paintings, toys, shop signs and jewellery.

Old orphanage (Burgerkinderenweeshuis) (C). – On the 18C façade of this house, also called **Huize Matthijs-Marijke,** a carved stone depicts Christ and children, between the founders of the orphanage.

House (Huis) of "'t Coemt al van God" (All comes from God) (D). – Lovely narrow façade with a crow-stepped gable, decorated with Renaissance medallions (1563).

Dalem Gate (Dalempoort) (E). – This lovely, small rampart gateway, square with a high roof topped by a pinnacle, dates from 1597; it was enlarged in 1770. It is the only gateway, which remains of the town's four entrances.
From here, one can see the tall wall **mill** called **De Hoop,** Hope (1764).

Buiten de Waterpoort. – This vast shaded esplanade stretches from the south of the old water-gate (Waterpoort), closed in 1894 to enlarge the road. The landing stage for boat tours is here.
There is a fine **view** over Dalem Gate, the mill and the river; to the southeast, on the opposite bank, one can see, amongst the greenery, the tall bell tower of Woudrichem Church and the pink brick Loevestein Castle.

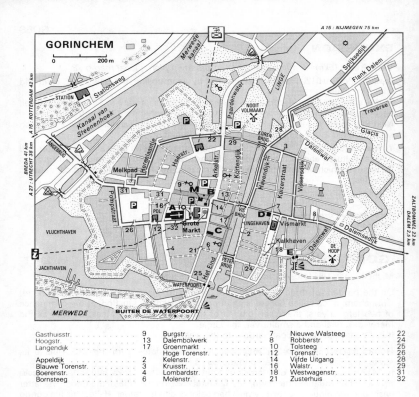

GORINCHEM

Gasthuisstr.	9	Burgstr.	7	Nieuwe Walsteeg	22		
Hoogstr.	13	Dalembolwerk	8	Robberstr.	24		
Langendijk	17	Groenmarkt	10	Tolsteeg	25		
		Hoge Torenstr.	12	Torenstr.	26		
Appeldijk	2	Kelenstr.	14	Vijfde Uitgang	28		
Blauwe Torenstr.	3	Kruisstr.	16	Walstr.	29		
Boerenstr.	4	Lombardstr.	18	Westwagenstr.	31		
Bornsteeg	6	Molenstr.	21	Zusterhuis	32		

EXCURSIONS

Leerdam. – Pop 18 499. *17km - 10½ miles to the northeast. Leave by Spijksedijk, take the motorway to Nijmegen and turn left towards Leerdam.*
This town, situated on the Linge, is the main glass-making centre in the Netherlands since the creation of its factory in 1878.

⊙ To the southwest, on the Oosterwijk road *(Lingedijk 28),* a small **National Glasswork Museum** (Nationaal Glasmuseum) is installed in a private home. This museum displays interesting collections of glass and crystal from different countries, notably from Leerdam (19 and 20C) but also from the United States and Finland (since the 18C).

Loevestein Castle. – *21km - 13 miles to the south. Leave by Westwagenstraat, turn left after the first bridge and return to the motorway towards Breda then a road to the left.*

Woudrichem. – Pop 13 291. At the confluence of the Rhine (Waal) and the Maas, this small town, commonly called **Workum,** is still enclosed in its encircling bastioned ramparts which have been turned into an esplanade. Formerly it belonged to the region of Heusden and Altena. It obtained its city charter in 1356. By the *Peace of Woudrichem* in 1419, John of Bavaria obtained important rights over his niece, Jacoba's *(qv)* territories.
Workum has a small pleasure boat harbour with a ferry for pedestrians that connects up with Loevestein Castle.
To the south one enters the town by **Koe Gate** (Koepoort). On the right is the squat **tower** of the Gothic church whose walls are decorated with medallions.
To the north near the 15C **prison gate** (Gevangenpoort), the **old town hall** (Oude Raadhuis, *Hoogstraat 47*) now a restaurant, has a graceful Renaissance façade with a crow-stepped gable and a flight of steps in front topped by two heraldic lions.
In the same street, at no 37, note a façade stone depicting an axe chopping wood, and opposite, two twin houses of 1593 and 1606, whose façade stones evoke by their sculpture a golden angel and a salamander, and by their inscriptions: To the Golden Angel and To the Salamander, their respective names.

⊙ **Loevestein Castle** (Slot Loevestein). – All that can be seen through the greenery are the high slate roofs of this solid fortress in pink brick, flanked with four square towers and surrounded by moats and ramparts. Loevestein Castle was built between 1357 and 1368 by Dirk Loef van Horne, lord of Altena. The Count of Holland, Albrecht van Beieren (of Bavaria), seized it in 1385 and surrounded it with an enclosure. In the 15C the castle was transformed into a prison by Jacoba who had just seized Gorkum *(qv).* In 1619 Grotius *(qv),* who had been taken prisoner the previous year, was imprisoned in Loevestein. There he devoted himself to the preparation of legal and theological works. His escape remains famous. He managed to escape in March 1621 by hiding in a chest which had been used to bring him books, and was then given shelter in Gorkum temporarily, before reaching France.
Inside the castle one can visit large rooms with lovely chimneypieces. In one of them is the chest in which Grotius escaped.

Michelin map **408** south of fold 10

Gouda (pronounced how-dah) owes its fame to the stained glass in the church, its cheese and its pipes. Situated at the confluence of the Hollandse IJssel and the Gouwe, this peaceful town is criss-crossed by several canals.

In the Middle Ages, Gouda, then called Ter Gouwe, developed under the protection of its castle, which was destroyed in 1577. It had received its city charter in 1272.

In the 15C, brewing and trading brought great prosperity to Gouda; while the 16C marked a decline. The town picked up again in the 17C due to the cheese trade and the manufacture of pipes introduced by English potters.

Today there is also the production of candles, Gouda having the biggest factory in the country, and pottery.

Gouda is the homeland of **Cornelis de Houtman** (c1565-99), who was in charge of an expedition to the East (1595-7) and founded the first Dutch trading post in East India (Indonesia) on the island of Java.

Gouda cheese. – Gouda, together with Edam, is one of the most famous cheeses in the Netherlands. Marketed in Gouda, it is a product either from a factory or from farms (its name then becomes *boerenkaas* meaning farm cheese).

Gouda is made with cow's milk either straight from the cow or pasturized (when it is made in a factory). It is either young, medium or old. The indication *volvet 48 +* means that its fat content is at least 48%. It is usually in the shape of a millstone with a diameter of 35cm - 14in.

Other specialities of the town are the *stroopwafels,* wafers filled with treacle.

⊙ **Boat Trips.** – Tours are organised on the Hollandse IJssel and towards Reeuwijk Lakes *(qv).*

★ **THE HEART OF THE TOWN** *time: 3 hours*

Markt (Z). – In the centre of the main square stands the town hall with its characteristic tall silhouette. Several markets take place in this square, particularly the ⊙ **cheese market** and **handicraft market.**

At no 27, the Arti Legi, houses the tourist information centre; Gouda pottery is displayed.

★ **Town Hall** (Stadhuis) (Z **H**). – *Illustration p 23.* This lovely mid-15C Gothic building, ⊙ restored in the 19 and 20C, has a very decorated sandstone façade on the south side with a gable, flanked by turrets and adorned with a small balcony. The staircase in front is in the Renaissance style (1603).

On the east side is a **carillon**, whose small figures perform every half hour; it depicts the scene of Count Floris V of Holland granting the city charter to Gouda in 1272.

Inside the Registrar's Office (Trouwzaal) is worth visiting; it is decorated with tapestries woven in Gouda in the 17C.

Weigh House (Waag) (Y **A**). – It is a classical construction of 1668 built by Pieter Post. The façade is decorated with a low relief depicting the weighing of cheese which formerly took place here.

Behind the weigh house the lovely **St Agnes Chapel** (Agnietenkapel) (Y **B**) has been restored.

★ **St John's** (St.-Janskerk) (Z **D**). – Founded in the 13C, St John's has been rebuilt twice ⊙ after the fires of 1438 and 1552.

With a small tower in front and surrounded by pointed gables, this church is the longest in the country, 123m - 403ft. The very luminous interior, is sober. Wooden barrel vaults top the three naves separated by short round pillars.

GOUDA

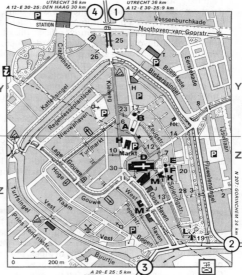

The main shopping streets are printed in a different colour in the list of streets.

★★★ **Stained glass** (Goudse Glazen). – St John's is renowned for its magnificent collection of 70 stained glass windows. 40 were spared by the Iconoclasts (qv), the others were made after the Reformation. The largest, of which there are 27, were donated by princes, prelates or rich bourgeois.

The 13 most remarkable stained glass windows, in the eastern part of the church, are attributed to the **Crabeth brothers** (Dirck and Wouter) who made them between 1555 and 1571 when the church was Catholic. They illustrate biblical subjects. The works of the Crabeth brothers are numbered:

  5: The Queen of Sheba before Solomon's throne
  6: Judith beheading Holophernes
  7: Dedication of Solomon's temple and the Last Supper
  8: Heliodorus, temple thief, chastened by the angels
12: Nativity
14: Sermon of St John the Baptist (patron of the church)
15: Baptism of Jesus (the oldest window, 1555)
16: First sermon of Jesus
18: Jesus replying to St John's disciples
22: Jesus driving the money-changers from the Temple (window donated by William the Silent and symbolising the Church's fight for purification)
23: Elijah's sacrifice and the Ablutions (donated by Margaret of Parma (qv), governor of the Low Countries at the time of the revolt)
24: St Philip preaching and baptising
30: Jonah cast up by the whale (tall window above the ambulatory, to the left of the chancel).

More recent stained glass windows which date from the Protestant period were put in between 1594 and 1603 on the western side. Donated by the free towns of Holland, they depict armorial bearings, historical events, allegories.

(After photo Stichting Fonds Goudse Glazen)

Stained glass window depicting William the Silent

Note numbers:
25: the raising of the siege of Leyden (in 1547) in the middle of floods; portrait of William the Silent; silhouette of Delft.
27: the Pharisee in the temple
28: the adultress in a monumental decor with deep perspective
28A (right aisle): Stained glass window by Charles Eyck placed in 1947 and evoking World War II and the Liberation.

The seven stained glass windows in the **chapel** (door under window 14 in the chancel) depict the Resurrection, Ascension, the Descent of the Holy Ghost, and are attributed to Dirck Crabeth or his pupil, Jan Dirckz Lonk, and come from a neighbouring convent.

⊙ The **organ** at the end of the church dates from 1736. The **new organ** in the chancel dates from 1974.

⊙ The 17C **carillon** by P. Hemony has been restored.

Interesting tombstones are strewn over the floor of the building.

★ **Het Catharina Gasthuis Municipal Museum** (Stedelijk Museum) (Z M¹). – Installed in
⊙ the governor's old mansion and St Catherine's Hospital (Gasthuis), this museum is a decorative arts museum (fine furnishings) and a regional art museum. Exhibitions are held here, as well.

To the north of the museum, there is a garden entered by a **portal** (1609) (Lazaruspoortje), which has a polychrome low relief depicting Lazarus the leper.

Near the hospital governors' former offices, the kitchen and 17 to 19C rooms, the **Great Hall** (Ruim) is devoted to the civic guards; there are paintings of groups (one by Ferdinand Bol), show-cases of gold and silversmith's work, among which a chalice offered in the 15C by Jacoba (qv).

A corridor contains torture instruments of the 16 and 17C.

On the upper floor there are collections of toys, the reconstitution of the surgeons' Guild Room, paintings by the Barbizon School and The Hague School (Mauve, Jacob Maris) as well as Isaac Israëls and Jan Toorop.

On the staircase there is a painting by Jan Steen, the *Pipe Smoker*.

In the old part (1542) one can see a portrait by Nicolaas Maes, a landscape by Van Goyen, and the former hospital rooms devoted to **religious art**: the *Annunciation*, and the *Baptism of St Eustace* by Pourbus the Elder (16C) and a collection of pewterware.

In a nearby room there is the reconstitution of a 17C town dispensary.

The neighbouring chapel has temporary exhibitions.

ADDITIONAL SIGHTS

⊙ **De Moriaan Municipal Museum** (Stedelijk Museum) (Z M²). – Under the sign of the Blackamoor (moriaan) evoking a tobacco shop, this Renaissance style house built c1625 has a lovely façade overlooking the picturesque Gouda canal.

It has been converted into a **Museum of Pipes and Pottery**. The tobacco shop of 1680 has been reconstructed. Fine collections of pipes, pottery, earthenware tiles 1600-1850 and pictures made of earthenware tiles are shown on several levels, in an elegant setting. One can also see the reconstructed potter's and a pipe maker' workshops.

Jeruzalemstraat (Z 7). – At the corner of Patersteeg is the **Jeruzalemkapel** (Z E), a 15C chapel.

Opposite, on the other corner is the former **orphanage** (Weeshuis) (Z F) of 1642, now a library, with a lovely façade with a voluted gable, and beside it a doorway topped by a low relief depicting two orphans.

On the opposite pavement, at no 2, an **old people's home** (Oude Mannenhuis) (Z K) opens by a door (1614), altered in the 18C.

At the far end of Spieringstraat is the **municipal park** where an 1832 **wall mill** stands (Molen't Slot) (Z L) which was formerly used for milling grain.

In the park there is a tree which was planted when Queen Wilhelmina reached majority.

EXCURSIONS

★ **Reeuwijk Lakes.** – *30km - 18½ miles to the north. Leave by Karnemelksloot. After the canal, take the 2nd road on the left and go to Platteweg.*

★ **Reeuwijk Lakes** (Reeuwijkse Plassen). – Even though these vast stretches of water are much appreciated by water sports enthusiasts, the road winding between the lakes goes through a captivating landscape.

After Sluipwijk, go in the direction of Bodegraven then Woerden.

Woerden. – Pop 27 226. Former important stronghold on the Old Rhine, Woerden was considered for a long time as "the key to Holland": strategically, occupying Woerden meant access to the country. In 1672 Louis XIV's armies commanded by the Duke of Montmorency-Luxembourg defeated William III's Dutch army. The town is still surrounded by a moat which edged its bastioned enclosure. A 15C **castle**, since 1872 turned into a quartermaster's store, is at the southern entrance to the town. There are imitation machicolations running along the façade.

⊙ In the old town hall there is a **municipal museum** (stadsmuseum).

Flanked by a turret it is a delightful small building (1501) with voluted gables and the 1st floor is completely glazed. An old pillory takes up the right part of the façade. Woerden also has a stage mill (1755), De Windhond (The Greyhound).

Schoonhoven. – *34km - 21 miles. Leave by Nieuwe Veerstal and follow the dike road, very narrow (passing difficult).* This road, which follows the Hollandse IJssel, offers picturesque **views**★ of the river with its marshy banks and thatched farmhouses.

Oudewater. – Pop 7 059. Homeland of Jacob **Arminius** (c1560-1609) *(qv)*, and the Primitive painter **Gerard David** (c1460-1523), who moved to Bruges in 1483, Oudewater is one of the Netherlands's oldest small towns.

⊙ Oudewater owes its fame to its **witches' scales,** installed in the **weigh house** (Heksenwaag), which houses a small witch museum (in the attic; the history of witchcraft is retraced via engravings and documents). This fine Renaissance building with crow-stepped gables and brick mosaic tympana is near Markt, which spans a canal.

In the 16C women accused of witchcraft came from afar to be weighed at Oudewater in the presence of the burgomaster of the town. If the woman's weight was not too light with respect to her size she was too heavy to ride a broomstick, so she was not a witch. They were then given a certificate of acquittal. All the people weighed in Oudewater were acquitted. The last certificate was issued in 1729.

Next to the weigh house, at no 14, note the Renaissance façade (1601) of Arminius's birthplace: the tympana are decorated with shells; a niche contains the statue of Fortune.

Dating from the town's prosperous era (end 16C) other façades are spread along the quiet streets like Wijdstraat. At no 3 Donkere Gaard, near Markt, there is a fine house. Near Markt, the Renaissance **town hall** (stadhuis) has a side façade preceded by a flight of steps and topped with a crow-stepped gable.

By the Gouda road, go to Haastrecht, then follow the valley of the Vlist towards Schoonhoven.

It is a picturesque **route**★. The road, shaded by willows, runs alongside the river with banks covered in abundant vegetation. Beautiful reed-covered roofed farmhouses with a conical haystack topped with a small roof, line the road.

Vlist. – Pop 9 561. Lovely wooden post mill.

On leaving Vlist, cross the river.

Schoonhoven. – Pop 10 775. This charming, small town at the confluence of the Vlist and the Lek, is known for its traditional silverware which continues to exist thanks to a few craftsmen. It is linked by a ferry *(veer)* to Lek's south bank.

A picturesque canal crosses the town.

The **town hall** (Stadhuis) stands on the canal's edge. Dating from the 15C, with a high roof topped by a pinnacle (carillon), it has been modernised.

On Dam, in the centre of the canal, is the **weigh house** (Waag), an original building of 1617 with a hipped roof. It is now a restaurant.

⊙ Near the weigh house there is a **Gold, Silver and Clock Museum** (Nederlands Goud-, Zilver-en Klokkenmuseum). It has a fine **collection**★ of wall clocks from Friesland and the Zaan, French dial cases, 18C timepieces as well as a collection of 17 to 20C silverware from several countries, and an important collection of watches.

To the south of the town, the gate, **Veerpoort** which dates from 1601, opens on to the Lek. Some lovely houses can be seen in the town, notably no 37 Lopikerstraat: the 1642 façade is decorated with a double crow-stepped gable and red shutters.

's-GRAVENHAGE See THE HAGUE

Michelin map 408 fold 6
Plan of built-up area in the current Michelin Red Guide Benelux

Capital of the province, main town in the northern region of the Netherlands, Groningen is at the extremity of the Hondsrug *(qv),* between a region of polders to the north and old peat bogs to the southeast.

HISTORICAL NOTES

Groningen is known of in 1000 AD. Fortified in the 12C it belonged to the Hanseatic League *(qv)* in the beginning of the 13C.

A convention concluded in 1251 with the neighbouring cantons made Groningen the only grain market in the region, bringing it six centuries of prosperity. Under the Bishop of Utrecht's authority the town passed into the hands of the Duke of Gelderland in 1515. Then, trying to escape from the Hapsburg authority, it finally gave in to Charles V in 1536. It joined the Union of Utrecht in 1579 and was taken by the Spanish in 1580 and then by Maurice of Nassau in 1594.

An era of prosperity followed with the construction from 1608-16, of a new enclosure (7km - 4½ miles) defended by 17 bastions.

In 1614 the university was founded; it very quickly acquired a great reputation and students came from all over Europe. Descartes chose it in 1645 to arbitrate in his conflicts with Dutch theologians.

In 1672 the town resisted against the troops of the Bishop of Munster, ally of Louis XIV. The fortifications, revised in 1698 by Coehoorn, were knocked down in 1874 to allow for the extension of the city. A few remains in Noorderplantsoen (**Y**) have been transformed into a garden.

The town of Groningen is the homeland of the painters **Jozef Israëls** (1827-1911), head of The Hague School *(qv)* and **Hendrik Willem Mesdag** (1831-1915), who was one of its members.

A dynamic town. – An important communications junction, Groningen is a stopping place on the way to Scandinavia. Due to its large canals, it is linked to the sea. Its port is installed on the Oosterhaven and the Zuiderhaven.

Groningen is a large industrial centre (metallurgy, hi-tech, printing, tobacco manufacture, potato flour factory). The town is the highest ranking in Western Europe for the production of sugar beet.

Groningen has built an important congress and exhibition centre, the **Martinihal,** near the racecourse, in the new quarters, which are developing to the south.

The surrounding lakes (Leekstermeer, Paterswoldse Meer, Zuidlaarder Meer) draw watersports enthusiasts.

It is also a university town (17 630 students in 1987).

GRONINGEN

Grote Markt	Z 19	A-Straat	Z 3	Noorderhaven Z.z.	Z 28
Herestr.	Z	de Brink	Z 6	Ossenmarkt	Y 31
Oosterstr.	Z	Brugstr.	Z 7	Paterswoldseweg	Z 35
Oude Boteringestr.	Z 32	Eeldersingel	Z 8	Rademarkt	Z 38
Oude Ebbingestr.	Y 34	Eendrachtskade	Z 12	Radesingel	Z 39
Vismarkt	Z 46	Emmaviaduct	Z 14	Schuitendiep	Z 40
		Friesestraatweg	Z 17	St. Jansstr.	Z 41
A-Kerkhof	Z 2	Gedempte Zuiderdiep	Z 18	Spilsluizen	Y 42
		Lopende Diep	Y 24	Verlengde Oosterstr.	Z 45
		Martinikerkhof	Z 26	Westerhaven	Z 49
		Noorderhaven N.z.	Y 27	Westersingel	Z 50

Groningen gas. – The town is considered as the Netherlands' power supply capital. Since 1945, oil has been exploited in the Drenthe near Schoonebeek *(qv)*. In 1959-60 gas was discovered at **Slochteren**, to the east of Groningen.

The province has very large deposits of natural gas. The reserves are estimated at more than 1 250 billion m³ - 44 142.5 billion f³ which makes it one of the greatest deposits in the world, with 29 reserves each one grouping several wells.

Half the gas is exported via pipelines to Belgium, France, Germany and Italy.

ⓣ **Boat trips (Rondvaart).** – *Departure opposite the station, near the canal* (Z).

AROUND GROTE MARKT *time: 1½ hours*

Grote Markt (Z 19). – Prolonged by Vismarkt, the fish market, this vast, very busy square where the town's main monuments stand, forms the city centre.

Grote Markt gives onto the different pedestrian precincts; the main shopping street is Herestraat.

ⓣ A **flea market** takes place here.

Town Hall (Stadhuis) (Z H). – In neo-classical style (1810), it is linked by a glassed-in footbridge to a modern annexe, which by its cubic mass, crushes the Gold Office.

★ **Gold Office** (Goudkantoor) (Z A). – This gracious Renaissance building built in 1635 has elegant façades with finely worked gables; the windows are topped by shells.

Originally the provincial tax collector's office, it was used in the 19C as a place to hallmark precious metal (*goud*: gold, *kantoor*: office).

ⓣ **St Martin's (Martinikerk)** (Z B). – Reconstructed in the 15C, the church is

ⓣ known for its tower, **Martini Tower**★ (Martinitoren) which is the pride of the people of Groningen. 96m - 315ft high with six stories, this bell tower is topped by a weather vane in the shape of a horse depicting St Martin's mount. It has a carillon cast by the Hemony brothers.

Inside the church, the chancel is decorated with 16C frescoes depicting scenes in the life of Christ.

From the top of Martini Tower there is an interesting **view** over Groningen and its canals, Grote Markt, the roofs of St Martin's, the Prinsenhof and its garden.

(After photo Bego, Groningen)

Martini Tower

ADDITIONAL SIGHTS

★ **Northern Shipping Museum (Noordelijk Scheepvaartmuseum)** (Z M²). – This museum is
ⓣ housed in two beautiful merchant's houses of the Middle Ages, Canter House (Canterhuis) on the right and Gothic House (Gotisch Huis) on the left.

It is devoted to inland water transport and coastal shipping in the northern region of the Netherlands, since the 6C.

The scale models of ships, navigational instruments, maps, paintings and ceramics are particularly well shown and retrace the stages which have marked the history of shipping: the brilliant period of the Hanseatic League to which Groningen belonged, the Dutch East and West India Companies, the activities relative to peat extraction and its transportation by boat, the coastal shipping of bricks and schooners which replaced the traditional galliots.

ⓣ **Netherlands Tobacco Museum (Niemeyer Tabaksmuseum)** (Z M²). – This museum is located at the back of the Gothic House, which also houses the Northern Shipping Museum *(see above)*.

A fine collection of pipes from all over Europe, snuffboxes and jars illustrate the use of tobacco over the centuries.

A 19C tobacco merchant's shop has been reconstituted.

ⓣ **Regional Museum (Groninger Museum)** (Z M¹). – It retraces the town's different historic periods as well as the province's. In the archaeological section one can see the finds excavated from the *terps (qv)*.

A section displays decorative art objects (Chinese and Japanese porcelain, silverware from Groningen).

In the fine arts department there are paintings by Rembrandt, his pupil Carel Fabritius, works of The Hague School *(qv)* and the Expressionist movement, De Ploeg (The Plough), as well as drawings and sculpture from the 16C to the present.

Temporary exhibitions on contemporary artists are held.

Martinikerkhof (Z 26). – This lovely square, laid out on the site of a 19C cemetery *(kerkhof),* is surrounded by renovated houses.

To the northeast is the **Provincial House** (Provinciehuis) (Z P) rebuilt in 1917 in the 17C style and flanked by an onion-shaped turret.

On its left, the Cardinaal House (Y C) has a small Renaissance façade (1559), whose gable is decorated with three heads: Alexander the Great, King David and Charlemagne. This façade is the reconstitution of a Groningen house, which was destroyed.

To the north of the square, the **Prinsenhof** (Y D), originally built for the Brethren of the Common Life *(qv)* became the Bishop of Groningen's residence in 1568. Preceded by a courtyard and a 17C portal, it is built onto the Gardepoort, a small gateway (1639). Behind the Prinsenhof there is a small 18C garden with two arbours and a rose garden. It opens on to the Turfsingel, a canal where peat *(turf)* was transported, via a gateway called the Zonnewijzerpoort which has an 18C **sundial** (Y N) on the garden side.

Beef Market (Ossenmarkt) (Y 31). – It is the former beef market. At no 5 there is a fine 18C **patrician house** (Y E); it is a good example of the local architectural style, with its wide façade with rows of rather narrow windows topped by shells.

Not far away, at the corner of Spilsluizen and Nieuwe Ebbingestraat, stand two 17C houses (Y F). The one on the left is also characteristic of the Groningen style.

On the canal's other side, a lovely sculptured stone depicting a stag (Y L) juts out from the wall of a house. At the corner of Spilsluizen and Oude Boteringestraat is the former **guard room** (Kortegaard) (Y K) with a portico (1534).

EXCURSIONS

Lauwersoog. – *27km - 16½ miles northwest by Friesestraatweg* (Z).

Aduard. – Pop 3 015. Of the old Cistercian abbey founded in 1163 only the refectory ⊘ remains. Built in 1300, it has become a **reformed church**. Although the façade is sober, the interior has interesting decorative details: Gothic bays alternating with blind arches with a brick background depicting geometric motifs, bays on the ground floor surrounded by ceramic cable moulding. The 18C furnishings are elegant: pulpit decorated with coats of arms, pews with carved backs, the lords' pews topped by a canopy with heraldic motifs, copper lecterns.

Leens. – Pop 3 574. **St Peter's** (Petruskerk), built in the 12 and 13C, houses a lovely ⊘ baroque **organ case★** (organ concerts) built by Hinsz in 1733.

Lauwersoog. – *Local map p 183.* Departure point for ferries to Schiermonnikoog *(qv),* Lauwersoog is situated near the **Lauwers Sea,** former sea gulf, which has been closed, like the Zuiderzee, by a dike completed in 1969 and around which polders are being laid out.

⊘ A small **museum** (Expozee) is housed in a large building.

Scale models, photographs, illuminated maps, film and slide projections give interesting documentation on the Lauwers Sea polders and the protection of the Wadden Sea.

★ Rural Churches. – *Round tour of 118km - 73 miles to the northeast. Leave Groningen by Damsterdiep* (Z) *– local map below.*

Each village in the province of Groningen has its brick church. Of the 12 or 13C, built in the transitional Romanesque-Gothic style, it is very simple architecturally but enhanced both outside and inside by harmonious brick motifs. Sometimes on a mound, called *wierd* here *(see terp; qv),* usually surrounded by a cemetery, it is hidden amongst large trees from which its saddleback roofed bell tower emerges. Its rustic charm is captivating.

Inside, the church has often kept a few frescoes, carved furnishings and hatchments. There are also farms of imposing size.

Garmerwolde. – The 13C vil- ⊘ lage **church** stands in an attractive enclosure near an isolated bell tower. The flat east end has bays outlined by recessed arches and a gable with blind arcading. The interior still has some 16C frescoes on the vaults and an 18C carved pulpit.

Ten Boer. – Pop 6 829. On a mound, a small 13C church, deconsecrated, topped by a pinnacle, has some lovely decoration, especially on the north side: bays outlined by recessed arches, medallions, multifoil blind arcading and gables both with reticulate brickwork.

Stedum. – Pop 2 008. Built on a mound surrounded by moats, the small, typical church with its tall saddleback roofed bell tower is picturesque. A frieze runs round the modillions sculptured with characters or heads of animals.

Loppersum. – Pop 3 993. This large Gothic **church** has two transepts with blind arcading on the gables.

The interior is interesting for its **frescoes★**, which decorate the upper part of the chancel vaults and the Lady Chapel. In the chapel south of the chancel there are numerous memorial slabs.

Zeerijp. – Next to its isolated bell tower, the **church** dating from the 14C has a gable in two parts with blind arcading and brick mosaic.

The interior is remarkable for its **domes★** with brick decoration which varies in each bay: chevrons, interlacing... Blind arcading decorates the end of the nave. The organ, the Renaissance pulpit, and hatchments are also worth seeing.

Leermens. – This 13C church has a flat east end decorated with blind arcading and a background decorated with brick motifs.

On arriving at Oosterwijtwerd, there is a large farmhouse with four roofs.

Krewerd. – This **church,** built on a mound, has vaults decorated with brick motifs. The organ dates from 1531.

Appingedam. – Pop 12 727. Renowned for its agricultural markets (April and October), it is a welcoming town with a long pedestrian precinct, Dijkstraat Promenade and crossed by a canal, the Damsterdiep. From the footbridge (Smalle brug) over the canal there is a fine **view★** of the overhanging kitchens and the town hall's pinnacle.

The **old town hall** (Raadhuis), flanked by a 19C bell tower, dates from 1630. The façade, with bays topped by shells, is decorated with a pelican, a statue of Justice and a voluted pediment. The 13C **church**, Nicolaikerk, has kept lovely frescoes, discovered when it was being restored.

Delfzijl. – Pop 24 042. A busy shipping port on Dollard Gulf, linked to Groningen by Eemskanaal, Delfzijl is an industrial city, whose main activities are petrochemistry and the manufacture of soda.

To the south of the town, at **Farmsum**, an aluminium foundry supplied with alumina from Surinam was the first installed in the Netherlands, in 1956. Delfzijl also has a large pleasure boat harbour; **boat trips** are organised.

From the dike on the bank of Dollard Gulf, there is a **view** over the harbour and the town, overlooked by a tall wall mill, called **Molen Adam** (1875).

On a square near the station, a monument topped by a swan, **Het Zwaantje**, commemorates the Resistance.

A small **statue of Maigret** on the lawns of the Damsterdiep *(600m - $\frac{1}{3}$ mile from the pumping station to the west of Eemskanaal, opposite the RWR warehouses),* is a reminder that Simenon (1903-89) passed by in 1929. It is believed that he created his most famous character, police inspector Maigret, while in Delfzijl.

Bierum. – Pop 4 298. On a mound there is a small 13C **church**, whose bell tower was reinforced by a flying buttress. The semi-circular end of the chancel dates from the 14C.

The interior is roofed with geometrically decorated ribbed domes on which a few traces of frescoes remain. The organ dates from 1793, the baptismal font from the early Middle Ages. Around the church the cemetery has remarkable 19C sculptured memorial slabs depicting symbols of life (trees) and time (hours glasses).

Eemshaven. – The new port, opened in 1973, was dug out of the Emma Polder and the Oost Polder, it has an industrial zone. To the east a power station, **Eemscentrale**, works with natural gas since 1976. It is planned that Eemshaven will import liquid gas, so as to economise the country's reserves.

Uithuizermeeden. – The **church** with a 13C nave and a transept (1705) has a white tower rebuilt in 1896-7. The pulpit was sculptured in the 18C.

★ Uithuizen. – To the east **Menkemaborg★** is a mansion hidden by large trees with a hundred or so herons' nests where the birds come to roost from February to June. A formal garden, a verdant maze, an orchard, a vegetable garden, and a rose garden surround it. At the back (14C) where the windows on the ground floor are taller, two other wings were added in the 17 and 18C. The interior is pleasantly furnished and decorated. The kitchen in the basement occupies the oldest part. There is an organ cabinet of 1777, collections of 17C Chinese porcelain, a canopied four-poster bed by Daniel Marot (1700-73), 18C armorial bearings and portraits of ancestors.

At Uithuizen, the **reformed church** (Hervormde Kerk) contains a remarkable organ built in 1701 by Arp Schnitger *(qv).*

Oldenzijl. – The small Romanesque church stands in a churchyard amongst the tombs, on a mound, surrounded by moats and a curtain of trees. The brick walls are pierced by a few small rose windows encircled with tori and the chancel is decorated with blind arches.

Return to Groningen by Garsthuizen, St.-Annerhuisjes, Ten Boer and ② of the town plan.

---

*Each year the **Michelin Red Guide Benelux***
revises its selection of hotels and restaurants
in the following categories
– pleasant, quiet, secluded
– with an exceptionally interesting or extensive view
– with gardens, tennis courts, swimming pool or equipped beach.

Michelin map **408** fold 10 – Local map p 73
Plan of built-up area in the current Michelin Red Guide Benelux

Historical capital of the Holland earldom and county town of North Holland province, Haarlem, situated on the Spaarne, is the birthplace of Frans Hals.
It is the centre of a large bulb growing region.

HISTORICAL NOTES

Haarlem was founded c10C on the edge of the offshore bar, near the interior seas, now disappeared, between Haarlem and Wijk (present Wijk aan Zee, qv).
Fortified in the 12C, Haarlem was the residence of the Counts of Holland. It obtained its city charter in 1245.
In the 13C its inhabitants took part in the Fifth Crusade and the capture of Damietta in 1219. The bells of the Great Church are still called *damiaatjes* in memory of this great deed. In the 14C Haarlem expanded but all that remains of its fortifications is the Amsterdam gateway (late 15C), to the east.

A bloody siege. – During the uprising against the Spanish, Haarlem was besieged for seven months (1572-3) by the troops of Dom Frederico of Toledo, son of the Duke of Alba.
During the winter, William the Silent managed to provide the town with supplies by the Beggars, who came on skates over Haarlem Lake, but despite the heroic defence by the whole population, the town had to surrender in June 1573; the inhabitants were massacred. It was only in 1577 that Haarlem sided with the States General.
The 17C marks the peak of Haarlem; the town took advantage of the fall of Flemish cities by developing the linen industry and made a fabric sold all over Europe under the name of holland (a plain weave linen).

Haarlem Lake (Haarlemmermeer). – Formed by peat exploitation, this great lake of about 18 000ha - 44 460 acres was a threat to Amsterdam and Leyden due to storms. As early as 1641, Leeghwater (qv) had suggested draining it by using windmills and making polders. The work was not undertaken until two centuries later when steam powered **pumps** gradually replaced windmills. Three pumping stations were installed (one being the one invented by Cruquius, qv) and the work was completed in 1852.
The present territory of Haarlem Lake, which has become a district borough, is on the average 4m - 13ft below sea level, and Schiphol Airport (qv), which is located there is 4.5m - 15ft below. The sea-clay under the old peat bogs is very fertile.

The meeting place of artists. – Haarlem is the town of **Claus Sluter** (c1345-1406), a sculptor who, working for the Dukes of Burgundy in the Charterhouse of Champmol near Dijon (see Michelin Green Guide to Burgundy) produced works of great realism.
In the 15C born in Haarlem were: the painter **Dirck Bouts** who went to live in Louvain (Belgium), **Jan Mostaert** (c1475-1555/6) a religious painter influenced by Italian art, while **Geertgen tot Sint Jans** (qv) came to live here.
In the 16C **Maerten van Heemskerck** (1498-1574) was the pupil of Van Scorel (qv) during his stay in Haarlem, from 1527-9. **Cornelis van Haarlem**, Mannerist painter (1562-1638) and **Willem Claesz. Heda** (1594-1680), famous for his still-lifes (p 24) were born in this town. The engraver **Hendrick Goltzius** (1558-1617), **Pieter Claesz.** (1597-1661), another specialist of still-lifes, and **Pieter Saenredam** (1597-1665) painter of luminous architecture, all ended their days here. **Hercules Seghers** (1589/90-1638) a remarkable landscape painter also lived here.
Born in Haarlem, **Lieven de Key** (c1560-1627) was a great Renaissance architect. **Bartholomeus van der Helst** (1613-70), **Philips Wouwerman** (1619-68) painter of horses, imitated by his brother Pieter, **Nicolaes Berchem** (1620-83) who, contrary to his father Pieter Claesz. painted landscapes and herds, were also born in Haarlem.
Salomon van Ruysdael, born in Naarden (c1600-70) settled in Haarlem. This serene painter, whose art is very near that of Van Goyen (qv) liked wooded shores reflected in calm water, and monochromes. His nephew and pupil **Jacob van Ruisdael** (1628/9-82) was born in Haarlem. He painted more tormented landscapes, already romantic with dark cliffs, waterfalls, trees menaced by storm, disquieting chiaroscuros. **Meindert Hobbema** (1638-1708) was his pupil.

Frans Hals. – This painter was born in Antwerp c1580, but his family went to live in Haarlem in 1591. Frans Hals became the portrait painter of the town's bourgeois at a time when the portrait and particularly, group portraits (guilds, brotherhoods) were in fashion.
Frans Hals disrupted traditions. In compositions which were formerly stilted, he introduced a certain disorder, natural attitudes. He was readily treated as sloppy, he did not hesitate to catch the arquebusiers unawares during their banquet. He enlivened his canvases with bright colours, a riot of colour on scarves and flags. His rapid but expressive brush strokes, which foreshadowed modern art, gave his models a life, a mobility which made his portraits real snapshots.
For a long time a frank cheerfulness radiated from his paintings, but after 1640 there was no longer the verve and fantasy in his works. In the famous group of regents and regentesses (p 110) the return to black and white, verticality, expressive faces, even disenchanted, left a sinister impression, a foretaste of the death which carried him away two years later (1666).
His style was not captured by his pupils: **Judith Leyster** (1609-60), the Fleming Adriaen Brouwer and **Adriaen van Ostade** (1610-85), painter of village scenes. The latter's pupils were his brother Isaack as well as Jan Steen (qv).

AROUND GROTE MARKT *time: 1½ hours*

★ Grote Markt (BY 32). – This great square is bordered by the Great Church, the town hall and the former Meat Market.

In the square there is a statue of **Laurens Coster** (1405-84) (his real name is Laurens Janszoon) considered in the Netherlands as the inventor of printing in *c*1430, that is to say about ten years before Gutenberg (who is thought to have completed the printing of the Bible by 1455). Coster is believed to have printed with moveable type, however, no evidence was kept.

★ Great Church or St Bavo's (Grote of St.-Bavokerk) (BY A). – This large 15C church, which should not be confused with the Catholic St Bavo's *(Leidsevaart),* is topped at the transept crossing by an elegant wooden lantern tower covered with lead, 80m - 262ft high.

Inside admire the short nave and, in the chancel, a lovely cedar-wood ribbed vault. Note, also, a 17C pulpit with a Gothic sounding board, wood choir stalls (1512) carved with amusing subjects, the copper lectern in the shape of a pelican (late 15C) and above all the lovely early 16C **chancel screen★**, backed by finely worked brass.

The **organ★** built by Christiaan Müller in 1738 has been decorated according to the drawings of Daniel Marot. For a long time it was considered as one of the best instruments in the world and it is said that Handel and Mozart (as a child) came to play it. International organ competitions are organised every two years in Haarlem *(see the chapter Practical Information at the end of the guide).*

★ Town Hall (Stadhuis) (BY H). – Flanked by a turret, it is a 14C Gothic building to which numerous alterations have been made: on the right an advancement over a gallery topped with a voluted gable (15 and 17C), on the left above a flight of steps, a Renaissance loggia.

HAARLEM

Inside on the 1st floor, the **Counts' Hall** (Gravenzaal) has kept its former style; the paintings which decorate it are copies of old frescoes from the Carmelite convent and depict the counts of Holland.

★ **Meat Market (Vleeshal) (BY B)**. – This elegant building in the Renaissance style, built in 1603 by Lieven de Key *(qv)* is topped by richly decorated dormer windows. Inside there are exhibits organised by the Frans Hals Museum.

★★★ FRANS HALS MUSEUM (BZ M²) *time: 1½ hours*

Since 1913 this museum has been installed in the former almshouse for old men built in 1608 by Lieven de Key. The façade is characteristic of this type of institution with on either side of the entrance a succession of low houses topped with a crow-stepped gable with window. The principal façade gives on to the main courtyard around which are the rooms.

Works by Frans Hals. – The eight paintings of civic guards and regents by Frans Hals constitute a remarkable collection making it possible to follow the evolution of the master's painting.
The first painting which marks the already brilliant beginnings of the painter dates only from 1616 when Hals was about 36 years old. It is the **Banquet of the Officers of the Haarlem Militia Company of St George** (no 123). The mobility of the characters and their personality are shown in an extraordinary way. The atmosphere is less restrained in the *Banquet of the Officers of the Haarlem Militia Company of St George* (no 124) and the *Officers of the Haarlem Militia Company of St Hadrian* (no 125), both painted in 1627 and rich in spontaneity and colour.
In the **Officers of the Haarlem Militia Company of St Hadrian** (no 126) of 1662, Frans Hals reached his greatest virtuosity.
In the **Officers of the Haarlem Militia Company of St George** (no 127) of 1639, with a self-portrait of the artist (2nd figure on the left, 2nd row) is the last of this genre.
In 1641 a tendency for restraint and solemnity appears in Frans Hals's work and predominates in the *Regents of St Elizabeth's Hospital* (no 128).
The somber colour of the garments underlines the expression on the faces and the very studied attitude of the hands.
In the same style, the *Regents of the Old Men's Home* (no 129) painted in 1664 is a daring study, a little cynical, of these six characters amongst whom Frans Hals had gone so far as to show a drunkard with his hat tilted back. Painted the same year, the painting of the **Regentesses of The Old Men's Home** (no 130) with furrowed hands, bony faces, unindulgent looks, communicate a sentiment of anguish and discomfort.

Other collections. – Apart from Frans Hals, the museum contains rich collections of paintings, furniture and *objets d'art.*
In the series of **old paintings,** first there are the works of Jan van Scorel including the famous *Baptism of Christ,* those of Maerten van Heemskerck and Cornelis van Haarlem *(Baptism of Christ).* The main 17C masters notably those of the Haarlem School are represented by landscapes of Esais Van de Velde, Van Goyen, Van Ostade, Salomon van Ruysdael and Jacob van Ruisdael, a scene by Ter Boch, animals by Wouwerman and Cuyp, still lifes by Pieter Claesz., Willem Heda, Floris van Schooten, Abraham van Beyeren. There are also some fine portraits by Verspronck (1597-1662). Note the fine collection of 17 and 18C silverware; a manuscript painted with a tulip by Judith Leyster, pupil of Hals, the reconstitution of an apothecary with Delftware jars and, in a room with Dutch gilded leather, an 18C **dollshouse.**
In a modern wing there are **modern and contemporary Dutch paintings,** notably by Isaac Israëls, Jan Sluyters (1881-1957) and the COBRA Group.
Opposite the museum, the lovely small houses with crow-stepped gables belonged to St Elizabeth's Hospital or **St.-Elisabeths Gasthuis (BZ D)**, whose regents Frans Hals painted.

ADDITIONAL SIGHTS

Teylers Museum (CY M¹). – This museum, the oldest in the Netherlands (1778), is devoted to science and the arts in accordance with the wishes of its founder Pieter Teyler.
Large rooms contain collections of physics and chemistry instruments, fossils and minerals.
However, the main interest of the museum is in a series of 4 000 **drawings★** from the 16 to 19C, from the Italian, Dutch and French Schools *(exhibited in rotation)* part of which belonged to Queen Christina of Sweden. Rembrandt and Michelangelo have signed some of these works.
The museum also has a collection of 19 and early 20C paintings.
At the corner of Damstraat stands the **weigh house** (Waag) **(CY E)**, built in 1598 in the Renaissance style and attributed to Lieven de Key.

Amsterdam Gate (Amsterdamse Poort) (CY F). – This late 15C structure, preceded on the town side by two turrets was also a water-gate commanding the Spaarne.

Almshouses (Hofjes). – Among the numerous charitable institutions, which the people of the wealthy town of Haarlem had as from the 15C, there is the **Proveniershuis (BZ K)** of 1592 which opens by a large doorway on Grote Houtstraat, the **Brouwershofje (BYZ L)** (1472) in Tuchthuisstraat and the **Hofje van Loo (BY N)** of 1489, visible from Barrevoetestraat.

ⓥ **St Bavo's Cathedral.** – *By Leidsevaart* (BYZ). The sacristy of this very large basilica, built between 1895 and 1906 by J.T. Cuypers, son of P.J.H. Cuypers *(qv)* in the style of the time, contains the **treasury**: a large collection of liturgical objects, mainly gold and silverware (15 to 20C). Note the sacerdotal ornaments (early 16C) which come from an old Beguinage in the town.

EXCURSIONS

ⓥ **De Cruquius Museum** (Cruquius Expo). – *7km - 4 miles to the southeast by Dreef* (BZ). *It is to the northeast of a large bridge on the road to Vijfhuizen. Local map p 73.*
This museum, on the edge of old Haarlem Lake *(p 108)*, is installed in one of the three pumping stations, which were used to drain it. The station bears the name of **Nicolaas Cruquius** (1678-1754) author of a project (1750), which intended to drain the lake.
The museum has interesting documentation on the protection of the country from the sea, the creation of polders and dams and the evolution in techniques for fighting water: scale model of Haarlem Lake, animated scale model showing the parts of the Netherlands which would be submerged by the sea in the absence of dikes and dams. There is also one of the original pumps of the Cruquius station.

Spaarndam. – *8km - 5 miles to the northeast by Spaarndamseweg* (CX), *which becomes Vondelweg, then after a bend, take Vergierdeweg on the right.*
The houses of this picturesque village, where one can eat smoked eel, huddle up along both sides of the dike. This is interspersed with several locks making it possible to link the Spaarne and the IJ. On one of these locks there is a statue of Hans Brinker. According to the legend the young boy plugged a hole he had discovered in a protection dike with his finger for a whole night and thus saved the town from being flooded. The origin of this anecdote: a children's book written in 1873 by the American novelist Mary Mapes Dodge, *Hans Brinker or the Silver Skates.*
Beyond this small monument is the pleasure boat harbour; a path makes it possible to walk alongside it and reach the Oost- et Westkolk dock; lovely restored houses.

★ **Zandvoort.** – Pop 15 709. *11km - 7 miles. Leave by Leidsevaart* (BYZ). Town plan in the current Michelin Red Guide Benelux.
It is one of the most busy seaside resorts in the Netherlands, mainly used by the inhabitants of Amsterdam and Haarlem. A large avenue runs along the dunes which overlook the beach.
The Zandvoort **motor-racing track** (4 226km - 2 637 miles long) is very well known. The Netherlands Grand Prix takes place here *(see the chapter Practical Information at the end of the guide).* Since 1976 Zandvoort has a **casino** installed in Hotel Bouwes, on Badhuisplein.

Beverwijk. – *35km - 21½ miles to the north by Verspronckweg* (BX).
Bloemendaal aan Zee. – It is Haarlem's family beach.
Bloemendaal. – Pop 17 579. Behind the chain of dunes, this is an elegant residential centre where the villas stretch over wooded hills.
In the open-air theatre or Openluchttheater *(Hoge Duin en Daalseweg 2)* performances are given in summer. Nearby is the highest dune in the country, **Het Kopje** (50m - 164ft). Further to the north are the ruins of the **Brederode Castle** (Kasteel Brederode), destroyed by the Spanish in 1573.

ⓥ **De Kennemerduinen National Park.** – *Reception pavilion (Informatiecentrum) at the southeast entry to the park.*
It is an estate of 1 250ha - 3 088 acres situated on the long line of dunes edging the North Sea, and criss-crossed by footpaths and cycling tracks. Near the small lakes numerous birds come to breed.

IJmuiden. – Famous for its locks, IJmuiden, situated at the far end of the North Sea canal, is also a seaside resort and ranks as Western Europe's first fishing port. About forty trawlers are fitted out here, sometimes, for herring fishing. The fish market auction is very large.
Three **locks★** (sluizen) make it possible for the biggest ships to sail up to Amsterdam. The north lock, the most recent, begun in 1919, was inaugurated on 29 April 1930. It is 400m - 1 312ft long, 40m - 131ft wide and 15m - 49ft deep.

Beverwijk. - Pop 34 809. This small wooded holiday centre has lovely dunes covered with forests which separate it from the seaside resort of **Wijk aan Zee.**

Times and charges for admission to sights described in the guide are listed at the end of the guide.

The sights are listed alphabetically in this section either under the place – town, village or area – in which they are situated or under their proper name.

Every sight for which there are times and charges is indicated by the symbol ⓥ in the margin in the main part of the guide.

★★ THE HAGUE

DEN HAAG or **'s-GRAVENHAGE** South Holland P

Michelin map ⁣408 fold 9
Plan of built-up area in the current Michelin Red Guide Benelux

Seat of the Netherlands's government, of the Parliament, a diplomatic centre, The Hague, whose official name is 's-Gravenhage (generally shortened to Den Haag), is, however, only, the provincial capital, the monarch being enthroned in Amsterdam since 1813. Near the sea, it is a pleasant residential town, quiet, airy, with a multitude of squares, parks (more than 700 public gardens) cut across by several lovely canals. Even though The Hague sprawls over a vast area and has a small population density, which has entitled it to being called the "biggest village in Europe", it is marked by a certain aristocratic charm and is considered as the most worldly and elegant town in the Netherlands.

It is the birthplace of William III (1650-1702), **Christiaan Huygens** (1629-95) the great physicist and astronomer and the **Jan** and **Nikolaas Tinbergen** brothers, born respectively in 1903 and 1907; one receiving the Nobel Prize for economics (1969) with the Norwegian R. Frisch, the other the Nobel Prize for medicine (1973) with the Austrians K. Lorenz and K. von Frisch.

The Hague is the seat of the Residentie Orchestra, located since 1987, in the very modern Dr. Anton Philips Hall (seating capacity 1 900) on the Spui (**AV**). That same year the Danstheater aan't Spui (**AV T**) was inaugurated (seating capacity 1 001), built to house the Nederlands Dans Theater ballet company.

HISTORICAL NOTES

A meet. – Up to the 13C, The Hague was just a hunting lodge set up by Count Floris IV of Holland in the middle of a forest which stretched up to Haarlem *(qv)*.

About 1250 his son, William II, who had been proclaimed King of the Romans (1247) by the Pope in his fight against Emperor Frederick II, built a castle on the site of the present Binnenhof *(p 113)*. Floris V completed the work of his father by adding the Knights' Hall *(p 113)*.

At the end of the 14C, abandoning Haarlem, the Count of Holland, Albert of Bavaria and his suite came to live in The Hague.

A village... . – 's-Gravenhage, the Count's Hedge or Die Haghe, the hedge, rapidly developed without being more than a place of residence and rest. The small cloth trade, which started in the 15C was not enough to make it a merchant town.

In the confederation of cities which was the Low Countries at that time, the other towns would not allow it within their council. However, it was in The Hague that Philip the Good, in 1432 and 1456 held the chapters of the Order of the Golden Fleece.

The absence of fortifications brought destruction upon the city: as from 1528 it was attacked and pillaged by Maarten van Rossum *(qv)*, famous captain of a Gelderland troop of mercenaries. In 1581, the act, declaring Philip II of Spain's disavowal by the States General of the United Provinces, was posted on the door of the Knights' Hall.

... which develops. – In the 17C, The Hague found peace and prosperity again. Seat of the States General of the United Provinces, then the government, it became an important centre of diplomatic negotiations. The main coalitions against Louis XIV were sealed here.

From the middle of the 17C to the end of the 18C wealthy mansions in the Renaissance and the baroque style were built round the medieval centre of the Binnenhof.

The French entered The Hague in 1795. Eleven years later the town had to cede its rank of capital to Amsterdam where Louis Bonaparte had installed his government.

In 1814 the government and the Court returned to The Hague. But the title of capital remained with Amsterdam, where the king had been enthroned the year before.

The 19C confirmed the residential character of the town which had become the favourite residence of colonials returning from Indonesia. This period marked it so profoundly that it is sometimes considered as the last example of the 19C.

Spinoza. – The great philosopher passed the last seven years of his life in The Hague; he died here in 1677. Born in Amsterdam in 1632, this Jew of Portugese origin was a brilliant scholar. In 1656 he had to flee from the Jewish community in Amsterdam. Because he contested the value of the sacred texts, they tried to assassinate him. He took refuge for a time in Ouderkerk aan de Amstel *(qv)*, then went to live in Rijnsburg near Leyden in 1660. For three years he devoted himself to philosophy, polishing lenses to earn his living.

After a few years spent in Voorburg, a suburb of The Hague, in 1670 he moved into a modest residence in Paviljoensgracht (**AV**).

It was only after his death that the *Opera Posthuma,* published in 1677 appeared in Latin; it included the **Ethica,** which became universally famous. His pantheistic doctrine whereby God is a Substance of which only two attributes, extension and thought, are known to us, was violently criticised.

The Hague School. – Between 1870 and 1890 a group of painters in The Hague tried to renew painting and notably the art of landscapes in the manner of the Barbizon School in France. Around their leader, **Jozef Israëls** *(qv)*, painter of fishing scenes and portraits, were grouped: **J.H. Weissenbruch** (1824-1903); **Jacob Maris** (1837-99) painter of dunes and beaches; **H.W. Mesdag** painter of numerous seascapes and the famous *Mesdag Panorama (p 115)*; **Anton Mauve** (1838-88) painter of the Gooi heathland *(p 126)*; **Albert Neuhuys** (1844-1914) painter of household interiors; **Bosboom** (1817-91) painter of church interiors; and **Blommers** (1845-1914) painter of the life of fishermen. Neuhuys and Mauve, having worked in Laren, are sometimes attached to the Laren School *(qv)*.

The Hague painters were not looking for brilliance of colour nor the virtuosity of the drawing. In their paintings the prevailing tint has grey or brown, the expression of a certain melancholy.

The diplomatic town. – The Hague was chosen several times as a centre for international negotiations: Peace Conferences (qv) in particular from 1899 to 1907. Finally the construction of the Peace Palace (1913) established its vocation as a diplomatic town.

It is the seat of the International Court of Justice, an organisation dependant on the UN, the Permanent Court of Arbitration and the Academy of International Law.

A number of companies have also made The Hague their headquarters: Royal Dutch (Shell), Aramco, Esso, Chevron.

The modern town. – The Hague belongs to the 20C through its urban expansion. The modern quarters, situated mainly to the southwest, are witness to a successful architectural effort. To the north, the Netherlands Conference Centre (p 118) has been opened to the public since 1969.

Many vast green spaces are a reminder of the primitive forest with marshes transformed into bodies of water. The residential quarters go right up to coastal dunes in a landscape of copses and meadows.

THE CENTRE time: $\frac{1}{2}$ day

Aristocratic residences line the wide avenues around the Binnenhof, the centre of the country's political life. Nearby shops are grouped in pedestrian precincts or covered passages: the town has numerous luxury shops and antique dealers.

Buitenhof (AV 16). – It is the outer courtyard of the old castle of the Counts of Holland. In the centre stands a statue of King William II.

★ **Binnenhof** (AUV). – Enter by the Stadtholder doorway to reach an inner courtyard (binnenhof) in the centre of which is the Knights' Hall. All around the buildings of different periods are, in a way, the emblem of the continuation of the Netherlands's government. They now house the First Chamber and the Ministry of General Affairs (north wing), part of the State Council (west wing) and the Second Chamber (south and east wing). Oldenbarnevelt (qv) was executed in this courtyard in 1619.

★ **Knights' Hall** (Ridderzaal). – An **exhibition** in the cellars of the Knights' Hall (no 8a) explains the origin and workings of the two chambers and the role of the head of state in the monarchy.

The Knights' Hall, destined to be a festival hall for Count William II of Holland, was completed c1280 by his son Count Floris V. The building, which looks very much like that of a church, was located in the prolongation of the old castle. Its façade with a pointed and finely worked gable is flanked by two slender turrets.

Inside, the great hall, restored, has recovered its Gothic vault with openwork beams. It is here that since 1904 (3rd Tuesday in September, p 198) the two chambers of the States General gather for a ceremonial opening session and listen to a speech (on the government's projects to be tackled during the upcoming year) made by the Queen who rides in a gold coach.

In 1907 the second Peace Conference took place here.

The back of the building, visible from the Binnenhof's second courtyard consists of the old castle built c1250 by Count William II. The main hall became, in 1511, the hall of sessions of the Holland and West Friesland Court, and was called the Roll Court.

First Chamber (Eerste Kamer). – Situated in the 17C north wing, in the **Stadtholders' Quarters** (or residence), bordered with a covered gallery, it is the former hall of the Holland and West Friesland States (17C).

Since 1848 it is used as a meeting hall for the Upper House or Senate, which consists of 75 members elected for four years by the twelve Provincial States. It has a wooden ceiling painted in the baroque style by two of Rubens's pupils: A. de Haan and N. Wielingh.

Truce Hall (Trêveszaal). – The Truce Hall, where in 1608 a twelve-year truce with Spain was prepared, is now used by the Council of Ministers. It was rebuilt in 1697 by Marot in the Louis XIV style.

Second Chamber (Tweede Kamer). – In the wing added by the Stadtholder William V at the end of the 18C, the former ballroom has been used since 1815 as the seat of the Lower Chamber (House of Commons or Representatives). Numbering 150 they are elected for four years by universal suffrage. The hall in the Louis XVI style has a balcony and several boxes.

Leave the Binnenhof by the 1634 Grenadiers' Doorway (Grenadierspoort).

★★ **Mauritshuis** (AU). – The Royal Picture Gallery is called Mauritshuis, after Prince John Maurice of Nassau (in Dutch: Johan Maurits van Nassau, qv) who had this elegant residence built in the 17C by Pieter Post, from plans by Jacob van Campen.

An important restoration, completed in 1987, has adapted the building to the requirements of a modern museum.

The exceptional quality of the canvases exhibited makes this museum one of the finest in the world, their relatively small number (about 300), forming a most agreeable collection to visit.

Ground floor. – It is devoted to foreign schools and the Flemish School.

The first room of the **Flemish School** (on right on entering) is remarkable with the pathetic *Descent from the Cross* by Rogier van der Weyden, the penetrating *Portrait of a Man* by Memling, *Christ Carrying the Cross* by Quentin Metsys.

DEN HAAG

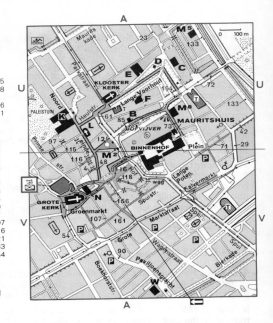

There are four lovely portraits by Holbein the Younger (16C), a touching young girl by the German Bartholomeus Bruyn, Holbein's contemporary; two portraits by Antonio Moro, one very vigorous of a silversmith.

Two rooms are reserved for **Rubens** and his contemporaries. *The Adoration of the Shepherds* by Jordaens, canvases by David Teniers are near a rich collection of works by Rubens: *Isabella Brant*, his first wife, *Hélèna Fourment*, his second, *Michel Ophovius*, bishop of 's-Hertogenbosch, and finally the famous *Adam and Eve in Paradise* where the two personages painted by Rubens can be seen against a landscape painted with charming meticulousness by Jan Bruegel (Velvet Bruegel).

1st floor. – Amongst the Dutch painters of the Golden Age, **Rembrandt** is the reigning master here *(galleries on the right).*

Between the portrait of the artist when he was 23 (1629), which holds one's attention by its meticulous precision of detail, its taste for scrupulous observation, and the portrait of 1669, one of his last works, with an overwhelming depth, one can see the whole evolution of the painter.

The Anatomy Lesson of Doctor Tulp (1632), his first group portrait painted when he was 26, brought him glory; the research in composition, the contrasts of light give the scene a dramatic intensity already characteristic.

The same emotion appears in the luminous *Susanna* of 1637, one of the rare nudes by Rembrandt, the *Simeon in the Temple* (1631) with its subdued muted light, or in the more fiery works like the pathetic *Saul and David* (1658); *The Two Negroes* (1661). The museum also has two admirable paintings by **Vermeer**, the *View of Delft* (c1658), "the most beautiful in the world" according to Marcel Proust and of which Van Gogh said "It's unbelievable", and the *Young Girl with a Turban* or *With a Pearl* (c1658). To these two masterpieces one can compare the *Diana,* one of the first paintings already showing the limpid and serene poetry of the Delft master.

The museum has a number of genre paintings: some Jan Steens, where the verve, malice, and delicacy bring charming anecdotes *(Merry Company),* some Van Ostades with scenes of country life *(The Violinist),* portraits by Frans Hals such as the brilliant *Head of a Child,* some Ter Borchs of great sensitivity, the *Young Mother* by Gerrit Dou...

There are also landscape painters; painters of rivers like Van Goyen, Van de Velde, the countryside, like Salomon van Ruysdael and his nephew Jacob van Ruisdael, skaters, like Avercamp, domestic animals, like Paulus Potter *(Young Bull).*

There are also some small gems: the famous *Goldfinch* which Carel Fabritius, Rembrandt's pupil, painted the year of his death at age 32.

Plein (AUV). – On this square, in the centre of which is the statue of William the Silent (1848), is the Ministry of Defence (Defensie). At no 23 stands a fine edifice built in the 18C from plans by Daniel Marot. In winter an antique market is held on the square.

Hofvijver (Court Lake) (AU). – From Korte Vijverberg, there is a lovely **view★** over the lake in which you can see the Mauritshuis reflected, the octagonal tower of the Prime Minister, the windows of the Truce Hall and the First Chamber. In the middle of the lake, which has a fountain, there is an island planted with trees.

Doelen (AU M⁸). – To the right of Korte Vijverberg are the former premises of the Archers' Company of St Sebastian (1636).

⊘ It houses **The Hague Historical Museum** (Haags Historisch Museum). While waiting for its definite reorganisation, the museum organises temporary exhibits concerning the city's history.

Take Lange Vijverberg.

At no 8 (**AU B**) there is a façade by Daniel Marot.

★ **Lange Voorhout** (AU). – Along the shaded avenues of Lange Voorhout with vast lawns there are some of the most beautiful patrician residences in The Hague. Most of them are occupied by embassies.

Nearby there is a big **antique market**. In the spring the lawns are covered with crocuses.

Paleis (AU C). – The former palace of Queen Emma (1858-1934), wife of William III and mother to Wilhelmina stands at the far end of the main avenue. Its elegant 18C façade is the work of Pieter de Swart. It was the home of a banker when Napoleon stayed in it in 1811.

In front of the Indes Mansion (nos 54-56), there is a lovely statuette of the **"Stroller"** (AU D) by the chronicler Elias.

No 34 (AU E). – This edifice was built in 1734-6 by Daniel Marot.

From 1813-4 William I, first king of the Netherlands, lived here. The building now houses the Supreme Court of Appeal.

At no 15, on the left, stands the building bought by Mesdag *(qv)* to house the **Pulchri Studio** company (AU F) of which he was the president as of 1889.

Kloosterkerk (AU). – This former convent chapel built in the 15 and 16C is used for organ concerts and choral services.

Noordeinde (AU). – This large street with antique shops crosses the square where the **Noordeinde Palace** (Paleis Noordeinde) (AU K) stands. Also called Het Oude Hof, this 16-17C building with two angled wings was occupied by Louise de Coligny, widow of William the Silent, by the princes Maurice and Frederick Henry, sons of the latter *(p 20)*, and by King William I. Queen Beatrix has installed her offices here.

Opposite there is an equestrian statue of William the Silent.

Return towards the south.

★ **Walloon Reformed Church** (Waals-Hervormde Kerk) (AU L). – It was built in 1807 by Louis Napoleon to be used by the French-speaking Protestant community of The Hague which formerly met in the castle chapel.

After the mid-16C the Protestant refugees, fleeing persecution in the Southern Netherlands (Belgium), established French-speaking parish communities. These increased in the 17C with Huguenots coming from France.

The cult is still practised today in **Walloon churches** *(qv)* which are dependent upon the Dutch Reformed Church *(qv)*.

De Plaats (AU 121). – In the centre of this square is the statue (1887) of Johan de Witt who was lynched here at the same time as his brother Cornelis *(qv)*.

★ **Prison Gate** (Gevangenpoort) (AUV M²). – This old curtain wall gate of the ducal castle houses a **museum** (Rijksmuseum Gevangenpoort) which contains a collection of torture instruments. Cornelis de Witt *(see above)* was imprisoned here before being killed on De Plaats.

Groenmarkt (AV). – It is the central square of The Hague where the town hall and the Great Church (Grote Kerk) stand. Numerous pedestrian precincts start from here, notably **Paleispromenade** (AUV) to the north, and **De Passage** (AV), the large covered passage built in 1880, to the south.

★ **Great Church or St Jacob's** (Grote- of St.-Jacobskerk) (AV). – Flanked by a tower with a carillon of 51 bells, this great brick hall-type (three naves of equal height) church (c1450) is roofed with a wooden vault.

In the chancel (c1500), there is the tomb of an admiral and the coat of arms of the knights of the Order of the Golden Fleece who held their chapter in this church in 1456. Several stained glass windows are worth seeing in the ambulatory: on one Charles V is shown kneeling at the Virgin's feet.

The pulpit of 1550 is beautifully sculptured.

Old Town Hall (Oude Raadhuis) (AV N). – This small building has kept a lovely 16C façade with crow-stepped gables. The 18C side façade is elegantly decorated. A modern wing has been added on the east side.

OUTSIDE THE CENTRE *time: ½ day – town plan p 116-117*

★ **Mesdag Panorama** (DY Q). – Installed in a rotunda on piles, lit by hidden windows, this extraordinary landscape of 120m - 394ft in circumference and 14m - 46ft high shows Scheveningen *(p 119)* as it was in 1881. The order for this immense canvas was given in 1880 to the painter **Hendrik Willem Mesdag** *(qv)*. In 1879 from the top of the highest dune in Scheveningen, he had already reproduced the landscape on a glass cylinder shown here.

This work was rapidly carried out: Mesdag painted the sky, the sea, the beach with boats; his wife, Sientje Mesdag van Houten, the village; Théophile de Bock, the dunes; Breitner, the cavalry; Blommers *(qv)*, the woman in costume and her child.

Despite the difference in technique it remains a unit; the perspective is marvellous, the sky over the sea of a very soft luminosity, while behind the village the bell towers of The Hague show up.

The spectator 14m - 46ft below this painting appears to be admiring the panorama from the top of a dune where real sand strewn with wreckage joins up with the bottom of the painting. In the absence of a port the flat-bottomed boats *(bommen)* were towed by horses.

In the entrance hall, added in 1910, paintings and watercolours by Mesdag and his wife are exhibited; note the lovely sombre tonalities.

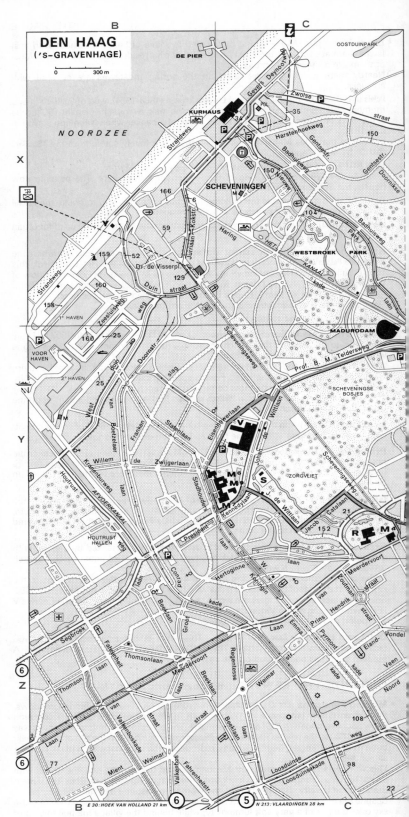

★ **Mesdag Museum** (CY M⁴). – Mesdag built this residence in 1869 to house his
⊘ collections. He bequeathed everything to the State in 1903.

In this museum an interesting comparison can be made between the Barbizon School
(mid-19C) with Millet, Daubigny, Corot, Théodore Rousseau, Courbet, and The Hague
School *(qv)* with Bosboom, Mauve, the Maris brothers, Jozef Israëls and obviously
Mesdag, the painter of seascapes. In the paintings of the two schools one finds fairly
sombre tones, often greyish and the taste for nature and landscapes.

⊙ **Peace Palace** (**Vredespaleis**) (**CY R**). – The Peace Palace was inaugurated a year before the beginning of World War I, on 28 August 1913.
On the initiative of Czar Nicholas II the first **Peace Conference** took place in The Hague (at Huis Ten Bosch) in 1899.
It was decided at that time to create a Permanent Court of Arbitration which was defined in 1907 during the Second Peace Conference which took place in the Knights' Hall *(p 113)*.

In the meantime the American industrialist and philanthropist, Andrew Carnegie, donated the funds to house this Court and equip it with a library, the Netherlands government donated a park and the French architect Cordonnier was put in charge of the construction.

In 1922 the palace became, in addition, the seat of the Permanent Court of International Justice which in 1946 became the **International Court of Justice** (the United Nation's main judicial organ). It also houses the Academy of International Law of The Hague, founded in 1923.

Each nation has contributed to the furnishings and decoration of the palace. The Japanese room, hung with sumptuous tapestries, is where the Administrative Council meets, and where French is the official language; the members sit round an immense table with seats decorated with the various countries' coat of arms. In the marble galleries, on the ground floor, one can see the bust of Grotius *(qv)* and some documents autographed by him.

Walk alongside **Zorgvliet Park** to see the **Het Catshuis (CY S)**, the Prime Minister's house which belonged to **Jacob Cats** *(qv)*.

Follow President Kennedylaan to reach the Municipal Museum.

★★Municipal Museum (Haags Gemeentemuseum) (CY M⁶). – Berlage *(qv)* built this ⊙ museum in 1935; the concrete structure has been covered by brick facing. A gallery leads to the rooms, which laid out in a very elaborate manner, surround a large interior courtyard.

The collections, very rich, consist mainly of ancient decorative arts, 19 and 20C sculpture and paintings.

The museum also has a section of musical instruments. An annexe (1962) houses temporary exhibitions and the costume museum.

Ground floor. – In the decorative arts section there is glassware from Venice (15 and 16C) and the Netherlands (17 and 18C), ceramics from Delft and Italy, silverware (15 to 19C), porcelain from The Hague (17 to 19C), and interiors of the 17 and 18C. Rooms are reserved for ceramics and glassware from Ancient times, Islam peoples and from China, furniture and gold and silverware from Indonesia from the time of the Dutch East India Company.

The collection of musical instruments (European as from the 16C and the whole world) is remarkable (concerts).

1st floor. – The museum houses works by great masters of the 19 and 20C.

The French School is well represented. There is a Courbet *(Bridge, House and Waterfall)*, a Sisley *(The Seine at Daybreak)* and three Monets *(The Louvre Quay, the Nets and Wisteria)*, a Signac *(Cassis, Cape Lombard)*; by Van Gogh, a *Self-Portrait* (1886), the *Poppy Fields* and two other canvases. One can also see: Picasso *(Woman With a Pot of Mustard, Harlequin, Sibyl)*, Braque, Léger, Marquet and two Dutch painters who became Parisians: Van Dongen and Jongkind.

The remarkable collection of Expressionists includes works by Kirchner, Jawlensky and Kandinsky.

One can also get an idea of Dutch pictorial production from the 19C to today; the Romantics with W. Nuyen, The Hague School (the Maris brothers, Jozef Israëls, Weissenbruch), the Amsterdam School (Breitner, Verster), modernism with Jan Toorop, a large collection of **Mondrians,** one of the pioneers of abstract art, and artists of the De Stijl movement *(qv)*.

Among the contemporary artists represented are: Karel Appel, Corneille, Constant, Schoonhoven amongst the Dutch, and amongst foreigners, Vasarely, Arp, Max Ernst, Henry Moore and Bacon.

The print room displays many of the works by the great engraver **M.C. Escher** (1898-1972), works of The Hague School, those of H. Werkman, and amongst numerous French artists, Daumier, Toulouse-Lautrec, Bresdin and Redon.

Since 1985 the municipal museum contains collections from the old Costume Museum of Lange Vijverberg. In their presentation emphasis has been placed on themes rather than on chronological evolution.

Temporary exhibitions are also organised.

⊙**Museon (CY M⁷).** – This modern museum presents, didactically, collections referring to the Earth's origins: geology, biology, ethnology, techniques, physics...

⊙**Omniversum (CY M⁹).** – This amphitheatre (seating capacity 300) shows films on a giant screen (840m² - 9 042sq ft) with the goal of familiarising the viewer to the world of science, astronomy and aeronautics. With its 2 projection systems (Omnimax 70mm and Digistar Planetarium projector) and 40 speakers, the spectator is offered an impressive show.

Netherlands Conference Centre (Nederlands Congresgebouw) (CY V). – Built from the plans of the architect J.J.P. Oud and carried out by his son between 1964 and 1968, the conference centre is a vast building with walls of sky-blue tiles and yellow bricks, overlooked by a triangular 17- storey tower.

The entrance, on the north side, is indicated by a large composition by Karel Appel in red and blue mosaic.

Among the many meeting rooms, the large conference centre (seating capacity 2 000) occupies three floors. It can be used for entertainment: concerts, theatre, ballets. In the basement the festival hall, which can hold 4 000 people, is used for banquets and exhibitions.

Prof. B.M. Teldersweg crosses Scheveningse Bosjes which separates The Hague from Scheveningen.

★ **Madurodam** (CY). – In memory of his son, who died in Dachau in 1945, Maduro built
⏱ this miniature town for children, which adults will find interesting as well – it is like
Gulliver in Lilliput.
Madurodam City is a sort of synthesis of the country, gathering together buildings,
monuments and characteristic sites.
It is a delight to stroll through, recognising the houses of Herengracht in Amsterdam,
Kinderdijk's windmills, the port of Rotterdam, Schiphol airport, fields of flowers, a
farmhouse of South Holland. Trains, cars, buses and boats travel round. At night it is
bright with lights.

ADDITIONAL SIGHTS

The Hague Woods (Haagse Bos) (EY). – Crossed by Leidsestraatweg, these woods
surround the royal palace, **Huis ten Bosch,** where the first Peace Conference *(p 118)* was
held in 1899.
This edifice was built in the 17C by Pieter Post for Amalia van Solms, widow of the
Prince-Stadtholder Frederick-Henry of Orange (3rd son of William the Silent). It is
inhabited by Queen Beatrix.

Westbroek Park (CX). – This park surrounded by lakes (canoeing) is famous for its
rose garden *(early July to late September)* where an international exhibition is held
annually.

St.-Annalands Clingendael (EXY). – This extensive park, with its meadows shaded
by majestic trees and strewn with lakes, was once on private grounds; there is a
Japanese garden.

Heilige Geesthofje (AV W). – Built in 1616, this almshouse, is a charming enclosure
with small low houses with crow-stepped dormer windows.
Opposite, near the house *(no 74)* where Spinoza ended his days, stands the statue of
the illustrious philosopher.

⏱ **Meermanno-Westreenianum Museum** (Rijksmuseum) (AU M[5]). – On Prinsessegracht,
lined with 18C rich patrician residences, this museum houses the Baron van
Westreenen's collections.
The ground floor is usually devoted to exhibitions about books.
On the 1st floor, in the library, there are **manuscripts and incunabula** from the medieval
period; the oldest dated books printed in the Low Countries were edited in 1473 in
Aalst (Belgium) and in Utrecht. The museum also contains: statuettes and papyrus
which was placed beside the dead from Egypt, Greek vases, Roman oil lamps, Gothic
ivory.

★★ SCHEVENINGEN

Belonging to The Hague administrative district, Scheveningen is an elegant seaside
resort with a very large and busy beach. It has often been devastated by storms: the
storm of 1570 submerged part of the village: the church, which, in the past, was
located in the town centre, is now near the beach. Today Scheveningen is protected
by many breakwaters and a high dike.

The beach. – It is a long and wide stretch of fine sand lined for 3km - 2 miles by a
boulevard, Strandweg, which is the continuation to the east of a pedestrian path.
Some important transformations have recently occurred on this seafront. Overlooking
the beach, the **Kurhaus** (CX) an imposing building (1885) contains a casino; events are
also held here.
⏱ The **Pier** (BX), a long promenade-jetty leads to four constructions built on piles offering
entertainment.
An observation tower (45m - 148ft) high offers a panorama stretching over the coast
and out to sea.

The port. – Beyond the lighthouse, towards the west, the fishing port remains very
busy.
Two interior docks (binnenhavens), have coasting vessels, ferry boats with services operating to England (Great Yarmouth), pleasure boats and a fleet of
trawlers.
The **obelisk** (BX Y) commemorates the place where William I *(qv)* landed in November 1813, from England to take possession of his throne.
First situated to the east of the port near the dunes, around Dr. de Visserplein as it is
shown on the Mesdag Panorama *(p 108),* the fishing village has grown with new
quarters to the south and west of the port: they are vast quadrilateral brick buildings
arranged round a courtyard with wide porches.
Old women remain faithful to the traditional costume: black dress and apron with a
black cape in winter (on Sundays it is pastel coloured) or a light-coloured shawl in
summer.
The headdress, placed on a metal headband fixed with two hairpins is distinctive: the
ends of the headband in the shape of an oval buckle of filigree gold stands up on the
top of the head. On Sundays the bonnet is of lace *(for more on the female costume
see p 30).*

⏱ **Boat trips.** – A day of competitive fishing at sea is organised. *Landing stage:
Dr. Lelykade* (BY 25).

EXCURSIONS

Wassenaar. – Pop 26 188. *12km - 7½ miles to the north; leave by ① on the town plan.* Residential suburban town of The Hague, Wassenaar has wealthy villas hidden amongst trees.

Zoetermeer. – Pop 85 349. *16km - 10 miles to the east; leave by ③ on the town plan.* This new town, built to relieve The Hague, will reach a population of 100 000 in its final phase.
It has been built since 1966 round a village, whose 18C **church** has kept a Gothic tower topped by a wooden spire (1642).
Zoeter Lake, formed by peat extraction, was drained in 1614.

Naaldwijk. – Pop 26 933. *16km - 10 miles to the south by ⑤ on the town plan.*
Cross the market-garden region of **Westland,** cut by canals, spread with thousands of greenhouses, orchards and gardens between The Hague, Hoek van Holland and the coastal dunes; flowers are cultivated as well as vegetables (tomatoes, salads, cucumbers).

⊙ **Naaldwijk.** – In the heart of Westland, this is a large horticultural centre and has **auctions** of cut flowers and potted plants.
On Wilhelminaplein, the main square, the old 17C **town hall** (raadhuis) has a baroque voluted gable. Not far away, behind the Gothic church, the **Holy Ghost Almshouse** (Heilige Geest Hofje) groups picturesque, 17C low houses with tall dormer windows lined
⊙ round a chapel of the same period, and now transformed into a **museum.** It evokes the history of Westland.

The times indicated in this guide
when given with the distance allow one to enjoy the scenery
when given for sightseeing are intended to give an idea
of the possible length or brevity of a visit.

HARDERWIJK Gelderland   Pop 33 866

Michelin map **408** fold 11

Harderwijk, a member of the Hanseatic League on the old Zuiderzee, has kept from its past a few picturesque lanes, the remains of its brick ramparts and its port, where one can eat excellent smoked eel.
On the edge of **Veluwe Lake** *(qv),* Harderwijk which has two pleasure boat harbours and a beach, attracts many tourists. The hinterland, which is part of the Veluwe *(qv)* and where dunes, forests and heathland stretch, is very attractive and includes several nature reserves.
The memory of the famous Swedish botanist **Carolus Linnaeus** (Carl von Linné 1707-78) is evoked in Harderwijk as he went to its university. Founded in 1647, this institution was abolished by Napoleon in 1811.
White ducks are bred in the vicinity.

⊙ **Boat trips.** – Boat trips are organised along Flevoland.

SIGHTS

★ **Dolfinarium.** – Near the pleasure boat harbour, next to the **Veluwestrand** leisure centre,
⊙ which has a beach, is this vast Dolfinarium. Amongst the marine mammals shown, one can see dolphins, sea lions, walruses, and seals.

Old town. – It has preserved a number of Renaissance houses (restored) and 18C patrician residences with rococo doors, witness to a rich past.

Vis Gate (Vispoort). – Enter on foot by this charming rampart gate (14 - 16C) which stands near Strandboulevard and gives access to the former fish market.

By Kleine Marktstraat on the right, one reaches Markt.

Markt. – The **town hall** (stadhuis) (1837) stands on the main square, with a portico and topped by a white pinnacle.

Follow **Donkerstraat,** a pedestrian precinct where there are several grand 18C mansions with rococo decorated doorways. In a street (Academiestraat), on the left, one can see the 16C Linnaeus Tower or **Linnaeustorentje** behind which was the university
⊙ garden. At the far end of Donkerstraat, at no 4, is **Veluwe Museum** installed in an 18C residence.
On the ground floor a room is devoted to Veluwe's *(qv)* past. The old gymnasium's rostrum illustrates the importance of education in Harderwijk's past; the part in front was occupied by examination candidates, while the upper seat was reserved for the director. The history of this famous university is evoked on the 1st floor where, notably, there are portraits of professors. Apart from Carolus Linnaeus, Herman Boerhaave *(qv)* and Constantijn Huygens *(qv)* received doctorates in Harderwijk. Coins from the Gelderland Mint, installed in Harderwijk from 1584 to 1806, Veluwe costumes and old Zuiderzee scale models of boats complete the museum's collections.
⊙ Taking Smeepoortstraat, a shopping street on the right, pass in front of the **Great Church** (Grote Kerk), a tall 14C building.
At the far end of the street, Bruggestraat (lovely 18C portals) returns to Markt.

EXCURSION

Elburg. – Pop 20 266. *20km - 12 miles to the northeast.*
This small town, which in the 14C was an active port on the Zuiderzee and belonged to the Hanseatic League, has kept its medieval character. It is still enclosed in its 14C quadrilateral high walls transformed into gardens and encircled by canals. Its streets, laid out like a checkerboard, notably the one which runs alongside the narrow De Beekstraat Canal are bordered with lovely houses. The narrow pavements are covered with black and white cobblestones.

Situated to the north and formerly open on to the sea, **Visch Gate** (Vischpoort), a 14C tower flanked by battlemented turrets, is the only town gateway which remains.

At the other end of the street is the **town hall** (stadhuis), which occupies the imposing buildings of a former convent of 1418 (Agnietenklooster). The **municipal museum** (Gemeentemuseum) is installed in the old Gothic chapel and part of the conventual buildings.

15C **St Nicholas** (St.-Nicolaaskerk), today Protestant, is overlooked by a massive square tower.

In the neighbouring street, Van Kinsbergenstraat, there are interesting houses, one of which is 15C and looks like a keep.

HARLINGEN Friesland   Pop 16 220

Michelin map **408** fold 4 – Local map p 183

Harlingen, Harns in Frisian, which already existed in the 9C under the name of Almenum, received its city charter in 1234. The dike, which protected it, having been submerged, was consolidated by Caspar (or Gaspar) de Robles, governor of the northern regions of the Low Countries in 1573.

The only seaport in Friesland. – Harlingen was formerly a great whaling port, with its boats sailing as far as Greenland until c1850.

Today, at the mouth of Harinxma Canal, it is a port from where dairy products are shipped to England, the departure point for the islands of Terschelling *(qv)* and Vlieland *(qv)* and a great shrimping centre.

Harlingen now also has two pleasure boat harbours.

Industries have been set up north and east of town; the largest tankers can berth at one of the docks.

Harlingen has a school of fluvial navigation and an educational institute for shipbuilding.

Each year there are Fishing Days *(Visserijdagen)* *(see the chapter Practical Information at the end of the guide)* and ring tournaments *(ringrijderij – qv)* as well as a naval review.

SIGHTS

The charm of its old streets makes Harlingen an attractive town. It is pleasant to stroll along the main street, Voorstraat and along the quays of the two old ports, the Noorderhaven and the Zuiderhaven. There are some interesting 16 to 18C façades.

★ **Noorderhaven.** – This dock, which has become a pleasure boat harbour, is lined with picturesque houses and warehouses.

On the north quay, there are some lovely façade stones.

On the south side stands the 18C **town hall** (stadhuis), topped by a low relief depicting the archangel St Michael; the back façade giving on to Voorstraat is flanked by a tower with a carillon.

Hannemahuis Museum (Gemeentemuseum). – *Voorstraat 56.* Installed in the Hannemahuis, an 18C residence, this museum is devoted to the history of Harlingen and its maritime past.

The regional furniture, the seascapes by Nicolaas Baur, painter born in Harlingen (1767-1820), engravings, collections of Chinese porcelain, Frisian silverware and scale models of ships, are all beautiful. A room, giving on to the garden, has a lovely collection of earthenware tiles grouped by motif.

At the far end of the street, near the canal, there is the statue of a schoolboy, Anton Wachter, hero of a series of novels by **Simon Vestdijk** (1898-1971), famous writer born in Harlingen; his works tended to describe middle class provincial life.

Stone Man (De Stenen Man). – At the top of a dike to the south of the port there is a monument crowned with two bronze heads, erected in 1774 in memory of the Governor Caspar de Robles *(see above).*

Behind the dike is Harlingen beach. Fine view over the port.

HAVELTE Drenthe   Pop 5 763

Michelin map **408** north of fold 12

This village in the Drenthe, with handsome regional farmhouses covered in thatch, has two *hunebeds (qv).*

★ **Hunebeds (D 53 and D 54).** – *Take the road to Frederiksoord to the north and opposite a café, there is a road on the right indicating "hunebedden".*

These two megalithic monuments lie in a lovely clearing covered in heather. One is still topped by seven enormous slabs in front of which, on the southeast, is a very conspicuous entrance. The other, smaller one, has a slightly curved shape.

HEERENVEEN Friesland   Pop 37 528

Michelin map 408 fold 5

Heerenveen was founded in the 16C by Frisian lords, hence its name which means: The Lords' Peat.

4km - 2½ miles to the south the flowered houses of **Oranjewoud** are hidden among the hundred year old trees of an old 17C Nassau Frisian property, crossed by small canals.

⊙ Two manor houses **Oranjewoud** and **Oranjestein** adorn this magnificent landscape *(access by Prins Bernhardlaan)*.

The lovely municipal park, De Overtuin, and paths in the woods make it a pleasant place for walks.

HEERLEN Limburg   Pop 93 888

Michelin map 408 fold 26 or 212 fold 2 (inset map)

This town was the main centre of the Netherlands's coal fields which cross Limburg, continue into Belgium, in the Maaseik region, and the Aachen basin in Germany. Mining started in 1896 and was abandoned in 1975. Nevertheless, a number of industries have established themselves in the region and Heerlen is becoming an important commercial centre.

The city possesses a modern quarter built round a vast pedestrian precinct, **Promenade**, and a theatre (Schouwburg), built in 1961.

The Romanesque church of St Pancras has for a tower the old keep of a castle built in 1389 by the Duke of Burgundy, Philip the Bold.

Coriovallum. – Heerlen, ancient Coriovallum, was a Roman camp on the great route going from Boulogne-sur-Mer to Cologne and passing by Maastricht. In 1C AD, another route crossed this Roman camp (Xanthus-Trier). Important Roman baths (2 to 4C) were found in Heerlen.

⊙ **Roman Baths (Thermenmuseum).** – There is a slide projection before visiting the Roman baths, the remains of which can be seen from a footbridge.

The museum also contains objects found during excavations: coins, bronze statuettes, pottery.

EXCURSION

Kerkrade. – Pop 52 827. *10km - 6 miles east of Heerlen.*

A frontier town and a mining centre going back to the Middle Ages, Kerkrade, since its mining activities were abandoned, is seeking to industrialise.

Every four years *(see the chapter Practical Information at the end of the guide)* an International Music Competition (Wereld Muziek Concours) is held here; it draws groups of amateur musicians.

⊙ To the east is old **Rolduc Abbey★** (Abdij Rolduc). *Go towards Herzogenrath and turn left before the railroad.*

Situated at the top of a slope of Wurm Valley which sets the frontier, the abbey is occupied today by a cultural centre, a gymnasium, a seminary and a museum.

The **abbey church** (abdijkerk) is surrounded by 17 and 18C buildings. Started in the early 12C, it has been restored several times, in particular in the 19C by Cuypers who replaced the Gothic chancel by a Romanesque one. On the west side, it has a façade with a massive porch tower flanked by two square towers.

Inside, on the level of the first and third bays of the nave a sort of transept takes shape in the side aisles. The **capitals★** in the nave are very varied. Note also the base of certain engaged columns in the side aisles. The heightened apse is trefoil in shape and built above a Romanesque crypt (remarkable capitals).

⊙ The **Mining Museum** (Mijnmuseum) inside the abbey contains interesting documentation on coal mines: geological information (collections of minerals, fossils), evocation of mine activities by machinery, instruments, scale models, photographs.

DEN HELDER North Holland   Pop 62 943

Michelin map 408 fold 3 – Local map p 183

Den Helder owes its importance to the depth of Marsdiep Channel, which separates it from Texel Island.

Originally **Huisduinen**, a simple fishing village, expanded eastwards. In 1500 the new town took the name of Den Helder.

It was the scene of a heroic exploit of Commander Lahure who, crossing the frozen Marsdiep at the head of 400 hussars belonging to Pichegru's army, captured the Dutch fleet blocked in the ice, in January 1795. In 1799 the British Commander, Abercromby landed with 24 000 men joining up with Russian reinforcements, however, he was defeated and went, no further than Alkmaar.

In 1811 Napoleon made Den Helder a stronghold. Today it is the Netherlands's chief naval base.

⊙ **Navy Museum (Helders Marinemuseum).** – This museum evokes the Royal Navy since 1813 with a selection of scale models, instruments, photos, uniforms, emblems, maps, paintings and engravings.

Worth noting, the section of a torpedo, a reconstituted ship's bridge, a periscope in working order. Films are shown.

EXCURSION

Schagen. – *27km - 16½ miles to the south.*
The road to Callantsoog runs alongside a dike behind which there are several beaches.

Ⓥ **Callantsoog.** – Pop 2 633. To the south there is a nature reserve, **Het Zwanewater** (Swan Lake).

The reserve stretches over 580ha - 1 432 acres amongst coastal dunes and the moors round two lakes which attract many birds. The best time to visit is around mid-May during nesting. From afar one can see the breeding grounds, generally set in reeds. The spoonbills *(illustration p 185)* arrive from Egypt or Spain at the end of February and leave again in July and August.

Schagen. – Pop 16 773. On Thursdays in summer *(see the chapter Practical Information at the end of the guide)* a colourful **market** (Westfriese markt) is held in this town where the costumes of West Friesland are worn.

's–HERTOGENBOSCH (DEN BOSCH) North Brabant Ⓟ   Pop 89 732

Michelin map 🇦🇹🇧🇪 fold 18 or 🇧🇪🇧🇪 folds 7 and 8
Plan of built-up area in the current Michelin Red Guide Benelux

Capital of the North Brabant province, 's-Hertogenbosch is also the seat of a Catholic bishopric. It differs from other towns in the country by its more southern character which can be seen in its tall stone cathedral and its noisy carnival *(see the chapter Practical Information at the end of the guide)*.

HISTORICAL NOTES

Vast forests, which stretched round, were the hunting ground of Duke Godefroy of Brabant, hence the name 's-Hertogen Bosch, the Duke's Wood. Today the town is usually called **Den Bosch**, the Woods. But marshland has replaced the forests.
The castle, built at the end of the 12C, was the centre around which the town grew. s'Hertogenbosch received its city charter about 1185 from Henry I, Duke of Brabant.
The town owes its prosperity to the wool and cloth trades.
In 1561 Philip II of Spain, who reigned over the Low Countries, made 's-Hertogenbosch a bishopric, dependent on the Archbishop of Mechlin.
Taken by the Spanish in 1579, the town only surrendered to the Prince of Orange Frederick-Henry, son of William the Silent, in 1629, after a long siege. Its 17C fortified wall is still clearly marked by a line of bastions and canals in the old moats.
Captured in 1794 by Pichegru after an 18-day siege, Den Bosch became the chief town of the Bouches-du-Rhin *département*.

The modern town. – 's-Hertogenbosch, an important road and rail junction, is well situated on the Zuid-Willemsvaart Canal and near the Maas. Numerous commercial and industrial establishments have developed here, in particular a Michelin tyre factory created in 1947.
The weekly cattle market, which takes place on Wednesdays in the **Brabanthallen,** is a particularly important one.
The inhabitants have several recreation areas: the **Zuiderplas** (64ha - 158 acres) where one can bathe, go sailing, row, fish, etc; **Oosterplas** (65ha - 160 acres) with a large lake (bathing) and the **Prins Hendrik Park (Y)** where there is a stag enclosure and another large lake, **De IJzeren Vrouw (Y).**
A new **Provincial House** (Provinciehuis) was built in 1968-71 to the southeast of the town.

A magician's art. – 's-Hertogenbosch is the birthplace of **Hieronymus Bosch** (c1450-1516) whose real name was Jeroen van Aeken. The life of this painter is not well known, except that he lived a comfortable life in this town.
Solitary genius, Hieronymus Bosch was not attached to any school. At the most one can see Flemish influence in his landscapes with distant perspectives, and the naturalistic tone given in scenes he painted (precision of plants, study of animals) and in the clear strokes and the somewhat archaic outline drawings of his characters.
But with this visionary painter, reality is put to the use of a prodigious imagination. Objects and animals take strange shapes, men and beasts fill fantastic scenes of a dream-like universe, even nightmarish, where it is impossible to distinguish hell from paradise.
Condemn the bad, denounce the ravages of sin was probably the intention of this mysterious artist who was as passionately interested in alchemy as ethics judging by the presence of numerous symbols in his works. His fantasy-like paintings were enhanced by the harmonious colours applied in fine, successive, slightly transparent coats.
His early works were mostly simple and sober, then later the compositions became more complex and the subjects more and more strange, such as in the most extraordinary of his works, the *Garden of Earthly Delights,* where the painter would have had no cause to envy the Surrealists. This last painting is in the Prado Museum in Madrid *(see Michelin Green Guide to Spain),* but one can see several works by Hieronymus Bosch in the Boymans-van Beuningen Museum in Rotterdam *(p 161).*
His only successor was Pieter Bruegel the Elder (c1529-69), who also showed a certain sense of satire and the unusual in his early works.

★★ ST JOHN'S CATHEDRAL (ST.-JANSKATHEDRAAL) (Z B) time: ¾ hour

⊙ It is one of the most beautiful religious buildings in the Netherlands. It was assigned to the Protestant faith from 1629-1810, date when Napoleon came and returned it to the Catholic faith. In 1929 it was given the status of basilica.

Built between 1330 and 1550 in the Brabant Gothic style, it has been much restored since the 19C.

It has a 13C belfry porch whose **carillon,** placed in 1925, has become famous for its concerts.

The cathedral seen from **Parade,** the square to the south, has impressive proportions and a wealth of ornamentation. The fantastic world of grotesque personages astride the flying buttresses may have inspired Hieronymus Bosch. Other amusing figures decorate the side chapels' gable spandrels.

The apse is superb with its numerous radiating chapels round the ambulatory. A lantern turret tops the transept crossing.

Interior. – The very luminous interior has a grandiose appearance with its five naves, 150 columns which, according to the characteristics of the Late Brabant Gothic, are a cluster of slender columns without capitals.

The last restoration, completed in 1985, has brought to light the vault frescoes, which are very varied. The oldest, in the chancel, dates from the first half of the 15C.

Note the canopy, slightly turned and finely worked, above a statue leaning against a pillar of the transept crossing.

The pulpit with its 16C Renaissance low reliefs, the 15C restored stalls and a 17C Renaissance organ case by Frans Symons of Leyden and Georg Schissler are worth seeing.

The copper baptismal font (1492), in the chapel on the left of the great organ, is the masterpiece of a Maastricht coppersmith.

In 1629, when Frederick-Henry, Prince of Orange seized s'Hertogenbosch, the canons left town for Brussels, taking with them the altarpieces which Hieronymus Bosch had painted for the cathedral.

The rood screen, which from 1610 to 1866, was at the transept crossing was replaced in 1985 by a black stone podium decorated with biblical scenes; the original is now in the Victoria and Albert Museum in London *(see Michelin Green Guide to London).*
Among the stained glass windows, all made after 1850, note the window in the north arm of the transept made by Marius de Leeuw (1965).

St Anthony's Chapel in the south arm of the transept has a fine **altarpiece**★ restored by the Antwerp School (*c*1500) which came from a local village. The six small scenes of the lower part, in rather naive fashion depict the birth and childhood of Jesus, but the main theme of the altarpiece is the Passion of Christ, with the Calvary in the centre. The figures carved in wood, notably the Virgin on the right panel (the Lamentation) are particularly remarkable for their expressions.

The Chapel of Our Lady, on the left of the belfry porch, has a miraculous statue of the Virgin (late 13C).

There are numerous memorial slabs on the cathedral floor.

ADDITIONAL SIGHTS

Markt (Z). – This very busy square is in the heart of the city, where one of the main shopping pedestrian precincts starts, **Hinthamerstraat** (Z).

In front of the town hall stands a statue (1929) of Hieronymus Bosch.

Town Hall (Stadhuis) (Z H). – Dating from the 15C it was given a classical façade in 1670. ⏱ Part of its **carillon** was cast by the Hemony brothers.

On the ground floor, the Registrars' Gallery (Trouwkamer) has lovely Cordoba leather hangings.

The 16C vaulted cellar (kelder) has been transformed into a café-restaurant.

De Moriaan (Z). – This building, which houses the tourist information centre (VVV), has, to the north of the Markt, a brick façade with a 13C crow-stepped gable.

★ **North Brabant Museum** (**Noordbrabants Museum**) (Z M¹). – Located in the governor's old ⏱ mansion (1768-9), the work of Pieter de Swarth, this museum evokes the province's history, the medieval town, the guilds, the Eighty Years' War, cults, popular traditions, archaeology...

Among excavated items discovered, there is an amber **statue** of Bacchus (*c*200 AD) found in a woman's tomb at Esch; there are also works by Van Gogh *(Study of a Brabant Peasant)* and by David Teniers the Younger *(The Four Seasons)*. Then one can see sculpture, decorative art objects (guilds' gold and silversmiths' work, rustic jewellery of the 18 and 19C) and costumes.

⏱ **Slager Museum** (Z M²). – It houses works by a family of painters, from Petrus Marinus Slager (1841-1912) to Tom Slager, born in 1918.

EXCURSIONS

Heeswijk-Dinther. – Pop 8 164. *14km - 8½ miles to the southeast by ③ on the town plan.*
⏱ Northwest of town stands the 14C **Heeswijk Castle** (Kasteel Heeswijk), set in the woods and surrounded by moats. It contains interesting furnishings and art objects.
⏱ At Heeswijk, a farmhouse museum, **De Meierijsche Museumboerderij** *(on Meerstraat 20)* retraces the life of Brabant peasants in 1900.

★ **Efteling.** – *25km - 15½ miles to the west. Leave by ⑥ on the town plan.*

Drunen. – Pop 17 080. To the south of the locality stretch the **Drunen dunes.**

Waalwijk. – Pop 28 557. Main centre of the Netherlands' leather and shoe industry, ⏱ Waalwijk has a **Dutch Leather and Shoe Museum** (Nederlands Leder en Schoenenmuseum; *Elzenweg 26*). An important collection of shoes from different countries (Japan, India, North America, Africa); reconstruction of a *c*1930 shoe factory and a 1870 tannery. Other display cases show the evolution of the European shoe.

★ **Efteling.** – *South of Kaatsheuvel.* This **country park** of 68ha - 168 acres offers numerous ⏱ diversions and restaurants: a lake (boating allowed), a swimming pool, playgrounds, etc.

A small steam train goes round the park.

The **fairy tale woods** *(Sprookjesbos; signposted)* are a magical world. Here the dwarfs cry round Snow White's glass coffin, the animals sing, the giant mushrooms play a harpsichord tune. Further on, in front of an oriental palace, a fakir zooms above on a flying carpet. Finally one visits a large haunted castle.

Zaltbommel. – Pop 9 375. *15km - 9 miles to the north. Leave by ① on the town plan.*
This old stronghold, beside the Waal, received its city charter in 1229.
On Markt, the **town hall** (stadhuis), restored, dates from 1763. At no 18 Boschstraat, next to a chemist shop, there is a Renaissance house with caryatids. This, the main street, leads to the 14C water gate, **Waterpoort.**
In Nonnenstraat, to the west of the main street, **the house of** (Huis van) **Maarten van Rossum** ⏱ *(qv)* has been converted into a **regional museum** (Streek Museum).
It has a picturesque façade (1535) with tympana decorated with medallions, corner turrets and crenellations. Inside there is an exhibition of objects from Roman times, discovered during excavations.
At the far end of Nieuwstraat is the 14C **Great Church or St Martin's** (Grote- of St.-Maartenskerk), restored and abundantly decorated, where the imposing 15C belfry porch, is 63m - 207ft high.
The dikes edging the Waal offer lovely views of the river.

Heusdsen. – Pop 5 710. *19km - 11½ miles to the northwest by ⑥ on the town plan.*
On the banks of the Maas, which here becomes the Bergse Maas, Heusden is an old stronghold fortified in 1581.
The town has been restored. Inside its ramparts, which have been transformed into an esplanade, it has some fine façades. Worth seeing is no 4 Hoogstraat (main street), a 17C house with very elaborate scrolls.

⊙ The **town hall** (stadhuis), rebuilt in 1956, has an automatic **carillon** and a Jack -o' the-clock. The **Vismarkt,** fish market, near the dock, is surrounded by 17C houses. A covered market (Visbank) of 1796 still stands.
Heusden has three post **mills.**

Rosmalen. – Pop 25 636. *6km - 3½ miles northeast by ② on the town plan.*

⊙ Set in an amusement park (steam train, airplanes, children's activities) is the **Autotron Transportation Museum.** It contains a fine collection of **automobiles**★ (250 out of the 400 are exhibited) formerly located at Drunen. On the ground floor each significant period in the automobile manufacturing's evolution is illustrated with examples: copy of the petrol powered motor car invented in 1885 by Benz in Germany, several De Dion-Bouton, Panhard & Levasseur, a Ford Model T (1909), Mercedes (1933) belonging to the ex-Kaiser of Germany Wilhelm II *(qv),* American-made limousines (1940s), a Tatra 600 (1947), a Daf (1958)... On the 1st floor are racing cars: note the 1978 Jameson Concorde, which was the most powerful car in the world (top speed 350km/h - 217mph). In the pavilion on the lake admire the Dutch motor cars by the Spyker (1899-1925) manufacture; the Spyker C4 had such qualities that it was nicknamed the Rolls Royce of the continent.

HILVERSUM North Holland   Pop 85 449

Michelin map ▓▓▓ fold 11 – Town plan in the current Michelin Red Guide Benelux

Hilversum in the picturesque moors and woods of the Gooi is, in a way, a large residential suburb of Amsterdam: it is a large built-up area with villas scattered amongst the trees.
In Hilversum and its surroundings to the north, towards Bussum, there are broadcasting stations and the seat of the Netherlands television installations and studios.

★ **Town Hall (Raadhuis).** – *To the north of town, Hoge Naarderweg.* Built between 1928 and 1932, it is the work of **Dudok** (1884-1974). For the most part it is a harmonious juxtaposition of cubic masses where the various different volumes fall nicely into place offering a play of horizontal and vertical lines overlooked by a tall clock tower. On the south side the clock tower is reflected in a lake. The bare walls are of a fairly discreet yellow tinted brick. The aim inside is that all should be functional and rational.

★ GOOI

Round tour of 62km - 38½ miles – allow a day – local map below

Leave Hilversum by ② on the town plan.

Soestdijk. – To the north of town is the **Royal Palace** (Koninklijk Paleis), residence of the Queen Mother (Princess Juliana). This former hunting lodge was used in the summer by the Dutch sovereigns until the marriage of Princess Juliana to Prince Bernhard of Lippe-Biesterfeld, when it became their residence.

Baarn. – Pop 24 764. Pleasant holiday resort near coniferous forests.

Near Laren one enters **Gooi.** This very wooded region of North Holland is in fact just an immense suburb with many wealthy looking houses tucked away in lovely parks where Dutch working in Amsterdam, have chosen to live. A few heathlands are spread about.

Laren. – Pop 12 043. A residential town on a very pleasant site, Laren is a painter's haven. At the end of the 19C the **Laren School** gathered together several painters under the guidance of Neuhuys and Anton Mauve, who were also members of The Hague School.

In the town's centre, around the villa (1911) of the American painter William Henry Singer (1868-1943) a cultural centre (Singer-museum en Concertzaal) was built in 1956 by the painter's widow. It includes a concert hall and a museum.

⊙ The **Singer Museum,** where exhibitions are held, has interesting collections; works by Singer with Impressionist tendencies, 17C Dutch paintings (Van Goyen, Jan Steen), the Laren, Amsterdam and The Hague Schools (Maris, Bosboom, Jozef Israëls, Breitner) and canvases by Van Gogh *(Spring in Asnières).* Sculpture is dispersed throughout the museum and garden.

Blaricum. – Pop 11 024. Lovely residential town in the heart of Gooi.

Huizen. – Pop 40 285. Since the closing of the Zuiderzee *(qv),* this town has become industrialised and has a large pleasure boat harbour.

Naarden. – Pop 16 305. It was the capital of Gooi. Washed by the Zuiderzee, the city was engulfed in the 12C. Naarden, rebuilt in the 14C, became an important stronghold, taken by the Spanish in 1572, by the French in 1673 and besieged in 1813.

Today it is a peaceful city still surrounded by its important system of **fortifications**★ in the shape of a twelve-pointed star and six bastions.

Dating from the 17C, they are surrounded by marshes.

⊘ The casemate of one of the bastions (Turfpoort) has been turned into a **museum,** Vestingmuseum *(Westwalstraat).*

The memory of John Amos **Comenius** (1592-1670), the educational reformer, is perpetuated in Naarden. Born in Moravia, this Czech humanist became bishop of the Bohemian Brothers or Moravian Brothers in 1648 *(qv).* Persecuted he fled to Poland, then in 1656 went to Amsterdam where he ended his eventful life. He devoted himself primarily to educational research. Founder of the educational methods concerning the development of a child's individual observation, in favour of playful methods, he was

⊘ one of the first to claim instruction for everyone. He is buried in the **old Walloon church** of Naarden (Comenius Mausoleum; *Kloosterstraat 29*).

The **Spanish House** (Het Spaanse Huis) where the façade stone evokes the massacre of

⊘ the townspeople by the Spanish in 1572, contains the **Comenius Museum** *(Turfpoortstraat).*

⊘ The 1601 **town hall** is a fine Renaissance building with crow-stepped gables. The interior, is embellished with old furnishings and 17C paintings; it has a scale model of the 17C fortifications.

★ **Muiden.** – Pop 6 820. Near this small harbour used frequently by pleasure

⊘ boats is **Muiden Castle**★ (Muiderslot) standing on the banks of the IJ Lake (IJmeer) and at the mouth of the Vecht. It is an old brick fortress with heavy corner towers, surrounded by a moat; its massive silhouette is visible from afar.

Built *c*1205 to defend the mouth of the Vecht, it was rebuilt by Floris V, Count of Holland. He was assassinated here in 1296 by the nobles, who felt he granted to many privileges to the common people.

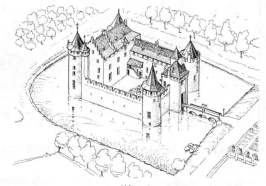

(After photo Aerophoto - Schiphol b.v.)

Muiden Castle in Muiden

Starting in 1621 the castle sheltered an intellectual and literary circle, the **Muiderkring,** which gathered round the owner of the premises, the historian and poet **P.C. Hooft** (1581-1647) and brought together musicians, writers and the poets Vondel and Constantijn Huygens.

The castle contains 17C furniture, paintings, weapons and armour.

Bussum. – Pop 32 540. An important residential town on the edge of Gooi Lake (Gooimeer).

On leaving Bussum, turn right towards 's-Graveland.

's-Graveland. – Pop 9 084. In the vicinity of this town, there are a number of fine manor-houses. **Tromp Manor** (Trompenburg) is the most elegant with its gracious silhouette reflected in the waters of the lake. Built by Admiral Cornelis Tromp, son of the famous Admiral *(qv),* it is a rectangular building linked to a pavilion with a dome.

Return to Hilversum by ④ on the town plan.

HINDELOOPEN Friesland

Michelin map **408** fold 4 – Local map p 169

This small town (Hynljippen), on the banks of IJssel Lake, is one of the eleven cities of Friesland. Member of the Hanseatic League, it was formerly very prosperous due to its trade with Norway.

Away from the road, with its lanes winding between houses and gardens, its footbridges spanning small canals, the tranquility of Hindeloopen is roused in the summer by the presence of many pleasure boats.

Furniture and costumes. – Since the 18C Hindeloopen's furniture is covered with rich colours where red and a dull green prevail. The colours as well as the motifs and shapes are inspired by styles used by sailors in the Far East and in Scandinavia during their long journeys. The Hindeloopen community lived in a closed milieu and each drawing had a ritual meaning.

The costumes also owed much to the Far East: made of cotton cloth with large foliage in reds, greens or blues on a white background *(sits, p 30).*

★ **Museum (Hidde Nijland Stichting).** – Located near the church, this museum captivates by

⊘ its reconstituted interiors, collections of fine traditional costumes and a series of tiles or earthenware pictures evoking great ships of the past.

★★ DE HOGE VELUWE NATIONAL PARK

(NATIONAAL PARK DE HOGE VELUWE) Gelderland

Michelin map **408** fold 12

The De Hoge Veluwe National Park, which covers 5 400ha - 13 338 acres, is a beautiful nature reserve with a famous museum.

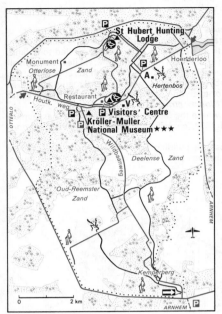

★★★ KRÖLLER-MÜLLER NATIONAL MUSEUM (RIJKSMUSEUM)

time: 3 hours

⊘ Built from the plans of Henry van de Velde, this museum, inaugurated in 1938, owes its name to its founder Willem Kröller and his wife Hélène, born Müller. A Sculpture Park was added in 1960 and a new wing in 1977. It houses an important collection of paintings and sculpture including works by Van Gogh.

To the right of the main entrance is the **sculpture room** (Beeldenzaal): *The Rider and Horse* by **Marini** (1952) is near works by Zadkine and a tapestry by Fernand Léger.

Then, in a succession of rooms, early 20C paintings can be admired.

By **Mondrian** *(qv)* there is a bluish composition of 1913 followed by works in more classical tones by this same artist. The paintings by Van der Leck are followed by works of the **Constructivists** (Strzeminsky) and **Futurists** (Ballà, Severini). **Cubism** is represented by Picasso, Braque, Juan Gris and Fernand Léger *(Soldiers Playing Cards,* 1917).

Grouped round a patio are a rich collection of works by **Van Gogh** dating for the most part from 1889-90: *The Olive Grove, Old Man in Sorrow, The Good Samaritain,* after a painting by Delacroix, *Cypress with a Star, Café Terrace at Night, The Bridge at Arles, Willows at Sunset, The Postman Roulin,* and *L'Arlésienne,* copied from a drawing by his friend Gauguin. There are also works of 1887 like the *Sunflowers,* which was Mrs Kröller's first acquisition and a *Bouquet of Flowers in a Blue Vase,* as well as drawings, a study of a *Weaver,* a *Cemetery, Cypresses.* Other paintings of more somber hue show Van Gogh's earliest style: *Potato Eaters,* the *Weaver's Workshop.*

Opposite the patio there are works by James Ensor, Charley Toorop and a few Pointillist canvases by Seurat *(Ile Chahut)* and Signac. In another room, next to the **French Impressionists,** (Cézanne, Renoir and Monet), there is a landscape by Jongkind. Strange Symbolist works are signed by the Dutch, Jan Toorop *(The Three Brides,* 1893), father of Charley.

Then there are Dutch painters of the Golden Age (Avercamp, Van Goyen, Van de Velde the Younger) and masters of the 16C such as Bruyn the Elder *(Portrait of a Woman with a Carnation,* with a vanitas on the reverse side*),* a *Venus and Amor* (1525) by Hans Baldung Grien, which one can compare with Cranach's.

The museum also displays Greek ceramics, Chinese and Japanese porcelain and 19C ceramics (Mendes da Costa).

In the **new wing,** the presentation of contemporary sculpture representing various styles, such as Minimal Art, the Zero Group and Arte Povera, alternates with temporary exhibitions of contemporary sculpture and architecture.

★ **Sculpture Park** (Beeldenpark). – *Access by the Kröller-Müller Museum.*

⊘ Extending over 10ha - 25 acres this tree-shaded park exhibits more than 90 sculptures by contemporary artists under the shade of the trees.

On leaving the museum one can see: a polyester by Marta Pan (1961) (**B**), *Niobe Weeping on the Ground* by Permeke (1951) (**C**), the thoughtful *Penelope,* by Bourdelle (1912) (**D**), *The Air* by Maillol (1939) (**E**).

Further on, a **pavilion** designed by Rietveld in 1953 has small or fragile sculptures (Barbara Hepworth). Nearby there is a *Walking Man* by Giacometti (1960) **(F)**.
A great number of sculptures are spread round the woods. Amongst the most varied creations there are: the *Concette Spaziale Nature, 5 Spheres,* by Lucio Fontana (1965) **(G)**, and the gigantic *Trowl,* by Claes Oldenburg (1971). One can also look round the **Enamel Garden** by Dubuffet (1975), a vast white honey-combed construction.
Finally one can see the work of Richard Serra, *Spin Out,* consisting of three steel plates carefully arranged in the hollow of a dune **(H)**.

★ PARK *time: 1½ hours*

Clusters of tall beech and oak trees broken up by clearings, pine and birch woods alternate with heathlands, sand dunes and lakes.
The park contains numerous animals (red deer, moufflons, wild boars, roe deer and a great variety of birds). One can watch them from an **observation post** (Wildkansel) **(A)** or from the place called **Vogelvijvers (V)**. Period recommended for watching the animals: winter and spring until end May, in the late afternoon.
Good roads cross the park, as well as cycling paths and pleasant footpaths. It is forbidden to leave certain roads from mid-September to mid-October.

De Aanschouw Visitors' Centre (Bezoekers Centrum). – The centre contains documentation on the park and the Kröller-Müller Museum; as well as an exhibition on the history of the park, its landscapes, its flora and fauna and recreational possibilities.

St Hubert's Hunting Lodge (Jachtslot St.-Hubertus). – This pavilion was built (1914-20) with Berlage's designs. Mrs Kröller died here in 1939, her husband in 1941.

(After photo Tegelmuseum, Otterlo)

17 and 18C ceramic tiles, Museum of Ceramic Tiles in Otterlo

Otterlo. – *1km - ½ mile from the west entrance to De Hoge Veluwe National Park.*
Otterloo has a **Museum of Ceramic Tiles** (Tegelmuseum "It Noflik Sté"), which houses a large collection of Dutch earthenware tiles, for ornamental tiling and facings, from the 14C to today: polychrome as from *c*1600, blue from about 1620, blue and violet in the 18 and 19C. Although 16C tiles, the influence of Italian earthenware and then Chinese porcelain are apparent, in the 17C typical Dutch themes appear. Landscapes and pastoral scenes were much appreciated in the 18C; note the mantelpiece covered with tiles painted with biblical subjects (late 18C) which came from the Zaan region *(p 182)*.
In addition there are paintings with blue, violet or polychrome tiles (18 to 20C) and a collection of tiles from abroad.

★ HOORN North Holland   Pop 53 788

Michelin map **408** folds 10 and 11
Plan of built-up area in the current Michelin Red Guide Benelux

One of the most characteristic ports of the old Zuiderzee, Hoorn, on the banks of IJssel Lake opposite the future Markerwaard Polder *(qv)*, is devoted to pleasure boating; it is also a very busy commercial centre.
Between Hoorn and Medemblik there is a **tourist train** (Stoomtram Hoorn Medemblik); the journey can be combined with a boat trip from Medemblik to Enkhuizen *(qv)*. The equipment is picturesque and varied (steam trains and rail cars) forming a sort of museum on wheels.
Wednesdays in season *(see the chapter Practical Information at the end of the guide)* there is a **market** (Maxi-Markt): folklore dancing, performances and concerts.

HISTORICAL NOTES

Founded *c*1300 round a natural harbour, Hoorn rapidly became the main settlement in Western Friesland. It owed its prosperity to overseas trade and fishing. It was in Hoorn that the first large fishing net for herrings was woven in 1416, the beginning of the flourishing fishing net industry.
To the north, wide canals made into gardens, outline the site of the moats of the early 16C ramparts.
In October 1573 just outside the harbour the famous naval battle, the Battle of the Zuiderzee, took place; the Dutch fleet defeated the Spanish Admiral Bossu.
In the 17C Hoorn lived its days of glory as administrative and commercial centre of all Holland, north of Amsterdam. It was also one of the six ports or *kamer* of the Dutch East India Company *(qv)*.

HOORN★

It was the time of **Willem Schouten** (1580-1625): the first to round the southern tip of South America, south of the Strait of Magellan; he gave the last headland of the Tierra del Fuego the name of his home town: Cape Horn.

Jan Pieterszoon Coen (1587-1629), also born in Hoorn, was the Governor General of the Dutch East Indies from 1617-23 and from 1627-9. He founded Batavia (today Jakarta) and is considered the founder of the colonial empire of the Dutch East Indies (Indonesia).

The decline felt in the 18C by the Dutch was particularly strong in Hoorn, which had to wait two centuries before recovering.

★THE OLD QUARTER *time: 3 hours*

The town began here: old façades follow one another, many decorated with lovely sculptured stones many of which have navigational themes.

Onder de Boompjes (Y 34). – To the far east of the quay, an old warehouse (Y A) of 1606 is decorated with a sculptured façade stone depicting two ships of the Dutch India Company.

To the far west, the **Doelen (Y)** home of the archers' guild, has a central façade (1615) with a fine porch topped by a low relief (martyr of St Sebastian, patron saint of the archers).

Korte Achterstraat (Y 22). – A narrow street; where at no 4 one can see the porch of the old orphanage or **Weeshuis (Y B)**. A memorial stone recalls that Admiral Bossu was emprisoned in Hoorn.

Not far away, in Muntstraat, at no 4, there is a house with a voluted gable with the letters VOC indicating that it once belonged to the Dutch East India Company (Verenigde Oostindische Compagnie).

Nieuwstraat (VZ 31). – In this shopping street stands the **old town hall** (stadhuis) (Y F) with its double crow-stepped gabled façade (1613), housing the tourist information centre.

The house, at no 17, presents a façade with Poseidon and Aphrodite accompanied by dolphins.

Kerkplein (Z 16). – At no 39 opposite a church (no longer used), the **De Boterhal** or butter market, formerly St John's almshouse (St.-Jans Gasthuis), is a fine 1563 residence with a gable decorated with sculptures.

Kerkstraat (Z 18). – At no 1 there is a fine 1660 façade.

★**Rode Steen (Z).** – This picturesque square is overlooked by the West Friesland Museum and by the weigh house. In the centre stands a 19C statue of Jan Pieterszoon Coen *(see above).*

The house at no 2 has a façade stone depicting a blacksmith, hence its name: *In Dyser Man* (To the Iron Man).

⊙**West Friesland Museum** (Westfries Museum) **(Z M¹).** – Built in 1632 the museum, is an elegant edifice in the baroque style. Its tall **façade★** is imposing with its large windows, very colourful coats of arms (House of Orange and West Friesland) and cornices topped by lions holding the armorial bearings belonging to seven towns of the region. It was the seat of the States' College: consisting of delegates from seven important towns, it governed West Friesland and the Noorderkwartier (Northern Quarter).

In the entrance note a lovely gate (1729).

In the basement there is an exhibition of excavated objects (Bronze Age tombs...).

On the ground floor there is a fine hall (Grote Voorzaal) decorated with a lovely chimney and guild paintings; the beams are supported by corbels sculptured with coats of arms of the region's towns.

On the 1st floor, the rooms decorated with lovely furniture and *objets d'art* reproduce the refined setting of the wealthy interiors, of the 17 and 18C including a great number of items brought back from the Far East by the Dutch India Company.

The 2nd floor is dedicated to Hoorn's maritime activities. There is a **portrait of Admiral De Ruyter** by Ferdinand Bol (1667). Amongst the scale models of ships, there is a flute (a fly-boat) built in Hoorn in 1595. A small section of regional, naive paintings shows the work of contemporary artists.

In the attic there are shop signs, scale models of mills and ships, pottery.

Weigh House (Waag) **(Z).** – Probably the work of Hendrick de Keyser, it is a fine 1609 building in blue stone, which today houses a restaurant. In a niche, a unicorn holds a shield depicting a cornucopia.

(After photo Westfriesmuseum)

Portrait of Admiral De Ruyter by F. Bol,
West Friesland Museum

HOORN

Grote Oost (Z). – In this street the houses near the square are very steeply inclined and topped with imposing sculptured balustrades in the rococo style.

East Church (Oosterkerk) (Z L). – This restored church dates from the 15 and 16C; a façade, added in the early 17C, was topped with a charming wooden pinnacle. Concerts are held here.

Bossu Houses (Bossuhuizen) (Z D). – On their façades they have a frieze in relief depicting the sea battle of 1573, in which Admiral Bossu was defeated. The left façade is very typical of old shops in Hoorn, with a ground floor topped by tall narrow windows separated by carved wood pilasters.

Oude Doelenkade (Z 35). – On the Binnenhaven quay, or inside harbour, there is a row of old warehouses, note nos 21 and 19 (Z E) with their façade stones depicting boating scenes.

★ **Veermanskade** (Z 45). – This quay is lined with a lovely series of restored houses. Most of them old merchants' residences have the typical façade of Hoorn, with carved wood pilasters. Some have lovely façade stones and are topped by crow-stepped or bell gables (p 48).
Note the birthplace of the navigator **Willem Bontekoe** (1587-1630); the façade displays a spotted cow (*koe: cow; bonte: spotted*).

Hoofd Tower (Hoofdtoren) (Z). – Built in 1532 to keep watch over the port's main (*hoofd*) entrance; in 1651 it was topped by a wooden pinnacle. On the other side of the tower a sculpture depicts a unicorn. Since 1968 a trio of ship's boys – bronze sculpture by Jan van Druten – contemplate the port from the foot of the tower. They are the heroes of a children's novel by Johan Fabricius dedicated to Bontekoe.

Bierkade (Z 6). – Interesting façades (nos 10 and 13) (Z K) line this beer quay (*bier: beer*).

HULST Zeeland   Pop 18 548

Michelin map 408 fold 16 or 212 fold 14

At the frontier with Belgium, Hulst is a small town with cheerful, colourful houses and streets paved with pink brick. It is an old fortified town which was located on an important defence line made up of 13 bastions.
In the past it was the capital of the said Quatre-Metiers region (*mestiers* meaning administrative district) comprising Axel, Assenede and Boechout (these last two cities became Belgian in 1830).
From the 17C Hulst has kept its grassy ramparts with numerous bastions, crowned with fine trees, surrounded by moats and made into an esplanade.

Reynard's city. – The surroundings of Hulst are evoked in the Dutch tale written in the mid-13C and inspired by the medieval epic *Reynard the Fox*.
Near Ghent Gateway (Gentsepoort) a monument in honour of Reynard has been erected (Reinaertmonument).

SIGHTS

Grote Markt. – The **town hall** (stadhuis) with a perron flanked by a square tower, dates from the 16C.

The **St Willibrord Basilica** (St.-Willibrordusbasiliek) is a fine Gothic edifice. Its tower (restored) has an excellent carillon. For more than a century (1807-1931), the church was used by both Catholics and Protestants: the chancel and ambulatory being reserved for the first, the nave for the second.

Dubbele Gateway (Dubbele Poort). – Near one of the town's gateways, important excavations have uncovered the remains of this early 16C gateway. A water gate as well, it stood over a navigable tunnel giving access to a military port.

From the top of the nearby ramparts, one can see the crow-stepped gable and octagonal turret of the old **Ter Duinen Abbey refuge,** the ruins of which are in Belgium. This refuge houses a **museum** (Streekmuseum "De vier Ambachten") of local and regional history.

Windmill (Stadsmolen). – On the ramparts, it was built by the garrison in 1792.

EXCURSION

Terneuzen. – Pop 35 411. *24km - 15 miles to the northwest*. This port at the mouth of the Scheldt commands the entrance to Ghent Canal in Terneuzen.

Accommodating ships of up to 70 000 metric tons, it has three **locks,** the most important being 290m - 951ft long and 40m - 131ft wide.

In this complex of locks one can examine their workings closely.

★ HUNEBEDS Drenthe and Groningen

Michelin map **408** folds 6 and 13

A prehistoric funerary monument, a *hunebed* is a kind of covered passage formed more or less by an alignment of several dolmens. It has a side entrance usually orientated to the south. Megaliths of this type, which exist in the Netherlands, are grouped in the Drenthe where 53 have been registered and numbered (D 1, D 2...). Only one is not included, that of Noordlaren *(qv)* which is in the province of Groningen (G 1).

Imposing dimensions. – The smallest *hunebeds* are not less than 7m - 23ft long whereas a length of 25m - 82ft is usual. The biggest covered alleyway is near Borger: the slabs which form it weigh more than 20 metric tons. The rocks used to build *hunebeds* are erratic boulders from the **Hondsrug** (Dog's back), a frontal moraine from a Scandinavian glacier, which extended from Groningen to Emmen. At present *hunebeds* have lost their original aspect. In early days, in fact, the *hunebed* was hidden under a small burial mound, the earth being held up by a ring of upright stones; the

Emmen's reconstructed hunebed (detail)

space between these uprights was filled in by small rocks. In Emmen *(qv)* and especially south of Schoonoord *(qv)* one can see reconstructed *hunebeds*.

A funerary function. – Hunebeds prove that prehistoric life existed in the Drenthe from 3 000 or 2 000BC. They were used as collective burial chambers. Dishes, plates, tools and even jewellery were placed next to the bodies. Consequently the excavations made under the *hunebeds* have been very fruitful. The objects discovered, notably pottery, have made it possible to connect *hunebeds* with the civilisation known as Bell-Beaker folk.

★ HUNEBED ROAD

From Emmen to Noordlaren

52km - 32 miles – allow 1 day – local map p 133

Emmen. – *Description p 90.*

Klijndijk. – *Go towards Valthe on the right.* On leaving the village turn right on to a sandy path, then left. Skirting the woods one reaches a long *hunebed* where two capstones remain.

Valthe. – On leaving the village towards the northeast, on the right before a petrol station, a lane marked *hunebed (about 400m - ¼ mile)* leads to *hunebed* D 37, surrounded by oaks. It is in fact two covered alleyways one of which has been knocked down by three large oaks.

> *Going towards Odoorn, on the left after a wood, there is a small lane marked hunebed which leads to hunebed D 34.*

Set among heather, it is a small covered alleyway with two half-fallen down slabs.

Odoorn. – Pop 12 269. At Odoorn, centre of a sheep rearing region, a very important sheep market is held annually.

At **Exloo** *(4km - 2½ miles north of Odoorn)* the shepherd's feast (Schaapscheerdersfeest) and an ancient handicrafts festival are held each year *(for these two events see the chapter Practical Information at the end of the guide).*

On leaving Odoorn, *hunebed* D 32 reached by a small path marked *hunebed,* is hidden behind a curtain of trees. It is topped by four capstones.

Borger. – Pop 12 498. *In the main street, take the road to Bronneger.* At the fork ⏲ there is the **National Hunebeds Information Centre** (Informatiecentrum) devoted to *hunebeds* and life during prehistoric times.

A little further on, surrounded by trees, is the Borger **hunebed★** (D 27), the biggest of all.
It is still topped by nine enormous capstones. Its entry on the south side is very visible.

Bronneger. – *In this hamlet, a path marked* hunebed *leads to an oak wood.* There are five small *hunebeds* (D 23/25 and D 21/22).

Drouwen. – The *hunebeds* (D 19/20) are on a rather bare mound, near the main road (they are visible from the road). One is surrounded by a circle of stones.

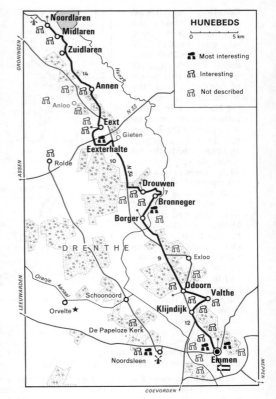

6km - 3½ miles to the north of Drouwen, go left towards Assen, then turn right towards Eext, before a small station (halte).

Eexterhalte. – Shortly after the fork, on the right there is a **hunebed★** (D 14) topped by six capstones. One can still see some of the stones encircling it.

Eext. – In this village, in line with a bend, a path on the left leads to a *hunebed* (D 13), which has kept its original appearance; set in a cavity at the top of a mound, it consists, of a square of uprights pressed closely together, and still has one of the capstones which served as the roof. Two stones set further apart mark the entrance, located, exceptionally, on the east side.

Annen. – Small *hunebed* (D 9) on the left of the road.

Zuidlaren. – Pop 10 424. Important tourist centre.

Midlaren. – The village has two *hunebeds. Turn left, between two houses, on to a dirt track called* Hunebedpad.
200m - 656ft away, after having crossed a road, and behind two houses shaded by large trees are two covered alleyways (D 3/D 4) each one made of several enormous slabs.

Noordlaren. – *Before reaching the mill, take a lane on the left marked* hunebed *which leads to a grove.* This *hunebed* (G 1), where there still remain two capstones resting on five uprights, is the only one in the Groningen province.

IJSSEL LAKE (IJSSELMEER)

Flevoland-Friesland-Gelderland-North Holland-Overijssel

Michelin map **408** folds 4, 10 and 11 – Local map p 134

IJssel Lake is the name that has been given to the Zuiderzee since it was cut off from the sea by the construction of a Barrier Dam in 1932.

HISTORICAL AND GEOGRAPHICAL NOTES

The old Zuiderzee. – The IJssel River formerly flowed into a series of small lakes. Enlarged progressively they developed into a large lake called **Lake Flevo** by the Romans and in the Middle Ages, known as **Almere** or Almari. In 1287 a tidal wave destroyed part of the north coast, enlarged the mouth of the Vlie, the lake's outlet and invaded the low-lying regions which surrounded it, turning it into a large gulf open to the North Sea. It owes its name of Zuiderzee or South Sea to the Danes.
From the 13 to 16C commercial ports developed such as Staveren, Kampen, Harderwijk, affiliated to the **Hanseatic League,** an association of towns in Northern Europe which had the monopoly of traffic in the Scandinavian countries. In the 17 and 18C, trade turned towards the Far East and brought prosperity to such towns as Amsterdam, Hoorn, Medemblik, Enkhuizen, etc.

Creation of IJssel Lake. – The idea of closing the Zuiderzee by a dike goes back to 1667 when **Hendrick Stevin** published a work in which he proposed this means of fighting against the devastation created by the North Sea. In 1825 a violent storm ravaged the coasts of the Zuiderzee. In 1891 a project was presented by the engineer **Dr. C. Lely** (1854-1929). It was only adopted by Parliament in 1918, following the terrible floods of 1916 and when Lely had become Minister of Public Works for the third time. The aim envisaged was triple: by the construction of a dike to put an end to the floods which menaced the banks of the Zuiderzee, make a reserve of fresh water to stop the increasing salinity of the soil, and with the creation of polders to gain 225 000ha - 555 750 acres of fertile land.

The work on IJssel Lake started in 1919; in 1924 the small Westerland Dam linking **Wieringen Island** to the continent was completed.

The Wieringermeer Polder. – From 1927 to 1930 this polder was made. It stretches over 20 000ha - 49 400 acres in a former gulf of the Zuiderzee, between Medemblik and the former Wieringen Island. Immediately after the drainage, the polder presented a surface of muddy clay, so in order to continue the work it was necessary, even before the end of pumping (600 million m^3 - 21 188.4 billion f^3 of water) to drain the future collection ditches.

In 1945, two weeks before their surrender, the Germans blew up the Wieringermeer Polder dike which then flooded. The water hollowed out two gaps of more than 30m - 98ft deep, engulfing a farm. These gaps could not be filled in and the dike, restored, had to be rerouted: it is the place called **De Gaper** (the Yawner). Again drained and returned to its former state, the polder is now a flourishing agricultural region.

Construction of the dike. – The Barrier Dam (Afsluitdijk) *(see below)* was undertaken in 1927 between the Frisian coast and the former Wieringen Island by means of an artificial island (Breezand) built between the two points.

With clay brought up from the bottom of the Zuiderzee, a dike was built, against which sand was deposited; the sand doubled by a layer of clay was collected on the spot by pumping. As the work advanced the current grew stronger increasing in violence, and so the closing of the last channels was properly done inspite of the great obstacles encountered.

The Barrier Dam was completed on 28 May 1932. 30km - 19 miles long and 90m - 295ft wide at sea level, it overlooks the sea by more than 7m - 23ft and forms a new lake, IJssel Lake.

Three large polders. – Once the Barrier Dam was completed, the creation of the second IJssel Lake polder was undertaken, the **Northeast Polder** *(qv)* and then the two **Flevoland★** polders *(p 96)*.

At present the development of a final IJssel Lake polder is being studied, the **Markerwaard** (about 40 000ha - 98 800 acres). To the north, part of the surrounding dike, completed, is used as a means of communication between Enkhuizen and Lelystad.

★★ BARRIER DAM (AFSLUITDIJK) 30km - 10½ miles

On the **Den Oever** side, at the dam's entrance, stands a **statue** of the engineer Lely on the left. On the seaward side the Barrier Dam has a breakwater which protects a bicycle path and a dual carriageway. Below the Barrier Dam on the IJssel Lake side, fishermen come to place their nets on the bottom of the lake, mainly to catch eels.

The **Stevin Lock** which bears the name of the engineer Stevin *(see above)*, forms the first group of locks for ships to pass through. They are also used to evacuate water.

At the point where the two sections of the Barrier Dam joined in 1932, there is now a **tower** with the inscription "A living nation builds for its future". From the top of this monument there is a **panorama** over Wadden Sea and IJssel Lake. Near this edifice a footbridge spans the road.

Further on, a viaduct built in 1970 makes cross traffic possible between the two ports of **Breezanddijk** and gives drivers the possibility of turning back.

Beyond **Lorentz Lock,** the second group of locks crossed by a viaduct, the Barrier Dam rejoins the eastern side of IJssel Lake.

Michelin map **408** fold 12 – Town plan in the current Michelin Red Guide Benelux

Kampen extends along the IJssel's west bank, near the mouth of the river. In the Middle Ages it was a very prosperous port due to the herring trade. It was a Hanseatic League city *(qv)* with commercial ties extending over the whole Baltic basin.
In the 16C there was a very rapid decline in the town brought about by the wars, which ruined the hinterland, and by the silting up of the IJssel. In the 19C a channel was made leading to the Zuiderzee but the closing of this sea reduced Kampen to the status of a river harbour.

Hendrick Avercamp (1585-1634). – This artist called the Mute of Kampen (due to his disability) came to work in the town in the early 17C. From his Flemish master Gilles van Coninxloo, he learnt Bruegel's style. But by the delicacy of the tones used, the presence of innumerable people and the serene atmosphere, his winter scenes have a surprising originality.
His nephew **Barent Avercamp** (1612-79) was his pupil and faithful imitator.

★ **Viewpoint.** – From the east bank of the IJssel, there is an overall view of the town, which is particularly beautiful at sunset. In the centre, the onion-shaped turret of the old town hall and the New Tower stand out, to the right the 14C Buiten Church (1), to the left St Nicholas and the large towers of the Corn Market Gateway.

⊘ **Boat trips.** – *Boat trips are organised to Urk, Enkhuizen or on the IJssel.*

Numbers in brown refer to the sight location on the map below.

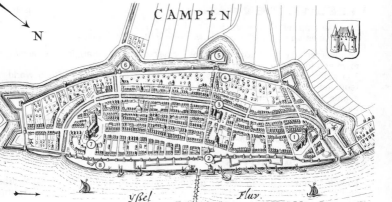

(After photo Stedelijk Museum, Kampen)

SIGHTS

⊘ **Old Town Hall (Oude Raadhuis) (2).** – A little crushed by the new 18C town hall, it is a small edifice of 1543 crowned with galleries and flanked at the back by a slightly leaning octagonal tower with an openwork onion-shaped dome. Its pinnacle gable is surrounded by bartizans. On the façade the statues were replaced at the beginning of the century.
The **Magistrates' Hall★** (Schepenzaal), with somber 16C oak wainscotting forming the seats, has an oak **bench** richly decorated with Renaissance style reliefs, next to a monumental **chimneypiece★** by Colijn de Nole (1545). Dominated by the head and coat of arms of Charles V, the chimneypiece has a gracious statue of Charity in its centre.

Old Butcher's Shop (Oude Vleeshuys). – *Oudestraat 119.* On the stone façade (1596) the town's coat of arms is engraved: two lions framing a fortified gateway.

⊘ **New Tower (Nieuwe Toren).** – It is a tall square tower, erected in the 17C, topped by an octagonal bell tower with a carillon cast by the famous Hemony brothers.

Gothic House (Gotische huis). – *On the right of the New Tower.* This elegant residence with a very tall façade, crowned with pinnacles and pierced with numerous windows,
⊘ contains the **municipal museum** (Stedelijk Museum). There is, notably, a collection of silverware of the boatmen's guild with a fine 1369 **goblet★** of horn and silver and costumes of the region (Kampereiland) which included former Schokland Island.

> *Pass under the New Tower and follow Nieuwe Markt to Burgwal, a quay running alongside Burgel Canal, which crosses the town; turn left.*

Broeder Church (Broederkerk) (3). – This is the former church of the Minorites (Franciscans).

Broederweg. – On the right side of this street, there is a Gothic chapel, a former Walloon church *(qv)* which in 1823 became a **Mennonite church** (4).

Monks' Gateway (Broederpoort) (5). – It is a lovely gateway with a voluted gable (1465) flanked by graceful turrets.

After the gateway, turn left.

Plantsoen. – This is the name of the pleasant park which follows the old ramparts: the moats form the Singelgracht.

Cloistered Monks' Gateway (Cellebroederspoort) (6). – An elegant building flanked by steeply pitched roofed towers, this gateway, which was part of the 15C walls, was altered in the 17C in the Renaissance style.

Go through the gateway and follow Cellebroedersweg then Geerstraat. By Boven Nieuwstraat, on the right, one reaches Muntplein.

⊘ **St Nicholas's (St.-Nicolaas) or Upper Church (Bovenkerk)** (7). – It is a vast Gothic edifice of the mid-14C, overlooked by a tower 70m - 230ft high.
The interior is vast: nave and four aisles, a wide transept and a large ambulatory with radiating chapels. Note the 16C chancel screen and a Late Gothic pulpit.
⊘ The **organ,** dating from 1676, was altered in 1741 by Hinsz.

Corn Market Gateway (Koornmarktspoort) (8). – It is the oldest gateway to the town. Dating from the 14C and situated on the old corn market (Koornmarkt) near St Nicholas, the gateway has kept its defensive character with a massive central keep flanked, since the 15C, by two squat towers.
The municipal museum holds exhibitions inside.

★ LEEUWARDEN Friesland P   Pop 85 191

Michelin map **408** folds 4 and 5 – Local map p 139
Plan of built-up area in the current Michelin Red Guide Benelux

Leeuwarden – Ljouwert for the Frisians – crisscrossed by canals, is an attractive, busy town and the Frisians' cultural centre.
The dairy industry is prosperous. The Frisian cow, a species with a world-wide reputation, has been immortalised on Zuiderplein by a famous bronze statue, a little larger than life, which the town's inhabitants familiarly call **Us Mem,** our mother (Z **A**).
In the immense Frieslandhal, the weekly (Fridays) cattle market (Z) and a show of prize bulls *(see the chapter Practical Information at the end of the guide)* are witness to the importance of Frisian stock-farming.

HISTORICAL NOTES

Founded from the linking of three mounds located on the edge of the old **Middelzee,** a sort of gulf, drained between the 14 and 18C, Leeuwarden gained some importance in the 12C when it was fortified.

Capital of Friesland. – A subject of dispute between the Counts of Holland and the Dukes of Saxony, who obeyed the German emperor, Friesland was given, in 1498 by Maximilian, to Duke **Albert of Saxony** who took up residence in Leeuwarden, which had become the capital. In 1516, under Charles V the town was fortified again.
After the independence of the United Provinces, Leeuwarden in 1584 became the residence of the **stadtholders** of Friesland and Groningen. The first was **William Louis** of Nassau (1560-1620) son of John of Nassau (brother of William the Silent). In 1675, under Henry Casimir II (1657-96), the Frisian stadtholdership became hereditary. **John William Friso** (1684-1711) received the title of Prince of Orange as a legacy from the Holland stadtholder (and king of England) William III. Friso's son **William IV** (1711-51) stadtholder of Friesland was chosen the first hereditary stadtholder of the whole country in 1747. The present dynasty in the Netherlands stems from him, the first king being his grandson William I *(see family tree p 20).*
In 1580 Leeuwarden received its new curtain wall and, in the beginning of the 17C, a few bastions to the north and west, which were razed in the 18C and today have been converted into an esplanade bordered by the Stadsgracht.
In 1876 Margarethe Geertruida Zelle was born here. Having learnt to dance in the Dutch Indies (Indonesia), she went to Paris in 1903 and became famous as a dancer under the name of **Mata Hari** (in Malayan: Eye of the Day). She was shot in 1917 for spying for the Germans.
Since 1909, Leeuwarden is the departure point of the famous **Eleven Towns Tour** (Elfstedentocht) a race where, when the Frisian canals are frozen, skaters compete over a distance of about 200km - 124 miles. The last race took place in 1986.

SIGHTS

Chancellery (Kanselarij) (YZ **B**). – These former law courts in the Renaissance style (1566) reveal, on Turfmarkt (peat market), a wide, heavily decorated façade, and topped by a slender dormer window with a statue of Charles V. The perron is flanked by heraldic lions. It is reminiscent of the town halls of Bolsward and Franeker.

★★ **Frisian Museum (Fries Museum)** (YZ M³). – Installed in a late 18C mansion, enlarged in
⊘ the 19 and 20C, this museum gives an excellent idea of Frisian civilisation.
On the ground floor the **gold and silversmith** section is remarkable, with 16C Leeuwarden plate, a nautilus made into a goblet in the 17C, rare in Friesland, brandywine goblets, the Popta treasure which shows 17C elegance and 18C rococo silverware.

LEEUWARDEN

The **archaeological** section concerns the *hunebed* period *(qv)*, the urnfield culture and the *terp* culture *(qv)*.

On the ground floor, interiors have been rebuilt, some decorated with 17C **earthenware tiles** made in Makkum, Bolsward and Harlingen. In the painting gallery (Schilderijenzaal) on the 1st floor there is a **Rembrandt;** it is the portrait of **Saskia** van Uilenburg, daughter of the burgomaster of Leeuwarden and the painter's fiancée (married in 1634). Several rooms are devoted to the 19C painter C. Bisschop, another room to Chinese porcelain and Frisian handicraft.

The **furniture** of Hindeloopen and Ameland are painted in bright colours.

On the 2nd floor: reconstitutions of old shops (apothecary, grocer, tobacconist) and an interior from Workum with walls covered with tiles in the Louis XVI style, 18 and 19C **costumes** some of which are from Hindeloopen *(qv)*, a gold and silversmith's workshop, and 17 to 19C Frisian pottery.

In the cellars, medieval sculptures and a Frisian kitchen of the 18 and 19C.

A new wing is devoted to temporary exhibitions.

Over de Kelders (Z 33). – One of the quays on this canal is dug out of cellars *(kelders)*. From the bridge to the north there is a fine view over the quays of Voorstreek and the bell tower of St Boniface.

The small **statue of Mata Hari** (Z D) was erected in 1976 for the anniversary of her birth.

Weigh House (Waag) (Z E). – On Waagplein, in the centre of the town, this is a 1598 building of red brick, the 1st floor cantoned with heraldic lions. Above them is a frieze sculptured with alternating motifs (flowers, animals, cherubs). The weighing of butter and cheese took place here up to 1884.

Weerd (Z). – This narrow street which plunges into Leeuwarden's old quarter is lined with lovely shops.

Hofplein (YZ 19). – The **town hall** (Z H) is on this square, a sober, classical building (1715) topped by a 17C carillon. At no 34 note a fine façade stone (1666) depicting Fortune.

In the town hall annexe, added in 1760, the Council Room (Raadzaal) has a façade with rococo decoration topped by the lion which appears on the town's coat of arms.

Opposite this is the **Hof** (YZ F), former residence of the Frisian stadtholders.

In the centre of the square there is a statue of William Louis, first hereditary stadtholder, called by the Frisians "Us Heit" (Our Father).

At no 35 a façade stone depicts a stork.

Eewal (Y). – This wide main road is lined with elegant 18C residences. Some still have lovely façade stones (no 52: sail boat, no 58: St James the Pilgrim).

⊙ **Great Church or Church of the Jacobins** (Grote- of Jacobijnerkerk) (Y K). – Dating from the 13C, this church was reconstructed in the 15 and 16C. Devastated by the revolutionaries in 1795, it was restored, notably in 1976.
Since 1588 it has been the Nassau Frisian mausoleum.

⊙ **Concerts** are given on the organ built in 1724-7 by Christiaen Müller *(qv)*.

Grote Kerkstraat (Y). – The tall house where Mata Hari probably lived has been converted into a **museum** (Fries Letterkundig Museum) (Y M¹).
Further on at no 43 there is a fine façade stone depicting a lion and a fortified castle, then near the corner of Doelestraat, at no 17, a fine baroque portal is decorated with garlands in the Frisian style.

★★ **Het Princessehof Museum** (Gemeentelijk Museum) (Y M²). – This 17C palace, decorated
⊙ with garlands and cherubs' heads was where Marie-Louise of Hesse-Kassel, widow of the Frisian stadtholder John William Friso, lived in the 18C. Her dining room can be seen on the ground floor.
The palace and the adjacent building (Papingastins) have been turned into the **Netherlands Ceramics Museum** (Algemeen ceramisch studiecentrum), particularly rich in oriental ware.

1st floor. – In the **Indonesian room** a typical Indonesian dwelling, the long house, is used to exhibit *martavanen,* large ceramic jars used for provisions.
The following rooms are devoted to **ceramics.**
From Japan one can see a selection of stoneware production with sober lines and from China the blue and white porcelain, exported in mass under the name of kraakporselein or Kraak porcelain by the Dutch East India Company *(qv).*
Thailand, Korea and Vietnam have produced fine works, sometimes influenced by the Chinese style.
The remarkable collection of **Chinese ceramics** makes it possible to follow its evolution. To begin with there was terracotta ware dating from the 3rd millenium BC. About 200BC under the Han dynasty (206BC - 220AD) glazed stoneware was made. Funerary objects are stamped with great realism. The **martavanen** *(see above),* large stoneware jars, were sold to Javanese traders from the 4 to 11C. The latter have fine enamel glazes which can be seen again on the translucent **porcelain** objects which began to be made in the 9C under the T'ang dynasty (618-906). A great variety in production characterises the Sung dynasty (960-1279) with monochrome porcelain sometimes crackled (white, green, celadon, flambé). Under the **Ming** dynasty (1368-1644) the great era of Chinese porcelain began. First blue and white, it was enriched with lovely designs with iridescent tones (yellow, green, violet, red). However, in the 16 and 17C production was limited to blue and white with Kraak porcelain, which included the large dishes called Swatow ware. Under the Ching (1644-1912), after a period when the blue became lighter, one reaches the 18C. Colours are intensified; the *Famille verte, noire* and above all *rose,* were much in demand by Europeans. The Chinese made porcelain to order for the Dutch East India Company with European inspired motifs (armorial devices, inscriptions).
The museum has a rich collection of **earthenware tiles** from the mid-16C to *c*1900. On the 1st floor there is an exhibition of tiles made in the Netherlands, some with geometric motifs, others decorated with people or scenes of daily life. Also on display are moulded bricks which covered the backs of chimneys or formed paving.

2nd floor. – Secondary collections of ceramics and earthenware tiles.

Ground floor. – A fine collection of **European ceramics**; 18C porcelain, Italian Renaissance majolica, Delftware.
There is also a room of art nouveau (18), galleries of modern ceramics with two drawings by Chagall.

Basement. – Here there are French **earthenware tiles** (terracotta in relief or with grooves covered with white glazing), and from Persia and Turkey (blue cobalt oxide and brown manganese form the glazes in relief). The Spanish *azulejos* of Moorish influence are made following two techniques: first the *cuerda seca* process (colours separated by a strip of manganese) then the *cuenca* process (tile with moulded relief).

⊙ **Oldehove** (Y). – This massive Gothic tower in brick was never completed due to the instability of the ground, which explains why it leans sharply.
The plan of the adjacent church, which was destroyed in 1595, is indicated on the square by coloured paving.
From the top of the tower, there is an overall **view** of the town and its main monuments. Nearby, the old wooded ramparts make a pleasant walk along **Stadsgracht** (Y), a wide canal which follows the shape of the bastions.

EXCURSIONS

Marssum. – *5km - 3 miles to the west by Harlingerstraatweg* (Y).
⊙ **Popta Castle** (Poptagasthuis) or Heringastate, preceded by a 17C gatehouse with voluted gables, houses 17 and 18C furnishings.
Nearby the **old almshouse** (Popta-Gasthuis) founded in 1711 is a picturesque group of low buildings with entry by a monumental portal.

Drachten. – *27km - 16½ miles to the southeast by Schrans* (Z).
In the Frisian countryside with rich meadows bordered by poplar trees, Drachten spreads with its great apartment complexes and brick houses. This town is a commercial and industrial centre with busy streets and pedestrian precincts, adorned with statues. It has numerous schools.

Terp Region (Terpenland). – *Round tour of 118km - 73 miles – local map below. Leave by Groningerstraatweg (Y). Turn left after 9km - 5½ miles.*

From the beginning of 5C BC and up to 12C AD in the low regions liable to sea or river flooding, the Frisians established their farmhouses and later their churches on man-made mounds called *terps.* There are still about a thousand of which two thirds are in the province of Friesland, and the rest in the province of Groningen where they are called *wierden.* Their average height is between 2 and 6m - 6½ and 19½ft, and their area between 1 and 12ha - 2½ to 29½ acres. The excavations have been very successful.

The tour covers a region where most of the villages have a *terp* with a church of tufa and brick with rustic charm, and a tower with a saddleback roof rising from a curtain of trees indicating its presence.

The typical Frisian countryside is scattered with lovely farmhouses with gables decorated with a *uilebord (qv)* and a few windmills.

Oenkerk. – This lovely for-est-like castle park, **Stania State,** is open to the public.

Oudkerk. – This village has a castle and a church on a *terp.*

⊘ **Rinsumageest.** – The **church,** built on a *terp,* has a Ro-manesque crypt with two elegantly sculptured capi-tals. The interior is typical of Frisian churches.

Dokkum. - *Description p 83.*

> *Follow the canal to the southeast.*

The route soon rises, the tree-lined canal becomes more pleasant.

> *Turn right towards Kollumerzwaag.*

Veenklooster. – Charming village with thatched cot-tages round a *brink (qv).*

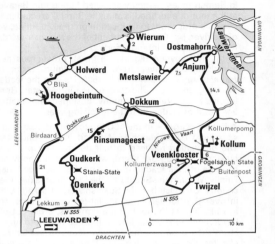

⊘ A fine alley leads to **Fogelsangh Castle** (Fogelsangh State) built in 1725; museum on the site of an abbey and surrounded by a park.

Twijzel. – All along the main road, which crosses this town for a couple of miles, stand a row of magnificent **farmhouses★.** Behind the pleasant façade, more urban than rural, an enormous barn, often covered with a thatched roof, is hidden *(illustration p 31).*

> *At Buitenpost, turn left.*

⊘ **Kollum.** – This town has a 15C Gothic **church** preceded by a 13C tower. The nave is separated from the side aisles by stocky columns. The vaults with painted ribs are decorated with naive frescoes, as is the north wall where one can see a St Christopher.

Oostmahorn. – From the top of the dike, there is an overall view of **Lauwers Sea** *(qv).* Like the Zuiderzee, this low-lying region was flooded by the sea in the 13C. To avoid floods and create new polders a barrier dam has been built. It has now become a lake with water-sports, (sailing...).

Anjum. – This village has kept an 1889 windmill. On a small *terp* there is a Romanesque church, enlarged in the Gothic style.

> *Take the road to Dokkum, then turn right towards Metslawier.*

Metslawier. – Grouped round the old Gothic church, the old, remarkably restored, houses form a harmonious whole.

Wierum. – This is a small harbour with modest homes; its church is built on an oval *terp* and surrounded by a cemetery.

A staircase leads to the top of the dike: **view** over the Wadden Sea *(qv),* which at low tide appears, here, like an immense beach. The islands of Ameland and Schiermon-nikoog stand out on the horizon.

Holwerd. – It is the departure point for boats going to Ameland Island *(qv).*

> *After Blija, turn left to Hoogebeintum.*

Hoogebeintum. – This village on the highest *terp* in Friesland (nearly 9m - 30ft above sea ⊘ level) has a **church** typical of the northern Netherlands with a bell tower with a saddle-back roof and surrounded by a cemetery. It offers a fine view over the neighbouring countryside.

The interior is interesting for the series of 16 **hatchments★** (from the 17 to the early 20C) which decorate the walls. On each carved wood panel, there is a coat of arms adorned with baroque motifs, symbols of death (scythe, hour glass, skulls and bones) and heads of cherubs in naive and rustic style.

There are also some lovely seignorial pews in wood, and on the ground numerous memorial slabs.

> *Reach Birdaard to the south and follow the Dokkumer Ee Canal towards the south. Via the village of Lekkum, Prof. Mr. P.S. Gerbrandyweg and Groningerstraatweg, one returns to Leeuwarden.*

Built on the Old Rhine (Oude Rijn), Leyden is an agreeable town crisscrossed by canals. It is famous for its university, the oldest in the country, and has numerous museums. It is also a prosperous town where graphic arts and the manufacture of building materials are important.

To the south of the town stretches the Vlietland, a large recreation area.

⊘ **Boat trips.** – Boat trips are organised on the Old Rhine, departure point: Oude Singel **(DY)** as far as Avifauna *(p 144)* and on the city's canals, departure point: Beestenmarkt **(CY)**.

HISTORICAL NOTES

In Roman times Leyden was called Lugdunum Batavorum. The medieval town grew at the foot of a fortified castle, the Burcht, erected in the 9C on an artificial mound. It owed its prosperity to its location on the Old Rhine, which was then the main branch of the river, but the displacement of the mouth towards Rotterdam reduced the town's role to that of an interior market.

In the 14C Leyden regained a great, prosperous period due to the linen industry introduced by weavers from Ypres (Belgium) taking refuge from the Black Death.

John of Leiden was born here in 1509. He was the leader of the Anabaptists, members of a religious sect, who took refuge in Münster, Germany in 1534, and where they formed a theocratic community. Beseiged, the Anabaptists had to surrender in 1535 and John of Leiden died the following year.

A heroic siege. – In the 16C the town was besieged twice by the Spanish. The first siege (end 1573 - March 1574) failed. The second, started a month later was terrible. The population reduced to half due to plague and starvation revolted against the burgomaster Van der Werff, who offered his body to the famished. Revived by the courage of their leader, the inhabitants continued their resistance.

Finally, William the Silent had the idea of breaking the dikes to flood the surrounding country. On 3 October, the Spanish were attacked by the Sea Beggars, who had sailed in over the flooded land on flat-bottomed boats; the Spaniards raised the siege, abandoning, at the foot of the ramparts, a big pot of beef stew. The inhabitants of Leyden were then supplied with bread and herring.

From then on a commemorative feast, **Leidens Ontzet,** takes place annually *(see the chapter Practical Information at the end of the guide)* with a historical procession, distribution of herring and white bread and eating of beef stew *(hutspot, qv)* in memory of the pot left by the Spanish.

To reward the town, William the Silent founded a university here.

Leyden University (1575). – It was the first in the Low Countries liberated from Spain and for a long time rivalled that of Louvain, which had remained Catholic; it very quickly acquired an European reputation due to its relatively tolerant spirit and the great minds it drew there: the Flemish humanist Justus Lipsius (1547-1606), the philologist Daniël Heinsius (1580-1655), the famous theologians Gomar, Arminius and Episcopius *(qv),* the Frenchmen Saumaise (1588-1653), philologist, and Joseph Scaliger (1540-1609) philosopher, the doctor and botanist **Boerhaave,** master of clinic education (1668-1738) and **Van Musschenbroek** (1692-1761), inventor in 1746 of the Leyden jar, the first electric condenser.

In 1637 **René Descartes** (1596-1650), published anonymously in Leyden, his *Discourse on Method* written in Utrecht, where he had formerly lived.

The influence of the university was increased by the fact that Leyden had become a great centre of printing in the 17C due to the illustrious **Elzevier** family; the family's first member, Louis who came from Louvain (Belgium) settled in Leyden in 1580.

The Protestant refuge. – In the 16 and 17C Leyden took in numerous Flemish and French Protestants (fled in 1685 because of the Revocation of the Edict of Nantes) as well as English.

In 1609 a hundred or so English Puritans arrived via Amsterdam, led by their spiritual leader **John Robinson** (c1575-1625), who had left their country under the menace of persecution. Former farmers from Scrooby, Nottinghamshire they had to adapt themselves to their new urban condition and applied themselves to various handicraft trades. A printing press published religious works exported to England and Scotland. Their stay became difficult and the Puritans decided to leave Leyden and go to America. Sailing from Delfshaven *(qv)* on the *Speedwell* they reached England and embarked on the *Mayflower* in Plymouth. The 102 emigrants amongst which there were 41 Puritans or **Pilgrim Fathers** landed in December 1620 on the southeast coast of Boston and founded Plymouth Colony, the first permanent settlement established in New England *(see Michelin Green Guide to New England).* Robinson intended on joining them later but died before.

LEYDEN PAINTERS

Leyden School. – From the 15 to the 17C a great number of painters were born in Leyden.

Geertgen tot Sint Jans (c1465-c95), who died in Haarlem, is the most gifted painter of the late 15C. Still turned towards the Middle Ages, he showed, however, a great virtuosity in the treatment of folds and gave a great deal of importance to landscape.

Cornelis Engebrechtsz. (1468-1533) remained Gothic as well, with crowded compositions and rather tormented linear painting (De Lakenhal Museum).

His pupil **Lucas van Leyden** (1489 or 1494-1533) is the great Renaissance painter. Influenced by Italian art, his *Last Judgment,* which can be seen in the De Lakenhal Museum *(p 142)* is a very fine work, by the balance of composition, sense of depth, elegant draughtsmanship and fine colours. Lucas van Leyden also originated the genre scene, using it for numerous engravings.

In the beginning of the 17C a few painters of the Leyden School painted *vanitas,* still lifes where certain specific objects: representing the arts and sciences (books, maps...), wealth (jewellery...), earthly pleasures (goblets, playing cards), death (skulls)... are depicted with great precision often with a moralistic message. These subjects were appreciated by Jan Davidsz. de Heem *(qv)* when he stayed here before going to Antwerp.

Jan van Goyen, born in Leyden in 1596 went to live in Haarlem in 1631 where he died (1656). He was a great painter of pale, monochromatic landscapes: immense skies covered with clouds, shimmering water and skilful use of light and shadow.

Son of **Willem van de Velde the Elder** (c1611-93), **Willem van de Velde the Younger** (1633-1707), specialised, like his father, in sea battles. The sun piercing through the clouds flooding light onto the sails and golden sterns of large warships and shimmering on a calm sea. The Van de Veldes ended their lives in London where they were called to be court painters to Charles II. Oddly enough, the Van de Veldes were artists of sea battles who changed from the Dutch side to the English side in the middle of the Dutch Wars.

Gerrit Dou (1613-75) is perhaps the most conscientious of all the intimist masters of Leyden. He took to chiaroscuro when in touch with his master, Rembrandt, but he mainly tried to render with the patience of a miniaturist and a stylistic touch, recalling his first trade as a glazier, scenes of bourgeois life (*Young Woman Dressing,* Boymans-van Beuningen Museum in Rotterdam).

His pupil **Frans van Mieris the Elder** (1635-81) depicted smiling people in refined interiors.

Gabriel Metsu (1629-67) genre painter, master in his manner of treating fabrics and the substance of objects, treated with great sensitivity slightly sentimental subjects (*The Sick Child,* Rijksmuseum, Amsterdam).

Contrary to his contemporaries, **Jan Steen** (1626-79) depicts very busy scenes with humour. His paintings are the theatre of the whole human comedy where somewhat dishevelled people indulge in various pleasures; they play music, drink, eat and play in a very unruly atmosphere (*Merry Company,* Mauritshuis in The Hague).

Rembrandt. – Rembrandt Harmensz. van Rijn was born in Leyden in 1606. Son of a miller he lived near the Rhine, hence his name Van Rijn. His childhood remains mysterious.

In 1620 he enrolled at Leyden University, but attracted by painting, he soon became an apprentice to Jacob van Swanenburgh, then, in 1623 in Amsterdam, to **Pieter Lastman** (1583-1633), a great admirer of Italy and Caravaggio.

Although he painted numerous portraits and even self-portraits, Rembrandt right from the start showed a leaning towards biblical history, which he first painted with minute detail typical of the Leyden School.

The artist, who never studied in Italy, contrary to the great painters of his time, adopted a very personal style. His chiaroscuro was not that of Caravaggio, where strong contrasts between light and shade existed, but an imperceptible change from shadow to people suffused with a warm light who occupied the centre of the painting. His works are steeped in a mysterious atmosphere from which an intense emotion and profound spirituality emanate.

Beginning in 1628 he took up etching and drawing, sometimes seeking inspiration from ordinary people (beggars, etc).

At the end of 1631, he settled in Amsterdam; it was then that he painted the famous **The Anatomy Lesson of Doctor Tulp** (1632). This group portrait brought glory to the young painter of 26. Orders started flowing in.

Rembrandt met Saskia *(qv)* whom he married in 1634. Several children were born (all died soon after birth), one of whom Titus, was born in 1641.

In 1639 he moved to a house in the Jewish quarter, the present House of Rembrandt.

In 1642 he painted his greatest work, the **Night Watch,** group portrait of members of the civic guard. This genre, which had already been revived by Frans Hals, is treated by Rembrandt with daring and complexity of technique up to then unequalled. However, not much interest was shown in this painting at the time, which became his most famous.

In addition, 1642 marked the beginning of the painter's misfortune: he lost his wife Saskia; he had already seen his parents die (in 1630 and 1640).

He painted numerous portraits including that of the young Titus (1655), a solemn *Self-Portrait* (1652) but the wealthy art patrons began to abandon him with the exception of the burgomaster Jan Six. In 1657 and 1658 he was unable to pay his debts and had to sell his house and goods. In 1661 his *Conspiracy of Julius Civilis,* ordered for the town hall was refused (National Museum of Stockholm). In 1662 he lost his mistress Hendrickje Stoffels.

The Sampling Officials of the Drapers Guild (1662) was his last group painting, but he still did some marvellous paintings like the *Jewish Bride* before passing away, forgotten, a year after his son Titus, in 1669. He had just completed his last self-portrait.

The Rijksmuseum *(p 51)* in Amsterdam has an exceptional collection of the master's works.

Among Rembrandt's numerous pupils in Amsterdam, there was the landscape painter **Philips Koninck** (1619-88) and several painters originating from Dordrecht *(qv)* or Leyden like Gerrit Dou.

THE OLD TOWN AND ITS MUSEUMS *time: 5 hours*

⊙ **De Valk Wall Mill (Molen) (CY M¹)**. – This wall mill, the last in Leyden, built in 1743, bears the name of a bird of prey *(valk:* falcon). It has seven floors the first ones were the living quarters; ten generations of millers succeeded each other until 1964. Restored, it has become a museum.

The tour includes the repair workshop, the forge, the drawing room (zondagkamer) and a retrospective of Dutch windmills.

In season its sails turn, but it no longer mills grain *(for more information on windmills see pp 33-34).*

★★ **National Museum of Ethnology (Rijksmuseum voor Volkenkunde) (CY M⁴)**. – Situated in ⊙ the former university hospital, this museum houses rich collections of non-western civilisations. The Asiatic and American departments stand out by their remarkable art works.

Ground floor. – The section on the right is devoted to **Java and Bali:** musical instruments (gamelan), openwork design puppets (wayang), paintings on paper; large 13C statues in basalt: **Ganeśa,** the elephant god on a crown of skulls, Durgà slaying the buffalo-demon.

1st floor. – The section on the right *(coming from the staircase)* deals with **Far Eastern civilisations:** Chinese ceramics, figures for the Chinese shadow theatre, Tibetan cult objects.

The Buddhist cult has produced some fine works of art: the **five bronze Buddhas** from Japan of the 17 and 18C, the 13C Chinese statue in polychrome wood of the bodhisattva (future Buddha) **Kuan Yin.**

To the left, after the African section where there are some fine **Benin bronzes** (Guinea), there is the **American department:** Peruvian mummies, Mexican pottery. Next to a Mayan stele of 766BC, the famous **Leiden Plate,** a minute jade plaque (320AD) engraved with a deity comes from Tikal in Guatemala; it was deciphered in 1900.

On the 1st floor there is a room devoted to Japan, another to Korea. Temporary exhibitions of Japanese prints take place here regularly.

★★ **De Lakenhal Municipal Museum (Stedelijk Museum) (CY M⁵)**. – Installed in the old cloth ⊙ merchants' hall (lakenhal), this is a museum of decorative arts (furniture, silverware, pewterware), which also contains a fine section of paintings. The whole history of the town unravels within these rooms.

On the 1st floor the **guild rooms** (gildekamers) have been reconstituted: the surgeons', civic guards', tailors', brewers' and clothmakers' rooms.

On the 2nd floor the town's religious history is evoked with an Old Catholic church *(qv),* and the execution of the Remonstrants *(qv)* in 1623.

On the ground floor there is a fine collection of glassware, furnished rooms (stijlkamers) in the Louis XV, Louix XVI and Renaissance styles.

In the **painting section,** numerous Leyden masters are shown.

By Cornelis Engebrechtsz. (room 17) there are two admirably detailed triptychs: *Crucifixion* and *Descent from the Cross,* as well as a small *Carrying of the Cross.* But the works of **Lucas van Leyden** dominate. In his luminous triptych of the **Last Judgment** painted with assurance of draughtsmanship, the painter knew how to free the figures from constraint and rigidity. The central panel shows the Son of Man enthroned in thick clouds for the Supreme Judgment. On the panels heaven and hell are painted; on the back, St Peter and St Paul.

Among the 17C Leyden painters exhibited are Gerrit Dou, Jan Steen (animated scenes) and refined works by Mieris the Elder.

The museum also possesses some fine 17C paintings: a still life by J. Davidsz. de Heem, *Horse Market* by Salomon van Ruysdael, *View of Leyden* by Van Goyen and an early work by Rembrandt.

To the south of **Turfmarkt (CY 53)** there is a lovely **view** over the harbour and the mill. Further on, from **Prinsessekade (CY 47)** there is an old warehouse **(CY A),** restored, giving on to Galgewater harbour.

★ **Rapenburg (CZ)**. – It is the most beautiful canal in Leyden, spanned by triple-arched bridges and lined with trees. On the west side there are some fine houses: nos 19, 21, 25, 29, 31, 61, 65.

★ **University (Academie) (CZ U¹)**. – Since the 16C the university's administrative offices are housed in the chapel of a former convent.

It has kept its old rooms and notably on the 1st floor, a sweating room where nervous students waited to take their exams.

⊙ **Botanical Garden (Hortus Botanicus) (CZ)**. – This botanical garden founded by the university in 1587 (the first in northern Europe) is a lovely spot, with flowers, rare plants and large trees. One can visit the orangery and the greenhouses.

★★ **National Museum of Antiquities (Rijksmuseum van Oudheden) (CYZ M⁶)**. – Apart from ⊙ the particularly rich Egyptology and Classical Antiquities sections, this museum has a collection of prehistoric and oriental antiquities.

Ground floor. – In the hall the Temple of Taffeh (Nubia) has been reconstructed, a gift to the Netherlands by the Egyptian State; it dates from the Augustan Age. In another room are Roman steles discovered in the Scheldt area (Zeeland), dedicated to the goddess Nehallenia. Also exhibited are Greek and Roman sculptures, notably the sarcophagus of Simpelveld (Limburg), a remarkable collection of Egyptian sculpture with the reconstitution of two tombs of the 5th and 19th dynasties, low reliefs from the tomb of Horemheb *(c*1330BC) and the famous statues of Maya and Merit *(c*1300BC).

1st floor. – Here there are collections of glassware (Egyptian, Roman, Syrian and Persian) and ceramics (Greece and Southern Italy) where the vases painted with mythological scenes of the classical period are at their apogee. The cult of the dead in Egypt is evoked by a great number of painted sarcophagi, mummies of men and animals, furniture and funerary urns.
Bronze statuettes, jewellery, amulets, pottery... give a fairly good overall view of decorative arts in Ancient Egypt. Egyptian art of Roman times and Coptic art are also evoked.
In one room an archaeological Panorama presented on tiers, gathers together objects of all the civilisations represented in the museum, classed by regions and in chronological order.

2nd floor. – Objects from excavations shown here (sculpture, everyday bronze objects, glassware, pottery, etc) illustrate Dutch archaeology.
From Roman times one can see, amongst other items, the gilded silver helmet from Peel swamp, the Merovingian treasure of Wieuwerd and the fibula from Dorestad (8AD).

Pieterskerkhof (CZ 42). – In the centre of this square, an old cemetery (kerkhof), St Peter's stands.

⏲ **St Peter's** (Pieterskerk) (**CZ B**). – It is a large and heavily built Gothic church with a nave and 4 aisles, whose construction began in the late 14C.
There are memorial slabs to the painter Jan Steen *(qv)* and Professor Boerhaave *(qv)* as well as the Puritan leader, John Robinson *(qv)*.

Jean Pesijnshofje (**CZ E**). – Built in 1683 on the site of John Robinson's house and intended for the members of the Walloon church *(qv)*, this almshouse took the name of its founder, Jean Pesijn, a merchant of Huguenot origin. There is a memorial slab to the memory of John Robinson.

LEIDEN

Breestr. .... CYZ
Donkersteeg .... CY 12
Haarlemmerstr. .... CDY

Aalmarkt .... CY 2
Apothekersdijk .... CY 3
Beestenmarkt .... CY 4
Binnenvestgracht .... CY 7
Burgsteeg .... DZ 8

Geregracht .... DZ 13
Hooglandse Kerkgracht .... DY 17
Hoogstr. .... CY 18
Houtstr. .... CZ 19
Kloksteeg .... CZ 22
Kort Rapenburg .... CY 24
Maarsmansteeg .... CYZ 29
Nieuwe Beestenmark .... CY 32
Nieuwsteeg .... CZ 33
Oude Herengracht .... DY 37
Papengracht .... CYZ 38
Pieterskerkgracht .... CZ 40

Pieterskerkhof .... CZ 42
Pieterskerkkoorsteeg .... CZ 43
Plantagelaan .... DZ 44
Plesmanlaan .... CY 46
Prinsessekade .... CY 47
Steenstr. .... CY 52
Turfmarkt .... CY 53
Utrechtsebrug .... DZ 54
Varkenmarkt .... CY 55
Vismarkt .... CZ 57
Voldersgracht .... DY 58
Volmolengracht .... DY 59

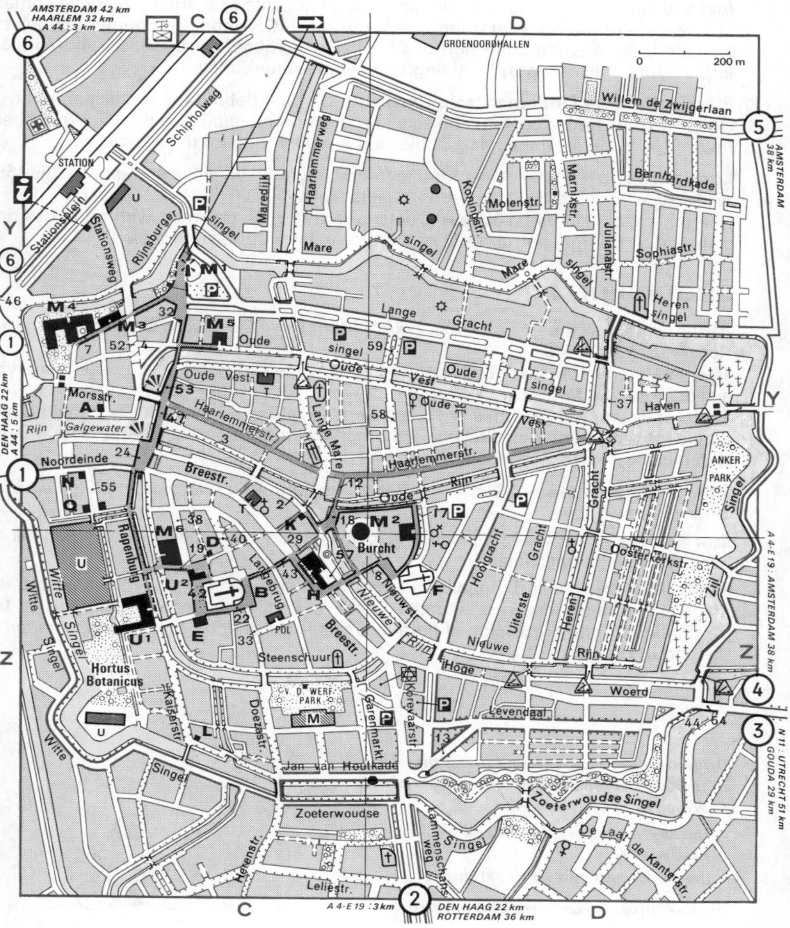

Gravensteen (CZ U²). – Once a prison, this building at present is the Law Faculty, and has a lovely classical façade on the church side.

Latin School (Latijnse School) (CZ D). – Founded in 1324, it has a Renaissance façade (1599).

By a narrow lane, Pieterskerkkoorsteeg, reach Breestraat.

Breestraat (CZ). – This, the town's main shopping street is very busy. At the point where one crosses it, there is a **blue stone** where executions took place.

Town Hall (Stadhuis) (CZ H). – Built c1600 and damaged in a fire in 1929, it was rebuilt in its original style. Preceded by a perron, it is topped with a highly decorated gable and a bell tower.

Vismarkt (CZ 57). – It is the old fish market.
At the beginning of Nieuwstraat one can see the 17C entrance doorway of the **Burcht** topped by a lion with the town's coat of arms (two keys). This fortress was built on an artificial mound at the confluence of the Old and New Rhine. There remains a wide curtain wall with crenellations and loopholes. Its watchpath offers a panorama over the town.

St Pancras's (St.-Pancraskerk) or Hooglandsekerk (DZ F). – On the outside of the transepts' arms, this 15C church has interesting Flamboyant style sculptured portals.

Hooglandse Kerkgracht (DY 17). – Near this filled-in canal, the old **orphanage** (Weeshuis) contains the National Museum of Geology and Mineralogy *(see below)*. The portal is topped by a low relief depicting orphans.

Weigh House (Waag) (CY K). – It was built by Pieter Post in 1657-9.

ADDITIONAL SIGHTS

⊘ **National Museum of Geology and Mineralogy (Rijksmuseum van Geologie en Mineralogie) (DY M²).** – It is installed in an old orphanage *(see above)*. On the 1st floor there is a fine **collection★** of meteorites, gems, fluorescent and volcanic stones.
On the 2nd floor the paleontology section includes numerous fossils of plants and animals.
There is also a sedimentological section (phenomenons affecting the earth's surface).

⊘ **Boerhaave Museum (Rijksmuseum voor de Geschiedenis der Natuurwetenschappen en van de Geneeskunde) (CY M³).** – The museum was named after the famous doctor, Boerhaave *(qv)* and contains scientific instruments and documents concerning the development of science and medicine, starting notably in the 17C. Among the numerous objects exhibited, there is the collection of Christiaan Huygens, astronomical and surgical instruments, microscopes, including Van Leeuwenhoek's, etc.

⊘ **Pilgrim Fathers Documentatie Centrum (CZ L).** – Behind the municipal Archives Office, a small house contains objects and documents regarding the Pilgrim Fathers *(qv)*; printing press, theological books and a scale model of the *Mayflower*.

Loridanshofje (CY N). – At no 1 Varkenmarkt (pig market) is the entrance to this 1656 almshouse, whose interior courtyard remains plain.
Nearby is the 1645 **Doelen Gateway** (Doelenpoort) (CY Q), crowned with an equestrian statue of St George, patron saint of the old Archery Company *(doelen)*.

EXCURSIONS

Alphen aan de Rijn. – Pop 57 184. *17km - 10½ miles to the east by ③ on the town plan. Access by boat p 140.*
This small industrial town built on the banks of the Old Rhine has a large park with ⊘ exotic birds, the **Avifauna.**
There are numerous aviaries with rare birds, a large lake with ducks dabbling and ⊘ ponds for pink flamingos. **Boat trips** are organised from the park to Braassemer Lake, which is located north of town.

Noordwijk aan Zee. – *18km - 11 miles to the northwest – local map p 73. Leave by ⑥ on the town plan.*

Katwijk aan Zee. - Near the bulbfields, this town is a very busy seaside resort with a long beach and wild dunes inland.

Noordwijk aan Zee. – A fashionable and very well equipped seaside resort, where the magnificent sandy beach is situated at the foot of high dunes. Noordwijk is the destination for the procession of floral floats *(see the chapter Practical Information at the end of the guide).*

Drive through Dutch towns using the plans in the current **Michelin Red Guide Benelux.**
Features indicated include:

- *throughroutes and by-passes*
- *new streets*
- *car parks and one-way systems*

All this information is revised annually.

Michelin map **408** fold 26 or **212** fold 1
Plan of built-up area in the current Michelin Red Guide Benelux

On the edge of three countries (Germany, Belgium, Netherlands), Maastricht is the capital of Limburg province. Situated on the banks of the Maas, it is separated from Belgium by Albert Canal.
It stands out from the rest of the Netherlands by its Mosan-type stone houses, its undulating countryside and its southern atmosphere.
It is a very busy town with numerous pedestrian precincts.

HISTORICAL NOTES

Maastricht came into being due to a fortified bridge built by the Romans on the Great Way from Bavay (in northern France) to Cologne, hence its name which means the Maas crossing (Mosae Trajectum).
St Servatius finding it safer than Tongeren (Belgium) transferred his bishopric here in 382. In 722 St Hubert moved it to Liège. The town already belonged to the Frank kings.
In 1204 it passed into the trusteeship of the Duke of Brabant who, in 1283, shared his power with the Prince-Bishop of Liège.
It was given its first defensive walls in 1229.

The sieges of Maastricht. – Maastricht having rallied in the revolt against the Spanish, the Spanish, led by the Duke of Parma, besieged the town in 1579, took it by surprise, devastated it and left only 400 people alive.
The United Provinces annexed the town in 1632.
In 1673, 40 000 French, commanded by Louis XIV appeared in front of Maastricht. The siege was terrible, the Dutch defense fierce. England contributed some 6 000 troops with the Duke of Monmouth commanding. But Vauban, who was directing the operations, won the victory for the French who left 8 000 men on the battlefield, amongst them **D'Artagnan** *(qv)*, officer of the musketeers.
The French captured Maastricht again in 1748, due to a clever move by Maurice de Saxe, Marshal of Saxony.
Taken by Kleber in 1794, Maastricht was annexed to France, as was Breda.
In 1814 the town became part of the Netherlands kingdom.
In 1830 the garrison resisted against the Belgians, thus obtaining the right to remain part of the Netherlands, but this was only confirmed by the Treaty of London in 1839. The fortifications were partly demolished in 1867.
During the occupation, Maastricht was the German communications centre in the west. One of the first towns liberated, in September 1944, only its bridges were damaged.

Maastricht today. – It is an important industrial centre specialising in ceramics, paper making, and cement.
The annual **carnival★** *(see the chapter Practical Information at the end of the guide)* draws great crowds which join in the general outburst of joy. All day and night practical jokes and comical games are played.

ⓥ **Boat trips.** – Boat trips are organised down the Maas to the Belgian frontier.

THE OLD TOWN *time: ½ day*

Vrijthof (AY). – This is the most important square in the town, a vast esplanade surrounded by cafés and restaurants and overlooked by two churches, St Servatius's and St John's.
To the south there is the Gothic façade of the **Spanish Government House** (Spaans Gouvernement) (AY A) where William the Silent *(qv)* was declared an outlaw by Philip II of Spain.
Numerous shopping pedestrian precincts start from this square.

★★ **St Servatius's Basilica (St.-Servaasbasiliek) (AY).** – This imposing monument, one of
ⓥ the oldest in the Netherlands, although often altered, was begun *c*1000 on the site of a 6C sanctuary. It then had one nave and side aisles, a transept and a flat east end. In the 12C it was enlarged on the one hand by the present chancel, flanked by two square towers and an apse, and, on the other hand, by a monumental **westwork**. The westwork is characteristic of the Rhenish-Mosan style *(p 22)*; the basilica is one of the first examples of this style. Topped by two towers and a central bell tower rebuilt by P.J.H. Cuypers in 1886 (and partly burnt down in 1955), it is decorated with Lombard
ⓥ arcading between which are twin arches. Its **carillon** is excellent.
In the 13C the lovely south portal or **royal portal★** was built and is now painted with vivid colours; the tympanum illustrates the life of the Virgin. In the 15C the side chapels and the north portal were added. The north portal gives on to cloisters also built in the 15C.
The whole building underwent extensive restoration in the late 19C.

Interior. – On the basilica's entrance portal there is a 15C statue of St Peter.
The interior suffers from the neo-Gothic polychrome added in the 19C. However, the **chancel★** vaults (restored) have recovered their 16C paintings. It is harmonious with its tall pillars and the gallery above the ambulatory.
Inside the westwork, on the 1st floor, is the Emperor's Room (Keizerszaal), topped by a dome. The **capitals★** of the westwork are interesting for their rich decoration.
Behind the modern statue of Charlemagne, venerated in the past in this church after his canonisation in 1165, one can see the remains of a 12C stone altar.

The last chapel on the north aisle, towards the transept, has a Sedes Sapientiae (Seat of Wisdom) and a seated Virgin and Child, of 13C Mosan type. Nearby is a doorway, formerly the main access to the church, opening onto cloisters. Outside it is topped by a lovely tympanum depicting Christ in Majesty.

The **crypt**, which is under the nave, contains the tomb of St Servatius, behind the grille is the sarcophagus of Charles of Lorraine son of the Carolingian King Louis IV of d'Outremer and on the old altar of St Peter, the sarcophagus of the Bishops Monulfus and Gondulfus, founders of the primitive church in the 6C, as well as two other bishops, Candidus and Valentinus.

The neighbouring crypt with square pillars, under the chancel, belonged to the 6C primitive church.

★★ **Treasury** (Kerkschat). – The ground floor (former sacristy) and the 1st floor of the ⏱ collegiate chapel (12C) house the treasury: a rich collection of liturgical objects, mainly gold and silversmiths' work, ivory, sacerdotal ornaments, paintings, altarpieces, statues.

There is notably a bust of St Servatius, a symbolic silver key decorated with foliated scrolls which would have been given to him by St Peter, the pectoral cross said to be of St Servatius (late 10C), pieces of oriental cloth (c600AD), a 15C Brussels altarpiece as well as a great number of reliquaries and shrines of the late 12C.

The most remarkable object is **St Servatius's shrine** called Noodkist (illustration p 22). In oak, covered with gilded copper, enamelled, chased and decorated with precious stones, it is an important work of the Mosan School (c1160); at each end Christ and St Servatius are depicted, on the sides, the apostles.

St John's (St.-Janskerk) (AY D). – This Gothic church, Protestant since 1632, was built by the canons of St Servatius to be used as a parish church. Dating from the 12C, it was enlarged in the 15C with a chancel and a tower 70m - 230ft high, decorated in the Utrecht style.

Take a few steps along Bonnefantenstraat.

From this street there is a fine viewpoint over a 17C house with crow-stepped gables (**AZ E**) and the botanical garden of the Natural History Museum, located on the other side of the canal.

Turn back and take Looiersgracht.

Grote Looiersstraat (AZ 16). – On this charming shaded square surrounded by old houses, a sculptured group depicts children listening to the popular Maastricht storyteller, Fons Olterdissen.

★ **South ramparts (Walmuur) (ABZ)**. – The defensive walls still preserved to the south of town and dominated by numerous towers, shaded by beautiful trees and surrounded by pleasant gardens, are one of Maastricht's charms. On the two sections which exist one can go round the watchpath from where there are fine views.

Follow the watchpath, then leave it to take a footbridge crossing the ring canal.

Monseigneur Nolenspark (BZ). – A lovely park laid out at the foot of the ramparts. Animals (deer, etc) are kept in enclosures.

Take the watchpath again.

From the top of the first tower one overlooks the lakes where swans and ducks swim. On the north side of the ramparts one can see the **Bejaardencentrum Molenhof (BZ F)** building. Beside it, near the Jeker, hides an old watermill.

Continuing, one reaches the **tower of five heads** (De Vijf Koppen) (**BZ K**) where one overlooks a vast lake.

Gate to Hell (Helpoort) (BZ L). – This gate, surrounded by two round towers, is a relic of the 13C curtain wall.

★ **Basilica of Our Lady (Onze Lieve Vrouwebasiliek) (BZ N)**. – This is the oldest monument ⏱ in town. It is thought that it is on the site of an old Roman temple where a cathedral was built at the time when Maastricht was the seat of a bishopric.

The edifice already existed in the year 1000. The very tall **westwork** which precedes the church, as is does at St Servatius, dates from this period. It is flanked by two round turrets; its upper part, added c1200 is decorated with Romanesque blind arcading. The nave and the beautiful apse date from the 12C.

Amongst interesting sculptures grouped under the left porch of the westwork, note the effigy of a bishop (c1200).

Inside, the **chancel**★★ with an ambulatory topped by a gallery, thus forming two rows of superimposed columns, like the one at St Servatius, is remarkable. Furthermore, the richly decorated capitals are very varied.

The nave, like that of Kerkrade (qv) has alternating thick and thin pillars supporting the vault, redone in the 18C. The transept was given pointed vaulting in the 15C. The organ case dates from 1652.

The church has two Romanesque crypts, one under the transept crossing (1018), the other under the westwork, and 16C cloisters.

⏱ **Treasury** (Kerkschat). – The treasury has precious reliquaries and shrines, ivory, liturgical ornaments including Bishop St Lambert's early 8C dalmatic.

Stokstraat (BYZ). – It is a pleasant pedestrian precinct where the lovely 17 and 18C restored houses, decorated with pediments, façade stones and signs, are now art, antique and print shops.

At no 28 there is a façade decorated with sculptured friezes.

To the west, on a small square called **Op de Thermen (BY Q)**, paving stones indicate the site of old Roman baths discovered here in 1840.

Dinghuis (BY R). – This former 16C law court is narrow and picturesque.

Markt (ABY). – On this busy main square a market takes place.
The **town hall** (Stadhuis) (ABY H), built 1659-65 by Pieter Post, who designed Huis ten Bosch in The Hague, is an imposing quadrilateral building preceded by a large perron ⊘ and topped by a bell tower with a **carillon.**

Return to Vrijthof by the pedestrian precinct crossing the shopping quarter.

ADDITIONAL SIGHTS

★ **Good Children Museum** (Bonnefantenmuseum) (AY M[1]). – This museum of archaeology, ⊘ history and art is installed in a building called "Entre-Deux" (Between-Two). The 2nd floor displays collections concerning archaeology and ancient art. The 1st floor is reserved for modern and contemporary art.
The archaeological section gives a good overall idea of prehistoric times (spiral-meander ware, flint quarry), Roman times (remains of Maastricht's Roman bridge) and the early Middle Ages in Limburg.
The local history section reveals: remains of Roman buildings, pottery and porcelain from local workshops (Sphinx collection) and a copy of a scale model of Maastricht made for Louis XV during the French occupation (1748-9).
The ancient art section has, apart from some works by Pieter Bruegel the Younger *(Census in Bethlehem),* Rubens, Harry met de Bles *(Repudiation of Hagar),* Velvet Bruegel, canvases of 17 and 18C regional painters, Italian painters (1300-1550) and an important collection of Mosan sculpture of the Middle Ages (fine wood statues of saints).
With respect to modern and contemporary art *(exhibited in rotation),* there are the painters Charles Eyck (born in Limburg in 1897), Aad de Haas (1920-72), Ger Lataster (born in 1920).
Belgium is represented by works of Ensor (1860-1949), Permeke (1886-1952) and the Flemish sculptor Oscar Jespers (1887-1970).

⊘ **Casemates** (Kazematten). – *By Tongersestraat (AZ).* Located in Waldeck Park, the casemates belong to a system of fortifications made between 1575 and 1825. A great deal of the surface work disappeared in 1867, but casemates remain, with galleries stretching over nearly 10km - 6 miles.
Some of it can be visited, including notably the **Waldeck Bastion** with domed vaults, stocks of powder and listening posts, reached by corridors and staircases.
Not far away, near the fortified walls there is a bronze statue of D'Artagnan *(qv).*

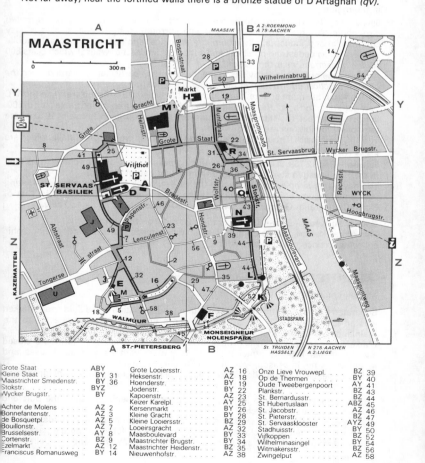

EXCURSIONS

★ **St Peter's Mount** (St.-Pietersberg). – *2km - 1 mile to the south by Sint Hubertuslaan and Luikerweg* (ABZ).

Between the valley of the Maas and the Jeker, St Peter's Mount rises to more than 100m - 328ft high.

It is above all famous for its **caves,** which come from old quarries which have been worked since Roman times. The stone, a sort of marl that hardens in the air, had been used for building numerous edifices in Maastricht. Today the galleries extend for more than 200km - 124 miles and are 12m - 39ft high. They were excavated by lowering the floor level so that now the oldest charcoal drawings covering the walls are near the roof. The rock sedimentary in origin, contains a large number of fossils. In 1780 the head of a prehistoric animal was found; it was called Mosasaurus (*Mosa:* the Maas). During all the troubled periods the caves have been used to shelter the people of Maastricht; they have kept traces of these periods of refuge.

The temperature is about 10°C-50°F and it is very humid.

⊘ **St Peter's Fort** (Fort St.-Pieter). – From the fort's (1701) terrace, there is an overall view of the town.

⊘ **Marl Caves - North Gallery** (Mergelgrotten - Noordelijk Gangenstelsel). – During World War II these caves sheltered Rembrandt's painting *The Night Watch.* There are graffiti here and amusing low reliefs like that of the Mosasaurus.

Continuing along the road then taking the second on the left, one reaches other caves.

⊘ **Zonneberg Caves** (Gangenstelsel Zonneberg). – They are very similar to the preceding ones, laden with history and filled with corridors covered with graffiti.

Susteren. - *35km - 21½ miles. Leave by ① on the town plan.*

Meerssen. – Pop 20 283. Former residence of the Frankish kings. In 870 a treaty was signed sharing Lotharingia, the domain of King Lothair II (855-869) between the two brothers Louis the German and Charles the Bald, the King of France (in 879 the whole of Lotharingia came into the hands of the German Emperor).

In the 13C Meerssen attracted the monks from the Abbey of St Remy in Rheims. They built the fine **basilica** of the Blessed Sacrament (13-14C). The chancel has a stone tabernacle in the Flamboyant Gothic style (early 16C), richly decorated, but unfortunately, greatly restored.

⊘ **Stein.** – Pop 26 445. Stein is the home of a small **archaeological museum** (Archeologisch reservaat; *Hoppenkampstraat 14a*). Built to house a megalithic tomb (*c*2800BC), the museum also has collections pertaining to prehistoric, Roman and Merovingian sites in the region

Sittard. – Pop 44 251. Sittard which obtained its city charter in 1243, was a very disputed stronghold. A large part of the city is still surrounded by ramparts. It is a busy commercial and industrial city (chemistry, electrical engineering, Volvo automobile factory). It has pedestrian precincts and a theatre (Stadsschouwburg) which seats 800 *(Wilhelminastraat, near the station).*

Amongst the numerous festivities in the town, note in particular the carnival *(see the chapter Practical Information at the end of the guide).*

On the **Markt,** the main square, there stands St Michael's (St.-Michielskerk), in the 17C baroque style, and a picturesque half-timbered house with a corbelled gable built *c*1500. In Rosmolenstraat, the **Kritzraedt House** (huis) is a lovely bourgeois house of 1620 where temporary exhibitions are held.

⊘ The 14C **Great Church** (Grote- of St.-Petruskerk) has carved wood Gothic stalls, which are probably the oldest in the country.

⊘ **Susteren.** – Pop 12 769. **St Amelberga's** (St.-Amelbergakerk), an old abbey church, was built in the Romanesque style probably during the first half of the 11C.

The nave, very simple, covered with a flat ceiling, leans on square pillars alternating with squat columns. The crypt, outside the apse was probably inspired by that of Essen Cathedral in Germany. It contains an 8C sarcophagus and a 13C calvary.

⊘ **Cadier en Keer.** – *5km-- 3 miles to the east by ④ on the town plan.*

The **African Museum** (Afrika-Centrum) exhibits interesting artistic and ethnographic collections concerning western Africa.

★ # MARKEN North Holland   Pop 2 094

Michelin map **408** fold 11

Separated from the continent in the 13C during the formation of the Zuiderzee, Marken was an island 2½km - 1½ miles from the shore until 1957. Now connected to the mainland, it is on the edge of the Gouw Sea (Gouwzee), a sort of interior sea.

Marken, whose population is Protestant, has from the beginning, formed a closed society. It has kept its atmosphere of days past with its wooden houses and inhabitants who, in season, wear the traditional costume.

Before IJssel Lake was made, the population earned its living from fishing; today it lives partly from tourism.

★ **The village.** – The village includes two quarters: Havenbuurt, near the port and ⊘ Kerkbuurt, around the church.

For protection against high tides, the houses are grouped on small mounds and built on piles which, before the closing of the Zuiderzee were left open for the passage of waves. Most of the houses are painted a somber green, with slightly corbelled side gables.

The **interiors,** painted and polished, are richly decorated with crockery and bibelots. Beds are fitted in alcoves where there is also a small drawer, which was used as a cradle.

★ **Costumes.** – The women wear over a striped petticoat a wide skirt and a black apron. The striped blouse, worn in summer, is covered with a corselet and a printed front. The headdress is just a gaily coloured lace and cotton skullcap from which a fringe of starched hair sometimes sticks out like a peak.
The men wear a short vest, baggy trousers tightened at the knees and black socks. The children more rarely wear a costume; boys and girls wear a skirt and bonnet, only the shapes and colours differ.
The costume worn on feast days, and particularly at Whitsun, is more refined.

★ MIDDELBURG Zeeland P   Pop 39 044

Michelin map 408 fold 15 or 212 fold 12 – Local map p 78

Middelburg used to be the pearl of Walcheren district. A very busy tourist centre, this old town is surrounded by canals and moats marking the limits of its fortified walls. Two 18C wall mills (A) still stand.

HISTORICAL NOTES

Formerly Middelburg was a prosperous commercial city, with its cloth trade and its importing of French wine from Argenteuil and Suresnes, shipped from the port of Rouen to Rouaansekaai *(p 150).*
The Sea Beggars captured it in 1574. In 1595 and 1692 the town was given its first line of fortifications with bastions. These have remained more or less intact up to today, but the only old gate which remains is **Koe Gate** (Koepoort) (**B A**) to the north.
It is said that a spectacle manufacturer of Middelburg, Zacharias Jansen invented the microscope in 1590 and the telescope in 1604. However, some people prefer to attribute the invention of the microscope to Van Leeuwenhoek.
Middelburg continued to prosper in the 17 and 18C due to the Dutch India Company which had a trading post here.
In 1940 a violent German bombardment destroyed the historic centre of the town. Its monuments have been rebuilt and it remains the great Walcheren market.
In July and August, on the Molenwater, one can watch a **ringrijderij,** a sort of horse show where the stake consists in unhooking a ring. On Vismarkt, in summer *(Thursdays),* there is an antique market and the first Saturday of each month, a flea market.

THE HEART OF TOWN

★ **Town Hall (Stadhuis)** (**A H**). – Overlooking **Markt** (**A**) or main square, where the market takes place *(Thursdays),* this imposing building, begun in 1452 by two architects of the Keldermans family from Mechlin (Belgium), is inspired by the Brussels town hall. Partly destroyed in May 1940, it has been rebuilt. The main façade is remarkable with its 1st floor pierced by ten Gothic windows with finely worked tympana. Between each window double niches have statues, remade in the 19C and depicting the Counts and Countesses of Zeeland back to back. The roof is decorated with 24 dormer windows and, on the left, the façade is prolonged by a pinnacled gable. The central perron was added in the 18C.
An octagonal turret, finely decorated and flanked by an openwork balustrade in the 17C, stands on the right.
A belfry 55m - 180ft high, cantoned with four pinnacles dominates the whole.
The interior contains antique furnishings, in particular the immense **Burgerzaal,** the former cloth hall.
Behind the town hall there is a lovely restored chapel called the **English Church** (Engelse Kerk) (**A B**).

★ **Abbey (Abdij)** (**B D**). – Today the seat of the provincial government of Zeeland, this vast monastic building was, in the 12C a Premonstrant abbey (order founded by St Norbert in 1120), a dependance of St Michael in Antwerp. It was secularised after the capture of the town by the Sea Beggars.
To the east, the defensive gate, the **Gist Gate** (Gistpoort) (**B E**) on Damplein, has a lovely 16C façade still marked by the Gothic style.

Abbey churches (Abdijkerken) (**B F**). – To the south of the abbey standing side by side are two churches.
The **Choral Church** (Koorkerk) with a 14C nave and apse has a 15C organ, whose case was renovated in the 16C.
The 16C **New Church** (Nieuwe Kerk) holds organ concerts in summer.
Against the Choral Church leans the **Lange Jan Tower.** This 14C octagonal construction in stone, crowned with a small 18C onion-shaped dome, rises 85m - 279ft. From the top there is a fine view over the abbey, the town and its canals.

★ **Zeeland Museum** (Zeeuws Museum) (**B M¹**). – It has been laid out in the old hostelery which is flanked by fine turrets. It has very varied regional collections.
In the archaeological section a room is devoted to the Celtic goddess **Nehallenia;** several votive steles dating from Roman times were found in 1647 in Domburg *(qv)* and in 1970 at Colijnsplaat (island of North Beveland). The goddess is often shown sitting, wearing a long dress and a wide-brimmed hat, accompanied by a dog and carrying a basket of fruit.

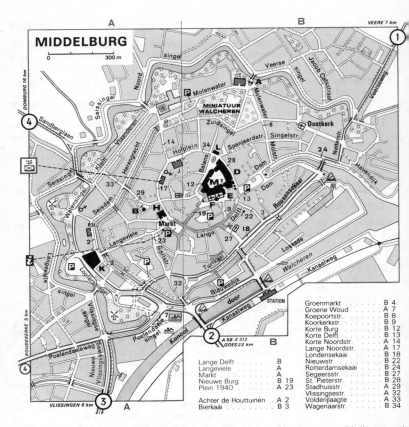

MIDDELBURG

Lange Delft . . . . . B	Groenmarkt . . . . . . B 4
Langeviele . . . . . A	Groene Woud . . . . . A 7
Markt . . . . A	Koepoortstr. . . . . . B 8
Nieuwe Burg . . . . B 19	Koorkerkstr. . . . . . B 9
Plein 1940 . . . . A 23	Korte Burg . . . . . B 12
	Korte Delft . . . . . B 13
	Korte Noordstr. . . . A 14
Achter de Houttuinen . A 2	Lange Noordstr. . . . A 17
Bierkaai . . . . . . B 3	Londensekaai . . . . . B 18
	Nieuwstr. . . . . . . B 22
	Rotterdamsekaai . . . B 24
	Segeersstr. . . . . . B 27
	St. Pieterstr. . . . . B 28
	Stadhuisstr. . . . . . A 29
	Vlissingsestr. . . . . A 32
	Volderijlaagte . . . . A 33
	Wagenaarstr. . . . . B 34

On the ground floor there is a collection of animal bones (stag, mammoth) discovered at the mouth of the Scheldt, and a roomful of rarities where notably a planetarium can be seen.

On the 1st floor, in a large room, there is a fine series of late 16 and early 17C **tapestries,** several illustrate Zeeland naval victories over the Spanish.

After having crossed the 17 and 18C decorative art rooms where Zeeland furniture and silverware, Chinese porcelain and Delftware can be admired, one reaches the attic which contains a remarkable collection of Zeeland **costumes** and headdresses; in a revolving show-case interior scenes are reconstituted.

ADDITIONAL SIGHTS

Kloveniersdoelen (A K). – It is the former arquebusiers' mansion, built in 1607 and 1611 in the Flemish Renaissance style. As from 1795 it was used as a military hospital. It has a very wide façade in brick streaked with white stone and brightened by painted shutters. The central voluted gable bears a sculptured low relief of arquebuses, cannon balls and topped by an eagle. The tall slate roof is pierced by dormer windows with painted shutters. Behind is an octagonal turret with an onion-shaped dome.

★**Miniature Walcheren** (Miniatuur Walcheren) (B). – It is an open-air scale model of ⊘ Walcheren Peninsula with its roads, dikes, ports and main buildings, made on a 1/20 scale.
Opposite stands the austere Koe Gate (1735).

The quays (B) – The **Rotterdamsekaai, Rouaansekaai** and **Londensekaai** are lined with fine rows of 18C houses, witness to the prosperity of that time.

Oost Church (Oostkerk) (B). – This octagonal church with an onion-shaped dome is of a fairly usual type amongst 17C Protestant buildings. Pieter Post was one of the architects who built it between 1646-67.

St.-Jorisdoelen (B L). – These old premises of the civic guard dating from 1582 were rebuilt in the original style in 1970. Similar to the old military hospital (Kloveniersdoelen), its central voluted gable is topped by a statue of St George (Sint Joris).

EXCURSION

Round tour of Walcheren. – *49km - 30 miles – allow 2 hours – local map p 78.*
    Leave by ④ on the town plan.
Domburg. – Pop 3 906. This seaside resort with a large beach situated at the foot of high dunes is very popular. To the west, the top of the highest dune offers an interesting **view** over Domburg and the coast.
The route follows the dunes which isolate Walcheren Peninsula from the sea. A few farmhouses surrounded by a curtain of trees line the route.

Westkapelle. – Pop 2 640. This town is on the western point of Walcheren Island, where the dunes are not strong enough to hold out against currents and are reinforced by **dikes.** These extend over 4km - 2½ miles and their highest crest is 7m - 23ft above sea level. In 1944 they were bombarded by the Allies, which caused flooding of the island and made it possible to evict the Germans. In 1945 the gaps were filled in. West-kapelle, a family seaside resort, has a beach facing south. The **lighthouse** is on the top of the bell tower of an old Gothic church destroyed by fire.

Zoutelande. – Small seaside resort.

Flushing (Vlissingen). – Pop 44 863. The only large port on the sea, at the mouth of the Scheldt, Flushing became important in the 14C due to its herring fishing trade. Philip II embarked here in 1559 when he finally left the Low Countries for Spain. From 1585 to 1616 the town was pledged to the English as a guarantee of the costs undertaken by the Earl of Leicester's army to uphold the United Provinces after the assassination of William the Silent.
A settlement was named after it in 1643, which was transformed into Flushing, in Queens, New York.
Admiral de Ruyter (1607-76), who was born in Flushing, distinguished himself during the third war against England (1672-4) and was mortally wounded during a battle near Syracuse.
The French artist **Constantin Guys** (1802-92) was also born in this town; he was war correspondent (Crimean War) for the *Illustrated London News.*
A fishing port, Flushing, which commands the entry to the Walcheren canal, is an industrial centre with large naval shipyards. Warships are moored here. A maritime terminal ensures a car ferry service to England (Sheerness) and with Flemish Zeeland (Breskens, *p 163*). Flushing also has a Naval College.
⊘ **Boat trips** are given along Walcheren.
The town's sea front consists of a long avenue doubled by an esplanade and called **Boulevard.** The 15C **Gevangen Tower** or prison tower is here. Down below stretches a large beach sheltered from the north winds. At the far end of Boulevard, on an old bastion built by Charles V, there is a small lighthouse and the statue of Admiral de Ruyter. From here you have a **view** over the port below and the **old Exchange** of 1635, a fine building with green shutters, topped by a pinnacle.

Return to Middelburg by ③ on the town plan.

★ NIJMEGEN Gelderland   Pop 146 639

Michelin map **408** fold 19
Plan of built-up area in the current Michelin Red Guide Benelux

The only town in the Netherlands built on several hills, Nijmegen is the gateway to the river region, due to its location on the Waal, main branch of the Rhine, and near the canal, the Maas-Waalkanaal.

HISTORICAL NOTES

An old Batavian oppidum, Nijmegen was conquered by the Romans under Emperor Augustus then burnt down in 70AD by the Roman, Cerialis, General of Emperor Vespasian who was trying to quell the **Batavian revolt** stirred up the year before by **Gaius Julius Civilis.** It subsequently became a prosperous Roman city called Ulpia Noviomagus. Charlemagne who considered the town one of his favourite places to stay, built himself a castle on the present Valkhof *(p 152)*. In the Middle Ages the town expanded west of this castle.
In the 14C it became a member of the Hanseatic League. In 1585 it was taken by Alessandro Farnese, Duke of Parma, but recaptured in 1591 by Maurice of Nassau.

The peace of Nijmegen. – After the French, under the leadership of Turenne, captured it without difficulty in 1672, Nijmegen gave its name to three treaties which were signed there between France, the United Provinces, Spain (1678) and the German Empire (1679). They mark the peak of Louis XIV's reign who, at the outcome of the war against the United Provinces, which had started in June 1672, annexed to France the Franche-Comté and a part of Flanders. The United Provinces remained intact.
It was during the preliminary conferences for these treaties that the French language began to impose itself as the diplomatic language (despite this the treaties were written in Latin as was customary). The first treaty written in French was that of Rastatt in 1714.
In February 1944 the town was bombarded by the Americans. At the time of the Battle of Arnheim *(qv)* in September, Nijmegen was in the midst of heavy fighting. The bridge over the Waal, Waalbrug, built in 1936, which the Germans were threatening to destroy, was saved by a young inhabitant of the town, Jan van Hoof. A tablet to his memory has been put up in the centre of the bridge, on the east side. A monument (Y **A**) at the southern entry to the bridge commemorates the liberation of the town. The Netherlands Catholic University founded in 1923 is, since 1949, installed in a campus to the south of the town on the road to Venlo.
Nijmegen is the birthplace of **St Peter Canisius** (1521-97) he was named doctor of the church, when he was canonised in 1925.

⊘ **Boat trips** (Y). – *Boat trips are offered on the Waal.*

SIGHTS

Grote Markt (Y **14**). – In the centre of the square the **weigh house★** (Waag) (Y **B**), built in 1612 in the Renaissance style, has a lovely façade with a perron where the red and black colouring of the shutters and the somber red brick merge harmoniously. The ground floor is now a restaurant.

There is also a bronze statue of **Mariken van Nieumeghen** (Y **D**), heroine of a late 15C religious drama in which, seduced by the devil, she followed him seven years before repenting. The hands of the statue have three iron rings with which the Pope had ordered Mariken to chain her neck and arms. They loosened themselves, when she had atoned for her sin.

Near the weigh house there is a group of four 17C houses (Y **E**). One, the **Kerkboog** is identifiable by its decorated gable (1605) above a vaulted passage; the passage leads to St Stephen's.

Near the chevet of the church, the old **Latin School** (Latijnse School) (Y **F**) is a fine building of 1554.

⊙ **St Stephen's** (St.-Stevenskerk) (Y **K**). – This large 13C Gothic church, enlarged in the 15C, is flanked by a massive square tower with an octagonal onion-shape domed
⊙ pinnacle (1604) which has an 18C **carillon.**

The interior contains some lovely **furnishings:** the back of the door of the south arm of the transept (1632), the lords' pews in the Renaissance style by Cornelis Hermansz Schaeff of Nijmegen and the Renaissance pulpit by Joost Jacobs.

Note also the 18C princes' pew decorated with the armorial bearings of the town
⊙ (eagles) and the province (lions), the **organ** built in the 18C by König and the copper chandeliers.

⊙ **Tower** (Toren). – *Access by the west façade.*

From the top (183 steps) there is a panorama over the town and the Waal. Note an old 15C curtain wall tower in Kronenburger Park (Y **L**).

The church's precinct has been restored; a flea market takes place here on Monday mornings. To the north there are some lovely houses with gables, **Kannunikenhuizen** (Y **N**) or the canons' houses.

⊙ **Municipal Museum** (Nijmeegs Museum "Commanderie van St.-Jan") (Y **M¹**). – This 15 and 16C brick building (restored) overlooking the Waal, is an old hospital. Founded in the 12C to shelter pilgrims going to the Holy Land, in the 13C, it came into the possession of the Order of the Hospital of St John of Jerusalem.

The town's history is unveiled in this museum where engravings, objects, scale models and paintings are pleasantly exhibited. The anonymous triptych depicting a Calvary (1526) with St Peter Canisius's family, a view of the Waal with the Valkhof by Van Goyen, the *Peace of Nijmegen* painted for Louis XIV in 1678, and the collections which belonged to corporations and guilds (silver chains, pewter pots) are particularly remarkable.

The museum also organises temporary exhibitions of ancient and modern art.

(After photo Nijmeegs Museum "Commanderie van St. Jan")

Chain of Office, Municipal Museum

⊙ **Town Hall** (Stadhuis) (Y **H**). – This fine 16 and 17C building, partly destroyed by the bombardments, was restored in 1953. It is flanked by an onion-shaped turret. The outside is decorated with statues carved by Albert Termote depicting the emperors who were Nijmegen's benefactors or who had played a part in its history. On the corner is a statue of the Virgin.

Inside there are lovely rooms decorated in the old style, the Aldermen's Room (Schepenhal), the Registrar's Office (Trouwzaal). In the **Truce Hall** (Trêveszaal) where the walls are covered with verdure tapestries, the treaties of 1678 and 1679 were signed. In the Council Room (Raadzaal) and the Great Hall (Burgerzaal) hang other tapestries.

Valkhof (Y). – This park has been laid out on the site of a castle built by Charlemagne. It took the name of "falcon's tower" because Louis the Pious, son of Charlemagne and heir to his father's empire, bred falcons here for hunting. The castle rebuilt by Frederick Barbarossa in the 12C was destroyed in the 18C.

St Martin's Chapel (St.-Maartenskapel) (Y **Q**). – In the centre of the park are the remains of the Romanesque chapel of Frederick Barbarossa's castle. There remains a finely decorated oven-vaulted apse at the chancel's entrance, two columns with foliated capitals, and blind arcades outside.

St Nicholas's Chapel★ (St.-Nicolaaskapel) (Y **R**). – Near a terrace from where there is an interesting **view** over the Waal, this old chapel of the Carolingian castle stands hidden behind trees. It was probably modified in the 11C. It has 16 sides and is topped by an octagonal turret. Inside one can see the pillars which encircle a central octagonal-shaped space. Upstairs there is a gallery with twin bays.

Belvedere (Y **S**). – It is the name of an old watch tower (1640) of the old curtain wall, now converted into a restaurant, the terrace offers a fine **view** over the Waal.

NIJMEGEN

Augustijnenstr.	Y 2	Passage Molenpoort	YZ 29	Keizer Karelpl.		Z 18
Bloemerstr.	Y	Plein 1944	Y 32	Mariënburg		Z 22
Broerstr.	Y	Ziekerstr.	Y	Mr. Franckenstr.		Z 24
Burchtstr.	Y			Nieuwe Ubbergseweg		Z 25
Lange Hezelstr.	Y	Bisschop Hamerstr.	Z 3	van Oldenbarnevelstr.		Z 27
Molenstr.	YZ	van Broeckhuysenstr.	YZ 4	Prins Hendrikstr.		Z 33
		Burg. Hustinxstr.	Z 6	van Schevichavenstr.		Z 34
		Doddendaal	Y 7	Stikke Hezelstr.		Z 42
		Grote Markt	Y 14	Voerweg		Y 44

🕐 **G.M Kam Museum (Rijksmuseum) (Z M²)**. – It contains Roman antiquities found mainly during excavations in Nijmegen and its surroundings.

The ground floor evokes Roman (pottery, bronzes, scale models) and Frankish (swords) Nijmegen. In the hall note a collection of ceramics as well as a finely worked silver goblet found in the Maas near Stevensweert (south of Roermond), a bronze portrait of the Emperor Trajan, a large goblet decorated with gladiators.

On the 1st floor there is a fine collection of Roman glass and domestic objects.

EXCURSIONS

🕐 **Heilig Land Stichting**. – *4km - 2½ miles to the southeast by Groesbeekseweg* (Z).
To the north of **Groesbeek**, the Holy Land Foundation (Heilig Land Stichting) is a sort of open-air Bible Museum.

Two signposted routes lead round a wood of 45ha - 111 acres where reconstructions evoke Palestine in biblical times.

Route A is devoted to daily life: Bedouin tents, farmhouses, villages and urban areas. Along route B the sites of the Passion of Christ are reproduced: the Garden of Olives, Pilate's palace, the Calvary, the Holy Sepulchre.

There is a neo-Byzantine church nearby.

Berg en Dal. – *6km - 3¾ miles to the east by Berg en Dalseweg* (Z).
This locality is located in a region appreciated for its wooded and undulating countryside.

🕐 The **African Museum** (Afrika Museum) is installed to the south. *Postweg 6.*
It contains a collection of sculpture including masks and objects used daily, laid out in a modern building, and reconstutions in the open-air (Ghana and Mali dwellings, houses on piles).

The **Duivelsberg**, a wooded hill 76m - 249ft high, is crisscrossed with paths. By following the signs "Pannekoeken" (restaurant) one reaches a car park. From there a signposted path leads to a belvedere: **view** over the German plain and Wijler Lake (Wijlermeer).

Doornenburg. – *18km - 11 miles to the northeast. Leave by Waalbrug* (Y) *and turn towards Bemmel and Gendt.*
🕐 This village has a 14C **castle** (Kasteel) rebuilt after World War II.
It is a tall square fortress surrounded by water, topped by turrets and linked by a footbridge to a fortified courtyard where there is a chapel and a farmhouse.

NORTHEAST POLDER (NOORDOOSTPOLDER) Flevoland   Pop 37 820

Michelin map 408 folds 11 and 12 – Local map p 134

It is the second polder made according to the Zuiderzee *(qv)* drainage plan.

Drainage. – The polder covers more than 48 000ha - 118 560 acres. Its surrounding dike built between 1937 and 1940 is 55km - 34 miles long. The polder was drained as from 1941 by three pumping stations situated at Vollenhove, Urk and Lemmer, which evacuated 1.5 billion m^3 – 52 971 billion f^3. Drainage canals were dug out and drainage completed in 1942.

The polder is attached to Urk (alt: 9m - 30ft high), an old island of the Zuiderzee, and includes the island of Schokland (alt: 3.5m - 11$\frac{1}{2}$ft high), which today is the culminating point of this territory where the lowest level is 5m - 16$\frac{1}{2}$ft below sea level.

Development. – After drainage 500km - 310$\frac{1}{2}$ miles of roads were constructed and a capital, **Emmeloord**, built in the centre of the polder.

The Northeast Polder is mainly devoted to agriculture. From 1942-62 the polder was soil improved, fertilized and 1 650 farmhouses were built on it. The smallest farms are grouped round villages, the larger ones have a dwelling house linked to a barn by a stable. In the meadows cows and sheep graze; the cultivation of wheat, potatoes and sugarbeet alternate with a few fields of flowers.

SIGHTS

Emmeloord. – The capital of the polder was built according to contemporary urban ideas. In the centre, the **water tower** (watertoren) built in 1957 provides drinking water for the whole polder and has a carillon of 48 bells.

From the summit the **view** stretches up to the Frisian coast, Urk and the electrical power station of East Flevoland.

Schokland. – *Between Ens and Nagele.* Formerly an island in the Zuiderzee, of elongated shape it included three villages which were abandoned in 1859; due to its low altitude the island was difficult to defend against the sea. The old church in the centre and its precincts have been converted into a **museum** (Museum Schokland).

Here one can learn about the region's medieval past evoked by the archaeological discoveries made during the polder's drainage, about its inhabitants in prehistoric times and its geological evolution.

Behind the presbytery there still remains part of the wooden stockade which protected the island from the onslaughts of the sea.Two stelae sealed onto the walls of the church and the presbytery show the water level reached during floods.

★**Urk.** – Pop 11 829. Zuiderzee's other island has been attached to land since the creation of the Northeast Polder. Today it is a small harbour much visited by tourists.

Urk is linked to Enkhuizen by **boat**.

Formerly specialising in eel fishing, Urk, whose inhabitants fish both in IJssel Lake and in the North Sea, now has the biggest fish market in the country. The **docks** have kept their picturesque appearance, with the stocky eel fishing trawlers painted in vivid colours.

Urk has kept from its insular past a few local traditions. The older inhabitants still wear the traditional costume: for the men, a black suit hiding a striped shirt; for the women, black skirt with a flowered or embroidered shirt front, a lace headdress worn on a metal headband ending in animal heads.

Near the church at the top of the mound, a terrace offers a **view** over IJssel Lake and the dike which protects the polder.

NUENEN North Brabant   Pop 20 619

Michelin map 408 fold 18 or 212 north of fold 18 (8km - 5 miles to the northeast of Eindhoven)

This town preserves the memory of **Vincent van Gogh** *(qv)* who, after having spent several months in the Drenthe, came to live, in the presbytery where his parents lived from December 1883 to November 1885. It was then that he really started applying himself to painting in oils before leaving for Antwerp. He painted several portraits of country people, which he used as studies for his great canvas *The Potato Eaters* (p 128).

SIGHTS

Monument to Van Gogh. – *On a small triangular square at the junction of the road to Mierlo, near a large lime tree surrounded by lime shoots.* Made by Hildo Krop in 1932, it is a sober black stone stela, engraved with a sun and lying on a round pedestal with an inscription concerning Van Gogh's stay here.

Presbytery (Het domineeshuis). – Just south of the monument, on the main street, at no 26 Berg is the house where Vincent van Gogh's father died in March 1885. It looks exactly as the artist painted it.

Van Gogh Documentation Centre (Van Gogh Documentatiecentrum). – Near the new town hall (Gemeentehuis) a small building has been specially constructed to house an exhibition of photos and documents concerning the painter's stay in Nuenen.

Mill (Molen). – *To the north, take a right off the main road towards 't Weefhuis (weaver's house).* Near a pond there is a mill perched on a mound.

Michelin map **408** fold 19 or **212** fold 20
Town plan in the current Michelin Red Guide Benelux

At the confluence of the Maas and the Roer, near the German and Dutch frontier, Roermond, the most important city in the centre of Limburg, is an industrial town (Philips, insulators, paper, chemistry, dairy products).
Due to its bishopric founded in 1559 it is also the religious capital of this very Catholic province.
Formerly Roermond was the county town of Upper Gelderland. It was granted its city rights in 1232 and was soon given a fortified wall of which the 14C **Ratten Tower** (Rattentoren) on the Buitenop, remains.
Roermond was one of the first towns captured in 1572 by William the Silent coming from Dillenburg and entering the country, but it was recaptured by the Spanish in October. Roermond then belonged to Austria, France, and only returned to the Netherlands Kingdom in 1815.
The town which greatly suffered in the last war has been partly rebuilt. It includes two pleasure boat harbours and vast stretches of water situated between the Maas and a side canal.

SIGHTS

⊙ **Church of Our Lady (O. L. Vrouwekerk) or Munsterkerk.** – *Munsterplein, in the town centre.*
It is the old church of a Cistercian abbey. In Rhenish style, it was started in 1218 in the transitional Romanesque-Gothic style and restored at the end of the 19C by Cuypers (who was born here in 1827).
On the west it is flanked by a massive porch framed by two towers with spires and topped by a dome flanked by two turrets at the transept crossing.
The trefoil plan of the western part, with the transept arms ending in semicircles, the apse's outside gallery, the roofs of the towers and turrets in the shape of bishops' mitres, and the decoration of Lombard arcading are characteristics typical of Rhenish edifices.
The church has a Brabant altarpiece (*c*1530) in carved and painted wood and at the transept crossing there is the tomb of the abbey's founders, the Count of Gelderland Gerald IV and his wife Margaret of Brabant.
Near the church, at the corner of Pollartstraat, the **Prinsenhof**, built between 1666-70 is the old palace of the stadtholders of Upper Gelderland, during Spanish rule.

Take Steenweg, the main shopping street and a pedestrian precinct.

⊙ **Cathedral (Kathedrale Kerk).** – Dedicated to St Christopher, it stands near Markt. Built in 1410 in regional Gothic style, it was damaged during the last war, but since restored. Opposite the cathedral there is a small 1764 **baroque house** (converted into a restaurant).

EXCURSION

★ **Thorn.** – Pop 2 621. *14km - 8½ miles southwest of Roermond. Leave by ⑤ on the town plan.*
Not far from the Belgian frontier, this large village built of pink brick, often painted white, has charm.
⊙ Near Plein de Wijngaard, its paving decorated with geometric motifs, stands the **church** (abdijkerk) preceded by a high brick tower striped with white stone.
This is the old church of a women's abbey founded at the end of the 10C by Ansfried (who became Bishop of Utrecht in 995) and his wife Hilsondis. Rebuilt at the end of the 13C in the Gothic style, it has preserved from Romanesque times two staircase turrets and a crypt on the west side. It was enlarged in the 15C, and transformed into the baroque style at the end of the 18C. It was restored by Cuypers at the end of the 19C.
The interior is surprisingly white. The eastern chancel, raised and decorated by a baroque altarpiece overlooks a Gothic crypt.
The chapels in the aisles have interesting low reliefs. In the south aisle there are charming 17 and 18C statues of saints in the folk art tradition.
At the end of the nave, a double flight of stairs leads to the canonesses's chancel. From here one reaches a small **museum** installed in the old chapterhouse and the archives both of the 14 and 15C: treasury (reliquaries, crowns), engravings, documents.
In the western crypt, which is Romanesque, there is a sculptured stone baptismal font (15C).

Take the main street (Akkerwal, Akker, Boekenderweg). At the second oratory (St.-Antoniuskapel) turn left.

On a small shady square, the 1673 **Chapel Under the Lime Trees** (Kapel onder de Linden) was enlarged in 1811. Inside, the oldest part on the east side has fine baroque decoration (stucco work, paintings) while the 19C part was decorated in the Empire style.

The Michelin Red Guide Benelux

revises annually its selection of establishments offering

- *a good but moderately priced meal*
- *prices with service included or net prices*
- *a plain menu for a modest price*
- *free overnight parking.*

Michelin map **408** folds 17, 24 and 25 – Local maps pp 79, 163 and 165
Plan of built-up area in the current Michelin Red Guide Benelux

The second biggest city in the kingdom because of population, Rotterdam, the world's
largest port, is located on the **Nieuwe Maas**, with 2 148ha - 5 306 acres of water
and 30km - 19 miles from the North Sea. Rotterdam, at the mouth of two important
waterways – Rhine, Maas and their tributaries – leading into the industrial heartland,
is the meeting point of maritime and fluvial traffic. The city of Rotterdam stretches on
both sides of the river and is linked by tunnels, bridges and a subway. It is part of the
Rijnmond a group of 23 municipalities part of **Randstad Holland** *(qv)*.
The university, named after Erasmus, was founded in 1973 by joining together the
School of Advanced Economic Studies and Social Sciences with the Faculty of
Medecine.
Destroyed during the last war, Rotterdam has been entirely rebuilt.

⊘ **Boat trips.** – Besides a visit to the port *(p 162)*, excursions are also organised in the
Delta, landing stage Willemsplein *(town plan p 160, DZ)*. In addition Rotterdam is the
departure point for cruises on the Rhine.

ROTTERDAM

HISTORICAL NOTES

Rotterdam was originally a small village built on the dike (dam) built on a small river, the Rotte. The town was still of little importance when Erasmus was born there.

Erasmus Roterodamus. – This was the way the great humanist Geert Geertsz. signed his name throughout his life. He was born here in 1469 but spent little time. As a child, Erasmus lived in Gouda, studied in Utrecht, then in the school of the Brethren of Common Life at Deventer and later at 's-Hertogenbosch.

An orphan with nowhere to turn, Erasmus became a monk in 1488 at the convent of Steyn, near Gouda, and studied the Antique world.

In 1493 having left the convent, he became secretary to the Bishop of Cambrai, whom he accompanied on his travels. He was, however, attracted by learning, and succeeded in getting a scholarship to study theology at the Sorbonne, while continuing to write many works.

During a stay in England, in 1499, he met Thomas More, the author of *Utopia,* who was to become his best friend. In 1502, fleeing the plague, which had spread through France, he arrived at the University of Louvain and soon became a professor there.

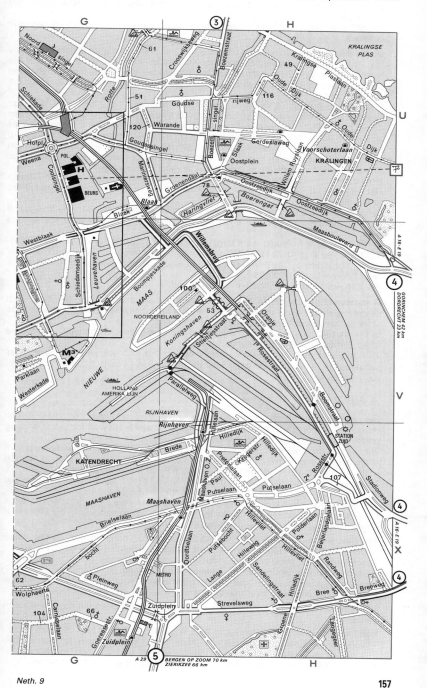

A tireless traveller, Erasmus was in Italy in 1506, where he published his **Adagia**, a commentary on quotations and proverbs from Antiquity; then in London in 1509 where he wrote and published two years later his **In Praise of Folly**. In Basle in 1514, Erasmus met Holbein who in 1515 illustrated an edition of *In Praise of Folly* and made several portraits of him.

When, in 1517, Luther put up the ninety-five theses which triggered the Reformation, Erasmus was in Louvain. He at first refused to take part in religious quarrels but, when the Faculty of Theology condemned Luther's Theses, his neutrality, brought him problems. After spending some months at Anderlecht, near Brussels in 1521, he left for Switzerland where he calmly continued with his literary endeavours and published, in 1526, an enlarged edition of his **Colloquia Familiaria**, satyric dialogues, which was very successful.

The Prince of Humanists died in Basel in 1536.

Expansion. – In 1572 the Spaniards pursued by the Sea Beggars, who had just captured Brielle, pleaded with the inhabitants of Rotterdam to be allowed entry. Once inside, Admiral Bossu allowed his troops to pillage the town. After this betrayal, Rotterdam joined the revolt. From 1576 to 1602 ports were constructed which were used by the Sea Beggars' fleet; the town rapidly surpassed its rival, Dordrecht, and became the second largest in Holland.

Nevertheless, when Rotterdam was captured by the French in 1794, its trade severely suffered.

Major dock work. – It was only after Belgium and the Netherlands separated in 1830 that Rotterdam once again became a transit port for the Rhine. As the depth of the river in the estuary (Brielse Maas) had become inadequate for the increasingly large ships, an access canal had to be built across the island of Voorne in 1830, the Voornsekanaal.

The Voornsekanaal, also, became insufficient and in 1863 the Minister Jan R. Thorbecke approved the plans drawn up by the young hydraulic engineer **Pieter Caland** (1826-1902) for the construction of a waterway crossing the sandy plains separating Rotterdam from the sea (North Sea). The **New Waterway** (Nieuwe Waterweg) a waterway 18km - 11 miles long and 11m - 36ft deep at low tide was dug out between 1866 and 1872, and is comparable to Amsterdam's Noordzeekanaal, without locks. The port of **Hoek van Holland** was built at the sea-end for passenger travel.

New docks started to be built on the south bank of the river towards 1870 (Binnen Dock, Entrepot Dock, Spoorweg Dock) which were bigger than the old ones and linked to the railway.

Between 1876 and 1878 two bridges were built across the Maas (Willems Bridge and Koninginne Bridge) as well as a railway viaduct 1 400m - 4 598ft wide spaning the river.

Three man-made harbours were dug, the Rijn Dock (1887-94), the Maas Dock (1898-1909) and the Waal Dock (1907-31), which became the largest artificial harbour in the world. Subsequently the port was extended along the right bank of the Maas, to the west (Merwe Dock, 1923-1932).

By 1886 Rotterdam had engulfed **Delfshaven** *(qv)*.

A martyred city. – On 14 May, 1940 Rotterdam suffered German bombings that destroyed almost all of the old town. Only the town hall, the central post office, the stock exchange and Erasmus's statue were spared.

In March 1943, Allied bombing completed the destruction. 280ha - 692 acres were razed, 30 000 houses and buildings set on fire.

The port was also bombed very badly during the last war and, moreover, was sabotaged in 1944 by the Germans who destroyed 7km - 4 miles of docks and 20% of the warehouses.

A NEW CITY

Reconstruction of the city. – Immediately after the war Rotterdam began rebuilding. Rational urban planning was adopted, which allowed for better spacing and a cultural and commercial city centre.

The population emigrated outside the city which led to the spectacular development of the built-up area. Many communities were set up almost overnight, such as **Hoogvliet** in the south and **Alexanderpolder** in the east, and Prins Alexanderpolder (1871).

The quarter south of the Maas was given a shopping centre, the **Zuidplein**, a theatre and an enormous sports complex, the **Ahoy** (concerts, exhibitions).

To facilitate the inhabitants' of this considerable urban area's leisure activities, large recreational facilities were set up nearby, in particular on a peninsula of the Maas near Brielle, to the west and to the northeast along the Rotte.

The new port. – *See also p 162.* In 1945 the reconstruction of the port started. It was decided to develop industry. A new port, **Botlek** was built in 1954 on the island of Rozenburg for the petro-chemical industries and the refineries.

When this became inadequate the **Europoort** had to be added.

Finally open-sea docks were built to berth giant tankers, south of New Waterway in the **Maasvlakte** area where an industrial zone was created around the port facilities.

Transportation. – There are 4 main urban road links between the north and south banks:

Maas Tunnel (Maastunnel). – Opened in 1942, it is 1 070m - 3 510ft long of which 550m - 1 804ft are under the river. Covered with yellow tiles, it has four separate galleries: two one-way roads for cars (6 000 an hour) placed side by side, and two upper levels for cyclists (8 000 an hour) and pedestrians (40 000 an hour) with eight escalators.

Benelux Tunnel (Beneluxtunnel). – This was built in 1967 to relieve some ·of the traffic from Maas Tunnel, which had become inadequate, and to allow a crossing between the two banks while avoiding the city centre. It is 1 300m - 4 265ft long and the river bed was dredged 22.5m - 74ft deep.

Willems Bridge (Willemsbrug). – This bridge was opened in 1982.

Van Brienenoord Bridge (Van Brienenoordbrug). – This bridge to the east dates from 1965. It has a single span 297m - 974ft long, rising 25m - 82ft above the water, and ends in a bascule bridge on the north side.

Moreover, the city has acquired an enormous quadrilateral ring road which enables traffic to avoid the city centre.

In 1968 the Rotterdam subway, the first in the country, was opened.

THE CENTRE

From the railway station
to the Boymans-van Beuningen Museum *time: about 5 hours*

The centre of the city is full of large buildings housing banks, offices and business concerns, amongst which many statues have been erected.

Stationsplein (DY). – With one's back to the **Centraal Station,** built in 1957, the **Wholesale Trade Centre** (Groothandelsgebouw) (**DY A**) can be seen on the right. Built in 1952, the massive building covering 2ha - 5 acres, has 200 firms and employs 5 000 people.

Kruisplein (DY 60). – To the right is the **Bouwcentrum** or **Building Centre** (**DY**) whose façade has an enormous reproduction of Picasso's **Sylvette**. Inside the building there are architectural exhibitions. On the side façade overlooking the Weena, note Henry Moore's brick **Relief** (1955).

De Doelen (DY). – It is an immense concert hall and congress centre built in 1966; the main auditorium seats 2 222 people.

To the north of Westersingel stands a statue symbolising the Rotterdam Resistance.

Schouwburgplein (DY 92). – Built over an underground car park, this square is an immense esplanade equipped with many benches.

On Korte Lijnbaan (**DY 57**) which branches off the square at the northeast angle, there is a headless statue by Rodin called **The Walking Man.**

★**Lijnbaan** (DY). – This is the shopping quarter's main street, built by Jacob B. Bakema from 1952-4, with pedestrian precincts and flower beds. One can stroll by pretty shops or relax in outdoor cafés.

Cross Lijnbaan to reach the town hall.

Note the charming little sculpture by Anne Grimdalen, **The Bear Cubs** (De Beertjes, 1956).

Opposite the town hall is the **War Memorial**. It was made by Mari Andriessen in 1957 and three generations are depicted.

Coolsingel (DY). – This is the city's main thoroughfare and the town hall, the post office and the stock exchange are situated here. There are many modern compositions on the sidewalks and building façades, as well as several statues. Shaded lawns make it a pleasant place to walk.

(After photo VVV, Rotterdam)

The Bear Cubs by Anne Grimdalen

⊙ **Town Hall** (Stadhuis) (**DY H**). – Built between 1914-20, a good example of period
⊙ architecture, it is one of the few edifices which was spared. It has an excellent **carillon.** Among other statues, in front of the building, is one of the great jurist, Grotius, by Hettema (1970). On the façade of the building opposite there is a mosaic (1954) (**DY C**) by Van Roode depicting Erasmus on his way to Basle.

The **post office** which dates from the same period as the town hall has a remarkable metallic framework inside.

Go south of the post office alongside the stock exchange.

The **stock exchange** (Beurs) (**DY**) was built 1936-40. The World Trade Centre (1987), an elliptically-shaped tower, is being built above the stock exchange.

Cross Rotte Canal.

The **Statue of Erasmus** on the parvis of St Lawrence's is the work of Hendrick de Keyser and was finished in 1622, after his death (1536). The church itself dates from the year of Erasmus's birth, 1469.

⊙ **St Lawrence's (Grote- of St.-Laurenskerk) (DY D)**. – Completed in 1646, with its truncated tower built into the transept, this Gothic church was destroyed in 1940. It now has, once more, a fine façade with a new bronze portal (1968) by Giacomo Manzù (War and Peace) and a chevet with Gothic tracery.

The **interior★** is spaciously conceived in the Gothic Brabant style, the severity of which is attenuated by the warm colours of the pannelled vaults, the copper chandeliers, the great red and gold organ (1973), and the 18C gilded ironwork of the sanctuary.

ROTTERDAM

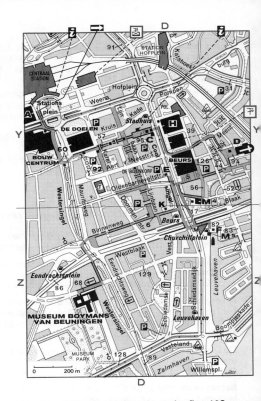

*For a pleasant stroll
in a town look
for the pedestrian streets
indicated on the town plans.*

The slightly protruding transept contains 17C admirals' tombs and a fine 16C organ case. The organ case in the chancel dates from 1725. The bronze baptismal font (1959) is by Han Petri.

Return to Coolsingel.

In front of a department store stands **Construction** (1957; **DY E**) by Naum Gabo.

Cross Coolsingel and bear left on Bulgersteyn, then right on Korte Hoogstraat.

★**Schielandshuis Historical Museum** (**Historisch Museum**) (**DY M⁴**). – Built between ⊙1662-5 to house the administrative centre of the Schieland dikes, this mansion (Schielandshuis) has a main façade in white ashlar stone, richly decorated and equipped with red shutters. The finely proportioned building was restored to hold the city's historical collection.

The ground floor and basement rooms are devoted to artistic production (paintings, gold and silversmith work, clockwork...). Three reconstructed interiors (Louis XVI, rococo and Regency styles) contain objects sought by 18C art collectors. Among the paintings worth noting are the interior scenes painted by H. Sorgh and C. Saftleven (both 17C artists) and, especially, the works of **Adriaen van der Werff** (1659-1722); his technique and the quality of his works – see *Self-Portrait in the Medallion* – brought this painter international recognition.

Note in the basement the ceramic tile scene *In Duijsent Vreesen* (*To Live 1 000 Fears*, *c*1600) where the green tone is evident and typical of the period's local production.

The 1st floor evokes institutions and municipal activities: more than 40 portraits of directors of The Dutch East India Company *(qv)*, 18 and 19C canvases (reflecting the importance of commercial activities.

The remains of the city's churches have a particular importance: Rotterdam lost all its old churches during the 1940 bombardment. The model of the wooden spire having topped St Lawrence's from 1619-45 was designed by Hendrick de Keyser *(qv)*.

The mezzanine exhibits the **Atlas van Stolk Collection** with engravings and drawings concerning the history of the Low Countries (displayed in part during temporary exhibitions).

Daily life (children's kitchen – 1853; reconstitution of a grocer's – 1910-68, etc) occupies the attic space.

Cross Blaak to reach Plein 1940.

At the north end of Leuvehaven, stands a statue by the Russian-born French sculptor, Zadkine, **Destroyed City** (1953) (**DZ F**), which symbolises the martyred city. The Prins Hendrik Maritime Museum *(p 162)* is located on Leuvehaven.

Return to Coolsingel.

On Coolsingel an amusing statue portrays **Monsieur Jacques** (**DZ K**) (1959), a typical citizen of Rotterdam by Wenckebach (1959).

Binnenwegplein (**DZ 6**). – Note **Het Ding** (the Thing; 1969) a giant mobile by the American artist George Rickey.

Westersingel (**DYZ**). – Down this avenue, with its many stretches of water surrounded by gardens, the remains of a ring canal, one reaches the Boymans-van Beuningen Museum.

★★★ Boymans-van Beuningen Museum. – On the edge of a park, this fine arts museum is in a building inaugurated in 1935, to which a wing was added in 1972. Besides an excellent collection of ancient art, the museum contains a large number of modern and contemporary works of art, engravings and drawings and a decorative arts section.

In 1958 the museum was enriched by the D.G. Van Beuningen donation, while in 1972 the Willem Van der Vorm Collection was given on loan. The Vitale Bloch bequest, a collection of paintings and drawings from the 15 to the mid-20C was acquired in 1978. The museum also organises temporary international exhibitions.

Ancient Art. – *Old building, 1st floor.* There is a remarkable collection of primitive art. *The Three Marys at the Open Sepulchre* is a major work by the **Van Eycks.** There are admirable paintings by **Hieronymus Bosch,** *The Marriage at Cana, St Christopher,* and in particular *The Prodigal Son* where one can appreciate the painter's poetic humour, his flights of imagination, and his mastery of colour. Note a Virgin and Child surrounded by angel musicians, *The Glorification of the Virgin,* a masterpiece by **Geertgen tot Sint Jans.** The Prophet Isaiah is shown on the left panel of the famous altarpiece by the **Master of the Annunciation of Aix** (Aix-en-Provence).

The Tower of Babel by **Bruegel the Elder,** the delightful *Portrait of a Young Scholar* in a red beret (1531) by **Jan Van Scorel,** and works by **Pieter Aertsen** etc represent the 16C.

17C painting is particularly interesting. There are two portraits by **Frans Hals;** church interiors with masterful use of light by **Pieter Saenredam** and **Emanuel de Witte;** a portrait by **Rembrandt** of his young son Titus; the distant horizons of **Hercules Seghers** and **Van Goyen;** and nature's atmosphere rendered by **Hobbema** and **Jacob van Ruisdael.** There are also interior scenes by **Jan Steen** and **Gerrit Dou.**

The **Rubens** collection has, among other sketches, a remarkable series on the theme of Achilles's life. In the fine group of Italian paintings from the 15 to 17C, there are works by the Venetians: Titian, Tintoretto and Veronese.

Willem Van der Vorm Collection (Verzameling). – It includes, notably, an interesting series of 17C paintings with Rubens, Van Dyck, Rembrandt *(Tobias and his Wife)* and many Dutch masters such as Gerrit Dou, Ter Borch *(Woman Spinning)* and Van de Velde with two seascapes.

19C French painting is represented by the Barbizon School. There are works by Daubigny, Théodore Rousseau and Corot *(Ville d'Avray).*

For the 18C, Hubert Robert, Chardin and Watteau should be mentioned for France, and the Venetian Francesco Guardi, for Italy.

Prints and Drawings. – *Old building, ground floor and print room on 1st floor.* This important collection, a part of which is exhibited during temporary exhibitions, covers the 15C to the present day. It includes works by Albrecht Dürer, Leonardo da Vinci, Rembrandt, Watteau, Cézanne and Picasso.

Modern and Contemporary Art. – *Old building, 1st floor and new wing.* It covers the period from 1850 to the present.

The Impressionist artists Monet, Sisley and Pissaro are represented as well as Signac, Van Gogh, Mondrian and Kandinsky *(Lyrisches).* Note the small 14-year old ballet dancer, a graceful statuette by Degas.

Among the Surrealist works there are paintings by Salvador Dali *(Sundial, Impressions of Africa)* and René Magritte *(The Red Model, Reproduction Forbidden).*

The contemporary art collection is exhibited on rotation; it includes sculptures by Richard Serra, Oldenburg, Joseph Beuys, Bruce Nauman and Walter De Maria, and Donald Judd and paintings by the Germans Kiefer and Penck, the Italians Cucchi, Clemente and Chia.

Dutch contemporary art is represented by Van Elk, Carel Visser, Rob van Koningsbruggen and René Daniels.

Among the contemporary trends are works by Milan Kunc and Salvo as well as sculptures by Thomas Schütte, Bazilebustamente and Niek Kamp.

Decorative Arts. – *Old building, ground floor.* The museum also has a very rich collection of *objets d'art;* glassware (17C), silverware, majolica and Persian, Turkish (13C), Spanish, Dutch, Italian (15-16C) and Delft earthenware.

DELFSHAVEN

From Delfshaven, Delft's *(qv)* old port, the Pilgrim Fathers *(qv)* embarked in 1620 for England from where they sailed for the New World.

Piet Hein was born here in 1577, the Admiral who distinguished himself in Mexico, in 1628, against the Spanish. The painter **Van Dongen** was born here in 1877 (d1968). He portrayed violently coloured female figures.

Voorhaven (EV 121). – It is a picturesque quay and has a chapel with a pinnacle known as the Pilgrim Fathers' Church, and a charming lever bridge.

★ De Dubbelde Palmboom Museum (EV M¹). – This museum has been remarkably installed in converted warehouses.

Photographs, scale models and a great variety of *objets d'art* and arts and crafts are shown throughout the five stories of the building to illustrate the history of Rotterdam. From the top storey, the city can be seen towards the east (orientation table); note below, opposite Coolhaven, the statue of Piet Hein (1870).

The Porters' House (Zakkendragershuis) (EV L). – To the north of Voorhaven, this old porters' house has been renovated and contains a tin smelting works where old methods are still used.

Nos 34 and 36 have interesting façade stones with sculptured animals.

ADDITIONAL SIGHTS

★ **Euromast** (F V). – This boldly designed tower was built in 1960 in Rotterdam Park, ⊘ close to Parkhaven.
From the terrace, which is 100m - 328ft high, there is a remarkable **view**★ of the city and the port.
⊘ The **Space Tower,** added in 1970, rises 180m - 591ft on an axis. The glass lift revolving around it holds 32 people who admire a **panorama**★★ stretching 30km - 19 miles in all directions, including the immense Delta formed by the Maas and the Rhine, hemming in the Europoort. At night the sight is extraordinary.

⊘ **Prins Hendrik Maritime Museum (Maritiem Museum)** (DZ M⁵). – Located on Leuvehaven, Rotterdam's first harbour basin onto the sea, this museum is devoted to European seafare in the past and present with special emphasis on the Netherlands. The main building houses not only the temporary exhibitions but scale models, paintings, maps, globes and navigational instruments as well.
In Leuvehaven note the Dutch ships used for inland navigation from 1850-1950 and especially the **Buffel** (1868), the Royal Navy's old ship. Cabins belonging to the different crew members are on view as well as the prison cells and the luxurious captain's cabin.

⊘ **Ethnographic Museum (Museum voor Volkenkunde)** (GV M³). – On the quays of the Nieuwe Maas, this museum which is in the old Royal Yacht Club building, is devoted to the cultures of non-Western peoples.

⊘ **Blijdorp Zoo (Diergaarde)** (EU). – In a floral park, this zoo contains an interesting collection of over 2 000 animals, including some rare species (okapies, etc). The Riviera-Hal includes aquariums, a vivarium (reptiles), a tropical hothouse and aviaries.

Kralingsebos (HU). – This wood surrounds a big lake (Kralingseplas) and has two **windmills** on the north side.
⊘ In one of them, **De Ster,** an old spice mill dating from 1740, rebuilt in 1969, snuff manufacture can be seen.

★★★ THE PORT

Port Activity. – Rotterdam with a total goods traffic for 1986 of about 256 million metric tons, is the world's largest port.
Petroleum and its byproducts account for about 115 million metric tons or about 45% of the total activity. Five important refineries (Shell, Esso, Texaco, Kuwait Petroleum Co. and BP) are situated between Rotterdam and the sea, beside docks capable of taking tankers of up to 350 000 metric tons. They can produce 90 million metric tons of petroleum byproducts and have engendered a powerful chemical industry. There are 33 million m³ - 1 165.3 billion f³ reserved for the storage of crude oil and its byproducts.
Maritime activity is supplemented by heavy **river traffic** on the Rhine as Rotterdam, due to its location, is a natural outlet for the Rhineland.
In 1986, 200 000 boats from the Rhine arrived in Rotterdam transporting 133 million metric tons of goods.

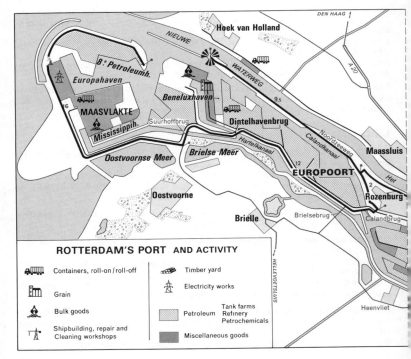

ROTTERDAM'S PORT AND ACTIVITY

⊟⫞ Containers, roll-on / roll-off

▦ Grain

♨ Bulk goods

Shipbuilding, repair and Cleaning workshops

⫞ Timber yard

⚡ Electricity works

▨ Petroleum — Tank farms, Refinery, Petrochemicals

▨ Miscellaneous goods

20km - 12 miles of quays are reserved for them in a 766ha - 1 892 acre dock area.
A part of these goods is transhiped directly onto Rhine barges.
Moreover, Rotterdam which is the home port or transit port for over 300 **regular international shipping lines**, in 1986 received about 33 000 sea-going vessels. The port facilities for these ships are quite impressive. 500 of them can dock along 40km - 25 miles of quays and 200 others by jetties and buoys. They can use 387 cranes of which 20 are floating ones.
The port facilities have had to adapt to **container** traffic as well as to the large number of ferries run by shipping companies between Rotterdam and British ports. **Roll on - roll off** of goods has also become very frequent with ships' holds directly accessible to trucks.
Sheds and warehouses cover a total space of 1 130 400 m² - 12 159 230sq ft.
Nevertheless, Rotterdam also has highly mechanised installations with vast storage capacities for **bulk goods** (minerals, grain, coal and fertilisers).

Nieuwe Maas

Short boat trip. – The boat sails down the Maas to Eem Dock. Landing stage: Willemsplein *(town plan, p 156: DZ)*.
The boat heads west, following the north bank. It passes on the right the park (Het Park) with Euromast. The air vents of Maas Tunnel can be seen.

Lloyd Kade. – This is the dock for ships trading with Indonesia.

Delfshaven. – This is Delft's old port *(qv)*.

Merwe Dock (Merwehaven). – This is the biggest dock for miscellaneous goods, on the north bank.

Schiedam. – *Description p 166.*

Wilhelmina Dock (Wilhelminahaven). – Naval repairs on a floating dock.

To the west the gulf, then **Wilton dock** (Wiltonhaven) can be seen; it is used for naval construction and repair workshops.

Here the boat turns round and crosses the river to sail back up the opposite bank towards Rotterdam.

Pernis. – Chemical industries, including petrochemical and artifical fertilisers.

Eem Dock (Eemhaven). – The boat enters into this vast series of docks specialised in container traffic and transhipment of goods.

Waal Dock (Waalhaven). – Originally built for iron and copper ore tankers, at present this dock also handles containers and miscellaneous goods.

Maas Dock (Maashaven). – Beyond Maas Tunnel, this grain dock, now supplanted by Botlek and Benelux Dock, also handles miscellaneous goods.

Rijn Dock (Rijnhaven). – This dock is lined by quays, where in the past, the great transatlantic liners of the Holland-America Line moored. Note the fine rectilinear constructions.

Long boat trip. – This tour goes all the way to Botlek. *Description of Vlaardingen and Botlek (p 164).*

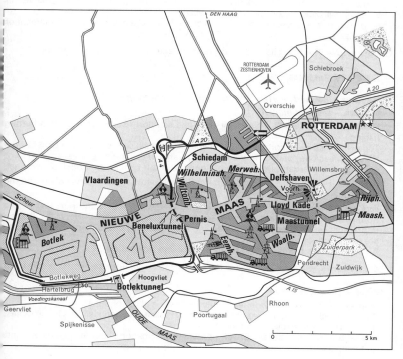

Europoort

The vast installations of Europoort, built between 1958 and 1975, cover 3 600ha - 8 892 acres on the south bank of New Waterway. Europoort continues to the west by Maasvlakte whose development dates from 1965-71. Some docks can take cargo boats drawing 21.95m - 72ft of water.

Car tour. – *79km - 49 miles to Maasvlakte. Leave by ① on the town plan and take Benelux Tunnel on the left.*
At the south exit there is a fine view of **Pernis** oil terminal.

Take the motorway on the right, running alongside a railway line.

Botlek Tunnel. – Opened in 1980 under the Oude Maas which comes from Dordrecht *(qv)*, this tunnel has a single carriageway 500m - 1 640ft long and 21m - 69ft below sea level. It supplements an old bridge.

Botlek. – It is a grain port and oil terminal. Moreover, it has installations for chemical products, bulk transport and naval repairs.

Leave the Europoort road opposite, and continue right to rejoin the river.

Rozenburg. – On the **Het Scheur**, the river's opposite bank, is the Maassluis *(see below)* industrial sector. Near the Rozenburg church there is a **windmill**.

Shortly afterwards leave the Europoort road on the left to take Noordzeeweg which runs between the New Waterway and Caland Canal (Calandkanaal).

On the left unloading facilities for oil tankers of different companies can be seen. The end of the road goes around an old radar station: there is a **view** of the Hoek van Holland *(p 160)*, Europoort and the estuary which is divided by a dike, towards the north, there is the entrance to the New Waterway leading to Rotterdam, and to the south, there is the entrance to Europoort – 30 000 ships pass through the estuary every year.

Return by the same route and take the bridge over the canal or Calandbrug, then go under Brielle Bridge (Brielsebrug) to reach Europoort.

To the right one goes alongside the oil terminals which have already been seen, and to the left **Hartel Canal**, which has recreational areas on either side of it; and on the edge of **Brielse Lake** (Brielse Meer) an artificial lake for pleasure boats dug out from an old branch of the Maas, the Brielse Maas.

Dintel Dock Bridge. – A bridge over an access canal to Dintel Dock, the mineral port. From this bridge one can occasionally see a ferry in **Benelux Dock,** which like Hoek van Holland, is a port for ferries between England (Kingston-upon-Hull) and the Netherlands.

Once over the Suurhoff Bridge (Suurhoffbrug), turn right towards Maasvlakte.

Oostvoornse Lake (Oostvoornse Meer). – This lake was created by the closing of the Brielse Gat in 1965; it has been adapted for swimming and sailing.

Maasvlakte. – Maasvlakte, meaning Maas plain, is composed of 2 700ha - 6 669 acres of sandy land reclaimed from the North Sea. At present in the **8th Petroleum Dock** (8th Petroleumhaven) there is a steam-generating station (Gemeentelijk Energiebedrijf or GEB), an oil terminal (Maasvlakte Olie Terminal) and a container terminal (Europe Container Terminal B.V.). Facilities for stocking and transhipment of minerals are in the **Mississippi Dock** (Mississippihaven) (E.M.O.)
A lighthouse has replaced that of Hoek van Holland, which, since the development of Maasvlakte, is too far from the sea. There is a beach to the west.

⊙ **Boat trip.** – The tour allows one to grasp the extent of the port installations.

EXCURSIONS

Hoek van Holland. – *31km - 19 miles by ① on the town plan.*

Schiedam. – *Description p 166.*

Vlaardingen. – Pop 75 430. This major river and sea port used to specialise in herring fishing.
Today it is also an important industrial and commercial centre. From the banks of the Nieuwe Maas one can look at the unending traffic of ocean-going ships coming to or going from Rotterdam. Downstream along the south bank is the Botlek oil terminal.

Maassluis. – Pop 32 890. This port is on Het Scheur, between the Nieuwe Maas and the New Waterway.

Hoek van Holland. – At the mouth of the New Waterway, this is the port just before Rotterdam for passenger travel and for ferries going to England (Harwich). It is an impressive sight to see the ships heading for Rotterdam or the North Sea. Opposite are the Europoort installations.
An artificial beach was created north of Hoek van Holland in 1971.

Oostvoorne. – *41km - 25½ miles to the southwest. Leave Rotterdam by ⑥ on the town plan.*

Brielle. – *Description p 72.*

Oostvoorne. – This is a seaside resort situated near a chain of dunes.
A 311ha - 768 acre nature reserve, the **Duinen van Voorne,** has been laid out in the dunes; the reserve is crisscrossed by paths.
A reception area (Bezoekerscentrum) provides information about the reserve's plants and animals.

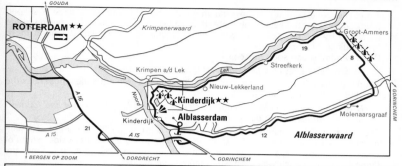

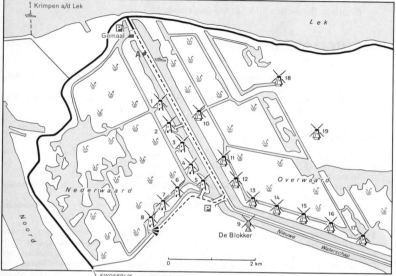

Windmills and polders. – *Round tour of 81km - 50 miles – about 3 hours – local map p 165.* Leave Rotterdam by ④ on the town plan and go towards Gorinchem and turn off towards Alblasserdam.

The narrow dike road follows the Noord, a stretch of water frequently used. Between the Noord and the Lek lies the **Alblasserwaard**. This old **waard** (low land surrounded by rivers) has a ring of dikes around it and has been made into a polder.

Alblasserdam. – Pop 17 053. This town has shipyards for naval construction.

Kinderdijk. – Kinderdijk means children's dike for it is said that during the great floods which occurred on St Elizabeth's feast day in 1421, the sea washed up on the dike a crib with a crying baby and a cat.

Towards the end of the village an opening between houses on the right gives a pretty **view** of the windmills which dot the plain.

★★ **Kinderdijk Windmills** (Molens van Kinderdijk). – *For details and illustrations of the different* ⊘ *kinds of windmills, see pp 33-34.*

Near the Nederwaard pumping station *(gemaal),* along the canals, amidst meadows and reeds stand 19 windmills. Their exceptional number, their size and the beauty of the marshy plain have made them famous. Up to 1950 they helped drain the Alblasserwaard.

Today their sails turn for tourists only on Windmill Days *(see the chapter Practical Information at the end of the guide)*

⊘ One can walk along the dikes or take a **boat trip** *(for departure point refer to A on the local map).*

The eight tall polder mills *(bovenkruier)* lined up towards the west are truncated-shaped brick drainage mills with rotating caps dating from 1738.

⊘ The second **windmill** can be visited.

A little further on there is a smaller hollow post mill, the *wipmolen* type, called De Blokker.

There are also eight windmills with rotating caps along the other canal, but octagonal in shape and thatched, dating from 1740. Hidden behind them are two other windmills built in 1740 and 1761.

Continue by car along the dike road which follows the Lek.

(After photo A.L.W. Hoenderkamp Gorinchem)

Polder mill (bovenkruier)

From Nieuw-Lekkerland on, just down to the right of the dike, large T-shaped farmhouses can be seen; they are thatched and have haystacks beside them protected by a little roof *(illustration p 32)*. Orchards are cultivated around these farmhouses.
Other windmills can soon be seen.

At Groot-Ammers take the Molenaarsgraaf road.

Soon four **windmills** appear in single file along a canal. Three are hollow post mills the fourth is an octagonal polder mill.

Further on rejoin the large canal which crosses the Alblasserwaard and follow it on the south side to Alblasserdam.

The **road**★ which is almost at water-level is picturesque. There are large hall-farmhouses *(p 30)* and windmills along the way in a very lush countryside. Some of these farmhouses have a safety exit a little above ground level, which led into the living room and which was used when there were floods.

Return to Rotterdam by ④ on the town plan.

SCHIEDAM South Holland   Pop 69 349

Michelin map **408** folds 17 and 24 (inset) – Local map p 163

Schiedam (pronounced sridam) is a typical small town whose centre is surrounded by canals, lined with several windmills.
Shipbuilding yards and numerous industries make it an animated town. But it is mainly juniper which brought its fame.

HISTORICAL NOTES

About 1260 a castle was built in Schiedam and one of its towers can be seen near the new town hall. It received its city rights in 1275. In 1574 the castle was destroyed by the inhabitants so that it would not fall into the hands of the Spanish.
Schiedam is the homeland of **St Lydwine** (1380-1433), a mystic whose life was retraced by J.K. Huysmans (*St Lydwine of Schiedam,* 1901).
The town has a large park, **Beatrix Park** to the north with lakes, and nearby the **Groenoord** open-air swimming-pool.

The juniper town. – Beginning in *c*1600 the inhabitants of Schiedam started to make alcohol from second-class wine brought from France. Then they made spirits from grain, and finally specialised in the distillation of juniper berries *(jenever)* making gin. Schiedam had nearly three hundred distilleries. Today, about ten distilleries use young juniper berries *(jonge jenever)* and old juniper berries *(oude jenever)* which make a more full-bodied gin. Called Jenever in the Netherlands, this kind of gin often presented in a stone jar or crock is called Hollands, distinguishing it from the American or British-made gin called London Dry gin.

SIGHTS

⊙ **Municipal Museum (Stedelijk Museum).** – *Hoogstraat 112.* Located in the centre of Hoogstraat, the town's main pedestrian street, the museum is installed in an old 1787 hospital (St.-Jacobs Gasthuis); it is a large building with a portico. Its collections concern prehistory, the history of the town, modern art (COBRA group, systematic painting, Pop Art and New Figurative Art).
In the basement, there is the **National Distillery Museum** (Nationaal Gedistilleerd Museum). Instruments, documents and scale models evoke the making of gin in the 19C; collection of miniature bottles.

Mills. – The town was formerly surrounded by 18 mills, mainly used for milling grain intended for the distilleries.
Four tall 18C stage mills *(illustration p 34)* exist along Noordvest, the canal marking the site of the old ramparts.

De Walvisch (The Whale). – Dating from 1794 this type of mill is found mostly in the south.

Continuing along the quay towards the north, one can see the three other mills.

De Drie Koornbloemen (The Three Corn Flowers). – This mill of 1770 was used to mill cattle food.

⊙ **De Vrijheid** (Freedom). – Started in 1785, it still mills grain.

De Noord (The North). – This mill of 1803 is thought to be the tallest in Europe (33.33m - 109ft including the cap, maximum height of sails 44.56m - 146ft). Its premises are used for tasting by an important distillery, whose buildings are opposite.

Porters' House (Zakkendragershuis). – *Take the road opposite the Municipal Museum and cross the Lange Haven, the town's central canal.* Fine view over the picturesque quays. Then follow the quay Oude Sluis, on the right. Behind the old Grain Exchange or **Korenbeurs,** there is a gracious 1725 building with a curving gable topped by a turret.

Maasboulevard. – From this boulevard near the pleasure boat harbour, there is an interesting **view** over the considerable comings and going's of ship traffic between Rotterdam and the sea.
The port of Pernis on the opposite bank, is linked to Schiedam by Benelux Tunnel.

SLUIS Zeeland

Michelin map **408** fold 15 or **212** fold 12

This small touristic town, pleasant and busy, is situated near the Belgian frontier. With Damme it was an outer harbour of Bruges in the 14C when it was at the mouth of the Zwin, today silted up. Its old French name, l'**Écluse** (the Lock) evokes the naval battle which took place here in 1340 at the beginning of the Hundred Years War. Edward III's English fleet repelled 190 French ships winning the first naval battle of that war.
The grassy mounds which one sees on entering the town are the remains of old ramparts, some of which have been turned into an esplanade.

SIGHTS

⊙ **Town Hall (Stadhuis).** – It is overlooked by a tall 14C **belfry,** the only one existing in the Netherlands. It is decorated with four turrets and a Jack-of the clock. From the top of the bell tower there is a fine **view** stretching over the plain. Sluis memorabilia can be seen in the staircase. The Council Room has a lovely 18C grille.

⊙ **De Brak Mill (Molen).** – This wall mill, destroyed in 1944, was rebuilt in 1951. Its three floors reached by steep ladders make it possible to understand how it works. From the handrail the **view** extends over the surrounding countryside and the Zwin.

EXCURSIONS

St.-Anna ter Muiden. – *2km - 1 mile to the northwest, near the frontier*. At the foot of the church's imposing 14C brick tower, the small triangular **square,** the rustic houses and the fountain form a charming picture. Note a thatched wooden barn at the far end of the square.

⊙ **Aardenburg.** – Pop 3 874. *8km - 5 miles to the southeast*. Its fine Gothic church, **St Bavo** (St.-Bavokerk), with characteristics of the Scheldt Gothic style (which developed in Belgium), contains 14 and 15C sarcophagi, with interesting paintings on their inside panels.

IJzendijke. – *22km - 14 miles to the east*. This old stronghold only has a small half-moon shaped bastion or ravelin remaining from its ramparts, covered with earth and surrounded by water. Nearby, there is a lovely windmill.
The pinnacle topped with a golden cock, which one sees in the middle of this small town, belongs to the oldest Protestant church (1612) in Zeeland.
⊙ At no 28 Grote Markt is the **Regional Museum** (Streekmuseum West Zeeuws Vlaanderen). Apart from a rustic interior of 1850 from Cadzand with its fine stove, there are instruments used in the cultivation of flax and madder and a section devoted to the Zeeland plough horses.

Breskens. – *29km - 18 miles to the north*. A fishing port at the mouth of the Western
⊙ Scheldt, Breskens is the departure point for the **Flushing** *(qv)* **ferry.** It also has a pleasure boat harbour. From the pedestrian Promenade laid out on top of the dune, between the fishing port and the ferry landing stage to the west, there are fine **views** over the beaches and the Scheldt.

SNEEK Friesland

Michelin map **408** fold 4 – Local map p 169
Town plan in the current Michelin Red Guide Benelux

Sneek (Snits for Frisians) is a small, active and very touristic town. In the Middle Ages it was a port on the Middelzee, an inland sea, since disappeared.

Gateway to the Frisian Lakes. – Sneek is situated in the centre of a region much appreciated for its lakes, in particular Sneeker Lake (Sneekermeer) which is used for different water sports.
Sneek has a pleasure boat harbour and several sailing schools. One can hire motorboats, sail boats, or participate in boating excursions in season *(apply to the VVV)*.
Every year regattas occur during the great **Sneekweek.** In addition, every summer for a fortnight, the **skûtsjesilen,** regattas with *skûts-jes* are held on the Frisian Lakes and IJssel Lake. Several Frisian towns have one of these old trading boats *(skûtsjes)* with dark brown sails and a wide and flat hull flanked by two leeboards. *See the chapter Practical Information at the end of the guide.*

SIGHTS

★ **Water-gate (Waterpoort).** – This elegant 1613 construction in brick decorated with sand-stone protected the entrance to the port. Its central part pierced with arcades and forming a bridge over the Geeuw is flanked by two turrets.

Water-gate

⊙ **Town Hall (Stadhuis).** – Dating from the 16C, modified in the 18C, it has a lovely rococo façade, with tall windows and green shutters, and a richly carved perron topped with heraldic lions.

⊙ **Navigation and Antiquities Museum** (Fries Scheepvaart Museum en Sneker Oudheidkamer). – *Kleinzand no 14.*

This museum is devoted to Frisian navigation, both fluvial and maritime, with a large collection of boat models used in the 18 and 19C, reconstituted pleasure boat interiors, 17, 18 and 19C paintings, sail and mast workshops, navigational instruments...

In the house, beside the canal, admire the lovely collection of Frisian silverware, especially from Sneek. Several rooms have been recreated including the delightful room, from a neighbouring farm, decorated with naive 18C Frisian landscape paintings.

★ FRISIAN LAKES (FRIESE MEREN)

Round tour of 134km - 83 miles – about 1 day – local map p 169

Leave Sneek by ④ on the town plan towards Bolsward.

Here and there one can see a church on an artificial mound, called *terp (qv)* hidden behind a screen of trees.

★ **Bolsward.** – *Description p 67.*

Near the Workum crossroads, take a small road towards Exmorra.

Exmorra is situated on the tourist route known under the name of Aldfaers Erf.

⊙ **Exmorra.** – In the small **museum** a country grocer's shop, a rural house and a classroom of 1885 have been reconstituted. Further on, the charming 13C church on a *terp,* surrounded by a cemetery, has been restored.

⊙ **Allingawier.** – Near the church with a saddleback roofed bell tower one can visit a typical old Friesland **farmhouse** named Yzeren Kou: a large building contains the huge barn and the stable; the annexe, the living quarters, are raised higher to leave room for the dairy.

Makkum. – It is a picturesque fishing port on the edge of IJssel Lake and crossed by a canal. It has naval shipyards.

Since the 17C tin-glazed earthenware is made here and above all tiles similar in style to those of Delft, but more rustic. On the main square, the **weigh house** (Waag) is a fine construction of 1698. It houses the tourist information centre (VVV) on the ground

Makkum's fishing port

⊙ floor and the **Museum of Frisian Ceramics** (Fries Aardewerkmuseum "De Waag") in the two attics and in the adjacent house. The museum displays objects used daily or for decorative purposes (plates, platters, hot plates) from 1600-1880. Note especially the objects (blue paintings on white backgrounds) from Makkum and Harlingen *(qv)* dating from the 18C, the period when Frisian earthenware was at its peak.

Among the painted tile scenes note the one of the chimney from a wealthy Makkum farmhouse and the scene depicting a Frisian earthenware factory in 1737 (a copy; the original is in the Rijksmuseum in Amsterdam).

⊙ In **Tichelaar's Royal Pottery and Tile Factory** (Tichelaars Aardewerk- en Tegelfabriek) one can see an exhibition of earthenware and visit the workshops.

A narrow road edged on one side by the dike and the other by a canal, which sometimes has herons, leads to Workum.

In Gaast, turn left to reach Ferwoude.

⊙ **Ferwoude.** – In this locality an old **farmhouse** and its carpentry workshop (1845) is open to the public. Opposite, the village church, topped by a pointed pinnacle, has been attractively repainted.

Workum. – *Description p 186.*

Hindeloopen. – *Description p 127.*

Stavoren. – *8.5km - 5¼ miles leaving from Koudum.* A fishing village, Stavoren (Starum in Frisian) has two pleasure boat harbours. It is linked to Enkhuizen by a boat service *(p 91).* In the past Stavoren was the capital of the Frisian kings, then a member of the Hanseatic League. Evangelised in the 9C by St Odulphus, it flourished in the 11C. Its port was excellent in the 14C. Then it silted up, as legend has it, because of a rich widow of Stavoren who ordered one of her ships' captain's to bring her a precious cargo. The latter returned to Stavoren with wheat: furious the widow had all the wheat thrown into the port.

After Koudum there is a fine **view,** from the lever bridge, over the two lakes on either side of the road.

One soon crosses the wooded region of **Gaasterland,** which stretches southwest of Balk.

Balk. – Near Sloter Lake (Slotermeer), this locality is crossed by a canal bordered with several lovely 18C houses, witness to a former prosperity due to its butter trade, for which Balk was the centre.

★**Sloten.** – Near Sloter Lake and at the end of the wooded Gaasterland region, Sloten (Sleat for the Frisians) an old fortified city, seems as though it was built on a reduced scale, which accentuates its charm; narrow streets, tiny 17 and 18C houses run alongside the small canal lined with lime trees.

Following the quays, where ducks waddle, one reaches **Lemster Gate** (Lemsterpoort), an old water-gate and its **mill** of 1755; lovely view over the canal and the lakes where yachts sail in season.

From the lever bridge near Spannenburg, there are lovely **views** over a wide canal which links the two lakes.

Joure. – Since the 17C this town has specialised in clock making. It also has a large firm dealing with tobacco, tea and coffee.

A few miles north of Joure, the road runs along a narrow strip of land between two lakes; there are some fine **views.** On the left **Sneeker Lake** (Sneekermeer) is one of the most frequented Frisian lakes.

Grouw. – Near a lake, it is a very animated water sports centre.

⊘ **Wieuwerd.** – The village **church** has a crypt with strange powers. Built in the 14C on a small *terp* surrounded by a cemetery, this small church, altered in the 19C was used as a tomb in the 17 and 18C for eleven people. The corpses were protected from decomposition by an antimonious gas which rose from the ground: four of the mummies are exhibited under a sheet of glass. To illustrate this phenomenon several birds, one of which in 1879 was a parrot, were suspended from the vault.

⊘ **Bozum.** – This charming village has a 12 and 13C **Romanesque church,** restored, built of tufa and brick in front of a tower with a saddleback roof, and lined on the west by a semicircle of lovely low houses. The inside is rustic and the paintings in the chancel (*c*1300) are very faded.

In the pond nearby there are often a multitude of mallards dabbling about.

Return to Sneek by ① on the town plan.

STADSKANAAL Groningen   Pop 33 506

Michelin map **408** fold 6

In this country of peat bogs, which have become ploughed fields and pastures, the villages follow one another along the main canals, forming a continuous road. Stadskanaal (canal-town) is one of them, and well merits its name.

EXCURSIONS

Ter Apel. – *20km - 12 miles to the southeast.*
⊘ Ter Apel, in the middle of a park with large beech trees, has an **old convent** (Museum Klooster) of which only the church and two wings of the cloisters remain.
One can visit the cloisters, the refectory and its cellar where sarcophagi, discovered in the cloisters's old courtyard, are lined up. The **church** has a Gothic rood screen of carved wood (1501) and stalls of the same period, with decorated misericords (picturesque figures). In the chancel note the fine gallery.

Nieuweschans. – *35km - 21¼ miles to the northeast.*
To the east of the province of Groningen near the German frontier, this small, quiet, village of low houses has been greatly restored.

★ STAPHORST Overijssel   Pop 13 308

Michelin map 408 fold 12

The localities near Staphorst and **Rouveen** have formed a separate world in the Netherlands. Their life is conducted by following the principles of severe Protestantism, a real barrier against the innovations of modern life: thus in 1971 vaccinations were forbidden, and even now cars are not allowed on Sundays during church services. Women, young and old alike, wear the traditional costume, but refuse to be photographed.

STAPHORST★

★ **The farmhouses.** – The two villages stretch out along a long road; lined up for more than 8km - 5 miles are picturesque thatched roofed farmhouses, all identical. Very trim, with their wooden sections painted green (doors) or blue (window frames, shelves for milk cans) they are of the hall-type *(p 31)* with the characteristic of having several doors all in line along the long side façade. On the right side of the farmhouse the shelf used for storing empty milk cans, finely carved, shows the inhabitants' need to decorate.

★ **Costumes.** – The very graceful, female costume is worn quite often. Somewhat dark (black shoes and stockings, pleated black skirt, blue or black apron), it is brightened by a bodice-front or *kraplap* with flowerets dotted over a black background, and with a matching bonnet. Over the bodice-front, a red tartan scarf (or blue if in mourning) is sometimes worn. In winter the costume is hidden under a blue cardigan. The older women still wear the head band with spiral rings antennae *(p 30)* which replaces the bonnet which is reserved for small girls. When the children leave school (about noon and 4pm) one sees little girls and adolescents bicycling about dressed in the traditional costume.

TIEL Gelderland	Pop 30 568

Michelin map **408** north of fold 18

Tiel is nicely situated on the banks of the Waal in the centre of the **Betuwe,** a region richly cultivated with fruit trees; the orchards form a magnificent sight in the spring. It formerly belonged to the Hanseatic League.
A parade celebrates the fruit and the harvest *(see the chapter Practical Information at the end of the guide).*

EXCURSION

Culemborg. – *19km - 11½ miles to the northwest.*
Buren. – Pop 9 367. This small town hemmed in by its ramparts has been restored. In 1492 it became the centre of an earldom, which by Anne of Buren, William the Silent's first wife, became part of the House of Orange's possessions.
The old **orphanage** (1613) is a fine building with green and red shutters, preceded by a sculptured porch. It contains the **Marechaussee Museum** (Museum der Koninklijke Mare-chaussee) retracing the history of the gendarmerie and the police in the Netherlands. Not far away, part of the curtain wall bordering the river has been turned into a promenade; lovely **views** over the river and the Betuwe orchards.
The main street, Voorstraat, is overlooked by a **church,** whose 15C square bell tower ends in a Renaissance style octagonal part, topped by a pinnacle. The **town hall,** rebuilt in the 18C, has a rococo portal. Nearby, built against the walls, is the small **Cart Museum** (Boerenwagenmuseum). *Achter Boonenburg 1.*
At the far end of Voorstraat is a brick **town gateway,** and a **wall mill** called The Prince of Orange (De Prins van Oranje), dating from 1716.
Culemborg. – Pop 20 607. This old city, which obtained its rights in 1318 and became the centre of an earldom in 1555, still has some of its walls. It is the birthplace of **Jan van Riebeeck** (1619-77), who in 1652 founded the Cape Colony (now known as Cape Town) for the Dutch East Indies Company, a stop-off on the way to India. On **Marktplein,** there is the town hall (stadhuis) in the Flamboyant Gothic style, preceded by a perron topped by heraldic lions.
The **interior gateway** (Binnenpoort), is the only gateway which remains from the old ramparts.

TILBURG North Brabant	Pop 153 625

Michelin map **408** folds 17 and 18 or **212** fold 7
Town plan in the current Michelin Red Guide Benelux

On Wilhelminakanaal, Tilburg is one of the largest populated towns in the country. It is a great textile centre. It has a Catholic university with Economic Science, Law, Social Science and Theological Faculties.
King William II lived in this town and died here in 1849.

SIGHTS

Stadhuisplein. – This is Tilburg's main square with pedestrian shopping precincts extending to the north. The town has grown recently and has modern monuments around the square.

Municipal Theatre (Stadsschouwburg). – Built in 1961 by the architects Bijvoet and Holt; part of it is in glass, next to windowless areas of brick forming concave like shapes.

Town Hall (Stadhuis). – A building with sober lines covered in black granite, by the architect Kraayvanger. It was added in 1971 to the old town hall, a crenellated building completed in 1849 and intended to be the palace of King William II.

Textile Museum (Nederlands Textielmuseum). – *Goirkestraat 96, to the north of the station.* This museum has an interesting presentation of the textile industry: machines and instruments for spinning and weaving, old and exotic fabrics, tapestries, lace and tools used in cottage industries in the 18 and 19C in the Netherlands.

EXCURSIONS

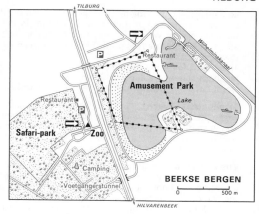

★ Beekse Bergen. – *4km - 2¼ miles to the south-east by ② on the town plan – local map below.* To the north of Hilvaren-beek, this recreational area stretches over 425ha - 1 050 acres. It has an amusement park, a wild animal reserve and a small zoo.

⊘ **Safari park**. – Sprawled over 100ha - 247 acres, the reserve has nearly 800 animals distributed in several enclosures separated by screens; lions, rhinoceroses, hy-

TILBURG

P

Restaurant

Amusement Park

Lake

Restaurant

P

Safari-park ▲ **Zoo**

Camping

Voetgangerstunnel

BEEKSE BERGEN

0   500 m

HILVARENBEEK

enas, cheetahs antilopes, zebras, baboons and different kinds of birds. The section with penguins, flamingos, squirrel monkeys and rare species are visited on foot.

Near the Safari park, a small **zoo** (Dierenland) has grouped together young animals for children to see.

⊘ **Amusement park** (Strandpark). – The 70ha - 173 acre lake (pedal-craft, canoes, bathing) and its surroundings (mini-golf, trampolines) offer many diversions. A cable-car (kabelbaan) goes over the whole area and makes it possible to get off on the bank opposite the entry; and a boat (rondvaartboot) goes round the lake.

★ Oisterwijk. – Pop 17 725. *10km - 6 miles to the east. Leave by ① on the town plan.*

It is a pleasant, shaded holiday resort, near wooded dunes, fields of heather and 60 small lakes.

An **old house** (1633) with an elegant gable is worth seeing in Kerkstraat *(nos 88-90)*. In front of the town hall, **De Lind** is a charming square planted with lime trees which lay out the traditional marriage way.

⊘ 1km - ½ mile to the southeast on the road to Oirschot near the open-air theatre, a **bird park** (Vogelpark) has been laid out in the pinewood: numerous exotic birds.

★★ UTRECHT Utrecht ℗   Pop 229 326

Michelin map 408 fold 11 – Local map p 176
Plan of access roads and bypasses in the current Michelin Red Guide Benelux

Utrecht is a religious metropolis – the Catholic primate of the Netherlands lives here – is intellectual due to its university and commercial due to its well-known international trade fair, founded in 1916. Furthermore, it is an important communication network junction.

⊘ Every year a Festival of Ancient Music is held here *(see the chapter Practical Information at the end of the guide).*

HISTORICAL NOTES

Utrecht was founded at the beginning of our era on the Rhine (now called Oude Rijn), which passed through the town at that time. Under the Roman Empire the town was called Trajectum (ford) from which it gets its present name.

In the 7C it was chosen as the seat of Friesland missions. **St Willibrord** (658-739), a Northumbrian, was made Bishop of the Frisians in 695, settled in Utrecht, Friesland then being considered a dangerous place. He died in Echternach in Luxembourg.

At the time of Charlemagne, who extended his empire northwards, the area became part of the Carolingian Empire. After the *Treaty of Meerssen (p 148),* Utrecht was subjected to the German emperors. Under their domination, Bishop Balderik (918-976) succeeded in enlarging the bishopric's jurisdiction. Having become very powerful, the bishops extended their sovereignty over the present-day provinces of Utrecht, Overijssel, Drenthe and Groningen: their territory was called the **Sticht**. The town received its city rights in 1122 and was surrounded by ramparts (rebuilt 14C).

Born in Utrecht in 1459, **Adrian VI**, tutor to Charles V and then a professor in Louvain (Belgium), was the only Dutch pope (1522-3).

Charles V took possession of the Sticht in 1528. Made an archbishopric by Philip II of Spain in 1559, the bishopric of Utrecht, from that time, covered all the main towns of the area, except 's-Hertogenbosch. However, the town's prosperity was coming to an end as the commercial centre had moved towards the coast.

In 1577 the inhabitants expelled the Spanish garrison.

In 1585, Elizabeth I, after signing the *Treaty of Nonsuch,* sent Robert Dudley, Earl of Leicester (*c*1532-88), to the Low Countries, to help the United Provinces against Spain. He was appointed Governor and chose to reside in Utrecht.

The Union of Utrecht. – In January 1579 the representatives of the states of Holland and Zeeland, and the territories of Groningen and Utrecht, and the stadtholder of Gelderland united to sign the *Union of Utrecht;* they decided that no separate agreement would be made with Philip II and that the Protestant religion would be the only one authorised in Holland and Zeeland; in the other regions, practice of the Catholic religion would not lead to prosecution. In the same year signatures were added by representatives from Overijssel, Friesland and Drenthe and some southern towns such as Antwerp.

This treaty, following the *Union of Arras* by which the Duke of Parma had forced the southern states to submit to Spain, was the cause of the split between South and North Low Countries (which later became the United Provinces).

Intellectual Utrecht. – In 1635, Descartes stayed in Utrecht *(Maliebaan 36 - 38)* and wrote the *Discourse on Method* which was published in Leyden.

The year 1636 was marked by the founding of Utrecht University, the second in the country after the one in Leyden. James Boswell studied civil law here in 1763-4, following in his father's footsteps.

The schism of the Old Catholics. – In the 15C a first schism shook the bishopric of Utrecht, where the chapter had retained the privilege of electing its bishops. In 1423, opposition to a pontifical candidate caused a bitter conflict between the partisans of the two opposing bishops.

In 1702 the Archbishop of Utrecht, Petrus Codde, accused of Jansenism, was dismissed from his duties by the pope. In 1723 the Chapter of Utrecht elected a successor, Cornelis Steenoven, without pontifical agreement. Thus, in 1724, the Old Catholics Church was formed in Utrecht. A large number of French Jansenists, fleeing to the Netherlands after the condemnation of their religion by the papal bull *Unigenitus* in 1717, became members of this independent church with Jansenist tendencies.

In 1870 a group of Germans, refusing the dogma of pontifical infallibility, joined the Church of Old Catholics in Utrecht. In 1889 a great meeting of members of this Church, coming from several countries, took place in Utrecht. This religion is still practised in the Netherlands where it has about 10 000 followers (as well as in the U.S., Switzerland, Germany, Austria...).

The Utrecht School of painting. – In the 16C a school of painting with a strong Italian influence developed in Utrecht.

Jan van Scorel (1495-1562) born near Alkmaar, lived in Utrecht, apart from a visit to Italy and a stay in Haarlem *(qv)*. He helped spread the Italian influence in his country; *The Baptism of Christ* (in the Frans Hals Museum in Haarlem) is one of his best works.

Maerten van Heemskerck *(qv)* his pupil, was also a Romanist painter (16C Northern European artists who were greatly influenced by the Italian Renaissance). Excellent portrait painter *(Portrait of a Young Scholar* in the Boymans-van Beuningen Museum in Rotterdam), Jan van Scorel also had as a pupil **Antoon Mor** (1517-76) who made his career particularly in Spain, under the name of **Antonio Moro,** where he painted with talent the court of Philip II.

In the beginning of the 17C, **Abraham Bloemaert** (1564-1651), born in Gorinchem, passed on his taste for Italian painting to many of his pupils: Hendrick Ter Brugghen or **Terbrugghen** (1588-1629) who, born in Deventer, worked mostly in Utrecht; on his return from Italy he was one of the first to take his inspiration from Caravaggism (those artists greatly influenced by Caravaggio's chiaroscuro), **Gerard van Honthorst** (1590-1656) born in Utrecht, also became, after a visit to Italy, a faithful imitator of Caravaggio; **Cornelis van Poelenburgh** (*c*1586-1667), who painted with precision, luminous landscapes scattered with Roman ruins. Not touched by these influences, **Jan Davidsz. de Heem** (1606-1683-4), who was born in Utrecht and lived in Leyden and then in Antwerp, specialised in the *vanitas* still lifes, especially paintings depicting a table loaded with plates, glasses and dishes of food. His son, Cornelis de Heem, imitated his subjects as well as his sophisticated style.

From the 17C to the present. – In the 17C Utrecht was a very important fortified town: a ring of canals, today, marks the site of the fortifications. The town was occupied by the armies of Louis XIV from 1672-4 and in 1712. Prepared in Utrecht's town hall in January 1712, the **Peace of Utrecht** was signed in 1713 in Zeist Castle *(p 177)* and brought an end to the Spanish War of Succession which, caused by the accession to the throne of Philip V, Louis XIV's grandson, had broken out in 1701.

In 1806 the King of Holland, Louis Bonaparte, stayed with his court in a private mansion in Utrecht *(at no 31 Drift - BX).*

The famous **Utrecht velvet** with its long strand and embossed ornamentation, used for covering walls, is no longer made in the area. It was a velvet woven with linen, goats' hair (which replaced silk) and cotton.

Utrecht has been expanding since the middle of the century and has many new quarters and buildings. Amongst many achievements there is a very large shopping centre, the Hoog Catharijne *(p 173),* a municipal theatre (1941) by Dudok, the Schröder House by Rietveld *(p 176)* and the Kanaleneiland (or island of canals) quarter to the west near the Amsterdam-Rijnkanaal and the music centre.

There are many statues in the town. Amongst them the fountain of the Muses' Feast (1959) by J.C. Hekman in front of the theatre, and Queen Wilhelmina by Mari Andriessen in Wilhelmina Park (1968). Others are cited in the text on the tour of the town.

The University of Utrecht, in a vast campus to the east (De Uithof), with approximately 24 000 students, is the largest university in the Netherlands.

Specialities of Utrecht include *spritsen,* a type of shortbread biscuit.

⊘ **Boat trips.** – Boat trips are organised on the city's canals, on the Vecht, Kromme Rijn and the Loosdrecht Lakes.

UTRECHT

★★ THE OLD TOWN time: ½ day

The very shaded **canals** (Oudegracht and Nieuwe Gracht) of Utrecht's centre are edged by quays which are much lower than the road level, on to which open vaulted cellars.

Vredenburg (AY). – Most of Utrecht's animation is concentrated on this large square which links the old town with the new quarters. The old fortress of Charles V stood here, the foundations having been found during the laying out of the square. A music centre (**AY Z**) with an original design by the architect Herzberger has stood here since 1978.

A market takes place on Wednesdays and Saturdays.

To the west, the new **Hoog Catharijne (AY)** shopping centre extends to the station. This vast urban complex includes shopping galleries with air-conditioning in the basement, a large hotel and the **Beatrixgebouw,** the main building of the Exhibition Palace (Jaarbeurs) where there are international fairs and a permanent commercial exhibition.

From Oudegracht bridge, there is a fine **view** over the canal.

★ **Oudegracht (AXY).** – Narrow, spanned by numerous bridges, this old canal which crosses the town from one end to the other, originally linked the Rhine to the Vecht. It is one of the city's animated centres, both on the upper quays and the lower quays, which are lined with shops and restaurants.

At the point where it forms a bend one can see the **Drakenborch (AY A)**, a house rebuilt in 1968 in the old style. Opposite at no 99, the 14C **Het Oudaen** house (**AY T**) has a tall façade topped by crenellations.

Cross the first bridge (Jansbrug).

The quay on the opposite side is reserved for pedestrians. One soon has a lovely **view**★ of the cathedral's tall bell tower (Dom Tower).

Return to the other quay.

On the bridge (Bakkerbrug) a statue has been raised in honour of Katrijn van Leemput, a heroic Utrecht woman, who distinguished herself fighting against the Spanish in 1577. On this bridge and along Oudegracht there is a flower market on Saturdays. Pass in front of the town hall, whose neo-classical façade (1826) conceals ruins dating from the Middle Ages.

Vismarkt (AY 54). – This is the old fish market. Several houses have façade stones: a golden falcon, three swords (at no 9), a boat (at no 10).

★ **National Museum "from the musical clock to the barrel organ"** (Nationaal Museum van Speelklok tot Pierement) (AY M¹). – Located in the old hall church, Buurkerk, this sonorous museum (the guide operates several instruments during the tour) presents a magnificent collection of 18 to 20C mechanical musical instruments.
Exhibited are old clocks and music boxes, player pianos and a type of organ which imitates orchestral instruments, similar to the Hupfeld automatic violin (1910).
The museum also houses a superb collection of barrel organs *(qv)*, small street organs and enormous fair or dance organs.

★★ **Dom Tower (Domtoren) (ABY).** – This bell tower was formerly linked by an arch to the nave of the cathedral, which was destroyed shortly after a church service in 1674, by a hurricane, which also devastated the town. Built between 1321-82 in the Gothic style, restored at the beginning of this century, it influenced many other bell towers in the country, of which it is the highest. Its three recessed floors, the first two are square and of brick, the last, octagonal and of stone, soar up to 112m - 367ft in height. It has a fine carillon, most of the bells having been cast by the Hemony brothers.
From the topmost gallery (465 steps), there is an immense and magnificent **panorama**★★ over the town and the province.

Domplein (BY 14). – This square extends between the Dom Tower, and the cathedral remains. A line of paving stones indicate the nave's old layout. In the centre of the square, there is a statue (1887) of Count **John of Nassau,** brother of William the Silent, who presided over the *Union of Utrecht.*

★ **Old Cathedral (Domkerk) (BY D).** – The tall silhouette of its transept stands miraculously preserved, hidden behind it is the chancel. Both are Gothic, built between 1254 and 1517 on the site of St Martin's Cathedral, destroyed by fire. The chancel with five chapels radiating round the ambulatory was inspired by that of Tournai Cathedral. Inside there are **funerary monuments,** in particular, in the second chapel, south side of the ambulatory, the black marble tomb of Bishop Guy of Avesnes, who died in 1379. The organ, built in 1831, is used for concerts.
The title of cathedral is now held by the church, Catharijnekerk (BY).

University (Rijksuniversiteit) (BY U). – Built at the end of the 19C in the neo-Renaissance style, it incorporates the cathedral's old **chapterhouse** (1409), the present great lecture hall or **Aula.** The *Union of Utrecht* was signed here. The seven coats of arms on the stained glass windows evoke the provinces and the signatory regions. On the wall seven tapestries woven in 1936 bear the emblems of the various faculties.

Cloisters (Kloostergang) (BY E). – A copy of a 10C runic stone of Jelling (Denmark), evoking the conversion of the Danes to Christianity, has been put up at the entrance to the cathedral cloisters. Around the cloisters, the gables over the Flamboyant tracery have low reliefs illustrating the life of St Martin, patron saint of the old cathedral. The **view** of the transept and the apse of the cathedral is very pretty.
To the south of the cloisters there is the old chapterhouse where the *Union of Utrecht* was signed.

Pausdam (BY 42). – At the junction of two canals, this is a peaceful square where the **Paushuize (BY F)** stands. This house, intended for Pope *(paus)* Adrian VI was only completed in 1523, the year of his death. On the left side there is a statue of Christ.

Nieuwe Gracht (B Y). – Similar to the Oudegracht, the new canal, is also lined by elegant residences. One can see Hof Gate (Hofpoort) (BY K), a 17C baroque doorway of the Law Courts, and at nos 35 and 37, lovely old houses.
Further on, at no 63, is the Het Catharijneconvent *(p 175).*
From the bridge, a fine **view** over the canal and Dom Tower can be had.

St Peter's (Pieterskerk) (BY L). – Assigned since 1656 to the Walloon Protestant cult *(p 108),* this interesting Romanesque church was built in 1048. It is one of the four churches in the shape of a cross which Bishop **Bernulphus** wished to build round the cathedral. Two of these churches have disappeared: abbey church of St Paul and St Maria, where only the cloisters remain. The two others, St Peter's and St John's are all that remain of the famous Bernulphus Cross.
The vaults in the transept are Gothic, but the nave in pure Romanesque style is roofed by a wooden barrel vault held up by ten red sandstone columns with plain capitals. Some of the columns have been moved to the end of the church and replaced by copies. The raised chancel is built over the crypt. Four **low reliefs**★ (*c*1170), found during the church's restoration, are embedded in the wall in front of the chancel. They concern the Judgment of Christ by Pilate, his death and resurrection.
The Romanesque baptismal font has corners decorated with heads.
In the chapel towards the left, which has oven vaulting, one can see the remains of Romanesque frescoes: the Virgin on the moon's crescent.
Concerts are given on the new organ at the end of the church.

★ **Crypt.** – The groined vaulting leans on thick columns decorated with grooves. In the apse there is a red sandstone sarcophagus which contains the remains of Bishop Bernulphus, founder of the church.

At no 8, on the corner of Achter St.-Pieter and Keistraat, there is a lovely house, **De Krakeling (BY N)**, with a façade (17C) of garlands.

Janskerkhof (BX). – On this square stands **St John's** (Janskerk) (BX Q) a restored Gothic church, and several elegant 17 and 18C houses, notably no 13. A flower market takes place here on Saturdays.

A small emblazoned building adjoins the church. In front of it is the **statue of Anne Frank** *(qv)* by Pieter d'Hont, sculptor born in Utrecht in 1917.

To the south of the square the Anatomy Institute is in the old restored **Statenkamer** (AX R) (former Franciscan cloisters), where the States General of the province met. In front one can see the statue of Professor Donders *(qv)* and further on the **statue of St Willibrord** by A. Termote, Dutch sculptor of Belgian origin (born in 1887).

House of the King of Portugal (Huis De Coninck van Poortugael) (AX S). – Dating from 1619, it has a charming Renaissance façade with a crow-stepped gable and above the ground floor, windows display the coat of arms of Nijmegen *(qv)* and Portugal around a man brandishing a sceptre, probably the King of Portugal.

ADDITIONAL SIGHTS

★ **Central Museum (Centraal Museum)** (BZ). – Housed in the old convent of St Agnes, the ◷ museum houses a rich section of paintings and decorative arts relating to Utrecht and its surroundings.

Ground floor. – Apart from a section on costumes (from the 2nd half of the 18C up to the present) the ground floor has six rooms with ancient furniture, from the Gothic to the Louis XVI style, and an interesting 17C dolls house.

Mezzanine and former stables. – The Van Baaren (mezzanine) collection includes late 19 to early 20C Dutch and French artists. To be noted are: J.B. Jongkind *(Full Moon)*, Van Gogh *(Underbrush)*, Fantin-Latour (portrait), Daubigny *(Iles Vierges at Bezons)*, J. Maris *(Five Mills)*, and I. Israëls *(At the Beach, c*1915).

Modern art (former stables) – mainly Dutch – encompasses the De Stijl *(qv)* movement to the present. Rietveld's armchairs, P. Koch's mysterious canvases, works by members of COBRA and a few of Bram Bogart's abstract paintings are worth admiring.

1st floor. – Devoted mainly to ancient art, this floor includes Primitives to the 18C with painters, from the Utrecht School (Jan van Scorel, Abraham Bloemaert) and Caravaggists (Terbrugghen – *The Calling of St Matthew* – Gerard van Honthorst). Several rooms are reserved for prints, drawings and silverware.

2nd floor. – The attic has an archaeological section with objects found in excavations dating from Roman and Carolingian times, and a historical part relating to Utrecht's medieval past (churches, walls) or the Golden Age (ceremonial entry of Maurice of Nassau in 1635).

The Muntenkabinet exhibits a rich collection of coins and medals.

In the basement, the **Utrecht boat** (*c*800) is worth seeing, a small craft of about 13 metric tons discovered in 1930.

Part of the museum, the **Van Renswoude Foundation,** built in 1756 as a school for orphans, has an imposing baroque façade on Agnietenstraat. Opposite, there is a fine group of low brick houses belonging to an almshouse, **Hofje van Pallaes** (1561). Next to it is another almshouse, **Beyerskameren,** founded at the end of the 16C.

★★ **Het Catharijneconvent Museum (Rijksmuseum)** (BY). – The old convent of St John of ◷ Malta contains collections of sacred art from Utrecht's Archbishopric Museum, Haarlem's Episcopal Museum and the Old Catholic Museum. The collections evoke Christianity in the Netherlands from its beginnings to the present. The **medieval art** section is the most important in the Netherlands.

The stages marking the evolution of Catholic and Protestant churches are shown in their historical context. Various themes are evoked: the churches (construction, style, decorative elements), the religious universe and the works of art it inspired, the different ceremonies, the role taken by faith in daily life, the relationship between the Church and the State.

Amongst the collections there are: altarpieces, gold and silversmiths' work, liturgical garments (15C cope of David of Burgundy), sculptures (Christ in bonds, of 1500, is particularly expressive), manuscripts and miniatures (the gospel-book of St Lebuinus incrusted with ivory and semi-precious stones), paintings (*Christ as Man of Sorrows* by Geertgen tot Sint Jans, the triptych of Jan van Scorel, the *Portrait of Stenius* by Frans Hals).

◷ **Dutch Railway Museum (Nederlands Spoorwegmuseum)** (BY M[2]). – The former Maliebaan Station is the setting for this museum.

Inside, paintings, documents and scale models reconstitute the history of the Dutch railways. Scale models, a film and mobile signals give an idea of present railway traffic. Outside on the tracks, no longer used, there are, in particular, shining steam engines and trams. One can see the reproduction of the engine *De Arend* (the eagle) which in 1839 with another engine *(De Snelheid)* drew the first train to run in the Netherlands, between Amsterdam and Haarlem.

◷ **University Museum (Universiteitsmuseum).** – *Biltstraat 166 by ② on the town plan.*
It assembles an interesting collection of **old instruments** formerly used by members of the university: astrolabes and sundials, air pumps, surgical instruments...

Through documents it also evokes distinguished members of the university like the physician **Frans Cornelis Donders** (1818-89), who researched and diagnosed the problems of the eye – nearsightedness, farsightedness and astigmatism; the quarrel between Descartes and **Voetius** (1589-1676) a Protestant theologian who was professor at the university, and the meteorologist Buys Ballot (1817-90).

Bruntenhof (BY V). – This picturesque line of low houses forms part of a 1621 almshouse.
The main entrance has a baroque portal.

St Mary's Cloisters (Kloostergang van St.-Marie) (AY W). – Only the Romanesque cloisters in brick remain of this church built in the 11C, one of the four churches of Bernulphus's Cross *(p 174)* which was destroyed in the 19C.

★★**Rietveld Schröder House (Huis).** – *Prins Hendriklaan 50, via Zonstraat* (BYZ). Restored
○ after the owner's death (Mrs Schröder, in 1985), this house, built in 1924, illustrates perfectly the architectural theories of the De Stijl movement to which Gerrit Rietveld (1888-1964) belonged.
In response to Mrs Schröder's demands, she attached a great deal of importance to communicating with nature (every room has a door to the outside), Rietveld created an open plan where the different elements placed at right angles determined the space. Breaking away from the traditional house, Rietveld limited himself to neutral tones – white and grey – for the large surfaces and primary colours for the linear details.
Visiting the interior enables one to appreciate the originality of the lay out both simple and clever. Where on the ground floor the rooms are clearly divided while, the 1st floor is a vast open space with sliding doors (living room, bedrooms).

EXCURSIONS

★★**Loosdrecht Lakes (Loosdrechtse Plassen).** – *Round tour of 70km - 43½ miles – allow 1 day – local map below. Leave Utrecht by ① on the town plan. Follow the signs to Hilversum A 27 until Darwindreef. Turn right, then right again towards Achttienhoven and Westbroek.*

Westbroek. – The pictur-
esque route is edged by canals spanned by small bridges, each one leading to a house surrounded by a charming garden.
Set between verdant strips of land bathed in soft sunlight, the **Loosdrecht Lakes**★★ stretch over more than 2 500ha - 6 175 acres their calm and wild beauty.
They have arisen from old peat bogs. Particularly favourable for water sports, they are served by numerous pleasure boat harbours.
The road is lined with villas.
After **Breukeleveen** one goes along the lake's edge; there is a fine **view.**

○ **Nieuw-Loosdrecht. - Sypesteyn Castle** (Kasteel Sypesteyn), rebuilt from 1912 to 1927 on the original plans, has been converted into a museum.
Displayed inside are fur-
niture, family portraits

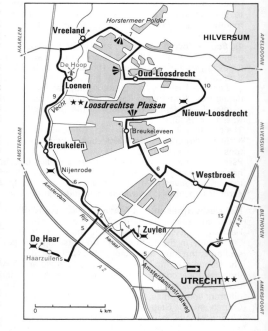

painted by N. Maes and C. Troost, old *objets d'art* and, in particular, Loosdrecht porcelain.

Oud-Loosdrecht. – This is the main tourist centre in the region. It has a large pleasure boat harbour.

Turn right then left towards Vreeland.

The road soon returns to the water; it has lovely **views.**

Vreeland. – An attractive **lever bridge** makes it possible to cross the Vecht, which one subsequently rejoins at Loenen aan de Vecht. The **Vecht**, formerly a great navigation way, since 1952, is doubled by the canal (Amsterdam-Rijnkanaal) from the Rhine to Amsterdam.

The road runs along this peaceful and winding river, on whose banks are charming villas and small manor houses surrounded by magnificent parks.

Loenen. – Pop 6 923. This small town with trim and flowered houses has a tall stage mill, with a handrail, called De Hoop (hope).

Breukelen. – Pop 10 731. In the 17C this locality gave its name to a quarter in New York founded by Dutch settlers: Breukelen, pronounced in English as Brooklyn.

To the south of Breukelen, there is a pleasant **route★** which offers views of lovely estates along the Vecht.

To the right of the road the 17C **Nijenrode Castle** (Kasteel Nijenrode) was restored at the beginning of the 20C. It has been laid out as a School of Advanced Commercial Studies.

De Haar Castle (Kasteel De Haar). – It stands to the west of **Haarzuilens** in the middle of a large park.

This castle is an enormous 14 and 15C brick construction. It was burnt by Louis XIV's troops in 1672-3, then rebuilt by Cuypers, as from 1892 in the original style.

The main building, with pepperpot roof towers, is surrounded by wide moats and linked to a large entrance fort by a covered bridge.

The interior, which is still inhabited in summer, contains the exceptional **collections★** of Baron van Zuilen van Nyevelt, notably lovely old furnishings, 16 and 17C tapestries, Persian carpets, paintings and ceramics.

In the main hall there is a 14C Virgin and Child.

Return to Haarzuilens, cross over the motorway and the canal, then turn right, then left to reach Oud-Zuilen.

Zuylen Castle (Slot Zuylen). – Situated near the Vecht at **Oud-Zuilen,** this **castle** is a solid medieval construction flanked by four octagonal towers. In the 18C it was enlarged with two wings.

Belle van Zuylen was born here in 1740, better known under the name of **Belle de Charrière.** This famous woman of letters, who wrote in French, a friend of Madame de Stael, Benjamin Constant and the diarist and biographer James Boswell *(Life of Johnson),* spent her childhood in the castle. After her marriage in 1766 she lived near Neuchâtel in Switzerland where she died in 1805. The castle houses ancient objects illustrating the daily life of the past, lovely furniture and a Chinese porcelain collection. One room is decorated with a large tapestry (1643) woven in Delft and depicting a landscape with a multitude of birds.

In the rooms where Belle de Charrière lived, a portrait of her by a Danish artist, a few books and engravings evoke the life of the writer.

Return to Utrecht by Amsterdamsestraatweg (AX).

Zeist. – Pop 59 873. *10km - 6 miles. Leave Utrecht by ② on the town plan.*
Zeist is an elegant and pleasant holiday resort amongst lovely woods.

In the centre of Zeist, a lane leads to **Zeist Castle** (Het Slot van Zeist) built in 1677. It presents temporary exhibitions. On either side of this lane there are 18C buildings of the **Moravian Brotherhood** community. This sect was revived in the beginning of the 18C by the Count of Zinzendorf (1700-60). On his land in Germany he sheltered the Moravian Brotherhood (or Bohemian Brotherhood), refugees from Bohemia and Moravia and disciples of Jan Hus, who had been burnt alive in 1415.

The members of this sect dedicate themselves to the mystical adoration of God and Christ, advocate the fraternity of all men, and live in a community. There are nearly 430 000 in the world.

★ VALKENBURG Limburg   Pop 17 696

Michelin map **408** fold 26 or **212** fold 1 – Local map p 179

Valkenburg is situated in the charming Geul Valley, between two branches of the river, a very old, little town, it belongs to the district borough of Valkenburg-Houthem. It is much frequented in the summer by holidaymakers attracted by the gentle hills surrounding its fine parks and its other attractions.

The town has preserved two fortified gateways: 14C **Grendel Gate** (Z A) and 15C **Berkel Gate** (Z B) with its footbridge.

The caves. – The hills round the town are composed of a marly soil, like St Peter's Mount *(qv)* near Maastricht, much esteemed for its building stone, which has been quarried.

A certain number of galleries 70km - $43\frac{1}{2}$ miles long can now be visited; they have made it possible to set up underground museums and other tourist attractions.

SIGHTS

Castle ruins (Kasteel-Ruïne) (Z). – The ruins of the castle of the Lords of Valkenburg dominate the city. Only parts of walls and broken arches still remain of this fortress. It was built in *c*1087 and was altered in the Gothic period. It was subjected to a great number of sieges, notably by the Count of Louvain (1122).

Louis XIV captured it in May 1672. It was taken back in December and razed to the ground the following year by order of the King-Statdholder William III.

Many legends are attached to the ruins, such as that of Walram and Reginald of Valkenburg, who were in love with Alix, the daughter of the Count of Juliers. Walram succeeded in marrying Alix but the young couple were assassinated by Reginald. From the top of the ruins there is a panorama over the town and the green Geul Valley.

★ Mining Museum (Steenkolenmijn Valkenburg). – *Access from Daelhemerweg (Z).*
A coal mine has been reconstituted in the galleries of an old quarry. The visit provides information on the methods of coal extraction as practised in Limburg before the last workings were closed.

VALKENBURG

A film provides a realistic picture of a coal mine. Then walk along the galleries where shown, in about twenty phases, are: the trains for the transportation of personnel or coal, the water pumps, the tunnel where the coal seam is extracted, with portable shaft supports, the evacuation of the coal and the different security systems.

⊙ **Municipal Caves (Gemeentegrot) (Z)**. – These are ancient marl quarries which were already known to the Romans. They were used for non-juring priests during the French Revolution and sheltered the population in time of war, notably in September 1944 on the town's liberation.

The sedimentary rock contains many fossils. The caves remain at a constant temperature of 14°C-57°F.

The walls are covered with charcoal drawings and low reliefs, some representing the animals whose fossils have been found, such as the Mosasaurus *(p 148)*; others represent artistic (Mona Lisa) or religious subjects.

As the stone was extracted lower and lower, some drawings are placed very high up.

⊙ **Fluwelen Caves (Fluwelengrot) (Z)**. – These caves are below the castle with which they communicate. They are named after their former owner, Fluwijn. Like the municipal caves, they are old quarries which housed refugees, who have left many drawings and low reliefs. Their temperature remains at 10°C-50°F.

⊙ **Wilhelmina Tower (Wilhelminatoren) (Z)**. – *Access either by car from Daelhemerweg, then turn left by chairlift* (kabelbaan). From the departure point of the chairlift, **caves** (Panorama-Grot) can be visited. A film on prehistoric times is shown.

From the top of the tower (160 steps), 30m - $98\frac{1}{2}$ feet high, there is a good view of the town's wooded surroundings.

⊙ **Roman Catacombs (Romeinse Katakomben) (YZ)**. – In the old quarries a dozen Roman catacombs have been reconstructed.

⊙ **Regional Museum (Streekmuseum) (Z M)**. – Objects found during excavations of the castle, paintings of the town, reconstructed workshops, mementoes of shooting companies are exhibited here.

★ SOUTHERN LIMBURG

Round tour of 58km - 36 miles – about $\frac{1}{2}$ day

Southern Limburg is a transitional region between the Dutch plains and the Ardennes hills jutting out between Belgium and Germany.

It is a rural area whose appearance is not marred by the region's coal mines. Its fertile plateaux, lush valleys, its fields shaded by apple trees, its hilltops from which can be seen vast stretches of countryside, form a pleasant landscape dotted with fine manor houses and picturesque white half-timbered farms *(p 32)*.

Leave Valkenburg *(p 177)* by ② on the town plan, eastwards in the direction of Gulpen.

The road follows the verdant Geul Valley.

Oud-Valkenburg. – On the left is the fine 17C **Schaloen Castle** (Kasteel Schaloen), restored in the 19C by Cuypers. The park is watered by a branch of the Geul. A little farther on, behind a chapel, is **Genhoes Castle** (Kasteel Genhoes), built in the 16 and 18C and surrounded by moats.

After Wijlre, notice on the left **Cartils Castle** (Kasteel), in the middle of a fine park.

Wittem. – Pop 7 583. On the right, the **castle** (Kasteel Wittem) is a 15C building, restored in the 19C in the neo-Gothic style. It is now a hotel-restaurant.

A road over the plateau leads to Vaals.

Vaals. – Pop 10 582. A resort which owes its animation to the proximity of the German frontier and Drielandenpunt.

A winding road climbs through the woods to Drielandenpunt. 500m - ½ mile before the end of the road, on the left, there is a fine **panorama★** of Aachen (Aix-la-Chapelle).

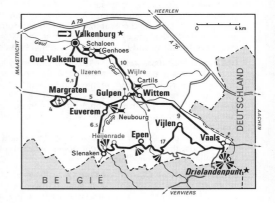

★ **Drielandenpunt.** – It is the meeting point *(punt)* of three *(drie)* countries' *(landen)* frontiers: Germany, Belgium and the Netherlands. It is also the highest point in the Netherlands being at 321m - 1 053ft. From the top of **Boudewijn Tower** (a metal building), there is a **panorama★** over the region, Aachen close by, Germany's Eifel Forests, and in the distance, towards the west, Maastricht.

Return towards Vaals and go to Vijlen.

Vijlen. – This village still has many half-timbered houses.

By a road through the woods one reaches the road from Vaals to Epen: pretty **view** over the hills to the south.

Epen. – Resort where several houses still have half-timbered walls.

Before reaching the church, turn left.

A fine half-timbered farmhouse can be seen on leaving the village.

The climb gives fine **views★** over the frontier hills to the south.

After Heijenrade there is a fine **view** on the right over Gulp Valley which one crosses at **Slenaken,** a small frontier village.

Then follow the river towards Gulpen. This is a pleasant drive through a landscape of lush fields.

Euverem. – In pools near the Gulp nearly 500 000 trout are raised every year. Some of them are sent to neighbouring fish ponds.

At the junction of the road from Gulpen to Maastricht, there is a **view** on the right of Neubourg Castle (Kasteel Neubourg). It lies at the bottom of a valley and is a vast building flanked by a square tower with an onion-shaped dome; it is now a hotel.

Gulpen. – Pop 7 029. A resort at the confluence of the Gulp and the Geul.

Margraten. – Pop 13 154. At the west of town lies the **Netherlands American Military Cemetery.** It was made in 1944 by the 9th American Army. On the left of the entrance a small museum retraces the episodes of the war. On the walls the names of the 1 722 missing are engraved.

In the cemetery, dominated by a tall tower (chapel inside) lie the graves of 8 301 soldiers marked out by crosses placed in a semi-circle; these soldiers fell during the breakthrough of the Siegfried Line.

Return to Valkenburg through IJzeren and Sibbe over the plain, entering by Daelhemerweg.

★ **VEERE** Zeeland Pop 4 801

Michelin map **408** fold 15 or **212** south of fold 2 – Local map p 78
Town plan in the current Michelin Red Guide Benelux

Veere is situated on **Veere Lake** (Veerse Meer), a former branch of the sea closed by a dam *(p 79)* which links Walcheren to North Beveland.
Veere was under the protection of the Lords of Borsele and was a flourishing port because of its wool trade with Scotland – it was in the early 16C that Veere became the port on the continent through which staple goods (exports of linen, salt and wool) passed. The port was gradually ruined by the War of Independence. Veere is twinned with Culross *(see Michelin Green Guide to Scotland).*
The dam has stopped any access to the North Sea by fishing boats, so Veere has become a sailing centre and a holiday resort.
With its paved alleyways, its monuments and its old brick houses, Veere has kept its character.

SIGHTS

Campveer Tower (Campveerse Toren). – This 15C tower is part of the town's old fortifications. It is built of brick and decorated with bands of white stone and has a crow-stepped gable. It is now a restaurant.

⊙ **★ Scotch Houses (Schotse Huizen).** – *Nos 25 and 27 on the quay (Kade).* Built in the 16C in the Gothic Flamboyant style, these two buildings were used as offices and warehouses by the Scottish wool merchants who lived in Veere. The tympana of the windows and doors are richly decorated. At no 25 the façade stone represents a lamb, symbol of the wool trade; at no 27 it shows an ostrich.

Inside there are Zeeland costumes, porcelain and furniture, including a *sterrekabinet* encrusted with designs of stars *(p 29)*. In a fine Gothic room there are the original statues of the lords and ladies of Veere, which had decorated the town hall.

⊙ **Old Town Hall (Oude stadhuis).** – This is a charming little two storey Gothic building made of sandstone. It was started in 1474. The openings on the 1st floor are separated by recesses surmounted by canopies, under which are statues, remade in 1934, of four lords and three ladies of Veere.

The roof is flanked with octagonal turrets and dominated by a 1591 onion-shaped belfry, crowned with a balustrade with pinnacles and small columns. Inside there is ⊙ a **carillon** of 48 bells.

In the audience chamber (Rechtszaal) on the ground floor, one of the oldest in the Netherlands, there is the silver gilt goblet which Emperor Charles V gave to Count Maximilian of Buren in 1546.

⊙ **Great Church or Church of Our Lady (Grote- of O.L. Vrouwekerk).** – A massive 14C structure, in front of which stands a large tower-porch, which was never completed. Next to the church is the **municipal fountain,** a lovely Gothic monument of 1551, composed of an octagonal rotunda with diagonal arches and small columns.

VENLO Limburg   Pop 63 598

Michelin map ▣ fold 19 or ▣ fold 20
Plan of built-up area in the current Michelin Red Guide Benelux

In the northern part of the province of Limburg, near the German-Dutch frontier, Venlo is a small industrial town on the banks of the Maas.

HISTORICAL NOTES

A legend of the Middle Ages gives 90AD as the date of Venlo's foundation by Valuas, chief of a Germanic tribe, the Bructeri. The name of the town's founder is commemorated at all the celebrations, parades and processions; the effigies of two giants representing Valuas and his wife are carried through the town.

Venlo was prosperous in the Middle Ages and was given city rights in 1343. In 1364 it became a member of the Hanseatic League.

Today it is the centre of a large market gardening area (asparagus mushrooms, flowers, tomatoes, gherkins), which stretches north to the outskirts of Grubbenvorst. The town's immediate surroundings are covered with hothouses.

The carnival *(see the chapter Practical Information at the end of the guide)* is a very lively one.

⊙ **Boat trips.** – Boat trips are organised on the Maas. Landing stage: Maaskade (Y).

SIGHTS

Town Hall (Stadhuis) (Y H). – In the middle of Markt, the town hall is a fine quadrilateral Renaissance building (*c*1600).

⊙ **St Martin's (St.-Martinuskerk) (Y).** – Dating from the beginning of the 15C, it was damaged during the last war but has been restored and its tower, which has a carillon of 48 bells, rebuilt.

The interior has interesting **furnishings★** and *objets d'art.*

The 15C Gothic **stalls** are carved to represent about twenty scenes of the Old and New Testaments; the misericords are decorated with various subjects (heads, evangelist symbols, fables, foliage). On the left of the triumphal arch note a 16C Virgin and Child; on the right a 17C Christ; in the chapel of Our Lady, north of the chancel, a carved 16C oak bench; in the chapel on the right of the chancel, a 15C limestone *Pietà.* In a south chapel there is an *Ecce Homo* painted by Jan van Cleef, a painter born in Venlo (1646-1716). The pulpit is baroque. A beautiful brass **baptismal font,** dating from 1621, stands at the back of the south side aisle.

In the same street (Grote Kerkstraat), at nos 19-21, there is the interesting façade of the **Schreurs House (Y D)** built in the Renaissance style (1588), topped by a voluted gable; on the 1st floor, blind arcades lean on two corbels carved with the head of a lion; note also the carved coat of arms and the medallions.

⊙ **Goltzius Museum (Goltziusmuseum) (Y M¹).** – This regional museum deals with archaeology, history and art.

The ground floor is devoted to prehistory, the Roman occupation and the town's history.

The 1st floor exhibits decorative arts. There are also collections of silverware, pewter, coins and weapons. The museum also organises temporary exhibitions.

VENLO

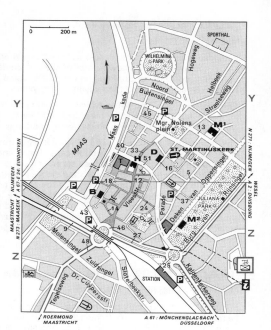

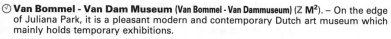

Ⓥ **Van Bommel - Van Dam Museum** (Van Bommel - Van Dammuseum) (Z M²). – On the edge of Juliana Park, it is a pleasant modern and contemporary Dutch art museum which mainly holds temporary exhibitions.

Romer House (Romerhuis) (Z B). – A 16C house with crow-stepped gable and pinnacles.

EXCURSION

Tegelen. – Pop 18 713. 4km - 2½ miles to the southwest by Tegelseweg (Z). This is a small industrial town well-known for its **Passion Plays** (Passiespelen) enacted every five years with all the population taking part (see the chapter Practical Information at the end of the guide).

Ⓥ Tegelen has a **museum** (museum Steyl); St Michaëlstraat 7.
Housed in the buildings of a missionary community, it contains artefacts from Indonesia, New Guinea, the Far East, Africa, Chinese objets d'art, butterflies and stuffed animals from all over the world.

Ⓥ Not far from the museum (Maashoek 2 b, Steijl), there is a **botanical garden** (Jochum-Hof). It is an open-air garden with plants from the north of Limburg and a tropical hothouse (Cacti, orchids, banana trees).

VENRAY Limburg   Pop 33 964

Michelin map 408 fold 19 or 212 south of fold 10

Ⓥ On Grote Markt, **St Peter's** (St.-Petrusbandenkerk), a large Gothic church, contains some interesting furnishings. Apart from the baroque pulpit note a fine late 15C brass lectern and a remarkable series of wooden **statues** and the one in stone of St Paul; the oldest is of St James (15C). The Apostles, with their attributes, stand against the pillars of the nave. In the aisles there is a series of saints (a beautiful St Lucy) which come from old altars no longer in existence. At the entrance there is a baroque statue of St Peter, shown as pope.

EXCURSION

Overloon. – 7km - 4 miles to the north. For three weeks in the autumn of 1944 the British and Americans fought a battle round this village to support the "Market Garden" operation (qv), one of the biggest tank battles of the war, often compared to the one at Caen because of the terrible artillery bombardment and the number of tanks involved.

Ⓥ The **National War and Resistance Museum** (Nederlands Nationaal Oorlogs- en Verzets-museum) is to the east of Overloon in the woods where the fighting occurred.
A signposted route is marked out in this 14ha - 34½ acre enclosure to display the large collection (70 items) of German and Allied material which remain from the battle: tanks, planes, one-man submarine, a complete V1, a pocket submarine, guns, land-mines, bombs, torpedoes, etc.
One then reaches a building with a gallery of hand guns and a large amount of graphic documentation about the Netherlands during the war.

Plan your own itinerary by looking
at the map of the principal sights (pp 4 to 6).

★ VOLENDAM North Holland Pop 24 251 (with Edam)

Michelin map **408** fold 11

Volendam stands on a small land-locked sea, Gouw Sea. It is equipped for eel fishing and is one of the best known ports of the old Zuiderzee. Its inhabitants wear the traditional costume in summer which has become Netherland's symbol abroad. Tourism is, also, an important activity of Volendam.

The village. – The long street, which runs along the top of the high dike, is just a line of shops, but behind and below the dike there are picturesque narrow alleyways winding between small brick houses with wooden gables.

★ **The traditional costume.** – The men wear black trousers with silver buttons, short jackets over striped shirts, and round caps. The women's costume *(illustration p 30)* consists of a black skirt with a striped apron or a striped skirt with a black apron, a shirt with a flowered front under a black short sleeved overblouse, a necklace of large coral beads with a gold clasp, hidden in winter by a blue and white shawl. When they are not wearing a pointed black bonnet they wear a lace cap for feast days, very tall with turned up wings, whose shape is famous. Men and women wear clogs or buckled shoes. Visitors should watch the congregation leaving after morning or evening service on Sundays or feast days when the couples cross the little wooden bridge in front of the Catholic church.

★★ WADDEN ISLANDS (Waddeneilanden)

Michelin map **408** folds 3, 4, 5 and 6 – Local map p 183

In the north of the country between the North Sea and the Wadden Sea (Waddenzee) lie the Wadden Islands: **Texel** (province of North Holland), the **Frisian Islands** of which the main ones are Vlieland, Terschelling, Ameland and Schiermonnikoog; and two smaller islands belonging to the province of Groningen: Rottumeroog and Rottumerplaat, which before 1950 were sometimes under water.

The formation of the islands and the Wadden Sea. – The islands' soil, formed during the Tertiary Era, was slightly modified, especially on Texel by the movement of a large Scandinavian glacier which covered the north of Europe in the Quaternary Era. But the Wadden Islands are, above all, along with the German and Danish islands which are an extension of them, the remains of an ancient chain of dunes, wind blown, which stretched as far as Jutland in Denmark.

As far back as the Roman epoch the sea had broken up the chain of dunes and invaded the flat hinterland forming the **Wadden Sea.** In the 13C this connected to a vast gulf which had just been formed, the Zuiderzee *(qv).*

Tides and currents. – The islands are still subject to the strong action of sea currents and the North Sea continues its insidious undermining process to the west of the islands. Numbered posts are planted in lines on the beaches making it possible to estimate the sand's movement, which breakwaters, built out perpendicularly from the coast, attempt to reduce.

The wind then accumulates the sand behind the dunes as well as to the southwesterly point of the islands, where it forms immense desert stretches.

To the east, the currents contribute to the filling up of the Wadden Sea. At low tide, the sea leaves huge stretches of mud or sand, called *wadden,* which are much appreciated by birds, but force ships to make large detours to avoid them and take marked channels.

The Wadden Sea can be crossed over by **fording** it (called *wadlopen*) with a guide.

Storms. – These have always been a threat to the Wadden Sea and its low-lying islands, which are only protected from the sea by a chain of dunes on the west and a dike on the east.

The small island of **Griend,** between Vlieland and Harlingen, was a prosperous island in the 13C; little by little it was worn away by the high tides, and had to be abandoned in the 18C. In 1851 part of Texel was covered by the sea.

Landscape. – The north of the islands have wonderful **beaches** of very white sand bordered by **dunes** on which abundant vegetation grows. They are particularly high and wide on Texel.

To the south the very flat coast is protected by a dike.

Inland the villages and **farms** are protected from the wind by thick curtains of trees. The farmhouses on the Frisian Islands have the same features as those of Friesland, whereas those of Texel are similar to the pyramid-shaped farmhouses of North Holland.

The countryside is generally subdivided into several **polders** separated by small dikes, where numerous herds of cows and a few horses graze. Texel specialises mainly in raising sheep.

There are also several small **ports** on the Wadden Sea. They were once the departure point for fishing and whaling, formerly the chief activity of Ameland.

Fauna and flora. – All these islands make up a kind of nature reserve for seabirds. Some come to lay their eggs: different types of gulls, spoonbills, pintail ducks.

In the autumn a great number of **migratory birds** from northern Europe (Scandinavia, Iceland) and from Siberia stop for a time on the Wadden Sea, which is rich in food of all kinds (fish and shellfish), then continue on their way to warmer climates (France, Spain, North Africa). This is so with the avocet. Others spend the winter on the Wadden Sea: they include among the waders a large number of different types of dunlins and oyster catchers.

Nature reserves have been laid out on each island; some of them are forbidden to visitors unaccompanied by a guide. The largest belong to the Forestry Department (Staatsbosbeheer).

Seals, which used to come in great numbers on the sand banks on the north side of the islands, are unfortunately decreasing.

Near the small ponds hidden in the dunes and on the dunes themselves, the **vegetation** is rich and exceptional. Among the most common species to be found are shrubs such as the sea buckthorn with its edible orange berries, Burnet rose, and grasses such as scurvy grass, Parnassus grass with white flowers and succulent plants such as milkwort.

Tourism on the islands. – Even if not interested in ornithology or botany, many tourists enjoy the natural beauty of the islands, hardly polluted (clear seas, wild dunes and a healthy climate), the calm (on two of the islands only public commercial vehicles are allowed), the signposted paths (for walking, bicycling, horse-riding) in the woods or on the dunes, and the possibilities for other activities such as fishing, sailing, etc.

The drawbacks. – The Wadden Islands are coveted: the army, for instance, has built several military bases (Texel, Terschelling, Vlieland) which have contributed to driving away some types of birds.

In addition very rich resources of natural gas have been found under the Wadden Sea: a drilling platform has already been built between Den Helder and Texel.

There is also a plan to unite all the islands to the mainland in order to create polders; this meets with much opposition.

Some practical advice. – The best way to get about on the islands, which are forbidden to cars, or across the nature reserves or dunes which have cycling paths (Boschplaat to Terschelling for example), is by bicycle. They can be hired on each island and in most villages. However, in season they are not always available, therefore, it is highly advisable to embark from the mainland with your own bicycle, which is accepted on all ships.

In season, it is recommended to reserve rooms through the island's tourist information centre. There are few hotels but private houses take lodgers.

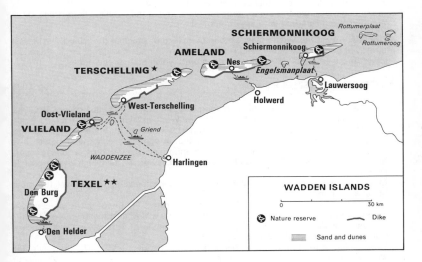

AMELAND Friesland   Pop 3 147

Access. – *From Holwerd.* This long island covering about 5 800ha - 14 326 acres with its large stretches of dunes, fine sandy beaches on the North Sea, and woods, is very frequented by tourists, including a large number of Germans who come here in the summer. A long bicycle track (20km - 12$\frac{1}{2}$ miles) crosses the island passing through woods and over dunes.

Like the other Wadden Islands, Ameland has its **nature reserves** for birds.

The inhabitants of Ameland formerly specialised in **whaling.** This activity was discontinued in the mid-19C but the captains' *(commandeurs)* houses can still be seen here and there on the island, and in some places whale bones are still used as fences. The farmhouses in Ameland are of the same type as the Frisian farmhouses *(p 31).*

Nes. – This is the island's chief locality, overlooked by an isolated **bell tower** with a saddleback roof, dating from 1732. In Doniastraat, there are several old captains' houses, **Commandeurshuizen,** one-storey houses with a small lean-to on the side, and where the entrance door is slightly off-centre. A cordon of bricks or a geometric frieze outline each floor. The façade anchors often show an old date.

To the east, on the road to Buren, past the new Catholic cemetery, the old **cemetery** is accessible by a small road on the left. It still has ancient steles, some decorated with a weeping willow, others are very narrow and nearly 2m - 6$\frac{1}{2}$ft high. Several graves of British airmen are grouped in this cemetery.

Ballum. – The **tower** of an old church stands in the village centre.
To the southeast, on Smitteweg, the **cemetery** has some attractive old gravestones, decorated with carved ships or weeping willows.

Hollum. – South of town a charming typical church with a saddleback roofed bell tower is surrounded by a **cemetery**, which has some 18C tombstones engraved with a fine ship.
Some charming captains' houses can be seen at Hollum. One of them has been
ⓥ made into a **museum** (Oudheidkamer 't Sorgdragershúske).
It has regional furniture and is walled with glazed tiles. There are varied collections – earthenware, pottery, costumes, and objects – pertaining to whaling.
ⓥ In Oranjeweg one can see the hangar sheltering the famous **redding-boot,** the lifeboat which was drawn on to the beach by a team of horses.

SCHIERMONNIKOOG Friesland   Pop 918

ⓥ **Access.** – *From Lauwersoog.* It is the smallest of Wadden Sea's inhabited islands: an area of 4 000ha - 9 880 acres, it is 16km - 10 miles long and 4km - 2½ miles wide and has recently become a national park.
The only town, Schiermonnikoog, has two large beaches and a small lake (pleasure boats), the Westerplas.
To the east, there is a nature reserve of 2 400ha - 5 928 acres: **De Oosterkwelder.**
With its wild scenery, its dunes, woods, beaches and its tranquillity, Schiermonnikoog is one of the most agreable of the Wadden Islands.
The island became Frisian in 1580. It belonged to different families between 1639 and 1858, it has belonged to the State since 1945.

Schiermonnikoog. – The houses of this small town are built among the trees. The town developed after Cistercian monks from Friesland settled here *c*1400. The name of the island derives from them, *schier* meaning grey, *monnik* monk and *oog* island. A statue of a monk on the green in the town centre is a reminder of its past.
Nearby, an arch made of two huge whale bones recalls the whale hunting of earlier
ⓥ times. The **museum** (Bezoekerscentrum de Oude Centrale) is housed in an old power station and contains documents concerning the island.
In Middenstreek, which runs towards the west, and in the parallel Langestreek, there are interesting **old houses** with assymmetrical roofs.

★ **Het Rif.** – Past the Westerplas, at the southwestern point of the island, lies a vast stretch of immaculate white sand reaching 1.5km - 1 mile in width. From it, there is a **view★** of the whole of Westerburenweg, a path which ends in the dunes.

★TERSCHELLING Friesland   Pop 4 595

ⓥ **Access.** – *From Harlingen.* This very long island (28km - 17½ miles) covers 10 000ha - 24 700 acres and is the second largest of the Wadden Islands, after Texel.
It welcomes many holidaymakers in summer, who enjoy its huge sandy beaches. Terschelling (pronounced Ter-srelling) has kept in some places its wild aspect. It is covered with vast areas of dunes where an abundant vegetation of various grasses, flowers and moss grow. It also has several **nature reserves,** of which the largest is De Boschplaat.
Many bicycle paths cover the island, which makes it possible to discover the most unusual scenery.
The **farmhouses** of Frisian type *(p 31)* have the distinctive feature of barns pierced by a high portal where the carts enter, and which forms a kind of transept.
The **cranberry wine** *(cranberrywijn)* has been a speciality of Terschelling ever since a sailor found a barrel of it washed up on the dunes.
Terschelling is the homeland of **Willem Barents** or Barentsz (*c*1555-97), the navigator who, while trying to seek a northeast passage to India, discovered Novaya Zemlya in 1594 and Spitsbergen in 1596. The portion of the Arctic Ocean, which lies between these two archipelagos bears his name, the Barents Sea. On his third expedition (1596-7), his boat was caught in the ice. He spent the winter in Novaya Zemlya in a hut made from boat planks, and died in the attempt to reach inhabited land. In 1871 his ship's log was found.

West-Terschelling. – The capital of the island is a small port well situated in a large bay. It is overlooked by a square tower 54m - 174ft high, the **Brandaris,** a lighthouse built in 1594 to replace the bell tower (used as a lighthouse) of St Brandarius Chapel which, located on the island's southwest side, had been engulfed by waves.
At the foot of the tower lies a large **cemetery.** The 19 and early 20C steles, engraved with naively depicted boats, recall the maritime past of its inhabitants. One of the steles, in the middle of the cemetery, recalls the episode during which on 3 January 1880, five of the island's life saver's tried to pick up the survivors from the wreck of the *Queen of Mistley.*

ⓥ **'t Behouden Huys Municipal Museum** (Gemeente Museum). – *Commandeurstraat no 30.* This pleasant regional museum is housed in two dwellings (1668) with charming crow-stepped gables, which belonged to the Dutch India Company. It bears the name of the hut in which Willem Barents spent the winter. At the entrance and at no 14 of the same street, note the fine sculptured paving stones.
The reconstructed interior with its furniture, household items, costumed figures, gives a picture of local life. The attic and the small adjoining house exhibit objects pertaining to the navy and whaling.

Formerum. – A small **windmill,** De Koffiemolen (the coffee mill) is worth seeing. It has a thatched roof and dates from 1876; and is now used to mill grain.

Hoorn. – This 13C church built of brick in the Frisian style is surrounded by gravestones. The oldest date from the 19C and are topped by a low relief depicting a ship.

★ **De Boschplaat.** – *Access forbidden to cars but bicycles allowed (bicycle paths in the* ⊘ *western part).*

This nature reserve, which can be visited by wagon *(huifkar)* or guided tour covers 4 400ha - 10 868 acres of the island's eastern point, which is uninhabited. On the dunes and near the estuaries, large numbers of birds come to nest. The vegetation is most remarkable, as unique types of halophyte plants can be found (those growing on salty soil).

★★ TEXEL North Holland   Pop 12 691

⊘ **Access.** – *From Den Helder.*
Texel (pronounced Tessel) is 24km - 15 miles long and 9km - 5½ miles wide and is the largest of the Wadden Islands.
The capital, **Den Burg,** is in the centre. **De Koog,** to the west, gives access to the main beach. **Oudeschild** is a small fishing and pleasure port. **De Cocksdorp** is the most northern locality.
After agriculture and tourism the island's main activity is sheep breeding (about 25 000 head).

Bird Island. – Birds are one of the most interesting features of Texel. The most varied species live here, lay their eggs and hatch them on the dunes or on the fresh water lakes here.
⊘ Texel has several **nature reserves★** belonging to the State.
Pedestrians only have access to the signposted paths.

De Eijerlandse duinen. – These dunes belonged to an island, Eyerlandt, which has been joined to Texel since 1629 by a sand bar. Numerous birds nest here from the end of March to the end of July, especially eiders which provide the down to make eiderdowns.

De Slufter. – This is a large area surrounded by dunes, linked to the sea by a gap. The vegetation growing here is impregnated with salt. About forty different species of birds nest here.
From the top of the dunes, at the end of the Slufterweg, which can be reached by a stairway, there is a **view★** over this amazing wild landscape which in July and August is covered with a mauve flower called sea lavender.

De Muy. – This is a partly marshy area in the hollow of the dunes, where nearly fifty species of birds nest, especially white spoonbills with their characteristic beak, and the grey heron. There are interesting plants (orchids, pyrola, and Parnassus grass).

De Westerduinen. – On these dunes, near the beach, herring gulls nest.

De Geul. – This lake was formed in the dunes at the end of the last century. Several other small lakes have formed since. In the reeds one can see the spoonbill, the grey heron and the pintail duck.
Nearby interesting plants grow on the dunes and marshes.

(After photo Staatsbosbeheer)

A spoonbill on Texel

A fine viewpoint can be had over the reserve from the belvedere built on the **Mokweg.**

⊘ **EcoMare.** – *Ruyslaan 92. Access by De Koog road and the crossroads numbered 13.*
In these dunes northwest of Den Burg a building houses this centre as well as a small **Natural History Museum** (Natuurhistorisch Museum) concerning Texel.
The first section is about the island's evolution, from its geological formation during the Ice Age, up to its transformation into polders, and from its prehistoric inhabitants until the present tourist invasion.
In another section, the nature reserves' flora and fauna can be studied with the help of dioramas, show cases with stuffed birds and photographs of plants. Aquariums, shell collections, reproductions of the sea bed evoke the maritime environment of the island.
The seals, which were once very common in the Wadden Sea, play in the salt water
⊘ ponds outside; their **meal time** can be viewed.

⊘ **Oudheidkamer.** – *In Den Burg, in Kogerstraat, on a small shady square called Stenenplaats.*
This house, built in 1599, with a pinnacled gable contains a museum of paintings and costumes recalling local life.

⊘ **Wagon and Agricultural Museum (Wagen- en Agrarisch museum).** – *At De Waal, north of Den Burg.*
There is a collection of wagons and carriages which have been used on the island. Some of the Frisian sledges are especially elegant.

VLIELAND Friesland   Pop 1 038

⊘**Access.** – *From Harlingen or from Terschelling.*
This island, composed of dunes and woods, covering 5 100ha - 12 597 acres is 20km - 12½ miles long with a maximum width of 2.5km - 1½ miles. There is only one small town, Oost-Vlieland. A single main road crosses it from east to west. Only the army at the western end and tourists in season come and spoil the peace of this wild countryside.

Oost-Vlieland. – In Dorpsstraat, the main street, there are a few old houses. On the
⊘south side of the street a house called **Tromp's House** (Huys) has been made into a museum.
This is a typical island home, with panelled rooms, some painted blue, with fine furniture and porcelain and earthenware collections.
⊘A small **reception centre** (Bezoekerscentrum) has been fitted out near the church.
Photographs provide documentation on the islands' flora and fauna and especially about the main species of birds which live on the shores.
⊘The **church** contains whale bones.
The **cemetery** beside the church contains some interesting carved funerary steles, as well as graves of Commonwealth soldiers killed during World War II.
From the hill on which the lighthouse (vuurtoren) stands, west of town, there is a **view**★ over the island, Oost-Vlieland, the dark green woods forming a contrast to the pale colour of the dunes, and Wadden Sea, where at each low tide vast stretches of mud flats appear, covered with flocks of birds.

Funerary stele in Vlieland

WORKUM Friesland

Michelin map 408 fold 4 – Local map p 169

This small town (Warkum in Frisian) was once a prosperous port where the eel trade flourished. Now it is a large holiday and water sports centre.
It is well-known for its glazed pottery which is brown in colour and often decorated with a frieze of white scrolls.
Workum still has several interesting houses with crow-stepped or bell-shaped gables *(klokgevel).*

Merk. – It has a picturesque collection of old buildings.

Town Hall (Stadhuis). – This has a tall 18C façade. On the left is the old town hall, a small Renaissance building decorated with carved stone.

⊘**St Gertrude's** (St.-Gertrudiskerk). – This large Gothic church was built in the 16 and 17C and has an imposing separate **bell tower** crowned with a tiny onion-shaped dome.
Inside the church there is a fine 18C pulpit and nine painted biers illustrating the activities of the guilds. They were used to carry the bodies of guild members to the cemetery.

Weigh House (Waag). – A fine 17C building with stepped dormer windows. Inside is a
⊘small **Antiquities Museum** (Oudheidkamer).

★ ZAAN REGION (ZAANSTREEK) North Holland

Michelin map 408 folds 10 and 27 (inset) – Local map p 187

This region which crosses the Zaan waterway, includes localities, which since 1974 have been grouped together to form the district of **Zaanstad** (pop 128 388).
Originally the inhabitants made their living by fishing. In 1592 Cornelis Corneliszoon built the first windmill for sawing wood. Then industrial **mills** developed. It is said that soon there were more than 500 in the region. This facilitated the development of naval construction. The shipyards in the region were so well known that Czar **Peter the Great** came incognito in 1697 to undergo a period of training with a shipbuilder.
Many windmills still exist. Most of them are built on top of large workshops and stand very high: their sails are driven from a platform *(illustration p 34).*
The **houses** were once built in a very particular style which spread over the district. Now most of the old houses still existing have been reassembled in the Zaan Quarter.

★ZAAN QUARTER (DE ZAANSE SCHANS)

This quarter has taken its name, De Zaanse Schans, from a redoubt built at the end of the 16C as a protection against Spanish troops and which no longer exists.
Since 1950 a village has been laid out here consisting of 17 and 18C houses and public buildings brought in from different localities, especially from Zaandam. They have been reconstituted and restored to form a kind of open-air museum.
The village is inhabited and its windmills are still active. It is built along a dike, **Kalverringdijk,** beside which runs a ditch crossed by little humpbacked bridges. Some of the houses border secondary canals, along which run paths such as Zeilenmakerspad *(p 187).*

Most of the houses are of wood with gables of different shapes. These are painted green or tarred black and their doors, windows and gables are outlined in white. On top of each gable is a small wooden ornament, the *makelaar*.

Several of the houses, shops and windmills can be visited.

South of the village and bridge there is an oil mill, called **De Ooievaar** (the stork).

⊘ **Boat trips.** – Boat trips are organised along the Zaan. *Landing stage on the local map above.*

⊘ **Wooden Shoe Workshop** (Klompenmakerij) (K). – The traditional way of making wooden shoes is shown.

Zeilenmakerspad. – On this path there is a tiny **hollow post mill** (A) or wipmolen.

⊘ At no 4, a 17C house called In de Gecroonde Duijvekater (the crowned bread-roll), there is a **Bakery Museum** (Bakkerrijmuseum) (B).

⊘ **Catharina Hoeve Cheese Dairy** (Kaasmakerij) (C). – Gouda and Edam are made here, traditionally.

⊘ **Theekoepel** (D). – It is a pavilion in the form of a rotunda at the bottom of a garden, once a tea house (theekoepel), it now houses a **pewter foundry.**

⊘ **Clock Museum** (Uurwerkenmuseum) (E). – A collection of all different types of clocks made in the country.

⊘ **Albert Heijn Grocery** (Kruidenierswinkel) (F). – A charming old shop in a 19C house selling out-moded products (sugar candy, etc).

⊘ **Het Noorderhuis** (G). – In this 18C house with its neck-shaped gable *(p 48)* one can visit the grand drawing room and a room with costumed figures illustrating wedding preparations.

De Huisman. – An 18C mustard mill with a rotating cap *(p 33)*.

⊘ **De Poelenburg.** – This saw mill dates from 1869 and is the **paltrok**-type *(paltrok-molen)*: it is built above the big workshop which turns with the mill when the sails are oriented to face the wind. Its name derives from its large moveable base like the *Pfalzrock,* a dress worn by the ladies of the Palatinate who were once refugees in the Netherlands.

⊘ **De Kat** (The cat). – It is a mill for grinding colours.

⊘ **De Zoeker** (The seeker). – In this oil mill, salad oil is made by grinding many types of seeds.

ADDITIONAL SIGHTS

⊘ **Zaandijk.** – On the opposite bank of the Zaan, this town has the **Zaan Region Antiquities Museum** (Zaanlandse Oudheidkamer).

It is in the brick built house of a rich 18C merchant and consists of a drawing room with 19C furniture and a "good year room", a room added to the house when business prospered, with a tiled chimney.

⊘ To the south is a 17C flour mill called **De Dood** (death).

⊘ **Koog aan de Zaan.** – In this small town there is a **Windmill Museum** (Molenmuseum). It is in a charming park and showns different types of ladders, tools, millers' garments, documents and engravings of the 17 to 19C.

Zaandam. – This industrial town on the Zaan has, since 1876, been served by the North Sea Canal (Noordzeekanaal).

Peter the Great's House (het Czaar-Peterhuisje), where he lived in 1697, can be seen on Krimp, no 23. It is built of wood but in 1895 it was enclosed by a brick construction, a gift of Czar Nicholas II.

Michelin map **408** fold 16 or **212** fold 3 – Local map p 78

Zierikzee, main centre of **Schouwen-Duiveland** Island, was once a small prosperous port on the Gouwe, formerly a strait which separated Schouwen from Duiveland. It was a member of the Hanseatic League and was also the residence of the Counts of Zeeland. It was made famous by the bravery of the Spaniards, led by Requesens, who captured it in 1576, after crossing Keeten canal in mid-winter.

Its decline began at the end of the 16C. It has preserved its historic character with a number of 16 to 18C houses.

Schouwen-Duiveland is linked to Goeree-Overflakkee by the dams, Brouwers *(qv)* and Grevelingen *(qv)* and to North Beveland by the Eastern Scheldt Dam and Zeeland Bridge *(qv)*.

⊙ **Boat trips.** – Zierikzee is the departure point for boat trips on Eastern Scheldt. *Landing stage* (Z) *on the port* (haven).

ZIERIKZEE

SIGHTS

★ **North Port Gate (Noordhavenpoort)** (Z B). – It is in fact a double gate with a double 16C Renaissance gable on the town side, and an older crow-stepped gable on the outside. The **South Port Gate** (Zuidhavenpoort) (Z E) linked by a lever bridge, is a tall square tower, flanked by four corner turrets (14C).

Oude Haven (Z 27). – Elegant 17 and 18C houses stand along the quays of this old port.

Havenplein (Z 8). – On the north side of this square the **De Witte Sween** (the White Swan) House (Z N) dates from 1658. It has a baroque gable and was reconstructed after the catastrophe of 1953 *(p 16)*.
Built onto the church (Gasthuiskerk) lies the old 1651 **market place** (Beurs) (Z L), surrounded by a Renaissance gallery with Tuscan columns.

's-Gravensteen (Z M¹). – This old prison has a crow-stepped façade dating from
⊙ 1524, decorated with fine grilles. It contains a small **maritime museum** (maritiem museum).

⊙ **Town Hall (Stadhuis).** – It is an old covered meat hall. It still has a picturesque wooden **tower** topped with an ornamental onion-shaped dome (1550) surmounted by a statue
⊙ of Neptune. The tower has a **carillon.**
The building was modified several times and has a double corbelled gable. On the façade highly decorative anchors served to hold torches.
⊙ Inside there is a **museum** (Stadhuismuseum). It is devoted to the town's history and its surroundings, and is mainly housed in the Arquebusiers' Hall which has a fine timber roof.
Across from the town hall the 14C De Haene (the cock) House, often called the **Templars' House** or Tempeliershuis (Z S) is the oldest in the town. The influence of Bruges (Belgium) architecture can be seen in the ogee shaped moulding round the windows.

⊙ **St Lieven's Tower (St.-Lievensmonstertoren)** (Z A). – It is the bell tower of the old Gothic cathedral, which caught fire and was destroyed in 1832. It was built as of 1454 by a member of the Keldermans family, who, subsequently, worked on the Middelburg town hall. It is 56m - 184ft high and unfinished.
Next to it stands a great neo-classical church (1848) preceded by a portico.

Nobel Gate (Nobelpoort) (Y D). – To the north of town, it is a late 14C square gateway to the town; the exterior side is framed by two tall towers built later and topped with pepperpot roofs.
Nearby, towards the south, there is a tall 19C **windmill** (Y F) with a handrail called De Hoop (hope).

Michelin map **408** fold 12

Zutphen lies at the confluence of the IJssel, the Berkel and Twentekanaal, near the Veluwe *(qv)*.
It is the capital of the beautiful wooded region of the **Achterhoek** *(qv),* a pleasant old city.
It is an important commercial centre and its pedestrian precincts are very crowded on market days.

HISTORICAL NOTES

Zutphen, a county capital, was attached to the Gelderland in 1127. It was granted its city rights in 1190 and beginning in 1200 returned to the Bishop of Utrecht. In the 14C it was affiliated to the Hanseatic League and built an enclosing wall which was enlarged in the 15C.
It was then an important strategic point due to its easily defendable position in the surrounding marshes (the name Zutphen, sometimes spelt Zutfen, comes from Zuidveen, the southern peat-bog).
It became one of the richest towns in Gelderland and in the 16C another fortified wall was built, of which there are numerous remains. Nevertheless, it was captured by the Spaniards in 1572 and was not recaptured by Maurice of Nassau until 1591.
It was taken by the French in 1672 who occupied it for two years. They took it again a century later, in 1795.

★THE OLD TOWN *time: 3 hours*

's-Gravenhof. – On this square stands St Walburga's and the town hall. In 1946 the remains of the castle of the Counts ('s-Gravenhof) of Zutphen were found. Paving stones indicate its outline.

⊙ **St Walburga's** (St.-Walburgskerk). – Built in the beginning of the 13C in the Romanesque style, it was progressively enlarged in the Gothic style until the 16C. It was damaged in 1945 and a fire in 1948 destroyed the top of its tower. The tower, formerly covered with tufa, has been restored with limestone.
The outside of the church is very picturesque due to the angles formed by the different parts of the building, the many roofs and their assemblage and by the variety of materials used.
On the north side, the small 15C **Virgin portal** was rebuilt from 1890 to 1925.
Inside the vaults are covered with 14 and 15C frescoes. A fine 15C **chandelier★**, in wrought iron, hangs in the chancel. The plain pulpit dates from the 17C. The organ loft, also 17C, is, on the other hand, richly decorated. There is an interesting brass **baptismal font**. It was cast in Mechlin (Belgium) in 1527 and decorated with many figures of evangelists and saints; at the summit is a pelican.
The **library★** (librije), installed since 1564 south of the ambulatory of St Walburga's has kept its old appearance with its low vaults and numerous columns. It contains, in particular, 85 incunabula and manuscripts of which some are set out on the desks. On the spring of the arches there are carved corbels and on the columns numerous statuettes.

Town Hall (Stadhuis) (**H**). – This 15C building, much modified in 1716 and 1729, was built onto the old **meat hall** (Vleeshal) whose 15C façade can be seen on Lange Hofstraat. Inside, the **great hall** (Burgerzaal), has a fine timber ceiling.

Cross the ramparts.

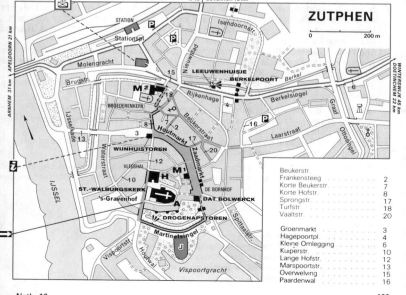

Beukerstr	
Frankensteeg	2
Korte Beukerstr.	7
Korte Hofstr.	8
Sprongstr.	17
Turfstr.	18
Vaaltstr.	20
Groenmarkt	3
Hagepoortpl.	4
Kleine Omlegging	6
Kuiperstr.	10
Lange Hofstr.	12
Marspoortstr.	13
Overwelving	15
Paardenwal	16

Martinetsingel. – Fine **view**★ over the south ramparts, behind which stands St Walburga's with its tower, on Drogenapstoren, and the gardens at the foot of the walls, watered by a canal.

★**Drogenapstoren.** – It is a very fine gateway built in 1444-6. The main building is square, crenelated, flanked by bartizans and topped by an octagonal turret.

Dat Bolwerck. – This fine Gothic house (1549), is topped by pinnacles.
Beside it is the old cavalry post or **Ruiter Kortegaard** of 1639 with a voluted gable.

Zaadmarkt. – On the old corn market, on the right at no 101, there is the doorway of an old **almshouse** (1723).

⊙**Henriette Polak Museum (M¹).** – It is laid out in a fine mansion called **De Wildeman,** which was modified in the 19C. It houses an interesting collection of paintings, sculptures and graphics by contemporary Dutch artists.
It includes the portrait of *Queen Wilhelmina* aged 10 by Mari Andriessen, and a *Portrait of a Child* by T. Sondaar-Dobbelmann.
On the 2nd floor in a secret chapel (1628), where Catholics took refuge, there is a 16C *Adoration of the Magi* from Jan van Scorel's workshop.

Houtmarkt. – On this old wood market stands **Wijnhuis Tower** (Wijnhuistoren), a slender
⊙ 17C Renaissance tower, which has a **carillon,** restored by the Hemony brothers.
A market is held here on Thursdays.

⊙**Municipal Museum (Stedelijk Museum) (M²).** – Installed in a secularized Dominican convent, it has a pretty garden on its south side, overlooked by the old convent church. On the ground floor there is clockwork, glassware, gold and silversmiths' work and paintings.
Note also a view of Zutphen and the IJssel attributed to Barent Avercamp, nephew of the famous painter, Hendrick Avercamp, whose style he imitated.
The 1st floor is devoted to temporary exhibitions. On the 2nd floor, there are varied collections concerning the town and its region (costumes 1780-1950, furnishings).
In the cellars are a lapidary museum, pottery and various finds discovered during excavations.

ADDITIONAL SIGHT

Berkel Gate (Berkelpoort). – A 15C watergate of brick, flanked by bartizans with arches spanning the Berkel. There is a good **view** of it from the footbridge to the west. Near the bridge, the **House of Lions** (Leeuwenhuisje) has a corbelled part supported by sculptured lions above the river.

EXCURSION

The old Zutphen county. – *44km - 27 miles to the southeast by the road to Winterswijk.*
Between Zutphen and the frontier lies the old Zutphen county, also called **Achterhoek,** an area of woods (conifers, oaks, beeches) and pastures crossed by quiet roads and fine forested avenues.

Vorden. – Pop 7 237. A small locality where two 19C **windmills** with hand-rails can be seen.
Vorden lies in the heart of the **eight manor-houses region** which lies hidden in the surrounding woods: Vorden, Hackfort, Kiefskamp, Wildenborch, Bramel, Onstein, Medler and Wiersse. In fact, in the region, there are a dozen of these small old brickbuilt manor-houses, mostly rebuilt in the 18C in a fairly austere style. They are witness to the interest of the great lords in these forested areas abounding with game. Many cannot be reached by car, but paths for pedestrians or bicycles marked *opengesteld* allow visitors to approach them.
The **Vorden Manor-house** (Kasteel Vorden) flanked by a crow-stepped square tower forms two wings on either side of an octagonal tower. It is now the town hall. Note the windows topped with shell-work.
The most imposing is **Hackfort** with two thick cylindrical towers. Next to it stands a **watermill** dating from about 1700.

Groenlo. – Pop 8 846. This is an old city watered by the Slinge and surrounded by the remains of ramparts. A famous beer is made here. The town surrendered to Prince Frederick Henry in 1627 only after a month's siege.
⊙ It has a small **regional museum** (Grolsch Museum), installed in a 17C farmhouse; it contains regional costumes, funerary urns, coins, etc.

Winterswijk. – Pop 27 937. This town, crossed by the Slinge, is near a peaceful wooded area, with big isolated farmhouses in a style close to that of the Twente farmhouses *(p 31).*

Each year
*the **Michelin Red Guide Benelux***
revises its selection of stars for cuisine (good cooking)
accompanied by a mention of the culinary specialities
and proposes a choice of simpler restaurants offering
a well prepared meal, often with regional specialities for a moderate price.

ZWOLLE Overijssel P

Michelin map 408 fold 12
Plan of built-up area in the current Michelin Red Guide Benelux

Pop 89 348

Zwolle has kept its special character inside its ring of canals.

HISTORICAL NOTES

It was a member of the Hanseatic League *(qv)* in the 13C, linked to the Zuiderzee by the Zwarte Water, and for a long time it remained the depot for traffic between the Netherlands and northern Germany.

After the Spaniards left in 1572, its 15C curtain wall was considerably strengthened due to its strategic position. The wall was destroyed in 1674 during the Third Dutch War and little remains apart from the Saxon Gate in the south and in the north Rode Tower, which was truncated in 1845. Today the ditches still surround the town and the pleasant gardens on the south and east sides mark the line of the ramparts and bastions.

Zwolle was, from 1810 to 1814, the main town of the French *département* of the Bouches-de-l'Yssel.

Thomas à Kempis (1379/80-1471), who was a pupil at the School of the Brethren of the Common Life in Deventer, and to whom is attributed the *Imitatio Christi (Imitation of Christ)* lived in a convent to the north of the town (in Agnietenberg).

Gerard Terborch or Ter Borch (1617-81) was born in Zwolle. This painter, like his contemporary Gerrit Dou *(qv)*, is above all the dignified and meticulous painter of cultivated and peaceful interior scenes where young women wear shiny satin dresses; he also made excellent portraits and minatures of notable people.

Zwolle has several industries (graphics, automobile, electro-technical, food and clogs).

The town's specialities are *zwolse balletjes,* sweets shaped like a small cushion with different flavours, and *blauwvingers,* shortbread in the form of fingers with chocolate tips.

ZWOLLE

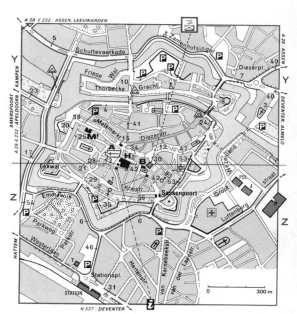

SIGHTS

★ **Overijssel Museum (Provinciaal Overijssels Museum) (YM¹).** – It has been set out in a 16C patrician residence where the roof is hidden behind an 18C balustrade, abundantly decorated with coats of arms and carved figures in the rococo style.

The refined interior with furniture from the 16 to 18C and well presented collections (ceramics, etc) is witness to the town's rich past. There is a remarkable collection of silverware from the Overijssel Province.

Great Church or St Michael's (Grote- of St.-Michaëlskerk) (Y A). – It is a hall-church with three naves, dating from the 14 and 15C, of Protestant worship. Unlike the neighbouring church of Our Lady, it does not possess the traditional great bell tower, which was the victim of successive disasters.

Inside note a remarkable early 17C carved pulpit and an organ loft of 1721. The organ is excellent. It was made by the **Schnitger** brothers *(qv)*, sons of a well-known German organ builder, who lived in Groningen; it has 4 000 pipes. There is also a small 17C clock with a statue of St Michael which makes a movement every half hour.

Attached to the left side of the fine 16C north portal there is a picturesque little building with a decorated pediment: the **Hoofdwacht** or guard room.

ZWOLLE

◷ **Town Hall (Stadhuis) (YZ H)**. – Beside the old building (15 and 19C) which had become too small, a new one has been built by the architect J.J. Konijnenburg.

The façades are punctuated by types of concrete buttresses on top of which appear a series of pointed red roofs. Inside the play of volumes and materials, and the arrangement of furniture make for a functional as well as aesthetic use of space.

The old part on the left, covered with mustard-yellow roughcast contains the **Aldermen's Hall** (Schepenzaal) dating from 1448. This old court room, now used for marriages, has a ceiling whose beams are held by 14 corbels with **sculptures★** depicting grotesque figures. Legend has it that the artists of Zwolle, rival town of Kampen, carved these heads to hold the governors of Kampen up to ridicule.

Note the brass chandeliers, and the small cupboards with locks fixed in the wall.

Above the 16C fireplace there is a picture of the *Last Judgment,* which is a reminder of the rooms original use.

On the terrace in front of the town hall there is a statue of *Adam* by Rodin.

The House of Charles V (Karel V-huis) (YZ B). – A medallion of Charles V's head can be seen on the gable, giving his name to this house built in 1571, which has a fine Renaissance façade decorated with pilasters, carved friezes and a voluted gable above which are recumbent gods.

Saxon Gate (Sassenpoort) (Z). – Built *c*1406, this gateway is the only one which still exists from the fortified town wall. Of red brick, it is flanked by four octagonal pointed turrets and topped by a spire.

Practical information

BEFORE STARTING

Tourist offices. – Before leaving consult the **Netherlands Board of Tourism** (NBT).

London : NBT, 25-28 Buckingham Gate, S.W. 1E 6LD; ☎ (01)-630-0451.

USA : **East Coast**: NBT, 355 Lexington Avenue, New York, NY, 10017; ☎ (212) 370-7367;
West Coast: NBT, 90 New Montgomery Street, San Francisco, Ca, 94105; ☎ (415) 543-6773;
Middle West: NBT, 225 North Michigan Avenue, Suite 326, Chicago III, 60601; ☎ (312) 819-0300.

Canada : NBT, 25 Adelaide Street East, Suite 710, Toronto, Ont, M5C 1Y2; ☎ (416) 363-1577.

Paris : NBT, 31-33 Avenue des Champs Elysées, 75008 Paris; ☎ (0) 1-42 25 41 25 (closed Saturdays).

Brussels: : NBT, Rue Ravenstein 68, 1000 Brussels; ☎ (0) 1-2-512-44-09.

In the Netherlands the **tourist information centres** are indicated by **i** or by **VVV** (Vereniging voor Vreemdelingenverkeer) (3 blue V's on a white triangle). They provide tourist information and a hotel booking service over the whole country.
The addresses of Netherland's main tourist offices are found in the Michelin Red Guide Benelux.

Currency. – The Dutch unit of currency is the guilder (abbreviated to fl) and it is composed of 100 cents: *stuiver* (5 cents), *dubbeltje* (10 cents), *kwartje* (25 cents), *guilder* (100 cents) *rijksdaalder* (2.50fl). There are no Dutch customs restrictions or special regulations regarding modest amounts of currency which may be taken into or brought out of the country. Special permission through a bank is required for large amounts. International credit cards are widely accepted.
British regulations are subject to alteration; enquire at your bank or travel agency. In January 1990 the rate of exchange was 3,15fl to £ 1 and 1,92fl to $ 1.

PASSPORTS, CUSTOMS, INSURANCE

Consulates. – **GB**: Postbus 548, 1007 AL Amsterdam, Koningslaan 44; ☎ (020) 76 43 43.
USA: Museumplein 19, 1017 DJ Amsterdam; ☎ (020) 79 03 21.
Canada: Sophialaan 7, 2514 JP Den Haag; ☎ (070) 61 41 11.

As administrative and customs formalities are subject to variation, those of you intending to visit the Netherlands should consult your local NBT or consulate.

EEC countries. – For visitors staying less than 3 months: a valid national identity card or passport is sufficient; no visa required.

USA and Canada. – For visitors staying less than 3 months: a valid passport; no visa required.

For the car, boats... . – **Private vehicles:** a valid registration certificate and if the vehicle is over 3 years old the current Test Certificate; a valid driving licence and/or an international driving licence; a certificate of Motor Insurance and Green Card, stating persons entitled to drive the car and nationality plate (USA, GB...).
As this information is subject to variation, we suggest you consult the Automobile Association or Royal Automobile Club or other motoring association for the latest information.
Cats and dogs: valid anti-rabies vaccination certificate given at least 30 days earlier.
Boats: no document is required for a tourist boat. If the boat enters the Netherlands by water one must go through customs at the nearest port (also on leaving).
Caravans: no formality is required provided one can produce a valid registration certificate.
Mopeds: the minimum age to ride a moped is 16. Helmets are obligatory, not only for the rider but also for any passenger. For mopeds the maximum speed in built-up areas is 30km/h - 19 mph and 40km/h - 25 mph outside them.

Insurance. – If you are a member of an international automobile club you can receive assistance. For information telephone ANWB (Royal Dutch Touring Club) in The Hague (070) 14 14 14.
Medical care given to EEC countries, insurance form E 110, E 111 or E 112 and with an international insurance form (make several copies).

Customs Offices. – At major points of entry they are usually open day and night.

HOW TO GET TO THE NETHERLANDS

By air. – Most major airlines (KLM, Air France, Pan Am, American Airlines, British Midlands...) fly directly into Schiphol Airport. Consult your local travel agency.

By sea. – From Great Britain ferries from Harwich to Hoek van Holland (Sealink/Zeeland Steamship Company); Hull to Rotterdam Europoort (North Sea Ferries); Sheerness to Flushing (Olau Line (UK) LTD); Great Yarmouth to Scheveningen (Norfolk Line). For address and telephone number of shipping company consult the current Michelin Red Guide Benelux.

By rail. – Booklets published in English available at information counters of main stations.

A FEW PRICES (autumn 1989)

florins

Petrol (per liter)	**1,62**
Petrol-super (per liter)	**1,69**
Oil (per liter)	**10,00**
Garage (overnight)	**9,00**
Postage:	
letters Western Europe	**0,75**
USA and Canada	**1,30**
post cards Western Europe	**0,55**
USA and Canada	**0,75**
Coffee, tea	**2,00-1,75**
Half pint of beer	**2,25**
Cigarettes (25 cigarettes)	**4,25**
Packet of pipe tobacco (50g)	**4,50**
Cigarillos (box of 20)	**8,00**
English or American newspaper	**3,00**
Cinema ticket (average price)	**12,00**
Theatre ticket (average price)	**30,00**
Local telephone call from call box	**0,25**
Tram, bus, subway (Amsterdam): "Strippenkaart"	**8,85**
Taxi fare (in town)	**3,80 + 2,40 per km**
Camping one night (family of 5 persons + car, caravan or tent)	**24,00**

ACCOMMODATIONS

Hotels and restaurants. – Consult the current Michelin Red Guide Benelux. Reservations can be made by contacting the Netherlands Reservation Centre (NRC), Postbus 404, 2260 AK Leidschendam; ☎ (070) 202500 or through the local VVV office (sign reads: –i– Nederland). Room will be paid to the VVV with a slight surcharge (commission).

Camping and caravanning. – Tourist information centres (VVV) supply a list of camping sites. They are officially classed from 1 to 4 stars (ANWB classification) corresponding to the nature and comfort of the site and private camping sites. Camping outside recognised sites is not allowed.

Youth hostels. – There are about 50 in all which are open all year round; you must be a member of a youth hostel organisation or hold an international youth hostel card. Apply to Stichting Nederlandse Jeugdherberg Centrale, Prof. Tulpplein 4, 1018 GX Amsterdam; ☎ (020) 551 31 33.

Hotels for the young. – The NBT has a leaflet with addresses of these hotels located in the country.

Electric current. – The usual voltage is 220; outlets standard European 2-prong. Remember to bring an adapter.

Tipping. – A service charge of 15%, V.A.T. (B.T.W.) and in certain areas the tourist tax *(toeristenbelasting)* are generally included in the bill. It is customary to give the waiter a tip for small services.

HELPFUL HINTS

Time. – The Netherlands, like the other Benelux countries, is in the Central European time zone; during the summer months the clocks are advanced 1 hour.

Working hours. – Usual opening times are as follows:

Banks: from 9am to 4 or 5pm; closed Saturdays and Sundays. Exchange offices (GWK) are open Mondays to Saturdays 8am to 8pm; Sundays 10am to 4pm (often located in railway stations); some department stores have exchange offices open Saturday mornings.

Post offices: from 9am to 5 or 6pm; closed Saturdays (except the morning in large towns) and Sundays.

Shops: from 8.30 or 9am to 5.30 or 6pm (earlier on Saturdays); closed Sundays and often Monday mornings. Most shops close once a week for one morning, afternoon or whole day.

Public holidays. – 1 January, Easter Sunday and Monday, 30 April (Queen's Day), Ascension Day, Whitsun and Whit Monday, 5 May (Liberation Day – every 5 years: 1990), 25 and 26 December.
In addition a local holiday, for example Carnival in the south *(p 197)*, can also cause different opening and closing times, enquire locally.

TOURISM FOR THE HANDICAPPED

Some of the sights described in this guide are accessible to handicapped people. The NBT offers a special brochure for the physically handicapped.
The **Michelin Red Guide Benelux** indicates rooms and facilities suitable for physically handicapped people.
Access to the Channel Ports (obtainable from Pauline Hephaistos Survey Projects, 39 Bradley Gardens, West Ealing, London W13 8H3) is a holiday guide for the physically handicapped.

MOTORING IN THE NETHERLANDS

Motorways. – The country has 1 905km - 1 189 miles of motorways *(Autosnelweg)* always free of charge. There are also numerous roads reserved for automobiles *(autoweg, sign of a white car on a blue background)* but they have crossroads, contrary to motorways.

Speed limits. – It is 120km/h - 74mph on motorways and *autoweg,* 100km/h - 62mph near large cities and certain sections of the motorway, 80km/h - 50mph on other roads and 50km/h - 31mph in built-up areas.

Accidents and breakdown services. – Wearing a **seat belt** is obligatory.
On most motorways **S.O.S. call boxes** are for drivers in difficulty. There are also ANWB (Alarmcentrale) telephone booths ☏ (070) 141414, people on call speak several languages.
In the case of a breakdown, one can be helped by the **road patrol** services *(Wegenwacht)* by telephoning 06-0888 (day and night) or by using the call boxes on the motorways.

Overtaking and priority. – Driving is on the **right**. At crossroads priority should be given to vehicles approaching from the right. The rule for roundabouts are: go round anticlockwise and allow priority to incoming traffic. Tramways can only be passed on the right, unless the space available is insufficient. They generally have priority.
Care should be taken with cyclists who often overtake on the right, and have priority over motorists who are changing direction.

Tourist routes. – The ANWB has marked out about 40 routes for cars. Indicated by hexagonal signposts, these routes (same word in Dutch) cover the most picturesque regions, each linking up main centres of interest in a tour of 80 to 150km – 50 to 94 miles.
A leaflet showing these routes and their main sights is on sale at the **ANWB** headquarters (Koninklijke Nederlandsche Toeristenbond, i.e. the Royal Dutch Touring Club, Wassenaarseweg 220, Postbus 93200, 2509 BA Den Haag) or in the touring club offices which exist in other towns in the country; price 2.50fl.
Other tourist routes are due to local initiative.

BICYCLING IN THE NETHERLANDS

There are about 11.7 million bicycles in the Netherlands (that is 2 bikes per 3 inhabitants) as well as 564 000 mopeds. Highways and roads are, therefore, very busy with cyclists, particularly at rush hour.

Cycle tracks. – The country is remarkably well equipped with cycle tracks (about 13 500km - 8 389 miles) which helps traffic as motorists can often use lanes reserved for them, in the same way as cyclists.

Road signs. – There are various different road signs, knowledge of which can be useful to both the motorist and cyclist:
– blue circular sign with a bicycle painted in white: obligatory track for cyclists and motorcyclists. It usually runs alongside the motorist's road.
– rectangular sign stating **Fietspad**: optional cyclist's track, forbidden to motorbikes.
– sign stating **Fietsers oversteken**: route or crossing for cyclists and motorcyclists, who should be careful of cars and drivers, who risk being surprised when seeing cycles emerging from a cycling track on to a roadway where they had no access before.

Hiring. – An office for hiring bikes can be found in most large **railway stations** (more than 100 stations). It is indicated by a blue and white square sign. *Price 2.75fl for 2 hours or 7fl per day.*
In towns, apart from numerous shops specialising in hiring, certain repair workshops have bicycles for hire *(fietsverhuur). Price: 10fl per day plus 200fl deposit.*
The bikes rarely have gear changes. Many have the traditional braking system by back-pedalling: it works by pushing on the pedals backwards which stops the movement of the back wheel. This system which is efficient but not very subtle, can surprise inexperienced foreigners.

Cycling tours. – The ANWB has marked out about a hundred tours from 25 to 50km - 15½ to 31 miles for bicycles *(fietsen)* and mopeds *(bromfietsen)* or for bicycles only. The tours are indicated either by blue rectangular road signs which have, in white, a hexagonal sign with a bicycle, like that used for motorists or by hexagonal white signs with indications in red. There is a leaflet for each tour.
In addition the ANWB, in collaboration with the Stichting Fiets association, edits 17 guides for cyclists, most of them including tours.

RAMBLING

The Staatsbosbeheer edits with the ANWB pamphlets called Voetspoorkaarten indicating footpaths and their characteristics.

WATERSPORTS AND FISHING

Watersports Federation: Koninklijk Nederlands Watersport Verbond, Van Eeghenstraat 94, Postbus 53034, 1007 RA Amsterdam, ☎ (020) 664 26 11.

A **pamphlet on watersports** is edited annually (enquire at local VVV or NBT office). Water charts published by the ANWB *(p 3)* or the Netherlands Hydrographic Service can be obtained by going through the ANWB.

Addresses of **sailing and windsurfing schools** are listed in a pamphlet available from the ANWB or the Watersports Federation *(see above)*.

For information concerning **angling** (permit, fishing season, etc) apply to the Nederlandse Vereniging van Sportvissersfederaties, Postbus 288, 3800 AG Amersfoort, ☎ (033) 63 49 24.

BOOKS TO READ

This is not an exhaustive list; some, which may be out of print will be available only in libraries. Exhibition catalogues have not been cited, they can be found in most large museum bookstores.

Of Dutch Ways by Helen Colijn (Harper & Row)

Holland by Adam Hopkins (Faber and Faber)

The Low Countries: History of the Northern and Southern Netherlands by J.A. Kossmann-Putto and E.H. Kossmann *(Flemish-Netherlands Foundation "Stichting ons Erfdeel VZW")*

The British and the Dutch by K.H.D. Haley *(George Philip)*

Dutch Painting by R.H. Fuchs *(Thames and Hudson)*

Dutch Art and Architecture: 1600-1800 by Jakob Rosenberg, Seymour Slive and E.H. ter Kuile *(Pelican History of Art)*

Guide to Dutch Art *(Ministry of Education, Arts and Sciences)*

Through the Dutch and Belgian Canals by Philip Bristow *(Nautical Books)*

The Pocket Guide to the Zuyder Zee Project by R.H.A. van Duin and G. de Kaste *(S. Schmidt-ter Neuzen)*

PRINCIPAL FESTIVALS (1)

Listed below are the most important festivals; others will be found, under the locality (see index). A detailed calendar of festivals appears in leaflets produced annually by the VVV (tourist information centres).

In February or March during Lent

Breda	**Carnival★**
Bergen op Zoom	Carnival
Eindhoven	Carnival
Venlo	Carnival
's-Hertogenbosch	Carnival
Maastricht	**Carnival★**
Sittard	Carnival

Late March to mid or late May

Keukenhof ... **National Floral Exhibition★★★** *(p 73)*

1 April (Saturday before if the 1st is a Sunday)

Brielle ... Historical Festival *(p 72)*

Mid-April to mid-September, Fridays

Alkmaar ... **Cheese Market★★** *(p 38)*

Last (or next to last) Saturday in April

Haarlem-Noordwijk ... Procession of floral floats *(p 72)*

Saturday before Whitsun

Exloo ... Shepherd's Feast *(p 132)*

June

Amsterdam, The Hague ... **Holland Festival★** (concerts, opera, ballet, theatre). To reserve apply to: Holland Festival, Kleine Gartmanplantsoen 21, 1071 RP Amsterdam; ☎ (020) 27 65 66 or to large travel agencies abroad

Early June

Dokkum ... St Boniface Pilgrimage *(p 84)*

Mid-June to late September

Tegelen ... Passion Plays *(1990; every 5 years) (p 181)*

Late June to late August, Thursdays

Schagen ... Market: Westfriese Markt

July

The Hague ... North Sea Jazz Festival

Haarlem ... International Organ Competition (even years only: 1st week in July) ☎ (023) 17 12 13 *(p 109)*

Kerkrade ... International Music Competition (1993: every 4 years) *(p 122)*

Early July to late August, Wednesdays

Hoorn ... Market 10am to 5pm *(p 129)*

Third Sunday in July

Exloo ... Ancient Handicrafts Festival *(p 132)*

July or August (2 weeks)

Frisian Lakes ... Regattas: *Skûtsjesilen (p 167)*

Early July to early August, Thursdays

Barneveld 408 fold 11 ... Old Veluwe Market

July, August, Saturday afternoons

Kinderdijk ... Windmill Days *(p 165)*

Late July-early August, Wednesday evenings

Markelo ... Country wedding *(p 82)*

Early August

Sneek ... Sneekweek Regattas *(p 167)*

---

(1) The fold on Michelin map 408 is given for all places listed pp 197-198 not mentioned in this guide.

1st Saturday in August **Rijnsburg** 408 fold 10 - **Noordwijk**	Procession of floral floats
Late August **Breda**	Taptoe: Military Music Festival *(p 68)*
Late August-early September **Utrecht** .... **Harlingen**	Festival of Ancient Music *(p 171)* Fishing Days *(p 121)*
1st Saturday in September **Aalsmeer-Amsterdam**	Procession of floral floats *(approximately 9am to 4pm) (p 72)*
1st Sunday in September **Zundert** 408 fold 17	Procession of floral floats
2nd Saturday in September **Tiel**	Harvest Fruit Parade *(2pm) (p 170)*
3rd Tuesday in September **The Hague**	Golden coach ride *(p 113)*
4th Wednesday in September **Odoorn**	Sheep market *(p 132)*
3 October (following Monday if the 3rd is a Sunday) **Leyden**	Leidens Ontzet: historical procession *(p 140)*
1st Wednesday in October **Leeuwarden**	Show of prize bulls *(p 136)*
Mid-October **Delft**	Antique Fair *(p 76)*
3rd Saturday after 5 December **Amsterdam**	St Nicholas's official entrance *(Prins Hendrik-kade) (p 43)*
From 1st Sunday of Advent to Epiphany **Denekamp**	Blowing of *midwinterhorens (p 95)*

Sports Competition

Automobile and motorcycle races. – Grand Prix of the Netherlands Formula 1 *(p 111)* is the most famous automobile competition in the country.
In Assen, in June, the Motorcycle Dutch Grand Prix *(p 65)* is held.
Cross-country motorcycling is very popular and races on ice are held in ice skating rinks.

Bicycle races. – The National Bicycle Day is held every year in May. The tour of 11 Friesland towns (depart from Bolsward) is held Whit Monday; Drenthe's 4 Days is held in July and Nijmegen's 4 Days (Fietsvierdaagse) is held in late July.

Water sports competition. – Throughout the country different water sports activities are held. The most spectacular are the **skûtsjesilen**, *skûtsjes* regattas on the Frisian Lakes *(qv)*. Among the other activities are Delta Week in June and Sneekweek *(p 167)* and National Surf Day.

Walking. – The 4-Day Walking Tour takes place in Apeldoorn (mid-July) and in Nijmegen (3rd week in July). The Frisian 11 Town Walking Tour lasts 5 days (depart from Leeuwarden) between mid-May and early June.

Traditional sports. – Archers Processions *(boogschieten)* are held the 1st Sunday in July in the Limburg.
Those who like ball games can watch **kaatsen** held in Frisian villages (early May-late September; important meets in August).
The annual pole vaulting *(polsstokspringen)* is held in Winsum (10km - 6 miles southwest of Leeuwarden) in August.

Times and charges for admission

Every sight for which there are times and charges listed below is indicated by the symbol ⊘ in the margin in the main part of the guide.

Due to the fluctuations in the cost of living and the constant change in the opening times, the information below is given only as a general indication.

The prices quoted below apply to individual adults with no reductions; charges for admission are given in florins (abbreviated to fl).

Groups should apply in advance in writing or at least telephone ahead; many places have special days for groups; many offer special rates for advanced bookings.

Churches are not visited during services. Opening and closing times are given only if they are limited and when the church's interior is worth visiting.

Enquire at the tourist information centre (VVV; for telephone number see the current Michelin Red Guide Benelux) for local religious holidays, market days etc.

When guided tours are indicated, the departure time of the last tour of the morning or afternoon will be up to an hour before the actual closing time. Most tours are conducted by Dutch speaking guides but in some cases the term "guided tours" may cover groups visiting with recorded commentaries. Some of the larger and more frequented sights may offer guided tours in other languages. Enquire at the ticket office or book stall. Other aids for the foreign tourist are notes, pamphlets or audio-guides.

Lecture tours are given regularly during the tourist season in Amsterdam, Breda, Groningen, The Hague, Leeuwarden, Leyden, Maastricht, Rotterdam and Utrecht. Apply to the tourist information centre.

The following opening times have been simplified. Open daily means open all the year round. When there is no mention of mornings or afternoons this means it is open all day without a lunch-time break. When telephone numbers are given, the local dialling code is indicated in brackets before hand.

a

AALSMEER

Flower Auction. – Open mornings only as of 7.30am; closed Saturdays, Sundays and holidays; 3fl.

AARDENBURG

St Bavo. – Open early April to late September mornings and afternoons; the rest of the year afternoons (2 to 4pm); closed Tuesdays; ☎ (01177) 1234.

ADUARD

Reformed Church. – Guided tours ($\frac{1}{2}$ hour) mornings and afternoons (Tuesdays afternoons only); closed Saturdays, Sundays and religious holidays; donation; ☎ (05903) 1724; apply to Burgemeester Seinenstraat 11.

ALKMAAR

Boat Trips. – Apply to Rederij Woltheus, Ark (boat) d'Elmara, Kanaalkade, opposite no 62; ☎ (072) 11 48 40.

Cheese Market. – Takes place mid-April to mid-September 10am to noon Fridays only; ☎ (072) 11 42 84.

Weigh House: Museum of Dutch Cheese. – Open early April to late October daily; closed Sundays; 2fl; ☎ (072) 11 42 84.

Town Hall. – Guided tours ($\frac{1}{2}$ hour) mornings and afternoons; closed Saturdays, Sundays and holidays as well as 8 October, 30 April and 5 May.

Great Church or St Lawrence's. – Open June, July and August only 10am to 3pm; 1fl.

Municipal Museum. – Open daily; closed mornings Sundays and holidays as well as all day Saturday, 1 January, Easter Sunday, Whitsun, and 25 December; 2fl; ☎ (072) 11 07 37.

Times and charges

ALLINGAWIER

Farmhouse. – Open daily early April to late October; 2.50fl; ☎ (05158) 1736.

ALPHEN AAN DE RIJN

Avifauna. – Open daily; 5fl. **Boat trips:** (1½ hours) Easter to mid-September as from noon, Sundays and holidays as from 10.30am; 4.50fl; for reservations apply ☎ (01720) 31106.

AMELAND see at Wadden Islands

AMERONGEN

Castle. – Open daily early April to late October; closed Saturday, Sunday and holiday mornings and all day Mondays; 5fl; ☎ (03434) 54212.

AMERSFOORT

Tower of Our Lady. – Open daily July to September; closed Sunday and holiday mornings and all day Monday; 1.50fl; ☎ (033) 635151.

St George's. – Open daily early June to early September; closed Sundays; 2fl; ☎ (033) 610441.

Antiques Market. – In Groenmarkt. Open early May to late August Saturdays only; closed holidays; ☎ (033) 635151.

Pewter Foundry. – In Kamperbinnen Gate west turret. Open daily Thursdays to Saturdays; closed holidays; ☎ (033) 635151.

Koppel Gate. – Open daily July and August; closed Saturday, Sunday and holiday mornings and all day Monday; ☎ (033) 635151. **Puppet Theatre:** Wednesdays and Saturdays 2.30pm; closed July and August; ☎ (033) 619629.

Flehite Museum. – Open daily; closed Saturday and Sunday mornings and all day Mondays and holidays; 2.50fl; ☎ (033) 619987.

AMSTERDAM

Taxi-boats. – ☎ (020) 750909.

Hiring of Bicycles. – Heja on Bestevaerstraat 39; Amstelstation on Julianaplein 1; Damstraat Rent A Bike on Pieter Jacobsz. Dwarsstraat 11; Macbike on Nieuw Uilenburgerstraat 116; ☎ (020) 266444.

Diamond Cutting Workshops. – About 15 workshops are open to tourists; apply to the tourist information centre.

Boat Trip. – Landing stages: indicated on the brochure "Cruising in Amsterdam"; trip time varies: 1 hour - 1½ hours; charge varies 8.50fl - 33fl; for information apply to the tourist information centre.

Royal Palace. – Open 1 week at Easter, early June to late August and the 1st or 2nd week in October 12.30 to 4pm; guided tours (1 hour) Wednesdays 2pm; 2.50fl; ☎ (020) 248698.

New Church. – Open 11am to 4pm; Sundays and holidays afternoons only; closed January and February; ☎ (020) 268168.

Museum of Amsterdam History. – Open daily 11am to 5pm; closed 1 January; 3.50fl; ☎ (020) 5231822.

Madame Tussaud's. – Open daily; 9.75fl, children 6.25fl; ☎ (020) 229949.

Mint Tower: Carillon. – **Concerts:** Fridays noon to 1pm.

Flower Market. – Open daily; closed Sundays and holidays.

Rijksmuseum. – Open daily 10am to 5pm; Sundays and holidays 1 to 5pm; closed Mondays (except holiday Mondays); 6.50fl; ☎ (020) 732121.

Vincent van Gogh National Museum. – Open daily; closed Sunday and holiday mornings and all day Monday; 6.50fl.

Municipal Museum. – Open daily 11am to 5pm; closed 1 January; 7fl.

Vondel Park. – Partly illuminated in season.

Amstelkring Museum "Our Lord in the Attic". – Guided tours (¾ hour) daily; closed Sunday and holiday mornings and 1 January; 3.50fl; ☎ (020) 246604.

Old Church. – Open daily Easter to October 11.30am to 4.30pm; the rest of the year 1 to 3pm; closed Sundays and holidays; 1fl; ☎ (020) 249183.

Rembrandt's House. – Open daily and holidays; closed Sunday mornings and 1 January; 3.50fl; ☎ (020) 249486.

Flea Market and Antique Market. – Both on Waterlooplein. **Antique Market:** Sundays mid-May to mid-September. **Flea Market:** open daily; closed Sundays.

Museum of Jewish History. – Open daily 11am to 5pm; closed Yom Kippur; 5fl; ☎ (020) 269945.

Portuguese Synagogue. – Open Easter to October mornings and afternoons (closed Sunday afternoons); the rest of the year guided tours (1 hour) only; closed Saturdays, holidays and Jewish holidays; 2.50fl; ☏ (020) 245 351.

Zuider Church Tower. – Entrance via Zandstraat. Open early June to mid-October Wednesdays 2 to 5pm; Thursdays and Fridays 11am to 2pm (4pm Saturdays); closed Sundays, Mondays and holidays; 1fl.

Allard Pierson Museum. – Open daily; closed Saturday, Sunday and holiday mornings, all day Monday, 1 January, and 30 April; 3.50fl; ☏ (020) 525 25 56.

Magere Bridge. – Illuminated at night all year round.

Anne Frank's House. – Open daily; closed 1 January, Yom Kippur and 25 December; 5fl; ☏ (020) 26 45 33.

Wester Church. – Closed temporarily for restoration.

Theatre Museum. – Open daily 11am to 5pm; closed Mondays, 1 January, 30 April and 25 December; 2.50fl; ☏ (020) 23 51 04.

Willet-Holthuysen Museum. – Open daily 11am to 5pm; closed 1 January; 1.75fl; ☏ (020) 523 1822.

Van Loon Museum. – Open all day Monday only; 5fl; ☏ (020) 24 52 55.

Fodor Museum. – Open daily 11am to 5pm; closed 1 January; 1fl; ☏ (020) 24 99 19.

Bible Museum. – Open daily; closed Sunday and holiday mornings and all day Monday, 1 January and 30 April; 3fl; ☏ (020) 24 24 36.

Concert Hall. – Sundays 11am to noon; 6fl.

Fruit and Vegetable Market. – Open Saturdays 10am to 3pm.

Artis. – Open daily; 15fl, children 8fl; ☏ (020) 523 34 00.

Tropical Museum. – Open daily; Saturdays, Sundays and holidays as of noon; closed 1 January, 30 April, 5 May and 25 December; 6fl, children 3fl; ☏ (020) 56 88 295.

Netherlands Maritime History Museum. – Open daily; closed Sunday and holiday mornings, all day Monday and 1 January; 5fl; ☏ (020) 52 32 222.

APELDOORN

Steam Train. – Departures twice a day early July to late August and Whitsun and fall term holidays; closed Sunday mornings and all day Saturday; 14fl Rtn; ☏ (055) 78 84 21 (Apeldoorn tourist information centre).

Het Loo Palace Museum. – Palace, gardens and park open daily; **East Wing, West Wing** (Museum of the Chancery of the Netherlands Orders of Knighthood) **and stables** afternoons only; **video film show** (25 min) in English early April to late October; closed Mondays (except holiday Mondays and 25 December; 7fl, children 5fl; **concerts:** last Friday of every month at 8.15pm; telephone for reservations ☏ (055) 21 22 44.

Marialust Historical Museum. – Open daily; closed Sunday and holiday mornings and all day Monday, 1 January, Easter Sunday, Whitsun and 25 December; ☏ (055) 21 61 29.

APPINGEDAM

Church. – Open daily mid-June to mid-September; closed Sundays and Mondays; ☏ (05960) 23313.

ARNHEM

Boat Trips. – Apply to Rederij Heymen, Kantoorschip (boat) Rijnkade.

Netherlands Open-Air Museum. – Open daily early April to late October; 7fl, children 4fl; ☏ (085) 57 61 11.

Great Church or St Eusebius. – To visit and for concert dates apply to the tourist information centre; ☏ (085) 420 330.

Municipal Museum. – Open daily 10am (11am Sundays and holidays) to 5pm; holidays closing times vary; closed Mondays and 1 January; ☏ (085) 51 24 31.

Burgers' Zoo and Safari Park. – Open daily; 15fl, children 11fl; ☏ (085) 42 45 34.

ASSEN

Drenthe Museum. – Open daily; closed Saturday, Sunday and holiday mornings, Mondays all day (except school holiday Mondays), 1 January and 25 December; 1fl; ☏ (05920) 12741.

ASTEN

National Carillon Museum. – Open daily (as of noon Saturday, Sunday and holidays) closed all day Mondays, 1 January, Carnival and 25 December; 4.50fl; ☏ (04936) 1865.

Nature Museum. – Open daily; closed Mondays, 1 January, Carnival and 25 December; 4fl; ☏ (04936) 1865.

BEEKSE BERGEN

Safari Park. – Open daily late March to late October; 11.50fl; ☎ (013) 36 00 32.

Amusement Park. – Open daily late April to mid-September and fall school holidays; 7.50fl; ☎ (013) 36 00 32.

BERGEN

Noordhollands Duin Nature Reserve. – Open sunrise to sunset; 1.50fl; ☎ (02208) 13100.

BERGEN AAN ZEE

Aquarium. – Open daily early April to late October; the rest of the year Saturdays, Sundays and school holidays 11am to 5pm; closed 25 December; 4.50fl, children 3.50fl; ☎ (02208) 12928.

BERG EN DAL

African Museum. – Open daily early April to late October; Saturdays, Sundays and holidays 11am to 5pm; the rest of the year Tuesdays to Sundays afternoons only; closed 25 December to 1 January; 5fl; ☎ (00095) 42044.

BERGEN OP ZOOM

Town Hall. – Open daily Mondays to Fridays; closed religious holidays, 1 January and 5 May; ☎ (01640) 66000.

Markiezenhof. – Open June to September 11am (2pm the rest of the year) to 5pm; closed Saturday, Sunday and holiday mornings, all day Monday, Easter Sunday, 25 December and 1 January; 3fl; ☎ (01640) 42930.

BIERUM

Church. – To visit apply to Mr. Van Heuvelen, Torenlaan 2; closed Sunday mornings.

BIESBOSCH National Park

Boat Trip. – Apply at: Drimmelen (Rederij de Zilvermeeuw, W. Vos, Avontuur and De Branding); Lage Zwaluwe (Rederij Biesboschtours); Geertruidenberg (Rederij De stad Geertruidenberg). Boats for hire in Biesbosch National Park.

BOLSWARD

Town Hall. – Open daily early July to late September; early April to late June and October mornings and afternoons; closed Saturdays, Sundays and holidays; 2fl; ☎ (05157) 3244.

St Martin's. – Open early April to late October mornings and afternoons by appointment only; apply to the sexton; closed Sundays and religious holidays; 2fl; ☎ (05157) 2274.

BORGER

National Hunebeds Information Centre. – Open daily early February to late October; Saturdays, Sundays and holidays afternoons only; 2.50fl; ☎ (05998) 36374.

BOZUM

Church. – To visit ring the doorbell.

BREDA

Great Church or Church of Our Lady. – Open daily early May to late October; Sundays afternoons only; the rest of the year apply to the church; ☎ (076) 21 82 67; 1.75fl; **carillon:** Tuesdays and Fridays, 10am in summer Saturday afternoons also; **organ concerts:** apply to the VVV.

Castle. – To visit apply to the VVV.

Ethnographical Museum. – Open daily; closed Sunday and holiday mornings and all day Monday; 3.50fl; ☎ (076) 47 22 10.

Town Hall. – Open daily; closed Saturdays, Sundays and holidays; ☎ (076) 24 20 75.

Municipal and Episcopal Museum. – Open daily Wednesdays to Saturdays; Sundays and Tuesdays 1 to 5pm; closed Mondays, 1 January and 25 December; 1.50fl; ☎ (076) 22 31 10.

De Beyerd. – Open daily; closed Saturday, Sunday and holiday mornings and all day Monday, 1 January, during Carnival, Easter Sunday, Whitsun and 25 December; 2fl; ☎ (076) 22 50 25.

Bouvigne Castle. – Open daily; closed Saturdays, Sundays and holidays; 0.75fl; ☎ (076) 63 10 00.

BRESKENS

Flushing Ferry. – Departure every ½ hour; only every hour Sundays; 7.50fl (car and driver), 5.25fl out of season.

BRIELLE

Tromp Museum. – Open daily Wednesdays to Saturdays; Mondays and Tuesdays open mornings and afternoons; closed Sundays and holidays; 0.50fl; ☎ (01810) 13 33 33.

Great Church or St Catherine's. – Open early June to late August mornings and afternoons, closed Saturday mornings; mid-May to early June and September afternoons only; closed Wednesdays; 1.50fl.

BROEK IN WATERLAND

Church. – Guided tour (½ hour), apply to the sexton at Leeteindre 2.

Cheese Dairy. – Open daily; closed Mondays and holidays; the best time to see the making of cheese is in the morning; ☎ (02903) 1454.

BOUVIGNE Castle see at BREDA

BROUWERSHAVEN

Church. – Open mid-May to mid-September Tuesdays to Saturdays 1.30 to 4.30pm; the rest of the year apply to Mrs. A. Rijnburg-Dalebout, Molenstraat 62.

BULBFIELDS

Airplane ride. – Time of trip: ¾ hour; apply at Luchtvaartmij. Kroonduif, Airport Zestienhoven, Rotterdam; 285fl for 3 people; ☎ (010) 415 7855.

Keukenhof. – Open late March to late May 8am to 6.30pm; 12.50fl, children 6fl; ☎ (02521) 19144.

Tulipshow. – Open daily late March to late May 8am to 6pm; 2fl; ☎ (02502) 7245.

BUREN

Marechaussee Museum. – Open daily late April to early October; Saturdays, Sundays and holidays afternoons only; closed Mondays; 3.50fl; ☎ (03447) 1256.

Cart Museum. – Open early May to early October 10am to 4pm (1.30 to 5pm Saturdays, Sundays and holidays); closed Mondays; 3.50fl; ☎ (03447) 1256.

c

CADIER EN KEER

African Museum. – Open daily afternoons only; closed Saturdays, 1 January and 25 December; 2fl; ☎ (04407) 1226.

CALLANTSOOG

Het Zwanewater. – Access: Zuidschinkeldijk 3. Open mid-March to late July 7am to 9pm; the rest of the year from sunrise to sunset; 1fl; ☎ (02248) 1467.

COEVORDEN

"Drenthe's Veste" Museum. – Open Mondays to Fridays mornings and afternoons; closed first Monday of the month and holidays; 1.25fl; ☎ (05240) 16225.

De CRUQUIUS see at HAARLEM

DELDEN

Twickel Castle Gardens. – Open mid-May to mid-October Wednesdays and Saturdays afternoons only; 3fl; ☎ (05407) 61300.

Salt Museum. – Open early May to late August Mondays to Fridays mornings and afternoons; September to April Tuesdays to Fridays afternoons only; closed Saturday (all day Saturday October to April) and Sunday mornings, Easter Sunday, Whitsun and 25 December; 2.50fl; ☎ (05407) 64546.

DELFT

Boat Trip on the Canals. – Departures every hour Easter to mid-October first departure at 10.30am, last departure 5.30pm; tour: $\frac{3}{4}$ hour; 6.50fl; ☎ (015) 12 63 85.

New Church. – Open Mondays to Fridays mornings and afternoons (4pm); all day Saturdays and mornings and afternoons holidays; closed Sundays; 2fl; ☎ (015) 12 30 25. **Access to the tower:** late April to early September daily Tuesdays to Saturdays; closed Sundays, Mondays (except mid-July to mid-August when also open) and holidays; 3.25fl.

Royal Netherlands Army Museum. – Open daily; closed Sunday and holiday mornings, all day Monday, 1 January, Easter Sunday, Whitsun and 25 December; 2fl; ☎ (015) 15 05 00.

Prinsenhof. – Open daily; closed Sunday mornings and all day Monday (except in June, July and August when open Monday afternoons, as well), 1 January, 25 December and days before exhibition opening; 3.50fl; ☎ (015) 60 23 57.

Old Church. – Open daily early April to early November; closed Sundays and holidays; 2fl; ☎ (015) 12 30 53.

Lambert van Meerten Museum. – Open daily; closed Sunday and holiday mornings and all day Monday (except in June, July and August when open Monday afternoons, as well), 1 January and 25 December; 3.50fl; ☎ (015) 60 23 58.

Nusantara Ethnographical Museum. – Same opening times and admissions fee as Lambert van Meerten Museum.

Paul Tetar van Elven Museum. – Guided tours (1 hour) May to October afternoons only; closed Sundays, Mondays and holidays; 2.50fl; ☎ (015) 13 22 67.

DELFZIJL

Boat Trips. – Apply to Mr. Duit Ripperdastraat 12 or to Mr Oosterveld, Menno Coendersbuurt 22, Termunterzijl.

DELTA

Delta Expo. – Open daily early April to late October; the rest of the year Wednesdays through Sundays only; closed 25 December; 10fl early April to late October (includes **boat tour**); 8fl the rest of the year (without boat tour); ☎ (01115) 2702.

DENEKAMP

Singraven Castle. – Guided tours (1 hour) Tuesdays to Fridays mid-April to late October 11am, 2, 3 and 4pm; closed holidays; 6fl; ☎ (05413) 2088.

Water Mill. – Open mid-April to late October Tuesdays to Saturdays mornings and afternoons; 2.50fl; ☎ (05413) 1372.

DEVENTER

Boat Trips. – In season only. Apply to Rederij Scheers, Worp 39 and Rederij Eureka, Bolwerksweg 1.

Museum. – In the weigh house. Open daily; closed Sunday mornings (all day holiday Sundays) all day Monday (except holiday Mondays, when open afternoons); 2.50fl.

Toy Museum. – Open daily; closed Sunday and holiday mornings, all day Monday, 1 January, Easter Sunday, Whitsun and 25 December; 2.50fl, children 1fl; ☎ (05700) 93 786.

Town Hall. – Open mornings and afternoons; closed Saturdays, Sundays and holidays; ☎ (05700) 93311.

Great Church or St Lebuin's. – Open daily; closed Wednesday afternoons out of season, Saturdays, Sundays and holidays; ☎ (05700) 12548. **Carillon:** for times ☎ (05700) 12548. **Organ concerts:** for times ☎ (05700) 25080. **Access to the tower:** open early July to early September afternoons only; 2.25fl.

Library. – In Buiskensklooster. Open Tuesdays and Fridays all day; Mondays, Wednesdays and Thursdays (9pm) afternoons only; closed Saturdays, Sundays and holidays; ☎ (05700) 93887.

DOESBURG

Boat Trips. – In July and August; apply to the VVV.

Great Church or Martin Church. – Open late April to mid-September afternoons; closed Sundays. To climb the tower apply to the VVV. **Carillon:** Wednesdays 10am.

Museum. – In the town hall. Open mornings and afternoons; closed Saturday, Sunday and holiday mornings, all day Monday, 1 January and 25 December; 1.50fl; ☎ (08334) 74265.

Mustard Factory. – Open 10am (11am Saturdays) to 4pm; closed Sundays and holidays (except Easter Monday, open 11am to 4pm); 1.50fl; ☎ (08334) 72230.

DOKKUM

Admiralty House Museum. – Open daily early March to early October; the rest of the year afternoons only; closed Sundays and holidays; 2fl; ☏ (01590) 3134.

Great Church or St Martin's. – Open July and August afternoons only; if closed apply to the sexton (Koster) Mr. J. Huisman, Op de Fetze 6.

DOORN

Castle. – Open daily mid-March to early November; Sundays and holidays afternoons only; 4.50fl; ☏ (03430) 12244.

DOORNENBURG

Castle. – Guided tours for times apply to Mr. Derksen ☏ (08812) 1456.

DOORWERTH

Doorwerth Castle and **Netherlands Hunting Museum.** – Open early April to late October daily Tuesdays to Fridays and Saturdays, Sundays and holidays afternoons only; the rest of the year Saturdays, Sundays and holidays afternoons only; closed 1 January and 25 December; 5fl; ☏ (085) 33 53 75.

DORDRECHT

Boat Trips. – For information (hours of departure) and reservations apply to Bezoekerscentrum "De Hollandse Biesbosch", Baanhoekweg 53, 3313 LP Dordrecht; ☏ (078) 21 13 11.

Great Church or Church of Our Lady. – Open early April to late October 10.30am to 4.30pm; closed Sunday mornings and all day Monday; ☏ (078) 14 46 60. **Carillon:** (1 hour) Fridays 11am, Saturdays 2pm; ☏ (01823) 3002. **Concerts:** in summer Thursdays 8pm. **Access to the tower:** November to April afternoons only (until 4pm); 1.50fl.

Simon van Gijn Museum. – Open daily; closed Sunday and holiday mornings, all day Monday 1 January and 25 December; 2.50fl; ☏ (078) 13 37 93. **Organ concerts:** The 1st Sunday of the month at 2.30pm.

Museum of Dordrecht. – Same opening times as Simon van Gijn Museum; 5fl; ☏ (078) 13 41 00.

DRIELANDENPUNT

Boudewijn Tower. – Open daily March to late October; 2fl; ☏ (04454) 2918.

EDAM

Museum of Edam. – Open daily early April to early October; closed Sunday mornings; 2fl; ☏ (02993) 71727.

Weigh House Exhibit. – Open daily early April to early October; ☏ (02993) 71727.

Great Church or St Nicholas's. – Open early April to early October afternoons only; ☏ (02993) 71727.

EFTELING

Country Park. – Open daily mid-April to mid or late October; 20fl; ☏ (04167) 80505.

EINDHOVEN

Evoluon. – Temporarily closed for restoration work; for times and charges ☏ (040) 73 29 98.

Van Abbe Museum. – Open Tuesdays to Sundays 11am to 5pm; closed Mondays except holiday Mondays; 5fl; ☏ (040) 38 97 30.

Animali. – Open daily; 6fl, children 4.75fl; ☏ (040) 11 37 38.

Kempenland Museum. – Open afternoons only; closed Mondays, 1 January and 25 December; 3fl; ☏ (040) 52 90 93.

ELBURG

Visch Gate. – Open mid-June to late August mornings and afternoons; closed Monday mornings and all day Saturdays, Sundays and holidays; 2.75 (combined ticket with Municipal Museum); ☏ (05250) 1341.

Municipal Museum. – Open daily; closed Monday mornings and all day Saturdays, Sundays and holidays; 2.75fl (combined ticket with Visch Gate); ☏ (05250) 1341.

St Nicholas. – Open July and August mornings and afternoons; closed Saturdays, Sundays and holidays; 1.50fl; ☏ (05250) 1520.

Times and charges

EMMELOORD

Water Tower. – Open 10am to 4pm mid-June to mid-September; closed Sundays and holidays; 1.50fl; ☎ (05270) 12000.

EMMEN

Zoological Garden. – Open daily; 15fl, children 12fl; ☎ (05910) 18800.

ENKHUIZEN

Boat Trips. – Towards Stavoren (1¼ hour) early July to early September 4 rides a day; early May to early July and early September 3 rides a day; 8.75fl (14.50fl Rtn). Information: Rederij NACO, Stationsplein Hoorn, ☎ (02290) 17341.

West Church or St Gommarus's. – For times and charges apply to the VVV ☎ (02280) 13164.

Dromedaris. – Open daily noon to 10pm; ☎ (02280) 12076.

Zuiderzee Museum. – **Indoor Museum:** open daily; 5fl; ☎ (02280) 10122. **Outdoor Museum:** only accessible by ferry departure every 15 min from the landing stage behind the train station or near the car park at the entrance to the dike linking Enkhuizen to Lelystad. Open daily late March to late October; last admission at 4pm; 9fl, children 7fl; ☎ (02280) 10122.

Weigh House Museum. – Open mornings and afternoons; closed Sunday and holiday mornings, all day Monday (except holiday Mondays); 1.25fl; ☎ (02280) 13382.

South Church. – For times and charges apply to the VVV ☎ (02280) 13164.

Summer Garden. – For times and charges apply to the VVV ☎ (02280) 13164.

ENSCHEDE

Twente Museum. – Open daily; closed Saturday, Sunday and holiday mornings, all day Monday and 1 January; 3fl; ☎ (053) 35 86 75.

Textile Industry Museum. – Open daily; closed Saturday, Sunday and holiday mornings, all day Monday, 1 January, Easter Sunday, Whitsun and 25 December; 1.50fl; ☎ (053) 31 90 93.

Museum of Natural History. – Open daily; closed Sunday and holiday mornings, all day Monday, 1 January, Easter Sunday, Whitsun and 25 December; 2.50fl; ☎ (053) 32 34 09.

EXMORRA

Museum. – Open daily early April to late October; 2.50fl; ☎ (05158) 1736.

FERWOUDE

Farmhouse. – Open daily early April to early November; 2.50fl.

FLEVOHOF

Amusement Park. – Open daily early April to late October; 17.50fl, children 12.50fl and 15fl; ☎ (03211) 1514.

FLUSHING

Boat Trips. – For information apply to the VVV ☎ (01184) 12345.

FRANEKER

Town Hall. – Open during office hours; closed Saturdays, Sundays and holidays; ☎ (05170) 8383.

Planetarium. – Guided tours (50 min) early May to late August mornings (closed Sundays and holidays) and afternoons; the rest of the year mornings and afternoons, closed Sundays, Mondays and holidays; 3.50fl; ☎ (05170) 3070.

't Coopmanshûs Museum. – Open daily; closed Sundays (all day Sundays October to March) and holiday mornings and all day Monday; 2.75fl; ☎ (05170) 2192.

You will find an index at the end of the guide listing all subjects referred to in the text (monuments, picturesque sites, points of interest, historical or geographical items, etc).

GARMERWOLDE

Church. – To visit apply to the sexton Mr. Westerhuis, Dorpsweg 62; ☎ (050) 41 77 94.

GIETHOORN

Tour of the Village. – Dinghy rental: 8fl an hour, 20fl per day; with a helmsman 6fl per person an hour; "punter" rental 10fl an hour, 30fl per day.

GOES

Steam Tramway. – Departures in season daily, closed Saturdays; departures spring and fall Sundays only; apply to the VVV or ☎ (01100) 28307.

Great Church or St Mary Magdalene. – Open early June to early September Tuesdays to Fridays 10am to 4pm; closed Mondays; ☎ (01100) 16768. **Organ concerts:** in season Tuesdays 12.30pm and some Saturday evenings as well.

GORINCHEM

Boat Trips. – Apply to Rederij Janihudi, ☎ (01833) 2183. Early July to mid-August Tuesdays, Wednesdays and Thursdays 1.30pm; 12.50fl.

Great Church or St Martin's. – Open early July to late August 2 to 4pm Wednesdays. **Access to the tower:** July and August Mondays 10am to noon and Saturdays 2 to 4pm; 1fl; ☎ (01830) 31525.

Bethlehem House. – Open Wednesdays to Sundays afternoons only; closed 1 January and 25 December; 2fl; ☎ (01830) 32821.

GOUDA

Boat Trips. – Apply to Rederij 't Groene Hart ☎ (01820) 25928; departure point: Bleekersingel.

Cheese Market and Handicraft Market. – Takes place July and August 9am to 12.30pm.

Town Hall. – Open daily Mondays to Fridays; 0.50fl; ☎ (01820) 88475.

St John's. – Open daily; certain holidays open afternoons only; closed 1 January, 25 and 26 December; 2.50fl; ☎ (01820) 12684. **Organ concerts:** early May to mid-September Wednesdays 8.15pm, July and August Thursdays as well at 12.30pm. **Carillon:** market days Thursday mornings and all day Saturday.

Het Catharina Gasthuis Municipal Museum. – Open daily; Sundays and holidays noon to 5pm; closed 1 January and 25 December; 3fl (combined ticket with De Moriaan Municipal Museum); ☎ (01820) 88440.

De Moriaan Municipal Museum. – Open daily Mondays to Fridays; Saturdays mornings and afternoons; Sundays and holidays noon to 5pm; closed 1 January and 25 December; 3fl (combined ticket with Het Catharina Gasthuis Municipal Museum); ☎ (01820) 88440.

GRAFT-DE RIJP

Church. – Open afternoons early June to late September; admission fee not available at the time of going to press.

GROESBEEK

Heilig Land Stichting. – Open daily Easter to early November; 7.50fl.

GROENLO

Regional Museum. – Open afternoons only; closed Saturdays, Sundays and holidays; 1.50fl; ☎ (05440) 63271.

GRONINGEN

Boat Trips. – Departures early June to late August Mondays to Saturdays 9.30 and 11.15am and 1.45, 3.30 and 5.15pm; duration of trip 75 min; 5.75fl, children 3.75fl; ☎ (050) 12 83 79.

Flea Market. – Open daily; closed Sundays and Mondays.

St Martin's. – Open late May to early September noon to 5pm; closed Sundays, Mondays and all holidays; 1fl; ☎ (050) 13 00 67. **Martini Tower:** open Good Friday to fall term holidays noon to 5pm; closed holidays; 1.50fl.

Northern Shipping Museum. – Open daily; closed Sunday and holiday mornings, all day Monday and 1 January, 30 April, 28 August and 25 December; 1.25fl; ☎ (050) 12 22 02.

Netherlands Tobacco Museum. – Same times and charges as the Northern Shipping Museum.

Regional Museum. – Open daily; closed Sunday and holiday mornings, all day Monday, 30 April and 28 August; 3fl; ☎ (050) 18 34 43.

De GROOTE PEEL

National Park. – Open daily early April to late October; ☎ (04951) 41497.

Museum. – Open daily early April to early November and Christmas and spring holidays; ☎ (04951) 41497.

h

HAARLEM

Great Church or St Bavo's. – Open daily; closed Sundays, 30 April and religious holidays; 1.50fl; ☎ (023) 32 43 99. **Organ concerts:** (time: 1 hour) mid-May to mid-October 8.15pm; late June to late August Thursdays also 3pm.

Town Hall. – Guided tours ($1\frac{1}{2}$ hours) by appointment only; apply to the mayor ☎ (023) 17 12 13.

Meat Market. – Open 11am (1pm Sundays and holidays) to 5pm; closed 1 January and 25 December; ☎ (023) 31 91 80.

Frans Hals Museum. – Open Mondays to Saturdays 11am to 5pm; Sundays and holidays 1 to 5pm; closed 1 January and 25 December; 4fl; ☎ (023) 31 91 80.

Teylers Museum. – Open daily; closed Sunday and holiday mornings and all day Monday, 1 January and 25 December; 4fl; ☎ (023) 31 90 10.

St Bavo's Cathedral. – Open 10am to 4pm (3.30pm early October to late February); closed Sundays, 1 January, 30 April, 5 May, Easter Monday, Whit Monday, 25 and 26 December; 1.50fl.

De Cruquius Museum. – Open daily early April to late November (closing time: 4pm October and November); closed 1 January and 25 and 26 December; 3.50fl; ☎ (023) 28 57 04.

HAARZUILENS

De Haar Castle. – Guided tours (1 hour castle; 1 hour park) early March to mid-August and mid-October to mid-November 11am (1pm Saturdays, Sundays and holidays) to 4pm (last admission); 7.50fl; ☎ (03407) 1275.

The HAGUE

Knights' Hall. – Guided tours Mondays to Saturdays 10am to 4pm (last admission: 3.55pm); Sundays also in July and August 10am to 4pm; closed public holidays (except Good Friday and Ascension Day); 1.50fl - 4.50fl (depending on tour's length), price of ticket includes audio-visual presentation Knights' Hall and First and Second Chambers (if not in session); apply to 8A Binnenhof; it is recommended that you reserve in advance ☎ (070) 64 61 44. **Exhibition:** same opening times as the Knights' Hall, admission free.

Mauritshuis. – Open Tuesdays to Saturdays 10am (11am Sundays and holidays) to 5pm; 1 January; 6.50fl; ☎ (070) 65 47 79.

The Hague Historical Museum. – Open noon to 4pm; closed Mondays, 1 January and 25 December; 2fl; ☎ (070) 64 69 40.

Antique Market. – Open early May to late September Thursdays 9am to 9pm.

Walloon Reformed Church. – Closed to the public.

Prison Gate. – Guided tours (1 hour) Mondays to Fridays 10am to 5pm (last admission 4pm) Saturdays, Sundays and holidays 1 to 5pm (early October to early April closed Saturdays, Sundays and holidays); 3.50fl; ☎ (070) 46 08 61.

Great Church or St Jacob's. – Open mid-May to early September 11am to 4pm; closed Sundays and holidays; ☎ (070) 64 39 90.

Mesdag Panorama. – Open Mondays to Fridays 10am (noon Saturdays, Sundays and holidays) to 5pm; 3fl; ☎ (070) 64 25 63.

Mesdag Museum. – Open daily; closed Sunday and holiday mornings, all day Monday and 1 January; 3.50fl; ☎ (070) 46 92 44.

Peace Palace. – Guided tours (2 hours) Mondays to Fridays 10 and 11am, noon, 2 and 3pm (4pm early June to early September); closed Saturdays, Sundays and holidays; 3fl; ☎ (070) 46 96 80.

Municipal Museum. – Open 11am to 5pm; closed Mondays, 1 January and 25 December; 5fl; ☎ (070) 51 41 81.

Museon. – Open 10am (noon Saturdays, Sundays and holidays) to 5pm; closed Mondays, 1 January and 25 December; 3fl; ☎ (070) 51 41 81.

Omniversum. – Films (1 hour) are shown Tuesdays to Thursdays 11am to 4pm (9pm Fridays, Saturdays, Sundays and holidays); closed Mondays; 13fl; for reservations ☎ (070) 54 54 54 (9am to noon). Audio-equipment can be rented (1fl per film).

Madurodam. – Open late March to late May 9am to 10pm; June, July and August 9am to 10.30pm; September 9am to 9pm; October to early January 9am to 6pm; closed 4 May as of 6pm; 9.50fl, children 5fl; ☎ (070) 55 39 00.

Meermannô-Westreenianum Museum. – Open 1 to 5pm; closed Sundays and holidays; ☎ (070) 46 27 00.

HARDERWIJK

Boat Trips. – Rides every hour early April to late August; landing stage, near the port: Strandboulevard.

Dolfinarium. – Open early March to late October 9am to 6pm (4pm last admission); 13fl, children 11fl; ☎ (03410) 16041.

Veluwe Museum. – Open daily Mondays to Fridays (Saturdays as well early May to late September 1 to 4pm); closed Sundays and holidays; 2.50fl; ☎ (03410) 14468.

Great Church. – For times and charges apply to the VVV; ☎ (03410) 12929.

HARLINGEN

Hannemahuis Museum. – Open daily Tuesdays to Saturdays mid-July to mid-October; the last fortnight in October Tuesdays to Fridays afternoons only; closed Sundays and holidays; 2fl ☎ (05178) 13658.

's-HEERENBERG

Bergh Castle. – Guided tours ($1\frac{1}{4}$ hours; for times and charges ☎ (08346) 61281.

HEERENVEEN

Oranjewoud and Oranjestein. – Not open to the public.

HEERLEN

Roman Baths. – Open daily; closed Saturday, Sunday and holiday mornings, all day Monday, 1 January, during Carnival, Easter Sunday, 30 April, Whitsun and 25 December; 2.50fl; ☎ (045) 76 45 81.

HEESWIJK-DINTHER

Heeswijk Castle. – To visit apply in advance from Easter to late October to Mr. and Mrs. Sleddens-Luykx, Kasteel 4, Heeswijk-Dinther, ☎ (04139) 2352; guided tours ($1\frac{1}{2}$ hours); 5fl.

De Meierijsche Museumboerderij. – Open early May to late September Wednesdays, Saturdays and Sundays afternoons only; 1.75fl; ☎ (04139) 1546.

Den HELDER

Navy Museum. – Open daily mid-January to early December; closed Saturday, Sunday and holiday mornings and all day Monday (except in June, July and August open in afternoons); 2.50fl; ☎ (02230) 57137.

HELMOND

Castle. – Open daily; closed Saturday, Sunday and holiday mornings, all day Monday, 1 January and during Carnival; 2.50fl; ☎ (04920) 47475.

's-HERTOGENBOSCH

St John's Cathedral. – Open daily; closed Saturday, Sunday and holiday mornings; ☎ (073) 14 41 70; organ concerts are held: for times apply to the VVV.

Town Hall: Carillon. – Concerts: Wednesdays 10am.

North Brabant Museum. – Open daily Tuesdays to Fridays; Saturdays 11am to 5pm; closed Sunday and holiday mornings, all day Monday, 1 January, during Carnival and 25 December; 5fl; ☎ (073) 13 96 64.

Slager Museum. – Open afternoons only; closed Mondays, Saturdays, 1 January Easter Sunday, Whitsun and 25 December; ☎ (073) 13 32 16.

HEUSDEN

Town Hall: Carillon. – Concerts: Thursday afternoons.

HINDELOOPEN

Museum. – Open daily early March to late October; closed Sunday and holiday mornings; 2.50fl; ☎ (05142) 1420.

HOEVEN

Simon Stevin Observatory. – Guided tours (1½ hours) all year round **Sundays** 1.30 and 3pm and Wednesdays and Saturdays 7.30pm; also Wednesdays at **3pm in** May and June; July and August every day (except Saturdays) 3pm and Fridays 11pm, as well; closed 1 January, Easter Sunday, Whitsun, 25 and 26 December; 4fl.

De HOGE VELUWE National Park

Kröller-Müller National Museum. – Open Tuesdays to Saturdays (and Easter Monday, Whit Monday and Ascension Day) 10am to 5pm; Sundays and holidays 11am (1pm early November to late March) to 5pm; closed Mondays and 1 January; ☎ (08382) 1041.

Sculpture Park. – Open early April to late October 10am (11am Sundays and holidays) to 4.30pm; closed Mondays; ☎ (08382) 1241.

Park. – Open 8am to sunset; 6fl per automobile plus 6.25fl per adult, 3fl per child (ticket price includes admission to all the sites in the park; Easter to late October bicycles available near the restaurant De Koperen Kop; ☎ (05768) 1441.

De Aanschouw Visitors' Centre. – Open early April to late October 10am to 5pm; the rest of the year Sundays and Christmas and spring term holidays 11am to 4pm; closed 1 January and 31 December; ☎ (08382) 1627 (for bicycle information and reservation, as well).

St Hubert's Hunting Lodge. – Guided tours (½ hour) early May to late October mornings and afternoons; ☎ (05768) 1441.

HOLTEN

Museum. – Open daily (as of noon Sundays and holidays) Easter to early November; 5fl; ☎ (05483) 61533.

HOOGEBEINTUM

Church. – Guided tours (¾ hour) early April to mid-October. Times and charges not available at the time of going to press.

HOORN

Tourist Train. – Ride (1 hour) in July and August two departures a day; May, June and September one departure a day Tuesdays to Saturdays; 15fl Rtn; ☎ (02290) 14862.

West Friesland Museum. – Open Mondays to Fridays 11am (2pm Saturdays, Sundays and holidays) to 5pm; closed 1 January and 25 December; 3.50fl; ☎ (02290) 15597.

HULST

Museum. – Open early May to late August afternoons only; closed Sundays except in July and August; 1.25fl; ☎ (01140) 89000.

i - k

IJZENDIJKE

Regional Museum. – Open all year round mornings and afternoons; Saturdays, Sundays and holidays afternoons only; 1fl; ☎ (01176) 1200.

KAMPEN

Boat Trips. – In July and August only; apply to the VVV ☎ (05202) 13500.

Old Town Hall. – Open Mondays to Thursdays mornings (as of 11am) and afternoons; Saturdays afternoons only early May to early September; closed Fridays, Sundays and holidays; 1fl; ☎ (05202) 92999.

New Tower. – Open early May to early September Wednesdays and Saturdays afternoons only; 1fl; ☎ (05202) 13500.

Municipal Museum. – In the Gothic House. Open mid-June to mid-September 11am (1pm Sundays) to 5pm; the rest of the year mornings (as of 11am) and afternoons; closed Sundays, Mondays, holidays and in January; 2fl; ☎ (05202) 13500.

St Nicholas's or Upper Church. – Open early June to early September daily Wednesdays to Fridays, Mondays and Tuesdays afternoons only; closed Saturdays, Sundays and holidays; ☎ (05202) 13608. **Organ concerts:** in summer Thursday nights and Saturday afternoons.

KAPELLE

Church. – Guided tours (½ hour) daily closed Sundays during services and holidays; ☎ (01102) 42938.

De KENNEMERDUINEN

National Park. – Open sunrise to sunset; 1.50fl; ☎ (023) 25 76 53.

KERKRADE

Rolduc Abbey. – To visit apply to Mr. Reynaerts, Centrum Rolduc, Heyendahllaan 82 ☎ (045) 45 77 44.

Mining Museum. – Open daily; closed Sunday mornings, Mondays, Saturdays (except July and August when open afternoons) and holidays; 2.50fl; ☎ (045) 45 71 38.

KETELHAVEN

Museum of Maritime Archaeology. – Open 10am (11am Saturdays, Sundays and holidays October to April) to 5pm; closed 25 December; 1.50fl; ☎ (03210) 13287.

KINDERDIJK

Windmills. – Illuminated at night the second whole week in September.

Boat Trip. – Trips are organised early May to late September daily (and holidays) departure every 20 min; closed Sundays; 2.50fl; ☎ (078) 132800.

Windmill. – The second windmill. Open daily (including holidays) early April to late September; closed Sundays; 2fl; ☎ (078) 132800.

KOLLUM

Church. – To visit apply to Van Bootsmalaan 6 or Witteveenstraat 13.

KOOG AAN DE ZAAN

Windmill Museum. – Open daily early April to early October; the rest of the year mornings and afternoons; closed Saturday, Sunday and holiday mornings and all day Monday, 1 January and 25 December; 2.50fl; ☎ (075) 288968.

KREWERD

Church. – To visit apply to Mr. M.A. Bos, Pastorieweg 8, ☎ (05960) 22347.

L

LAREN

Singer Museum. – Open daily; closed Sunday mornings (until noon) all day Monday, 1 January, 30 April and 25 December; 4.50fl; ☎ (02153) 15656.

LAUWERSOOG

Museum. – Open daily early April to late September; Saturdays, Sundays and holidays afternoons only; closed Mondays; 2.50fl; ☎ (05193) 9045.

LEEK

National Carriage Museum. – Open daily (and holidays) Easter to late September; closed Sunday mornings; 3.50fl; ☎ (05945) 12260.

LEENS

St Peters': Organ Concerts. – Mid-May to mid-October Saturdays 8.15pm.

LEERDAM

National Glasswork Museum. – Open Tuesdays to Fridays mornings and afternoons; early April to late October open, as well, Saturday, Sunday and holiday afternoons; closed 1 January, 25 and 26 December; 2.50fl; ☎ (03451) 13141.

LEERSUM

Leersumse Plassen. – Open mid-July to mid-March; guided tours early May to late July and after applying in advance; admission charged; ☎ (03434) 54777.

LEEUWARDEN

Frisian Museum. – Open daily; closed Sunday and holiday mornings, all day Monday, 1 January, 30 April and 25 December; 3fl; ☎ (058) 123001.

Great Church or Church of the Jacobins. – Open June, July and August Tuesdays to Fridays 2 to 4pm; closed holidays. **Organ concerts:** July and August times not available at the time of going to press.

Het Princessehof Museum. – Open daily; closed Sunday and holiday mornings; 1 January and 25 December; 3.50fl; ☎ (058) 12 74 38.

Oldehove. – Open early May to early October Tuesdays to Saturdays mornings and afternoons; closed holidays; 1fl; ☎ (058) 13 22 24.

Times and charges

LEYDEN

Boat Trips. – Canal rides mid-June to early September 11am, noon, 1.30, 2.45, 4 and 5pm; 6fl; for a ride on the Old Rhine to Avifauna, apply to the Avifauna Company.

De Valk Wall Mill. – Open daily; closed Sunday and holiday mornings, all day Monday, 1 January and 25 December; 3fl; ☎ (071) 25 46 39.

National Museum of Ethnology. – Open daily; closed Sunday and holiday mornings, all day Monday, 1 January and 3 October; 3.50fl; ☎ (071) 21 18 24.

De Lakenhal Municipal Museum. – Open daily; closed Sunday and holiday mornings, all day Monday, 1 January and 25 December; 2.50fl; ☎ (071) 25 46 20.

Botanical Garden. – Open daily; closed Saturdays (except early April to late September), 8 February, 3 October and 25-31 December; 1fl; ☎ (071) 27 51 88.

National Museum of Antiquities. – Open daily (Sundays and holidays as of noon); closed Mondays, 1 January, 3 October and 25 December; 3.50fl; ☎ (071) 14 62 46.

St Peter's. – Open daily afternoons; 1.50fl; ☎ (071) 12 43 19.

National Museum of Geology and Mineralogy. – Open daily; closed Sunday mornings, all day Saturdays and holidays; 3fl; ☎ (071) 14 38 44.

Boerhaave Museum. – Museum closed, to be relocated; new address: Lange St Agnietenstraat 10, 2312 WC Leiden; scheduled opening date 1991; ☎ (071) 21 42 24.

Pilgrim Fathers Documentatie Centrum. – Open daily; closed Saturdays, Sundays and holidays; ☎ (071) 12 01 91.

LOEVESTEIN

Castle. – Guided tours (50min) early April to late October daily Mondays to Fridays; Saturdays, Sundays and holidays (except Easter Monday, Whit Monday and Ascension Day open all day) afternoons only; last admission 4pm; 3.50fl; ☎ (01832) 1375.

LOPPERSUM

Church. – To visit apply to Mr. L. Aslander, Nieuwstraat 4.

MAASTRICHT

Boat Trips. – Trips are organised late April to late September apply to Rederij Stiphout, Maaspromenade 27, 6211 AS Maastricht; ☎ (043) 25 41 51.

St Servatius's Basilica. – Under restoration. **Carillon:** evenings July and August; ☎ (043) 43 15 32. **Treasury:** open daily; closed during Carnival and 25 December; 3.50fl.

Basilica of Our Lady. – Open daily Easter to mid-September; closed mornings Sundays and holidays; 2fl; ☎ (043) 25 18 51. **Treasury:** same times and charges as the basilica.

Town Hall: Carillon. – Concert (1 hour) Fridays at 11.30am.

Good Children Museum. – Open 10am (11am Saturdays and Sundays) to 5pm; closed Mondays, 1 January, during Carnival, Good Friday, 25 December; 5fl; ☎ (043) 25 16 55.

Casemates. – Guided tours (1 hour) July and August and school holidays at 2pm; 4fl; children: 2.25fl; ☎ (043) 25 21 21.

St Peter's Fort. – Same times and charges as the Casemates *(see above)*.

Marl Caves-North Gallery. – Guided tours (1 hour); 4fl; children 2.25fl; for information ☎ (043) 25 21 21.

Zonneberg Caves. – Guided tours (1 hour) early May to early September 10.45am (12.45pm Sundays) to 3.45pm; the rest of the year Sundays only 1.30 to 2.30pm; 4fl, children 2.25fl; ☎ (043) 25 21 21.

MAKKUM

Museum of Frisian Ceramics. – Open daily early May to mid-September; closed Sunday and holiday mornings; 2.50fl; ☎ (05158) 1422.

Tichelaar's Royal Pottery and Tile Factory. – Guided tours ($\frac{3}{4}$ hour) Mondays to Fridays; closed 1 January and 26 December; 3fl; ☎ (05158) 1341. Workshops open daily; closed Sundays.

MARKEN

Village. – Paying car park obligatory. **Interiors:** a few on the port can be visited.

MARSSUM

Popta Castle. – Guided tours (1 hour) early April to early October at 11am, 2 and 3pm; closed Saturdays, Sundays and holidays; 3fl; ☎ (05107) 1231. .

MEDEMBLIK

Radbod Castle. – Open daily mid-May to mid-September; closed Sunday and holiday mornings; 3fl; ☎ (02274) 1960.

MIDDELBURG

Town Hall. – Guided tours (1 hour) Mondays to Fridays mid-March to mid-October 10.30 to 11.15am and 1.30 to 4pm; mid-July to mid-August 11am to 4pm; closed holidays; 1.70fl; ☎ (01180) 26251.

Abbey. – Guided tours ($1\frac{1}{4}$ hours) Mondays to Fridays in July and August 11am, 1.30 and 3pm; May to November Mondays to Saturdays 1.30 and 3pm only; closed Ascension Day and Whit Monday; 5fl; ☎ (01180) 16851.

Abbey Churches. – Open early May to late October Mondays mornings and afternoons and daily Tuesdays to Saturdays; closed Sundays and holidays; ☎ (01180) 16851.

Lange Jan Tower. – Open daily mid-March to early October; closed Sundays; 1.35fl; ☎ (01180) 82255.

Zeeland Museum. – Open daily Tuesdays to Fridays; Saturdays to Mondays open afternoons only; closed 1 January and 25 December; 3.50fl; ☎ (01180) 26655.

Miniature Walcheren. – Open daily mid-March to mid-October; 4.50, children 2.50fl; ☎ (01180) 12525.

MIDWOLDE

Church. – Open Good Friday to late September mornings and afternoons; closed Sunday and Monday mornings and Easter; 1fl; ☎ (05945) 13649.

MUIDEN

Muiden Castle. – Guided tours (1 hour) daily early April to late September (last admission 4pm); the rest of the year every hour 10am to 3pm; Sundays and holidays open 1pm; closed Saturdays, 1 January, 25 and 26 December, 3.50fl.

NAALDWIJK

Auctions. – Open Mondays to Fridays 8am to noon; guided tours in English.

Museum. – Open Tuesdays and Thursdays 2 to 4.30pm; closed holidays; ☎ (01740) 29480.

NAARDEN

Museum. – Open daily the week before Easter to late October; closed Saturday, Sunday and holiday mornings (open at noon); 3fl; ☎ (02159) 45459.

Old Walloon Church. – Open mid-January to mid-December 4 to 5pm; closed Mondays; apply to Comenius Museum; ☎ (02159) 43045.

Comenius Museum. – In the Spanish House. Same opening times as the Old Walloon Church; ☎ (02159) 43045.

Town Hall. – Open afternoons Mondays to Fridays early May to early September; closed Saturdays, Sundays and holidays; ☎ (02159) 41354.

NIEUW-LOOSDRECHT

Sypesteyn Castle. – Guided tours (1 hour) early May to mid-September mornings and afternoons (last admission 4pm); closed Sunday and holiday mornings, all day Monday, 1 January and 25, 26 and 31 December; 5fl; ☎ (02158) 3208.

NIJMEGEN

Boat Trips. – In season; apply to Rederij Tonissen, "Waalorama", Waalkade; ☎ (080) 23 32 85.

St Stephen's. – Open mid-May to late September Mondays to Fridays mornings and afternoons (open all day mid-June to mid-August); Saturdays open 10am to 1pm; closed Sundays (except mid-June to mid-August when open afternoons); 1.25fl. **Carillon concerts:** Mondays 11am and early June to late August Thursdays at 7.30pm; **Organ concerts:** June to August Tuesdays at 8.30pm; 5fl. **Access to the tower:** 1fl.

Municipal Museum. – Open daily; closed Sunday and holiday mornings, 25 December; ☎ (080) 22 91 93.

Town Hall. – Guided tours (1 hour 15 min) afternoons Mondays to Fridays early May to late October; closed holidays; 2.50fl; ☎ (080) 29 24 03.

G. M. Kam Museum. – Open daily; closed Sunday and holiday afternoons, all day Monday and 25 December; ☎ (080) 22 06 19.

NUENEN

Van Gogh Documentation Centre. – Open mornings and afternoons; closed monthly 1st and 3rd Friday afternoon, all day Saturday, Sunday and holidays; 1fl; ☎ (040) 83 25 00.

OISTERWIJK

Bird Park. – Open daily Easter to fall term holidays; 6fl; ☎ (04242) 83449.

OLDENZAAL

St Plecheln's Basilica. – Open early June to late August Tuesdays and Thursdays 2 to 3pm and Wednesdays 2 to 4pm; closed holidays; ☎ (05410) 12808.

Het Palthe Huis Museum. – Open mornings and afternoons; closed Saturday and Sunday mornings, all day Monday, 1 January, during Carnival, Easter Sunday, Whitsun, 25 December; 3fl; ☎ (05410) 13482.

OOSTERBEEK

Airborne Museum. – Open 11am (noon Sundays and holidays) to 5pm; closed 1 January and 25 December; 3fl; ☎ (085) 33 77 10.

OOTMARSUM

St Simon and St Judas. – Open early May to early October mornings and afternoons (3 to 4.30pm); closed Sunday and holiday mornings and all day Saturday; ☎ (05419) 2183.

OTTERLO

Museum of Ceramic Tiles. – Open Tuesdays to Saturdays mornings and afternoons; Sundays and holidays 2 to 4pm; closed Mondays, 1 January and 25 December; 3fl; ☎ (08382) 1519.

OUDENBOSCH

Museum of Pontifical Zouaves. – Open early May to late September Tuesdays and Thursdays and the 1st and 3rd Sunday of the month; 1fl; ☎ (01652) 13448.

OUDEWATER

Weigh House. – Open daily early April to early November; closed Sunday and holiday mornings (open as of noon) and all day Monday; 2fl; ☎ (03486) 3400.

OUD-ZUILEN

Zuylen Castle. – Guided tours (1 hour) mid-May to mid-September 10 and 11am and 2, 3 and 4pm; Sundays and holidays additional tour at 1pm; the rest of the year Saturdays, Sundays and holidays afternoons only; closed Friday afternoons and all day Monday; 5fl; ☎ (030) 44 02 55.

OVERLOON

National War and Resistance Museum. – Open daily; closed 1 January, 24, 25 and 31 December; 6fl; ☎ (04788) 1820.

RAAMSDONKSVEER

National Automobile Museum. – Closed for restoration work: scheduled opening date 1990. Open daily 9am (11am Sundays and holidays) to 4.45pm; admission fee not available at the time of going to press; ☎ (01621) 85400.

RENESSE

Moermond Mansion. – Guided tour ($1\frac{1}{2}$ hours) of the garden mid-June to early September Thursday evenings and Saturday afternoons; 1.50fl (tickets available at Renesse VVV).

RHENEN

Ouwehands Dierenpark Zoological Garden. – Open daily; 14fl; ☎ (08376) 19110.

Cunera Church. – Open mid-June to mid-September 2 to 3.30pm; closed Saturdays, Sundays, Mondays and holidays; 1fl; ☎ (08376) 14093.

RINSUMAGEEST

Church. – Apply to the sexton (1 Juckemawei) or at 2 Juckemawei; ☎ (05111) 3399.

ROERMOND

Church of Our Lady or Munsterkerk. – Open Fridays mornings and afternoons and all day Saturdays; closed holidays; ☎ (04750) 34924.

Cathedral. – Guided tours ($\frac{3}{4}$ hour) early April to early October Saturday afternoons only; apply in advance to the VVV ☎ (04750) 33205.

ROSENDAAL

Golden Rose Museum. – Open afternoons only; closed Mondays, 1 January, Carnival, Easter Sunday, Whitsun, and 25 December; 1.50fl; ☎ (01650) 36916.

ROSENDAEL

Rosendael Castle. – Open 10am (11am Sundays) to 6pm early June to late August; closed Mondays in June; September and October Sundays only 11am to 6pm; 4fl, children 1.50fl; ☎ (085) 420944.

ROSMALEN

Autotron Transportation Museum. – Open daily late March to early October; 11.50fl, children 9.75fl; ☎ (04192) 19050.

ROTTERDAM

Boat trips. – Excursion (9 hours) in the Delta July and August Wednesdays and Thursdays; departure 10am; 37.50fl, children 18.75fl; apply to Spido BV, Willemsplein; ☎ (010) 4135400. For cruises on the Rhine apply to Keulen-Düsseldorfer German-Rhine line. Groenendaal 49a.

Town Hall. – Guided tours (1$\frac{1}{2}$ hours) daily; closed Saturdays, Sundays and holidays; ☎ (010) 4172459. **Carillon:** concerts Tuesdays and Thursdays noon to 1pm.

St Lawrence's. – Open daily early May to early October Tuesdays and Sundays; the rest of the year daily Tuesdays, Wednesdays, Fridays and Saturdays and Thursdays as well noon to 2pm; closed holidays.

Schielandshuis Historical Museum. – Open daily Tuesdays to Saturdays; closed Sunday mornings, all day Monday (except holiday Mondays), 1 January and 30 April; 2.50fl (includes admission to De Dubbelde Palmboom Museum and The Porters' House; ☎ (010) 4334188.

Boymans-van Beuningen Museum. – Open 10am (11am Sundays and holidays) to 5pm; closed Mondays, 1 January and 30 April; 3.50fl; ☎ (010) 4419475.

De Dubbelde Palmboom Museum. – Same times and charges as Schielandshuis Historical Museum.

The Porters' House. – Open Tuesdays to Saturdays 10am (11am Sundays and holidays) to 5pm; closed Mondays (except holiday Mondays); combined ticket with Schielandshuis Historical Museum; ☎ (010) 4334188.

Euromast. – Open mid-March to mid-October 10am to 9pm (6pm the rest of the year; 8fl, children 4fl. **Space Tower:** mid-March to mid-October 10am to 9pm; the rest of the year 11am to 4pm; closed January and February except for the weekend; 3fl, children 2fl; ☎ (010) 4364811.

Prins Hendrik Maritime Museum. – Open early May to late December 10am (11am Sundays and holidays) to 5pm; closed Mondays; 3.50fl; ☎ (010) 4132680.

Ethnographic Museum. – Open 10am (11am Sundays and holidays) to 5pm; closed Mondays, 1 January and 30 April; 3.50fl; ☎ (010) 4111055.

Blijdorp Zoo. – Open daily; 12fl, children 7fl; ☎ (010) 4654333.

De Ster. – Open daily early April to late November Tuesdays and Wednesdays; the rest of the year Wednesdays only; closed 1 January, 25, 26 and 31 December; ☎ (010) 4526287.

Short Boat Trip. – Duration of tour 1$\frac{1}{4}$ hours early April to late September 9.30am to 3.30pm every $\frac{3}{4}$ hour and at 5pm; in March and October 10 and 11.30am and 1 and 2.30pm; the rest of the year 11am and 2pm; 11.50fl, children 5.75fl; apply to Spido BV, Willemsplein; ☎ (010) 4135400.

Long Boat Trip. – Duration of tour 2$\frac{1}{4}$ hours. Runs early April to late September 10am and 12.30pm; 19fl, children 9.50fl apply to Spido BV, Willemsplein; ☎ (010) 4135400.

Boat Trip. – Europoort. Duration of the tour 6 hours. Tuesdays 11am July and August; 35fl, children 17.50fl; apply to Spido BV, Willemsplein; ☎ (010) 4135400.

s

SCHEVENINGEN

Pier. – Open daily (until 10pm July and August); 1fl.

Boat Trips. – For reservations apply to Rederij Vrolijk, Doorniksestraat 7; ☎ (070) 514021.

SCHIEDAM

Municipal Museum. – Closed for restoration work: scheduled opening date: 1990. Open daily Tuesdays to Saturdays; Sundays and holidays afternoons only; closed 1 January and 25 December; ☎ (010) 4269066.

De Vrijheid. – Open Saturdays 11am to 4pm; closed holidays; ☎ (010) 4733000.

SCHIERMONNIKOOG see at Wadden Islands

SCHIPHOL

Aviodome. – Open daily early May to early October; the rest of the year daily Tuesdays to Fridays, holidays, Saturdays and Sundays as of noon; closed 1 January and 25 December; 6fl, children 4.50fl; ☎ (020) 6041521.

SCHOKLAND

Museum. – Open daily (as of 11am Saturdays, Sundays and holidays); closed Mondays early October to late March, 1 January and 25 December; 3fl; ☎ (05275) 1396.

SCHOONHOVEN

Gold, Silver and Clock Museum. – Open noon to 5pm; closed Mondays, 1 January and 25 December; 3fl; ☎ (01823) 5612.

SITTARD

Great Church. – Open daily until 3.30pm; closed Saturdays and Sundays.

SLUIS

Town Hall. – Open mid-May to mid-September mornings and afternoons; 1fl; ☎ (01178) 1700.

De Brak Mill. – Open daily Easter to mid-September; closed Fridays; 2.15fl; ☎ (01178) 1810.

SNEEK

Town Hall. – Guided tours (20 min) Mondays to Fridays early July to mid-August 2 to 4pm; closed holidays; ☎ (05150) 85373.

Navigation and Antiquities Museum. – Open mornings and afternoons; closed Sundays, Easter Monday, Whit Monday, 25 and 26 December; 2fl; ☎ (05150) 14057.

De STEEG

Middachten Castle. – Guided tours (1 hour castle; 1 hour garden). Castle for opening times ☎ (08309) 54998; 5fl. Garden mid-May to mid-September 10.30am to 4.30pm; 5fl.

STEIN

Archaeological Museum. – Guided tours ($\frac{1}{2}$ hour) by appointment only apply in advance ☎ (04490) 32850.

SUSTEREN

St Amelberga's. – Apply to Mr. L.M.G. Pesgens, Pasteur Tijssenstraat 5; ☎ (04499) 1473.

t

TEGELEN

Museum. – Open daily mid-March to mid-October; the rest of the year Tuesdays to Saturdays afternoons only; closed Sunday and holiday mornings; 1 January, Good Friday and 25 December; 2fl; ☎ (077) 768294.

Botanical Garden. – Open Easter to late October daily 11am to 5pm; closed 1 January and during Carnival; 4fl; ☎ (077) 733020.

TER APEL

Old Convent. – Guided tours ($\frac{1}{2}$ hour) mornings (except Sundays and holidays) and afternoons; closed Mondays and 25 December; 2,50fl; ☎ (05995) 1370.

TERSCHELLING see at Wadden Islands

TEXEL see at Wadden Islands

THORN

Church. – Open daily Maundy Thursday to late October; 2fl; ☎ (04756) 2761.

TILBURG

Textile Museum. – Open daily (as of noon Saturdays, Sundays and holidays); closed Mondays, 1 January, Easter Sunday, Whitsun, 30 April, 5 May, 24, 25 and 31 December; 5fl; ☎ (013) 36 74 75.

u - v

UITHUIZEN

Menkemaborg. – Open mornings and afternoons; closed Mondays early October to late March and January; 2.50fl; ☎ (05953) 1970.

UITHUIZERMEEDEN

Church. – To visit and access to the tower apply to J. Veenstra, Paaptilsterweg 3.

URK

Boat to Enkhuizen. – Departure point near the railway station. No automobiles, bicycles only (5.50fl, 8fl Rtn). Early July to late August departure 9.30am, 1.15 and 4.45pm; May, June and late August to early September departure 9.30am and 2.30pm; closed Sundays; 9fl, 15fl Rtn; for reservations ☎ (05277) 3407.

UTRECHT

Boat Trips. – Landing stage: Oudegracht. For rides on the canals (1 hour) late March to late October on the Vecht ($8\frac{1}{2}$ hours) and the Kromme Rijn ($1\frac{1}{2}$ hours); apply to Utrechts Rondvaartbedrijf; ☎ (030) 31 93 77. Information concerning boat trips on Loosdrecht Lakes apply to Watersportbedrijf Wolfrat, Oud Loosdrechtsedijk 165, 1231LV Loosdrecht; ☎ (02158) 3309.

National Museum "from the musical clock to the barrel organ". – Guided tours (1 hour) and demonstrations daily; closed Sunday mornings and all day Mondays; 6fl; ☎ (030) 312799.

Dom Tower. – Guided tours (1 hour) daily Mondays to Fridays early April to early November; Saturdays, Sundays and holidays all year round noon to 5pm; 1.50fl; ☎ (030) 91 95 40.

Old Cathedral. – Open daily early May to late September; the rest of the year 11am to 4pm; closed Sunday mornings; ☎ (030) 31 04 03.

University. – Open daily; closed Saturdays, Sundays and holidays; ☎ (030) 39 42 52.

St Peter's. – Open mid-June to mid-September Tuesdays to Fridays 11am to 4.30pm, Saturdays 10am to 1pm; closed Sundays, Mondays and holidays; 1fl; for organ concerts enquire locally; ☎ (030) 311485.

Central Museum. – Open daily; closed Sunday and holiday mornings, all day Monday, 1 January and 25 December; 4fl; ☎ (030) 31 55 41.

Het Catharijneconvent Museum. – Open daily; Saturdays, Sundays and holidays as of 11am; closed Mondays and 1 January; 3.50fl; ☎ (030) 31 38 35.

Dutch Railway Museum. – Open daily; closed Sunday and holiday mornings, all day Monday, 1 January, Easter Sunday, Whitsun and 25 December; 7.50fl, children 4fl; ☎ (030) 30 62 06.

University Museum. – Open daily; closed Sunday mornings, all day Saturday and holidays; ☎ (030) 73 13 05.

Rietveld Schröder House. – Guided tours (1 hour) by appointment only; ☎ (030) 517926; closed Mondays, 1 January and 25 December; 7.50fl.

VALKENBURG

Castle Ruins. – Open daily 1 week before Easter to fall term holidays; 1.50fl; ☎ (04406) 12727.

Mining Museum. – Guided tours ($1\frac{1}{2}$ hours) daily 1 week before Easter to early November; the rest of the year Saturdays 2pm; closed 1 January, during Carnival and 25 December; 7.25fl; ☎ (030) 12491.

Times and charges

Municipal Caves. – Guided tours (1 hour on foot, $\frac{1}{2}$ hour by train) daily 1 week before Easter to early November; the rest of the year daily at 2pm (3.30pm Saturdays and Sundays); closed 1 January, during Carnival and 25 December; 4.25fl, children 2.25fl; ☎ (04406) 12271.

Fluwelen Caves. – Guided tours (50 min) daily 1 week before Easter to fall term holidays; combined ticket with Castle Ruins *(p 217)* 4.50fl, children 2fl; ☎ (04406) 12727.

Wilhelmina Tower. – Open daily Easter to late October; 2fl; ☎ (04406) 12023. Via chairlift Easter to Whitsun 1 to 5pm and Whitsun to mid-September and fall term holidays 10am to 7pm. **Caves Panorama-Grot.** – Guided tours (40min) July and August daily; Easter to late June and September and fall term holidays afternoons only; 3fl.

Roman Catacombs. – Guided tours (45 min) daily early April to early October; the rest of the year 3pm; holidays all day; closed 1 January, during Carnival and 25 December; 4fl, children 2fl; ☎ (04406) 12554.

Regional Museum. – Closed temporarily for restoration work; ☎ (04406) 13064.

VEENKLOOSTER

Fogelsangh Castle: Museum. – Open early May to late September mornings and afternoons; closed Sunday and holiday mornings; 2fl; ☎ (05113) 1970.

VEERE

Scotch Houses. – Open daily early April to late October; closed Monday and Saturday mornings, all day Sundays and holidays; 2fl; ☎ (01181) 1744.

Old Town Hall. – Open early June to late September noon (11am early July to early September) to 5pm; closed Sundays and holidays; 2fl; ☎ (01181) 1951. **Carillon:** concerts (1 hour) May to October 3pm and early June to late August 7pm, as well; the rest of the year 3pm every two weeks.

Great Church or Church of Our Lady. – Open daily (as well as holidays) mid-April to mid-October; closed Sunday mornings; 2.25fl; ☎ (01189) 2390.

VELUWEZOOM National Park

De Heurne Reception Centre. – Open Wednesday afternoons and Saturdays, Sundays, holidays and school holidays all day; ☎ (08309) 51023.

VENLO

Boat Trips. – In July and August; apply to the VVV or Rederij 't Veerhuis ☎ (04759) 1318.

St Martin's. – Open mornings and afternoons; closed Sunday mornings and during Carnival; ☎ (077) 51 24 39.

Goltzius Museum. – Open daily; closed Saturday and Sunday mornings, all day Monday and holidays; 2.50fl; ☎ (077) 59 67 62.

Van Bommel - Van Dam Museum. – Open daily; closed Saturday, Sunday and holiday mornings, all day Monday and 1 January, during Carnival, Good Friday, Easter Sunday and 25 December; 2.50fl; ☎ (077) 51 34 57.

VENRAY

St Peter's. – Open Wednesdays to Saturdays 2 to 4pm; closed 25 and 26 December; ☎ (04780) 10505.

VLIELAND see Wadden Islands

VLISSINGEN see Flushing

WAALWIJK

Dutch Leather and Shoe Museum. – Open daily; Saturdays, Sundays and holidays noon to 4pm; closed Mondays, 1 January, Easter Sunday, Whitsun and 25 December; 4fl; ☎ (04160) 32738.

WADDEN Islands

Fording the Wadden Sea. – Walking tours are conducted early April to late October (weather permitting); 10-28fl; for information apply to: Dijkstra Wadlooptochten, Hoofdstraat 118, 9968 AH Pieterburen; ☎ (05952) 345.

Ameland

Access. – Reservations needed for cars: Wagenborg's Passagiersdiensten, Reeweg, 9163 ZL Ness, Ameland, ☎ (05191) 6111. Bicycles for hire in each locality. Access to the main beach (Badstrand) by bus from the landing stage.

Museum. – In Hollum. Open early April to late October mornings and afternoons, Saturdays and Sundays afternoons only; the rest of the year afternoons only, closed all day Saturdays and Sundays; 2.50fl; ☎ (05191) 4477.

Redding-Boot. – Demonstrations 7 to 8 a year.

Schiermonnikoog

Access. – Crossing takes approximately $\frac{3}{4}$ hour; 12fl Rtn. No automobiles allowed on the island; bicycles for hire at Schiermonnikoog.

Museum. – Open early April to late October Tuesdays and Thursdays mornings and afternoons, Mondays, Wednesdays and Fridays 1.30 to 5pm and 7 to 9pm, Saturday afternoons only; closed Sundays and holidays; 1fl; ☎ (05195) 1641.

Terschelling

Access. – Crossing: $1\frac{1}{2}$ hours, 2 to 3 times a day; 30fl (for the car average price 140fl) reserve in advance to Rederij Doeksen, ☎ (05620) 6111. For crossings between Vlieland and Terschelling see at Vlieland (below). Bicycles for hire in most localities; car rentals apply to Autoverhuur Visser, Westerburen 15, Midsland, ☎ (05620) 8966.

't Behouden Huys Municipal Museum. – Open early April to late October and Christmas and spring holidays; closed Saturdays (except mid-June to early September) and Sundays; 3fl; ☎ (05620) 8031.

De Boschplaat. – To tour in a wagon apply in Den Hoorn (Huifkarbedrijf Terpstra Dorpsstraat 20, Hoorn, ☎ (05620) 8837; 17.50-22.50fl. For guided tours apply to the tourist information centre (VVV) in West-Terschelling.

Texel

Access. – Crossing takes approximately 20min; no reservations for automobiles taken.

Nature Reserves. – Guided tours in four Staatsbosbeheer reserves: Slufter Reserve early April to late August 8am; Muy and Geul Reserves early April to late August 11am; Westerduinen Reserve early May to mid-July 11am. Apply for reservations 9am to 5pm at EcoMare, Ruyslaan 92, 1796 AZ De Koog-Texel, ☎ (02220) 17741 (early November to early April closed Sundays). Boots and binoculars are recommended.

EcoMare. – Open daily; closed Sundays early November to early April, 1 January and 25 December; 5fl, children 3fl. **Seals** fed at 11am and 3pm; ☎ (02228) 741.

Oudheidkamer. – Open early April to early November 10am to 12.30pm and 1.15 to 3pm; closed Saturdays and Sundays; 2fl; ☎ (02220) 17741.

Wagon and Agricultural Museum. – Open daily mid-May to mid-September closed Sunday and Monday mornings; mid-September to mid-October afternoons only; 3fl; ☎ (02220) 18622.

Vlieland

Access. – From Harlingen (crossing: $1\frac{1}{2}$ hours) 2 to 3 crossings a day. From Terschelling in July and August 2 crossings 3 days a week, September 1 day a week. From Texel daily early May to late September. No cars allowed on the island. Bicycles for hire: Dorpsstraat nos 8 and 113 or Havenweg 7.

Tromp's House. – Open early May to late September mornings and afternoons; early October to late April afternoons only; early November to late March Wednesdays to Saturdays afternoons only; 2.50fl; ☎ (05621) 1600.

Reception Centre. – Same times and charges as Tromp's House; ☎ (05621) 1700.

Church. – Apply to the tourist information centre (VVV).

WIEUWERD

Church. – Open early April to mid-October mornings and afternoons; closed Sundays; 2fl; ☎ (05104) 226.

WIJK BIJ DUURSTEDE

Museum. – Open daily afternoons; closed Mondays and 25 December; 2fl; ☎ (03435) 71448.

WILLEMSTAD

Mauritshuis. – Open daily (as of 8.15am) Mondays, Tuesdays and Thursdays; Wednesdays and Fridays mornings and afternoons; closed Saturdays, Sundays and holidays.

WITMARSUM

Church. – Apply to Mr. D. de Boer, Arumerweg 36; ☎ (05175) 1959.

Times and charges

WOERDEN

Municipal Museum. – Open afternoons and Wednesday mornings, as well; closed holidays; 1fl; ☎ (03480) 28415.

WORKUM

St Gertrude's. – Open daily mid-May to late August; early September to early October and early April to mid-May afternoons only; closed Sundays and holidays; 1fl; ☎ (05151) 1976.

Antiquities Museum. – Open daily early March to mid-October Tuesdays to Fridays; afternoons only Saturdays and Mondays (closed all day September to mid-October); 1.50fl; ☎ (05151) 1300.

WOUW

Church. – Open Wednesdays and Thursdays mornings and afternoons; ☎ (01658) 1649.

#

ZAANDIJK

Zaan Region Antiquities Museum. – Guided tours (1 hour) mornings and afternoons; closed Mondays and Saturdays; 2.50fl; ☎ (075) 21 76 26.

De Dood. – Open all day Saturdays (unless Saturday is a holiday); 2.50fl; ☎ (075) 215148.

ZAAN REGION

Boat Trips. – From early April to early October daily every hour; 6fl.

Wooden Shoe Workshop. – Open daily.

Bakery Museum. – Open early March to late November daily; the rest of the year Saturdays, Sundays and holidays only; closed Mondays; 1fl.

Catharina Hoeve Cheese Dairy. – Open daily 8am to 7pm.

Pewter Foundry. – Open daily early April to late October; the rest of the year Saturdays and Sundays only; closed Wednesdays.

Clock Museum. – Open daily early March to late November; the rest of the year Sundays and holidays only; closed Mondays (except in July and August); 2fl.

Albert Heijn Grocery. – Open early March to late October mornings and afternoons; closed Sundays; 0.50fl.

Het Noorderhuis. – Open daily early March to late October mornings and afternoons; the rest of the year Saturdays, Sundays and holidays only; closed Mondays (except in July and August); 1fl.

De Poelenburg. – Open early April to late September the 2nd Saturday of the month only; 2.50fl.

De Kat. – Open daily early April to late October; the rest of the year Saturdays, Sundays and holidays only; closed Mondays; 2.50fl.

De Zoeker. – Open early March to late October Mondays only; 2.50fl.

ZALTBOMMEL

Regional Museum. – Open mornings and afternoons; closed Saturday (all day Saturday early October to late March), Sunday and holiday mornings, all day Monday, and Easter Sunday, Whitsun and 25 December; 2fl; ☎ (04180) 12617.

ZEERIJP

Church. – If closed see information posted near the door.

ZIERIKZEE

Boat Trips. – From Easter to late September. For information: Rederij den Breejen, Mantelmeeuwstraat 13, 4301 WT Zierikzee; ☎ (01110) 14995.

Maritime Museum. – Open daily early May to early October and all school holidays; closed Sundays, 1 January, Easter Monday, Ascension Day, Whit Monday, 25 and 26 December; 1.50fl; ☎ (01110) 13151.

Town Hall. – Open mornings and afternoons; closed Saturdays, Sundays and holidays. **Carillon:** Thursdays 10.30am. **Museum:** Open early May to mid-September mornings and afternoons; closed Saturdays, Sundays and holidays; 1.50fl; ☎ (01110) 13151.

St Lieven's Tower. – Open early May to mid-October 11am to 5pm; the rest of the year Saturdays, Sundays and holidays only 11am to 5pm; closed holidays; 2fl; ☎ (01110) 15046.

ZUTPHEN

St Walburga's. – Guided tours (1 hour) – including library – early May to late June and the last fortnight in September Mondays 2 to 3pm and Tuesdays to Saturdays 11am and 2 to 3pm; late June to mid-September Tuesdays to Saturdays 10.30am to 4pm; closed Monday mornings and all day Sundays and holidays; 2.50fl; ☎ (05750) 14178.

Henriette Polak Museum. – Open 11am to 5pm; closed Saturday, Sunday and holiday mornings, all day Monday, 1 January, Easter Sunday, Whitsun, 30 April, 5 May and 25 December; 2fl; ☎ (05750) 16878.

Wijnhuis Tower: Carillon. – Thursdays and Saturdays 11am to noon; ☎ (05750) 19355.

Municipal Museum. – Open 11am to 5pm (4pm certain holidays); closed Saturday and Sunday mornings, all day Monday, 1 January, Easter Sunday, Whitsun and 25 December; 2fl; ☎ (05750) 16878.

ZWOLLE

Overijssel Museum. – Open daily; closed Sunday and holiday mornings, all day Monday, 1 January, Easter Sunday, Whitsun and 25 December; 2fl; ☎ (038) 14650.

Great Church or St Michael's. – Open July and August Wednesdays 10am to 4pm, Fridays 10am to 1pm (noon organ concert), Saturdays 2 to 4pm; ☎ (038) 21 75 96.

Town Hall. – Open daily; closed Saturdays, Sundays and holidays.

Index

223

225

MANUFACTURE FRANÇAISE DES PNEUMATIQUES MICHELIN

Société en commandite par actions au capital de 875 000 000 de francs

Place des Carmes-Déchaux - 63 Clermont-Ferrand (France)

R.C.S. Clermont-Fd B 855 200 507

© Michelin et Cie, Propriétaires-Éditeurs, 1990

Dépôt légal 2ᵉ trim. 1990 – ISBN 2.06.015.551-7 – ISSN 0763-1383

Printed in France 01-90-16

Photocomposition: COUPÉ S.A. Sautron - Impression: HÉRISSEY, Évreux n° 50394